Frames that Speak

Mapping the Past

The titles published in this series are listed at *brill.com/mtp*

Frames that Speak

Cartouches on Early Modern Maps

By

Chet Van Duzer

BRILL

LEIDEN | BOSTON

This book was realised with the generous support of the Kislak Family Foundation and CITCO.

Cover illustration: Detail of Philipp Johann von Strahlenberg, *Nova descriptio geographica Tattariae Magnae, tam orientalis quam occidentalis in particularibus et generalibus territoriis una cum delineatione totius Imperii Russici imprimis Siberiae accurate ostensa* (Stockholm, 1730), Warsaw, Biblioteka Narodowa, ZZK 6 700. Courtesy of the Biblioteka Narodowa.

The Library of Congress Cataloging-in-Publication Data is available online at https://catalog.loc.gov
LC record available at https://lccn.loc.gov/2023006708

Typeface for the Latin, Greek, and Cyrillic scripts: "Brill". See and download: brill.com/brill-typeface.

ISSN 2589-9945
ISBN 978-90-04-50518-6 (hardback)
ISBN 978-90-04-52383-8 (e-book)

Contents

Acknowledgments

It is a pleasure to express my gratitude to the many people who contributed to this book in various ways. One of the inspirations for the project was my discussions with Lauren Beck of the wonderfully rich cartouche on a manuscript map of North America attributed to Claude Bernou, analyzed below, which was part of our 2017 map exhibition titled "Canada before Confederation"—thank you, Lauren, and thanks also to the Canada History Fund and to CITCO for supporting the project.[1] Additional inspiration came from my work studying Urbano Monte's manuscript world map of 1587 at Stanford: I still remember exactly where I was sitting in Green Library when I discovered that Monte had copied the design of one of his cartouches from that on the 1558 map *Septemtrionalium regionum* printed by Michele Tramezzino. I thank David Rumsey for the research fellowship that gave me time to study Monte's map and its sources.[2]

I am grateful to the American Bibliographical Society for a Charles J. Tanenbaum Fellowship in Cartographical Bibliography that afforded me time to do research for the book at the Newberry Library and the John Carter Brown Library in 2018–2019. I thank Jim Akerman of the Newberry Library for his advice during my research there, and Neil Safier and the staff of the John Carter Brown Library for supporting and facilitating my research for several months in 2019.

I am indebted to Marcy Bidney, Curator, and Jovanka Ristic, Reference Librarian, at the American Geographical Society Library in Milwaukee, for their assistance during a visit to the library in April of 2019; and to Reinder Storm, Curator of Maps at the University of Amsterdam, for his amiable and generous help consulting cartouches in the summer of 2019.

I am also grateful to the Huntington Library for an Alan Jutzi Fellowship which enabled me to study the decreasing use of elaborately decorated cartouches in August of 2021.

As always, Eric Frazier, Marianna Stell, and Amanda Zimmerman in the Rare Book and Special Collections Division of the Library of Congress have been very generous in their help with my research, as has Mike Klein in the Geography and Map Division. I am indebted to them.

Numerous librarians helped this project forward by checking maps to see whether a cartouche was hand-colored and also by supplying images, and I am grateful for their help. I would like to express my particular gratitude to Barry Ruderman, Alex Clausen, and Jorge Chavez of Barry Lawrence Ruderman Antique Maps for generously furnishing images both for my research and for use in the book.

I am grateful to Amanda Luyster for our conversations about cartouches early in the project, and to Andrew Kapochunas for sharing his collection of cartouche images with me.

And I thank friends and colleagues for reading draft chapters of the book and giving me the opportunity to benefit from their corrections and suggestions: Pedro Germano Leal, David Ramírez Palacios, Jim Akerman, Andrés Veléz Posada, Ad Stijnman, Alexander Nagel, Juliet Wiersema, Wulf Bodenstein, Günter Schilder, David Buisseret, Bronwen Wilson, Jaime Humberto Borja Gómez, Reinder Storm, Sjoerd de Meer, Maria Berbara, Francesca Fiorani, Stella Chrysochoou, Paolo Militello, Kevin Wittman Rodríguez, Catherine Hofmann, Nadine Orenstein, Jean-Marc Besse, Jeffrey Jaynes, Howard Golden, Jan Mokre, John Stapleton, Jamel Ostwald, Markus Heinz, Sarah Tyacke, Laurence Worms, Ashley Baynton-Williams, Frans De Bruyn, Marcia Yonemoto, Rosario López Parra, Mary Pedley, Jean B. Archer, Júnia Furtado, Michael Buehler, and Ian Folwer. I also thank Brill's two anonymous readers for their suggestions.

I owe special thanks to Michael Ritter for generously sharing with me his knowledge of the dates and states of Matthäus Seutter's maps.

I thank my friends at the Society for the History of Discoveries, particularly Wesley Brown, for some crucial logistical help.

And finally, I offer my effusive thanks to the Kislak Family Foundation and to CITCO for their financial support that allowed this book to be published with all of the color images it needed, and also to be in Open Access, allowing anyone in the world to explore for free the stimulating world of cartouches. I hope that readers who enjoy the book will share my gratitude to them.

Chet Van Duzer

---

1   See Lauren's essay on Bernou's map in our exhibition catalog, Chet Van Duzer and Lauren Beck, *Canada Before Confederation: Maps at the Exhibition* (Wilmington, DE: Vernon Press, 2017), pp. 155–168.

2   See Chet Van Duzer, "Urbano Monte's World Maps: Sources and Development," *Imago temporis* 14 (2020), pp. 415–435, esp. 425–426.

Figures

Introduction

1 Definition of "Cartouche"

To write a book about a subject whose name is not widely known, which lacks a good definition, and about which there is no systematic investigation, entails certain challenges. But there are excellent incentives for confronting those challenges to study cartographic cartouches, the framed texts or images that adorn maps. Cartouches are usually the most visually engaging elements of maps and are of great art historical interest; moreover, cartouches are in fact one of the most important spaces on historic maps. Through their decoration and symbolism the cartographer often reveals his or her interests and beliefs in a way that does not happen elsewhere on the map. That is, cartouches can be venues for a privileged communication between the cartographer and his audience, a breaking of the fourth wall if you will, that can epitomize or give essential clues about the larger meaning of a map. As J.B. Harley has remarked, "The cartouche is the *pictura loquens* of cartography. Like the emblematic title page or frontispiece, it serves to abstract and epitomize some of the meaning of the work as a whole. A cartouche may thus be decorative, illustrative, programmatical, propagandist, doctrinal or controversial."[1] Stephanie Pratt has declared that "far from being marginal, the cartouche constitutes the map," a provocative statement based on Jacques Derrida's discussion of the meaning of "supplement."[2] As such, cartouches and their history deserve careful study.

The decorative frames that are cartouches have been used in other media besides maps, including architecture, grave monuments, non-cartographic prints, and the title pages of books.[3] Earlier definitions of "cartouche" in a cartographic context have limited them to particular shapes, such as a scroll,[4] or a shield,[5] and placed too

1 See J.B. Harley, "Power and Legitimation in the English Geographical Atlases of the Eighteenth Century," in John A. Wolter and Ronald E. Grim, eds., *Images of the World: The Atlas Through History* (Washington, DC: Library of Congress, 1997), pp. 161–204, at 184. Also see Harley's "Meaning and Ambiguity in Tudor Cartography," in Sarah Tyacke, ed., *English Map-Making, 1500–1650: Historical Essays* (London: The British Library Reference Division Publications, 1984), pp. 22–45, at 36. For brief general discussions of cartouches see François de Dainville, *Le langage des géographes: termes, signes, couleurs des cartes anciennes: 1500–1800* (Paris: A. et J. Picard, 1964), pp. 64–67; George Kish, "Cartouches: Notes on Decorative Maps," *LSA, The University of Michigan* 4.3 (Spring, 1981), pp. 3–10; J.H. Andrews, *Maps in Those Days: Cartographic Methods before 1850* (Dublin: Four Courts Press, 2009), pp. 452–461; and Jean-Marc Besse and Nicolas Verdier, "Cartouche," in Matthew H. Edney and Mary Sponberg Pedley, eds., *The History of Cartography*, vol. 4, *Cartography in the European Enlightenment* (Chicago and London: University of Chicago Press, 2019), pp. 244–251. Also see Martin Brückner, "The 'New England' Cartouche: Tablets, Tableaux, and Theatricality in Eighteenth-Century Cartography," in Martha J. McNamara and Georgia B. Barnhill, eds., *New Views of New England: Studies in Material and Visual Culture, 1680–1830* (Boston: The Colonial Society of Massachusetts, 2012), pp. 214–243.

2 Stephanie Pratt, "From the Margins: The Native American Personage in the Cartouche and Decorative Borders of Maps," *Word & Image* 12.4 (1996), pp. 349–365, at 362. To my mind, Jacques Derrida's claim that the cartouche is "a place of exile on the map" in *The Truth in Painting*, trans. Geoff Bennington and Ian MacLeod (Chicago: University of Chicago Press, 1987), p. 190, is simply mistaken.

3 Denis Diderot, ed., *Encyclopédie, ou, Dictionnaire raisonné des sciences, des arts et des métiers* (Paris: Briasson, 1751–65), vol. 2, pp. 731–733, s.v. "cartouche"; Margery Corbett, "The Cartouche in English Engraving in the 16th and 17th Centuries," *Motif* 10 (1962–63), pp. 61–76; Margherita Azzi-Visentini, "Strapwork and Cartouches," in Alain Charles Gruber, ed., *The History of Decorative Arts* (New York: Abbeville Press, 1994–1996), vol. 1, *The Renaissance and Mannerism in Europe*, trans. John Goodman, pp. 347–431; Rebecca Zorach, "Ornament and the 'School of Fontainebleau,'" in her *Blood, Milk, Ink, Gold: Abundance and Excess in the French Renaissance* (Chicago and London: University of Chicago Press, 2005), pp. 140–158 and 268–271; Caroline Heering, "Evolution et mutation du cartouche dans l'art de nos régions du XVIe au XVIIIe siècle," in *Actes du 8e Congrès de l'Association des Cercles francophones d'Histoire et d'Archéologie de Belgique et 55e Congrès de la Fédération des Cercles d'Archéologie et d'Histoire de Belgique, Namur, 28–31 août 2008* (Namur: Presses Universitaires de Namur, 2011), pp. 857–868; and the same author's "Entre cadre et support. Formes et fonctions du motif du cartouche dans la gravure d'ornement," in Michaël Decrossas and Lucie Fléjou, eds., *Ornements: XVe–XIXe siècles: chefs-d'oeuvre de la Bibliothèque de l'INHA, collections Jacques Doucet* (Paris: Institut National d'Histoire de l'Art; Mare et Martin, 2014), pp. 176–189.

4 Antoine Furetière, *Dictionnaire universel, contenant generalement tous les mots françois tant vieux que modernes, et les termes de toutes les sciences et des arts* (The Hague: Heers, 1690), vol. 1, p. 394: *C'est un rouleau de carte, ou sa representation, dont la sculpture & et la graveure font divers ornemens, au milieu duquel on met quelque inscription ou devise. Les titres des cartes geographiques sont écrits dans des cartouches, fort historiées*, that is, "It is a roll of paper, or a representation thereof, in which there are various ornaments of sculpture and engraving, in the middle of which is put some inscription or motto. The titles of the maps are written in cartouches, heavily decorated."

5 Jürgen Bollmann, *Lexikon der Kartographie und Geomatik: in zwei Bänden* (Heidelberg: Spektrum, Akad. Verl., 2001–2002), vol. 2, p. 48: *Kartusche, E cartouche, eine schildförmige, von reich verziertem Dekor begrenzte Fläche …. Auf historischen Karten wurden vom 16. bus zum Anfang des 18. Jhs. meist die Titel, manchmal auch weitere Inschriften und Widmungen, teilweise auch die Zeichenerklärung dekorativ als Kartuschen gestaltet*, that is, "Cartouche, a shield-shaped area

much emphasis on title cartouches,[6] that is, cartouches that contain the title of the map and the cartographer's name. The title cartouche is special, for it frames some of the map's metadata to separate it from the cartographic data, and thus participates more than some other textual cartouches in that direct communication between cartographer and viewer. But other cartouches that do not include title information are just as important, and just as fully cartouches, as these.

The definition I have developed is "a framed device on a map containing text or decorative elements, together with associated adjacent imagery." The framing aspect seems to me essential. The French word *cartouche* comes from the Italian *cartoccio*, a paper container, and the French word is used for a few different types of containers. This idea of containment and framing is particularly clear in its use in Egyptology, where the cartouche is an oval frame that encloses and protects the hieroglyphic characters that form a king's name, or sometimes the name of a divinity.[7] The word "compartment," which as we will see below, was used in English for cartographic cartouches before the adoption of the French word, also involves separation and containment. Without a frame, a text or image is just a text or image, not a cartouche.

The frame that is essential to a cartouche can be created various ways. For example, the frame can be an area left blank for the text amid the waves of the ocean; in some cases the frame is incomplete, but still qualifies, as in the case of Didier Robert de Vaugondy's *Carte du Royaume de France*, printed in 1758: the frame around the title information is formed by the landscape and two trees, but the trees do not quite meet at the top.[8] The Spanish military

engineer and cartographer Francisco Requena (1743–1824) created a wonderfully poetic cartouche frame in a map of the Japurá River in Colombia and Brazil (Fig. 1). The top of the frame is the upper edge of the map; the left-hand side is formed by a tall tree—a Brazil nut tree, *Bertholletia excelsa*—at the base of which are two indigenous men, a hunting dog, and a European man firing a musket to the right across a river at some waterfowl. The birds, startled by the shot, fly up into the air, and the undulating lines they form, together with some clouds above them, form the right-hand section of the frame.[9]

It is also important to emphasize that the decorative elements adjacent to the frame are to be considered part of the cartouche. In the cartouche in North America on Pieter van den Keere's world map of *c.*1611, Amerigo Vespucci, Ferdinand Magellan, and Christopher Columbus are all outside the frame, but clearly form part of the decorative element that is the cartouche (Fig. 2). In some cases the decorative elements associated with the frame can extend quite some distance from it, so that the cartouche acquires an enormous size, even while the frame is relatively small. Thus although the frame is an essential element of a cartouche, the associated decorative elements that form part of the cartouche can occupy a much larger part of the map than the frame.

Descriptive texts that are not contained within a frame of some sort may be called legends or simply texts; decorative scenes that are not associated with a frame may be called vignettes. Banderoles, which are small banners that contain the names of regions, I count as cartouches because they are framed.

---

delimited by richly ornamented decor .... On historical maps from the 16th to the beginning of the 18th centuries they were usually used for the titles, sometimes also other inscriptions and dedications, and sometimes the explanation of the symbols was decoratively designed as a cartouche."

6   Norman J.W. Thrower, *Maps and Man* (Englewood Cliffs, NJ: Prentice Hall, 1972), p. 168, defines cartouche as a "feature of a map or chart, often a decorative inset, containing the title, legend, or scale, or all of these items"; Joachim Neumann, *Enzyklopädisches Wörterbuch Kartographie in 25 Sprachen = Encyclopedic Dictionary of Cartography in 25 Languages* (Munich: KG Saur, 1997), p. 46, no. 21.23, defines it as "An embellishment of a map, often in the form of a scroll, which encloses a title, legend, or name."

7   On cartouches in Egyptian hieroglyphic writing see Cathie Spieser, "Cartouche," in Elizabeth Frood and Willeke Wendrich., eds., *UCLA Encyclopedia of Egyptology* (Los Angeles: UCLA, 2010) (online publication).

8   A high-resolution image of Robert de Vaugondy's *Carte du Royaume de France* is available at https://searchworks.stanford.edu. Below we will examine other maps by Didier Robert de Vaugondy (*c.*1723–1786) and his father Gilles Robert de Vaugondy (1688–1766).

9   I thank Dr. Pedro Lage Viana, Curador do Herbário do Museu Paraense Emílio Goeldi, Belém, Brazil, for identifying the tree. Francisco Requena's 1788 manuscript map of the Japurá River is titled *Mapa de una parte del Rio Yapurá*, and a high-resolution image of it is available at https://loc.gov. On the donation of Requena's maps to the Library of Congress see Lawrence Martin, "South American Cartographic Treasures," *The Library of Congress Quarterly Journal of Current Acquisitions* 1.3 (1944), pp. 30–39; and Lawrence Martin and Walter W. Ristow, "South American Historical Maps," in Walter W. Ristow, ed., *A la Carte: Selected Papers on Maps and Atlases* (Washington, DC: Library of Congress, 1972), pp. 189–203, esp. 198–200. On Requena himself see Eric Beerman, "Bosquejo biográfico de Don Francisco Requena y su Descripción de la Provincia de Guayaquil en 1774," *Revista del Archivo Histórico de Guayas* 14 (1978), pp. 3–22; and Eric Beerman, "Pintor y cartógrafo en las amazonas, Francisco Requena," *Anales, Museo de América* 2 (1994), pp. 83–97. On his trip to the Japurá River see Michele Cohen, "Diario del viaje al Yapura por Francisco Requena, 1782," *Suplemento del Anuario de Estudios Americanos. Sección Historiografía y Bibliografía Americanistas* 45.2 (1988), pp. 3–68.

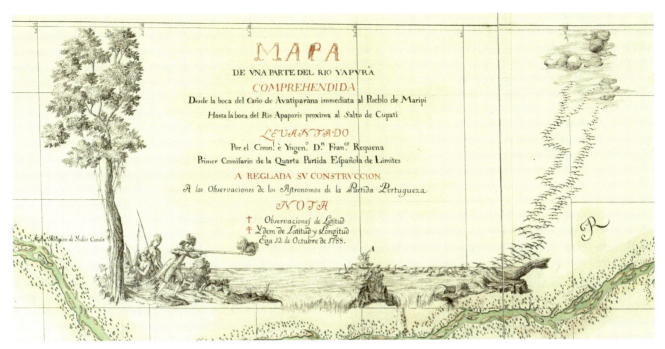

FIGURE 1   The title cartouche on Francesco Requena's manuscript *Mapa de una parte del Rio Yapurá*, 1788
LIBRARY OF CONGRESS, G5292.J2 1788 .R4. COURTESY OF THE LIBRARY OF CONGRESS

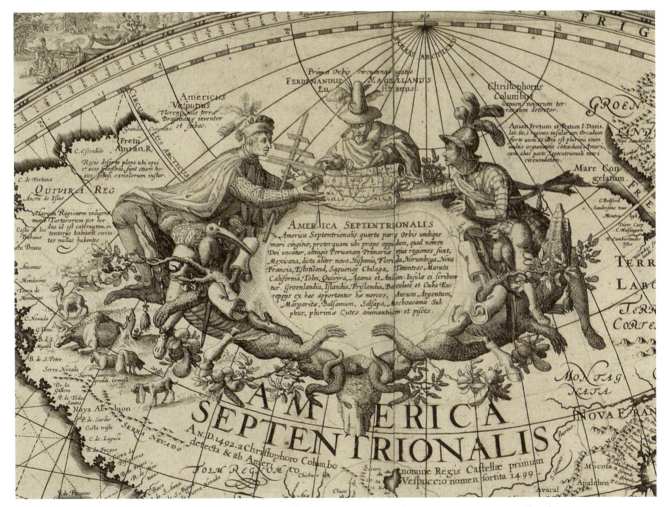

FIGURE 2   The cartouche in North America from Pieter van den Keere, *Nova totius orbis mappa, ex optimis auctoribus desumta*
(Amsterdam, *c.*1611)
SAN FRANCISCO, SUTRO LIBRARY, G3200 1611.K43. COURTESY OF THE SUTRO LIBRARY

2   Names for Cartouches

Before "cartouche" was borrowed from French, the word "compartment" was used in English for these framed spaces on maps. The word is employed in this sense by William Folkingham in his *Feudigraphia: The Synopsis or Epitome of Surveying Methodized* (London: Printed for Richard Moore, 1610), where he discusses how to decorate a map. He writes:[10]

"Compartiments are Blankes or Figures bordered with Anticke Boscage or Crotesko-woorke [i.e. grotesques], wherein Evidences or other Memorables may be abreviated. And these may bee contrived in Parallelograms, Squares, Circles, Ovalls, Lunaries, or other mixt or voluntary proportions compassed and tricked *ad libitum*. Under this Title may also be rainged the Lordes-Coate with Crest and Mantells. And these Compartiments with the Scale, Carde and Kalender must bee bestowed in convenient spare and voide places."

Folkingham is describing a relatively simple style of cartouche decoration, with vegetal motifs and grotesques, as opposed to the more elaborate decorations involving people and symbolism. Arthur Burns also used the word "compartment" in the modern sense of "cartouche" in his instructions on how to make an estate map in his *Geodaesia Improved or, a New and Correct Method of Surveying Made Exceeding Easy* (Chester: printed for the author, 1771). It is worth quoting the passage as it shows that the instructions for beginners were much more basic than what was being done by the leading practitioners at this time, as we shall see below:[11]

"Having completed the Fields, &c. in the Map, make Choice of a Compartment, or Vacancy therein, at the Top, if possible, to draw the Coat of Arms belonging to the Gentleman that owns the Estate, with Shield, Crest, and Supporters; the Shield should be drawn so, that it may contain the Title, Township and County, or any thing else that is proper to denote the Situation thereof. The Art of drawing such Ornaments, will soon be obtained by assiduous Application, and some Instructions therein from a Limner, which the small Size of this Treatise prevented me to give in this Place. In another Compartment, or Vacancy, draw the Dividers, drawing Pen, the Scale you laid down the Map by, &c. Lastly, Draw the Mariner's Compass, with the Flower de Luce therein, pointing to the North exactly."

Many professional cartographers in the 1770s were making cartouches with elaborate allegory and political messages; the expectations for do-it-yourself map-makers were much more modest.

The word "cartouche" first appears in English in Randle Cotgrave's *A Dictionarie of the French and English Tongues* (London: Adam Islip, 1611)—but it is defined as a paper container (harking back to the Italian word *cartoccio*), with no mention of decorative frames, much less of maps:

"Cartouche: f. The cornet of paper whereinto Apothecaries, and Grocers put the parcels they retaile; also, a Cartouch, or full charge, for a pistoll, put up within a little paper, to be the redier for use; also, a peece of pastbboord, or thicke, paper, stuffed (in a round, or puddinglike forme) with bullets, &c, and to be shot out of a great peece; also, as Cartoche."

The word was used in French to describe the decoration of maps as early as 1748,[12] but it was not used in English for a decorative frame until 1824, when John Johnson in his *Typographia, or the Printers' Instructor* (London: Longman, Hurst, Rees, Orme, Brown & Green, 1824) uses it to describe the frame around a portrait of the printer John Day in the 1570 English edition of Euclid's *Geometry*.[13]

---

10   The passage is on p. 58 of Folkingham's book, and is also quoted by George Kish, "Cartouches: Notes on Decorative Maps," *LSA, The University of Michigan* 4.3 (Spring, 1981), pp. 3–10, at 5; and David Woodward, "Techniques of Map Engraving, Printing, and Coloring in the European Renaissance," in J.B. Harley and David Woodward, eds., *The History of Cartography*, vol. 3, *Cartography in the European Renaissance* (Chicago and London: University of Chicago Press, 2007), part 1, pp. 591–610, at 605. On Folkingham see E. Gordon Duff, *Bibliotheca Pepysiana: A Descriptive Catalogue of the Library of Samuel Pepys* (London: Sidgwick & Jackson, 1914–40), vol. 4, pp. 28–29.

11   This passage is on p. 240 of Burns's book, and he includes a sample estate map with a cartouche between pages 250 and 251. Burns's instructions were copied without attribution by William Davis in his *A Complete Treatise of Land Surveying* (London: printed for the author, 1798), pp. 197–198.

12   François de Dainville, *Le langage des géographes: termes, signes, couleurs des cartes anciennes, 1500–1800* (Paris: A. et J. Picard, 1964), p. 64; and Mary Sponberg Pedley, *The Commerce of Cartography: Making and Marketing Maps in Eighteenth-Century France and England* (Chicago: University of Chicago Press, 2005), p. 56.

13   Johnson in his *Typographia*, p. 540, writes of the portrait of Day that "The print itself has a large cartouch oval frame, with pinks and gillyflowers issuing from the four corners ...." The 1570 English edition of Euclid is *The Elements of Geometrie of the Most Auncient Philosopher Euclide of Megara* (London: John Daye, 1570). The portrait of Day is at the end of the book, and may be seen in the Library of Congress's digital version of the

The earliest use of "cartouche" in English specifically with reference to map decoration occurred under dramatic circumstances, in a lawsuit over land ownership in Canada. In 1621 James I of England (r. 1603–1625) granted to Sir William Alexander (1567–1640), later the first Earl of Stirling, a huge swath of land in eastern Canada that included all of Nova Scotia and also significant mackerel fishing rights, as part of an effort to encourage British settlement there. These lands could only be inherited by male heirs, and the eighth Earl of Stirling had no sons. Alexander Humphrys-Alexander (1783–1859) had descended from this line via a maternal grandmother, but he laid claim to these lands in eastern Canada on the basis of documents he adduced that were affixed to the back of a map of Canada. These documents attested to the existence of a later charter by Charles I that made the rights to the land inheritable by female descendants as well.[14] The map in question was Guillaume Delisle's *Carte du Canada ou de la Nouvelle France*, first published in 1703.[15] The claim went to trial; the matter naturally turned on the genuineness of the documents, and this question depended on the date of the map to which they were affixed.

Mathieu-Guillaume-Thérèse Villenave (1762–1846), a French man of letters and bibliophile, gave his opinion on the date of the map by way of a letter, and that letter was translated into English as part of the proceedings. In that translation, which was published in 1840, we read:[16]

"I have also the same maps, especially that of Canada, in which the denomination of first Geographer is wanting, and which has a "cartouche," (scroll or tablet) and engraved ornaments, different from the "cartouche" and ornaments of the map which contains the title of first Geographer to the King. And the two maps have, nevertheless, the same date, 1703!"

Given that the word "cartouche" is originally French, it is appropriate that it entered English language through a translation from that language, and the tentative nature of its use in this passage, requiring an explanation, is clear. It is fortuitous that the word was first used in English when the stakes were so high, with the ownership of more than a province of Canada hanging in the balance. The documents affixed to the back of the map were determined to be forgeries,[17] but Humphrys-Alexander was found not guilty of having forged them.

Another interesting and very appropriate word for "cartouche" appears on an eighteenth-century map of West Africa made by the heirs of Johann Baptist Homann in Nuremberg. The map is titled *Guinea propria, nec non Nigritiae vel Terrae Nigrorum maxima pars* ("Guinea Proper, with the Greater Part of Nigritia or the Land of the Blacks"), and was printed in 1743.[18] In the lower left-hand corner there is an elaborate scene of village life in Cape Mezurado, in modern Liberia; the scene qualifies as a cartouche because of the scales of miles (Italian, French, and German) which are framed by elephants' tusks in the foreground. In the margin beneath the scene there is a key that identifies the various elements of the illustration that are marked with letters.[19] The key begins with the phrase *Parergum hoc monstrat modum habitandi Nigrorum in Cap. Mezurado*, "This *parergon* shows the mode of dwelling of the blacks of Cape Mezurado."

"Parergon" means a work, especially an artwork, that is subordinate or supplementary to a main work,[20] and this

---

book at https://www.loc.gov/resource/rbc0001.2010english20856/?sp=992.

14 There is a concise summary of the history of this claim in "A Curious Story," *New York Times*, May 15, 1871, p. 4; for fuller accounts see William Turnbull, ed., *The Stirling Peerage: Trial of Alexander Humphrys or Alexander, Styling himself Earl of Stirling, before the High Court of Justiciary, for Forgery, on 29th April, 1839, and Four Following Days* (Edinburgh: William Blackwood and Sons; London: T. Cadell, 1839); and *Remarks on the Trial of the Earl of Stirling at Edinburgh, April 29th, 1839, for Forgery* (London: Lewis and Co., 1839 [i.e. 1840]); and William C. Townsend, *Modern State Trials: Revised and Illustrated with Essays and Notes* (London: Longman, Brown, Green, and Longmans, 1850), vol. 1, pp. 403–468.

15 On Delisle's map see Jean Delanglez, "The Sources of the Delisle Map of America, 1703," *Mid-America* 25 (1943), pp. 275–298; Ronald F. Lockmann, "North America in the Cartography of Guillaume Delisle," *Western Association of Map Libraries Information Bulletin* 10 (1978–1979), pp. 20–31; and Kenneth A. Kershaw, *Early Printed Maps of Canada* (Ancaster, Ontario: Kershaw Pub., 1993–1998), vol. 1, pp. 275–284.

16 *Remarks on the Trial* (see note 14), p. 120. Incidentally it was at this same time, 1839, that the word "cartographie" was invented in French: see J.B. Harley, "The Map and the Development of the History of Cartography," in J.B. Harley and David Woodward, eds., *The History of Cartography*, vol. 1, *Cartography in Prehistoric, Ancient, and Medieval Europe and the Mediterranean* (Chicago: University of Chicago Press, 1987), pp. 1–42, at 12–13.

17 See Townsend, *Modern State Trials* (see note 14), vol. 1, pp. 425–427.

18 A high-resolution image of Homann's map of Guinea is available on the website of the Library of Congress at https://loc.gov.

19 Much of the scene of village life on this map by the Heirs of Homann is based on K. De Putter's woodcut titled *Maisons des Negres du Cap Mezurado* in Jean Baptiste Labat's *Voyage du chevalier Des Marchais en Guinée, isles voisines, et a Cayenne, Fait en 1725, 1726, & 1727* (Amsterdam: Aux dépens de la Compagnie, 1731), vol. 1, illustrating chapter 16, "Du Cap Mesurado. Sa Description." This woodcut also has a lettered key at the bottom that identifies various elements in the scene. Below we will discuss the various sources that cartographers used for their cartouches.

20 For discussion of *parergon* as a supplementary work of art see Christopher S. Wood, *Albrecht Altdorfer and the Origins of*

is an interesting way to think about cartouches. Certainly they are subordinate to the map—there is no cartographic cartouche without a map—but at the same time, the word encourages us to think about the relationship between cartouche and map in a productive way, specifically about the ways in which a cartouche supplements a map, and how the supplement may be necessary to the map. Today "parergon" is the word in Czech for a cartographic cartouche, and the very closely related "parerga" is the word in Polish.

3 Two Ornamental Motifs of Sixteenth-Century Cartouches

We should distinguish between ornament and decoration. Decoration is the broad term "for the art we add to art," while "Ornament is decoration in which the visual pleasure of form significantly outweighs the communicative value of content."[21] All but the plainest cartouches communicate, and thus most are to be considered decoration, but they very often incorporate ornamentation. Two of the ornamental elements commonly used to create those decorations in the sixteenth and early seventeenth century are not very familiar today, and it is worth briefly reviewing their definitions and histories.

Strapwork consists of stylized ornamentation that imitates leather straps or ribbons or sheet metal, sometimes curling with three-dimensional effects, sometimes pierced

with holes, sometimes woven into geometric patterns. In cartographic cartouches, strapwork may be the only ornament, or it may serve as the support and framework for fantastic creatures called grotesques, about which more below.[22] This style of ornamentation originated in Italy in the fifteenth century, was popularized in the elaborate stucco frames created under the painter Rosso Fiorentino (1495–1540) in the 1530s for the Château de Fontainebleau southeast of Paris,[23] and embraced and disseminated in prints even more broadly across northern Europe by artists in Antwerp such as Cornelis Bos (c.1510–c.1555), Cornelis Floris II (1514–1575), and Hans Vredeman de Vries (1527–c.1607) from the middle of the sixteenth century.[24] As we will see further below, in some cases the works of these Antwerp artists were borrowed by cartographers for their maps.

Good examples of strapwork can be found in the cartouches in Abraham Ortelius's *Theatrum orbis terrarum*, the earliest atlas in the modern sense of the word, which was first published in Antwerp in 1570, and these can be easily explored in digitized exemplars of the book.[25]

Landscape (Chicago: University of Chicago Press, 1993), pp. 54–61; Christopher S. Wood, "'Curious Pictures' and the Art of Description," *Word & Image* 11.4 (1995), pp. 332–352, at 344; and Anna Degler, *Parergon: Attribut, Material und Fragment in der Bildästhetik des Quattrocento* (Paderborn: Wilhelm Fink, 2015). On the various meanings that have been ascribed to the term "parergon" see Paul Duro, "What Is a Parergon?" *Journal of Aesthetics and Art Criticism* 77.1 (2019), pp. 23–33. In a cartographic context the word is most famous for Abraham Ortelius's use of it as the title for the supplement of historical maps that he added to his atlas, the *Theatrum orbis terrarum*, in 1584. On Ortelius's *Parergon* see Peter H. Meurer, "Ortelius as the Father of Historical Cartography," in Marcel van den Broecke, Peter van der Krogt, and Peter Meurer, eds., *Abraham Ortelius and the First Atlas: Essays Commemorating the Quadricentennial of His Death, 1598–1998* (Utrecht: HES Publishers, 1998), pp. 133–159; and George Tolias, "Glose, contemplation et méditation: Histoire éditoriale et fonctions du *Parergon* d'Abraham Ortelius, 1579–1624," in *Les méditations cosmographiques à la Renaissance* (Paris: PUPS, 2009), pp. 157–186.

21   James Trilling, *Ornament: A Modern Perspective* (Seattle: University of Washington Press, 2003), p. 23. For discussion of the use of the word "ornament" in the Renaissance, see Mary E. Hazard, "An Essay to Amplify 'Ornament': Some Renaissance Theory and Practice," *Studies in English Literature* 16.1 (1976), pp. 15–32.

22   For discussion of the use of strapwork in cartouches see Azzi-Visentini, "Strapwork and Cartouches" (see note 3); and Femke Speelberg, "'Ordine con piu ornamento': Reconsidering the Origins of Strapwork Ornament in Relation to the Emancipation of the Ornamental Frame," in Ralph Dekoninck, Caroline Heering, and Michel Lefftz, eds., *Questions d'ornements, XVeᵉ–XVIIIeᵉ siècles* (Turnhout: Brepols, 2013), pp. 154–165.

23   For discussion of the cartouches designed for the Château de Fontainebleau see Zorach, "Ornament and the 'School of Fontainebleau'" (see note 3).

24   On Cornelis Bos see Sune Schéle, *Cornelis Bos: A Study of the Origins of the Netherland Grotesque* (Stockholm: Almqvist & Wiksell, 1965); on Floris see Antoinette Huysmans, Jan van Damme, and Carl van de Velde, *Cornelis Floris, 1514–1575: beeldhouwer, architect, ontwerper* (Brussels: Gemeentekrediet, 1996), review by Peter Fuhring in *Print Quarterly* 16.3 (1999), pp. 283–290. He made a model book of cartouches titled *Veelderleij veranderinghe van grotissen ende compertimenten ghemaeckt tot dienste van alle die de conste beminnen ende ghebruiken* (Antwerp: Hieronimus Cock, 1556). On Vredeman de Vries see Peter Fuhring, "Hans Vredeman de Vries und das Ornament als Vorlage und Modell," in Heiner Borggrefe et al., eds., *Hans Vredeman de Vries und die Renaissance im Norden* (Munich: Hirmer, 2002), pp. 61–70.

25   For background on Ortelius and his *Theatrum orbis terrarum* see Marcel van den Broecke, Peter van der Krogt, and Peter Meurer, eds., *Abraham Ortelius and the First Atlas: Essays Commemorating the Quadricentennial of his Death, 1598–1998* (Houten: HES, 1998). An exemplar of the 1570 edition with uncolored maps in the David Rumsey Map Collection at Stanford University at https://searchworks.stanford.edu/view/11403483, and an exemplar at the Library of Congress with hand-colored maps is available at https://www.loc.gov/resource/g3200m.gct00126/?st=gallery; Stanford also has a copy of the 1595 edition with hand-colored maps at https://searchworks.stanford.edu/view/201273.

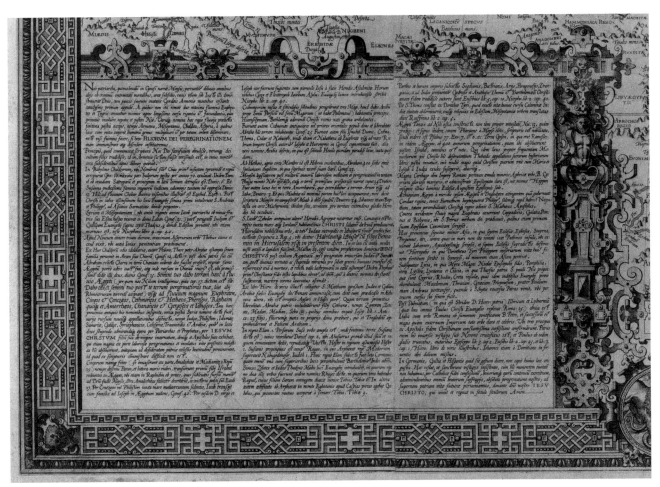

FIGURE 3   Cartouche showing strapwork decoration in its frame, from Christian Sgrooten, *Peregrinatio filiorum Dei* (Kalkar, 1572)
UNIVERSITÄTSBIBLIOTHEK BASEL, KARTENSLG AA 119–120. COURTESY OF THE UNIVERSITÄTSBIBLIOTHEK BASEL

I illustrate a slightly later cartouche here, from a map of the Holy Land and surrounding regions designed by the German cartographer Christian Sgrooten (*c.*1532–*c.*1608) and printed in Kalkar in 1572 (Fig. 3), about which more below. The strapwork along the top edge of the cartouche is shaded to show its three-dimensionality and supports some ornamental plants and two busts; that along the right-hand edge, also three-dimensional, is more convoluted and elaborate, and supports two lion heads and the upper half of a grotesque who holds two torches. The strapwork in the map's border, which forms the left-hand and lower border of the cartouche, is of a different character, two-dimensional and verging into a style of ornamentation called knotwork.[26]

The second ornamental element mentioned above is the grotesque. The Renaissance tradition of the grotesque was inspired by Roman models. In the late fifteenth century Nero's palace in Rome, the Domus Aurea, which had been buried under centuries of detritus, was rediscovered, and people lowered themselves on ropes through its broken roofs to see its frescoed ornamentation—so that the rooms had the feel of caves, or *grotti* in Italian. Artists adopted the Roman ornamentation into their works and thus gave them new life, and the name grotesque began to be applied to fanciful ornamental arrangements of garlands, reeds, acanthus, candelabras, and fantastic human and animal figures, with flimsy elements illogically supporting heavy ones, and the limbs of the humans and animals often terminating in plants or other decorations.[27]

26   For discussion of knotwork see Alain C. Gruber, "Interlace," in Alain C. Gruber and Margherita Azzi Visentini, eds., *The History of Decorative Arts*, trans. John Goodman (New York: Abbeville Press, 1994), vol. 1, *The Renaissance and Mannerism in Europe*, pp. 21–112 and 454–457.

27   For discussion of Renaissance grotesques see Schéle, *Cornelis Bos* (see note 24); Nicole Dacos, "Fortune des grotesques au XVIe siècle," in her *La découverte de la Domus Aurea et la formation des grotesques à la Renaissance* (London: Warburg Institute, 1969), pp. 121–135; Philippe Morel, *Les grotesques: les figures de l'imaginaire dans la peinture italienne de la fin de la Renaissance*

FIGURE 4   Cartouche with grotesques, detail of Johannes Franciscus Della Gatta, *Palestinae sive Terre Sancte descriptio* (Rome, 1557)
COURTESY OF THE RENAISSANCE EXPLORATION MAP COLLECTION, STANFORD UNIVERSITY

We see one good example of cartouche ornamentation emphasizing the grotesque in Fig. 4, a map of the Holy Land by Johannes Franciscus della Gatta titled *Palestinae sive Terre Sancte descriptio*, printed in Rome, probably in 1557.[28] The bodies of various beasts and monsters that surround the frame sprout into acanthus leaves; the

two-headed king at the top of the cartouche has acanthus leaves growing from his shoulders, and unconcernedly places his hands in the mouths of two sea monsters; on the lower right, a boy playing a lute sits on the head of a demon-like creature. The grotesque is a world of the fantastic and the impossible, monsters and metamorphoses—of logic abandoned in the interest of pure ornamentation. The monstrous nature of grotesques makes them particularly well suited to demarcating cartouche space from carto-graphic space, for they are startlingly different than the surrounding depictions of plains, rivers, cities, and seas. Grotesque ornamentation of cartouches declined in the early seventeenth century.

(Paris: Flammarion, 1997); and Maria Fabricius Hansen, *The Art of Transformation: Grotesques in Sixteenth-Century Italy* (Rome: Edizioni Quasar, 2018); also see Mark Dorrian, "On the Monstrous and the Grotesque," *Word & Image* 16.3 (2000), pp. 310–317. On polemics against grotesques during the Counter-Reformation see Damiano Acciarino, "Between Renaissance and Reformation: Grotesques and the Debate on Images," in Damiano Acciarino, ed., *Paradigms of Renaissance Grotesques* (Toronto: Centre for Reformation and Renaissance Studies, 2019), pp. 29–54.

28   On Franciscus's map of the Holy Land see R.V. Tooley, "Maps in Italian Atlases of the Sixteenth Century, Being a Comparative List of the Italian Maps Issued by Lafreri, Forlani, Duchetti, Bertelli and Others, Found in Atlases," *Imago Mundi* 3 (1939), pp. 12–47, p. 39, no. 434; and Eran Laor, *Maps of the Holy Land: Cartobibliography of Printed Maps, 1475–1900* (New York: A.R. Liss; Amsterdam: Meridian Pub. Co., 1986), p. 33, no. 249, with a full page illustration on p. 32.

4   Early Cartouches, and Some Cartouche Firsts

To my knowledge the early history and development of cartouches has never been investigated. Almost no ancient Greek or Roman maps survive, but we have a description indicating that maps in classical antiquity had descriptive

FIGURE 5   Detail of the cartouches in northwestern Africa on Giovanni da Carignano's nautical chart of *c.*1327, which before its destruction
was in Florence, Archivio di Stato, Carte nautiche 2
THIS COMPOSITE IMAGE COURTESY OF COLLEZIONE ALBERTO QUARTAPELLE

texts written on them; if these were framed, they would qualify as cartouches, but the question of whether they were written in frames remains unanswered. The Greek biographer Plutarch (*c.*46 CE–120 CE) writes in his life of Theseus:[29]

"Just as geographers, O Socius Senecio, crowd on to the outer edges of their maps the parts of the earth which elude their knowledge, with explanatory notes that "What lies beyond is sandy desert without water and full of wild beasts," or "blind marsh," or "Scythian cold," or "frozen sea"."

It is possible that these Greek cartographers wrote these texts about distant lands within frames, which would qualify them as cartouches, but we simply cannot be certain. One of the earliest surviving maps that clearly does have them is a hand-painted nautical chart made by the Genoese cartographer Giovanni da Carignano in about 1327. The chart, formerly in the Archivio di Stato in Florence, was destroyed during World War II, but may be studied in reproductions.[30] Carignano made ample use of cartouches on the chart as a way to make the texts legible by setting them on white backgrounds, which set them apart from the dark-colored geography (Fig. 5). These cartouches are as simple as could be: they are plain unornamented rectangular frames.

On the Catalan Atlas of *c.*1375, one of the most elaborately decorated medieval nautical charts to have survived, there are numerous unframed descriptive texts on land, whose lack of a frame disqualifies them from being cartouches, but the descriptive texts in the sea are in simple cartouches: the wavy lines representing the water give way to frames that afford the texts a white background

29   Plutarch *Theseus* 1.1; English translation from *Plutarch's Lives*, trans. Bernadotte Perrin (London: W. Heinemann; and New York: G.P. Putnam, 1914–26), vol. 1, pp. 3–4. In connection with this quotation from Plutarch see Dmitry A. Shcheglov, "Pomponius Mela's Chorography and Hellenistic Scientific Geography," in Alexander V. Podossinov, ed., *The Periphery of the Classical World in Ancient Geography and Cartography* (Leuven: Peeters, 2014), pp. 77–94.

30   Carignano's nautical chart is reproduced in Youssouf Kamal, *Monumenta cartographica Africae et Aegypti* (Cairo, 1926–1951), vol. IV, fasc. 1, ff. 1137v–1138r; in Theobald Fischer, *Raccolta di mappamondi e carte nautiche del XIII al XVI secolo* (Venice: F. Ongania, 1881), no. 3; and in Ramon J. Pujades i Bataller, *Les cartes portolanes: la representació medieval d'una mar solcada* (Barcelona: Institut Cartogràfic de Catalunya, 2007), on the accompanying CD, no. C6. For discussion of the chart see A.J. Duken, "Reconstruction of the Portolan Chart of G. Carignano (*c.*1310)," *Imago mundi* 40 (1988), pp. 86–95.

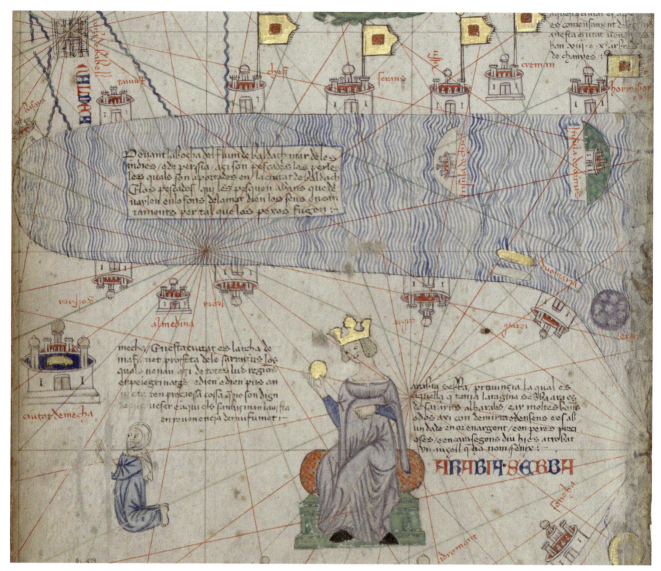

FIGURE 6   Detail of the Middle East showing a cartouche in the Persian Gulf and unframed descriptive texts on land in the Catalan Atlas
of *c.*1375

that makes them legible (Fig. 6).[31] These cartouches are purely practical, and have no decorative element.

The Venetian cartographer Fra Mauro, in his famous world map made in about 1455 and preserved in the Biblioteca Marciana in Venice,[32] uses a system similar to that in the Catalan Atlas: the descriptive texts on land are unframed, while those in the ocean are framed. But his cartouches, rather than being plain rectangles, are scroll-shaped, showing an early awareness of the ornamental possibilities that these frames offer (Fig. 7). The anonymous cartographer of the so-called "Genoese" world map of 1457 also used scroll-shaped cartouches, but unlike Fra

31   The Catalan Atlas is in Paris, Bibliothèque nationale de France, MS Espagnol 30. It has been reproduced in multiple facsimile editions, including *Mapamundi del año 1375* (Barcelona: S.A. Ebrisa, 1983), and more recently *El món i els dies: L'Atles Català* (Barcelona: Enciclopèdia Catalana, 2005); the atlas is also reproduced in Pujades, *Les cartes portolanes* (see note 30), on the accompanying CD, number C16. Good zoomable images of the panels that compose the atlas may be consulted at https://gallica.bnf.fr.

32   On Fra Mauro's map see Piero Falchetta, *Fra Mauro's World Map* (Turnhout: Brepols, 2006); and Angelo Cattaneo, *Fra Mauro's Mappa Mundi and Fifteenth-Century Venetian Culture* (Turnhout: Brepols, 2011).

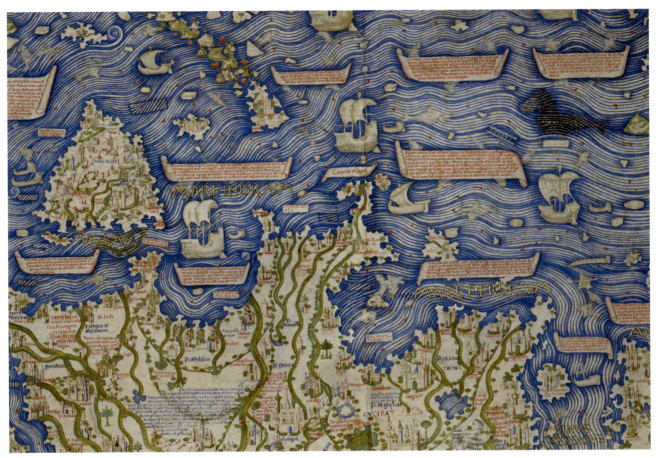

FIGURE 7   Detail of the Indian Ocean on Fra Mauro's *mappamundi* of *c.*1455, showing multiple scroll-shaped cartouches
VENICE, BIBLIOTECA NAZIONALE MARCIANA. BY PERMISSION OF THE MINISTERO DI CULTURA, BIBLIOTECA NAZIONALE
MARCIANA. FURTHER REPRODUCTION IS PROHIBITED

Mauro, thought that descriptive texts on land, as well as those in the sea, required framing.[33]

An important cartographer whose appreciation of the utility of cartouches has not heretofore been recognized is Henricus Martellus, a German who worked in Florence in the second half of the fifteenth century. Of the 43 surviving Latin manuscripts of Ptolemy's *Geography*,[34] in the vast majority—in fact in all but three of them—the cartographers write their descriptive texts and the names of oceans on the blue of the water, using white or black paint for contrast, but without cartouches. Martellus departed from this tradition by using scroll-shaped cartouches in the maps of the two surviving manuscripts of the *Geography* that he made (Fig. 8).[35] Martellus's appreciation of cartouches is also evident in the maps he made to illustrate his *Insularium*, a book about the world's islands.

---

33   The so-called Genoese map is in Florence, Biblioteca Nazionale Centrale, Portolano 1; for discussion of it see Edward Luther Stevenson, *Genoese World Map, 1457* (New York: American Geographical Society and Hispanic Society of America, 1912), p. 25; and there is a facsimile edition with commentary by Angelo Cattaneo, *Mappa mundi 1457* (Rome: Treccani, 2008). Stevenson's facsimile of the map may be viewed in high resolution at https://loc.gov.

34   Marcel Destombes, *Mappemondes, A.D. 1200–1500* (Amsterdam: N. Israel, 1964), pp. 247–248, lists 42 Latin manuscripts of Ptolemy's *Geography*, but does not include the Wilczek-Brown Codex at the John Carter Brown Library, call number Codex Z 1 3-SIZE.

35   The two manuscripts of Ptolemy's *Geography* whose maps were made by Martellus are in Vatican City, Biblioteca Apostolica Vaticana, Vat. lat. 7289; and Florence, Biblioteca Nazionale Centrale, Magliabechiano XIII 16. On these two manuscripts see Sebastiano Gentile, ed., *Firenze e la scoperta dell'America: umanesimo e geografia nel '400 fiorentino* (Florence: L.S. Olschki, 1992), pp. 240–243 and 247, with plates 47–48; and Chet Van Duzer, *Henricus Martellus's World Map at Yale (c.1491): Multispectral Imaging, Sources, Influence* (New York: Springer, 2019), pp. 4–5 and 5–8. The third manuscript whose maps have cartouches is in Helsinki, National Library, Nordenskiöld Collection, MS Misc. 1; high-resolution images of its maps may be viewed by searching in https://www.doria.fi for "N_Mscr_1", and a digital version of the manuscript may be downloaded in sections by going to https://www.doria.fi/handle/10024/69925.

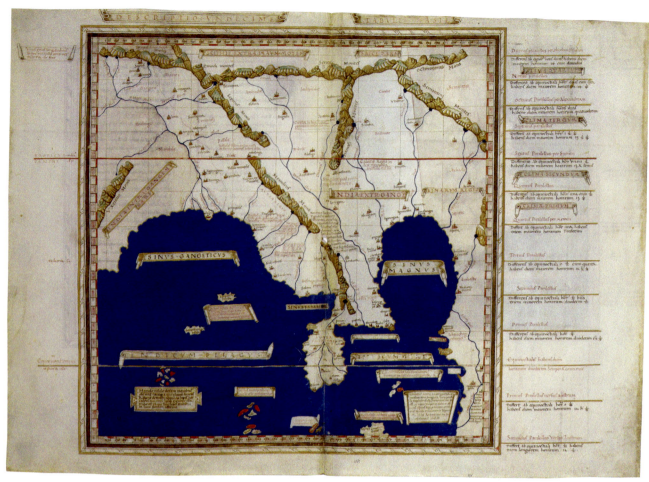

FIGURE 8   Numerous cartouches in the eleventh map of Asia in a manuscript of Ptolemy's *Geography* whose maps were made by Henricus
             Martellus
             FLORENCE, BIBLIOTECA NAZIONALE CENTRALE, MAGLIABECHIANO XIII 16, FF. 156V–157R. BY PERMISSION OF THE
             BIBLIOTECA NAZIONALE CENTRALE DI FIRENZE

In his working manuscript for the book, the maps have no cartouches, as we see in the map of Taprobana (Fig. 9), but in a luxury copy he made for a wealthy client, the same map abounds with cartouches (Fig. 10).[36] Martellus seems to have recognized both the legibility that cartouches afford to descriptive texts and the visual interest they confer on maps.

The first cartographer to use cartouches to hide his ignorance of a region's specific geography seems to have been Johannes Ruysch (c.1460–1533), who made a new world map that incorporated recent discoveries for the 1508 edition of Ptolemy's *Geography*; the map also appears

in some copies of the 1507 edition.[37] Ruysch has several descriptive texts on his map that are framed merely by the wave pattern that surrounds the open space in which the text is written. But the two cartouches that run down the western coasts of South America and the landmass to the north that represents Cuba[38] are framed as scrolls, and the locations of these cartouches, covering the western coasts of the two landmasses, allow Ruysch to avoid

---

36   On the Florence and Chantilly manuscripts of Martellus's island book see Van Duzer, *Henricus Martellus's World Map at Yale* (see note 35), pp. 10–12 and 13–15, respectively.

---

37   On Ruysch's world map see John Boyd Thacher, *The Continent of America: Its Discovery and Its Baptism* (New York: William Evarts Benjamin, 1896), pp. 209–219; Bradford F. Swan, "The Ruysch Map of the World (1507–1508)," *Papers of the Bibliographical Society of America* 45 (1951), pp. 219–236; Donald L. McGuirk, Jr., "Ruysch World Map: Census and Commentary," *Imago Mundi* 41 (1989), pp. 133–141; and Peter Meurer, "Der Maler und Katrograph Johann Ruysch," *Geschichte in Köln* 49 (2002), pp. 85–104.

38   Donald L. McGuirk, Jr., "The Depiction of Cuba on the Ruysch World Map," *Terrae Incognitae* 20 (1988), pp. 89–97.

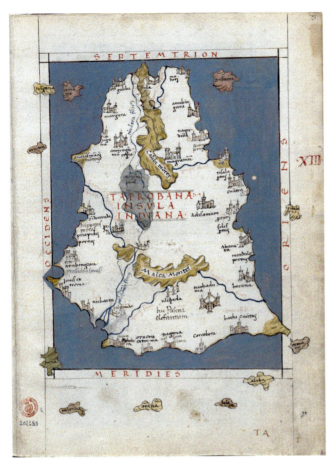

FIGURE 9   The cartoucheless map of Taprobana in Martellus's
working copy of his island book
FLORENCE, BIBLIOTECA MEDICEA LAURENZIANA,
PLUT. 29.25, F. 75R. BY PERMISSION OF THE
BIBLIOTECA MEDICEA LAURENZIANA

FIGURE 10   Abundant cartouches in the map of Taprobana in a
luxury copy of Martellus's island book
CHANTILLY, BIBLIOTHÈQUE DU MUSÉE CONDÉ,
MS 698 (483), F. 74R. © RMN-GRAND PALAIS / ART
RESOURCE, NY

drawing coastlines that he did not know—that is, they allow him to conceal his ignorance of those coastlines (Fig. 11). Indeed, the text in the southern cartouche ends by saying that Spanish sailors did not see all of the land, "nor up to this time have they surveyed further than this limit. Therefore here it is left unfinished, especially since it is not known in which direction it tends."[39] In fact he did not leave the coast unfinished, as he says, but rather covered it with this cartouche. As we will see below, other cartographers used cartouches in this same way to conceal their ignorance of a region's geography, particularly during the sixteenth century.

Two of the earliest artistically elaborate cartographic cartouches appear on Martin Waldseemüller's *Carta marina* of 1516, a woodcut wall map printed on twelve sheets that survives in just one exemplar.[40] The map has many cartouches containing descriptive texts, the majority of which are simple rectangular frames, while some of them have very rudimentary strapwork ornamentation

39   The legend on Ruysch's map is translated by Thacher, *The Continent of America* (see note 37), p. 214; and is transcribed and translated by Gaetano Ferro, Luisa Faldini, Marica Milanesi, and Gianni Eugenio Viola, *Columbian Iconography*, trans. Luciano F. Farina and Carla Onorato Wysokinski (Rome: Istituto poligrafico e Zecca dello Stato, Libreria dello Stato, 1996), p. 437.

40   The unique surviving exemplar of Waldseemüller's *Carta marina* is in the Jay I. Kislak Collection at the Library of Congress. For discussion of the map see my "Waldseemüller's World Maps of 1507 and 1516: Sources and Development of his Cartographical Thought," *The Portolan* 85 (Winter, 2012), pp. 8–20; and my "The Carta Marina, 1516," in John Hessler and Chet Van Duzer, *Seeing the World Anew: The Radical Vision of Martin Waldseemüller's 1507 & 1516 World Maps* (Washington, DC: Library of Congress and Delray Beach, FL: Levenger Press, 2012), pp. 49–68. I transcribe and translate all of the descriptive texts on the map in my book *Martin Waldseemüller's Carta marina of 1516: Study and Transcription of the Long Legends* (New York: Springer, 2020), which is available in Open Access.

FIGURE 11   Detail of the New World and relevant cartouches in a hand-colored exemplar of the world map by Johannes Ruysch from the 1508
Rome edition of Ptolemy's *Geography*
LIBRARY OF CONGRESS, GEOGRAPHY AND MAP DIVISION, G1005 1508 VAULT : FOL., COURTESY OF THE LIBRARY OF
CONGRESS

that looks like strips of leather or wrought iron, and is very common in sixteenth-century cartouches. But the map contains two cartouches that are elaborately decorated. The first contains Waldseemüller's statement of his privilege to print the map (Fig. 12), which is decorated with ropework and vegetal motifs; the second is the cartographer's long address to the reader that discusses his reasons for making the map and lists the sources he used (Fig. 13). This latter cartouche has ropework decoration, vegetal motifs, and two dragons at the top. It is important to note that Waldseemüller uses these two elaborate cartouches for the two texts that contain metadata about the map (about its genesis and printing), indicating his clear consciousness of the different nature of these texts in comparison with the descriptive texts in the other plain

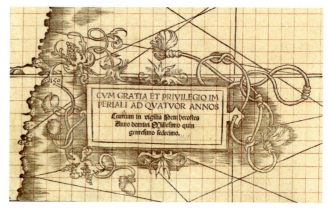

FIGURE 12   Detail of Martin Waldseemüller's *Carta marina* of 1516 showing the elaborate cartouche indicating Waldseemüller's right to print the map
LIBRARY OF CONGRESS, GEOGRAPHY AND MAP DIVISION, JAY I. KISLAK COLLECTION. COURTESY OF THE LIBRARY OF CONGRESS

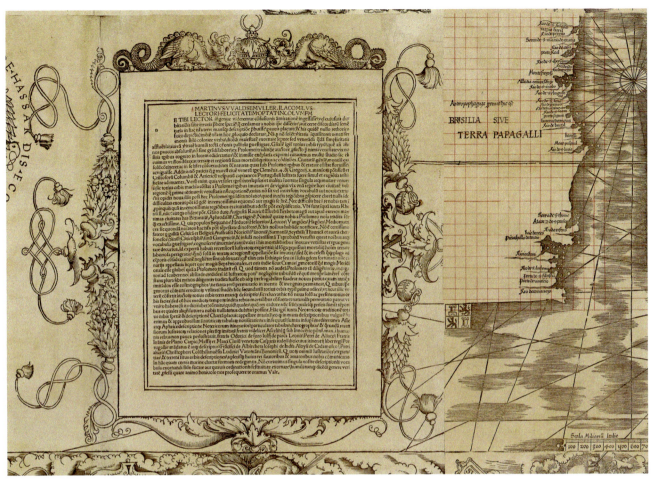

FIGURE 13　Detail of Martin Waldseemüller's *Carta marina* of 1516 showing the elaborate cartouche containing Waldseemüller's address to the reader, reasons for making the *Carta marina*, and list of his sources
LIBRARY OF CONGRESS, GEOGRAPHY AND MAP DIVISION, JAY I. KISLAK COLLECTION. COURTESY OF THE LIBRARY OF CONGRESS

cartouches. That is, Waldseemüller deploys special decorations around the two texts in which he communicates most directly with the viewer, informing him or her about his work.

An early example of a heavily ornamented title cartouche appears on a large map-view of the city of Augsburg that was surveyed by Jörg Seld (*c.*1454–1527) between 1514 and 1516, cut on eight woodblocks by Hans Weiditz (1495–1537), and printed in Augsburg in 1521.[41] The long title is surrounded by a frame with floral and vegetal motifs, and surrounding that frame there are larger vegetal

designs, and at the top, two grotesques in the form of satyrs who are blowing cornucopias and whose bodies dissolve into the vegetal design.

The earliest cartouche I know that contains an inset map is an outlier: it is a detail map of the Holy Land that appears above an anonymous fifteenth-century *mappamundi*, and I am not familiar with any other examples from that century.[42] The earliest sixteenth-century example of such a cartouche—there are earlier maps that have unframed inset maps—is a small anonymous map of Malta printed in 1565 that shows the attack that Soliman

---

41　Jörg Seld's map of Augsburg is titled *Sacri Romani Imperii, urbs Augusta Vindelicorum Caes. Augusto olim dedicate* …; the map is listed by Franz Grenacher, "Guide to the Cartographic History of the Imperial City of Augsburg," *Imago Mundi* 22 (1968), pp. 85–106, at 87; for discussion and a good image of the map see Peter Barber, *The Map Book* (New York: Walker & Company, 2005), pp. 86–89. One of the few surviving copies of the map is in the British Library, Maps *30415.(6.). On Seld see Norbert Lieb, *Jörg Seld, Goldschmied und Bürger von Augsburg: Ein Meisterleben im Abend des Mittelalters* (Munich: Schnell und Steiner, 1947).

42　The *mappamundi* with the inset map of the Holy Land is in Wolfenbüttel, Herzog August Bibliothek, Cod. Guelf. 442 Helmst., Vorderseite. For discussion and illustration of the map see Jörg-Geerd Arentzen, *Imago mundi cartographica* (Munich: W. Fink, 1984), pp. 128–129, 212, 276, and plate 36; Christian Heitzmann, *Europas Weltbild in alten Karten: Globalisierung im Zeitalter der Entdeckungen* (Wiesbaden: Harrassowitz in Kommission, 2006), pp. 36–37; and Chet Van Duzer and Ilya Dines, *Apocalyptic Cartography: Thematic Maps and the End of the World in a Fifteenth-Century Manuscript* (Leiden: Brill, 2016), pp. 115 and 181, with a color illustration on p. 199.

FIGURE 14   An anonymous map of Malta with an early inset map of Europe, *Gewisse verseychniss der insel und Ports Malta* (Nuremberg: Mathias Zündten, 1565)
UNIVERSITÄTSBIBLIOTHEK BASEL, KARTENSLG AA 80. COURTESY OF THE UNIVERSITÄTSBIBLIOTHEK BASEL

the Magnificent, Sultan of the Ottoman Empire, directed against the island during the Great Siege of Malta that same year (Fig. 14).[43] The inset map in the lower left gives the larger cartographic context of the main map, showing all of Europe; its frame has a grotesque at the top, and just as the larger map has its title cartouche in a vertical rectangle at the left, so does the inset map. This suggests that the cartographer was conscious of the nestedness of his map-within-a-map composition.

The earliest cartouches I know whose decoration tells a story are those on a large and elaborate map titled *Peregrinatio filiorum Dei* ("The Wanderings of the Sons of God"), which was designed by Christian Sgrooten and engraved by Joannes and Lucas van Doetecum, and printed in Kalkar in 1572.[44] The map depicts the region from the cen-

tral Mediterranean east and south to the Persian Gulf, that is, the Holy Land and the areas to which the descendants of Noah spread first. It was printed on ten sheets which when assembled measure 98 × 169 cm (more than 3 × 5.5 feet), and it survives in only one exemplar. The map has an impressive set of six cartouches along its upper border. In the upper left corner of the map there is a cartouche decorated with strapwork and vegetal motifs that

---

43   The map of Malta is titled *Gewisse verseychniss der insel und Ports Malta* (Nuremberg: Mathias Zündten, 1565), and there are copies in the British Library, Maps C.7.e.2.(43.), and Basel University Library, Kartenslg AA 80.

44   The map *Peregrinatio filiorum Dei* survives in just one exemplar, in the Basel University Library, Kartenslg AA 119–120, and high-resolution image of the northern and southern halves of the map are available via the UB Basel's online catalog. For discussion of

the map see Fernand van Ortroy, "Chrétien Sgrooten, cartographe, XVIᵉ siècle," *Annales de l'Académie Royal d'Archéologie de Belgique* 71 (1923), pp. 150–306, at 217–219; Carl C. Bernoulli, "Ein Karteninkunabelnband der öffentlichen Bibliothek der Universität Basel," *Verhandlungen der Naturforschenden Gesellscheft in Basel* 18.1 (1905), pp. 58–82, at 79, nos. 119–120, reprinted in *Acta cartograhica* 27 (1981), pp. 358–382; Günter Schilder, *Monumenta cartographica Neerlandica* (Alphen aan den Rijn: Canaletto, 1986–2013), vol. 1, p. 4; Robert W. Karrow, Jr., *Mapmakers of the Sixteenth Century and their Maps: Bio-Bibliographies of the Cartographers of Abraham Ortelius, 1570* (Chicago: Published for The Newberry Library by Speculum Orbis Press, 1993), p. 485; and Henk Nalis, *The New Hollstein: Dutch and Flemish Etchings, Engravings and Woodcuts 1450–1700: The Van Doetecum Family* (Rotterdam: Sound and Vision Interactive, 1998), vol. 3, pp. 85–96, entry 598.

FIGURE 15   Cartouche showing the Resurrection, from Christian Sgrooten, *Peregrinatio filiorum Dei*, 1572
UNIVERSITÄTSBIBLIOTHEK BASEL, KARTENSLG AA 119–120. COURTESY OF THE UNIVERSITÄTSBIBLIOTHEK BASEL

contains Sgrooten's dedication to the Dutch statesman Viglius Zuichemus, and above, his emblem and motto *Vita mortalium vigilia*, "The life of mortals is a vigil."[45] To the right there is a small frame decorated with strapwork containing a quotation from Revelation 6 about the resurrection of the dead at the End of Days. From that frame there arises a system of clouds that encloses a detailed depiction of the Resurrection, with angels helping many of the newly risen, and Christ at the center surrounded by worshippers and holding a cross and a quill pen, the latter indicating his connection with the words of Revelation (Fig. 15).

Further to the right there is a small oval cartouche illustrating the martyrdom of St. John the Baptist, whose feast day is March 6. In the center along the upper border of the map is an oval cartouche of the Crucifixion, and to the right of that, a cartouche depicting the martyrdom of St. Stephen, which is recounted in Acts 7. And finally in the upper right-hand corner of the map there is a very large representation of the Last Judgment, framed by clouds like the scene of the Resurrection; at the top above Christ the words *Judicium Extremum*, "Final Judgment," are inscribed in the clouds. Christ is surrounded by saints, and around his head are the words *Venite benedicti patris mei*, "Come to me, the blessed in my father." Below the saints, wingless angles blow trumpets and show open

books—no doubt the Bible—to hordes of sinners below, many of whom beg for mercy. Flames jet from an unseen source down to the lower right, carrying the damned downward, and in the midst of the flames are words from Matthew 25, *Discedite a me maledicti in ignem aeternum*, "Go away from me, O damned, to eternal fire."

In short, while the map itself shows the region from which the sons of Noah and Christianity first spread, the cartouches at the top of the map show the Crucifixion and the end of Christian history in the Resurrection and Last Judgment. These cartouches are an essential part of the history Sgrooten is trying to tell in the map. Although Sgrooten seems not to have made additional cartouches in which narration and history played such a large role, the cartouches in his two manuscript atlases, produced in the 1590s, are extraordinary in the artistic refinement and elaboration of their strapwork, human figures, and grotesques.[46]

---

45   This same motto of Viglius Zuichemus appears in Hadrianus Junius, *Hadriani Iunii medici Emblemata* (Antwerp: ex officina Christophori Plantini, 1565), p. 11.

46   Sgrooten's two atlases are in Brussels, Bibliothèque Royale, MS 21596, made in 1573, and Madrid, Biblioteca Nacional de España, RES/266, made c.1592. For discussion of the atlases see Alphonse Bayot, "Les deux atlas manuscrits de Chrétien Sgrooten," *Revue des Bibliothèques & Archives de Belgique* 5.3 (1907), pp. 183–204; F.C. Wieder, *Nederlandsche historisch-geographische documenten in Spanje: uitkomsten van twee maanden onderzoek* (Leiden: Brill, 1915), pp. 33–66; Leo Bagrow, *A. Ortelii catalogus cartographorum* (Gotha: Justus Perthes, 1928–30), vol. 1, pp. 58–69; Christian Sgrooten, *Die Karten deutscher Länder im Brüsseler Atlas des Christian s'Grooten* (1573), ed. Hans Mortensen and Arend Lang (Göttingen: Vandenhoeck & Ruprecht, 1959); Christian Sgrooten, *Kaarten van de Nederlanden*, ed. S.J. Fockema Andreae

5   The Sources of Cartouches

Before continuing with our examination of the history of cartouches it is worth pausing to consider the sources that cartographers were using for their cartouches. How would a cartographer trained in copying the outlines of lands and place names go about creating an artistic cartouche? One option was to hire a specialized artist to design the cartouche.[47] For example, Marijn Schapelhouman has shown that the artist Pieter Jansz. provided artwork for more than twenty cartouches on maps by Joan Blaeu between 1635 and 1654.[48] As far as the price of custom cartouches, Mary Pedley has gathered evidence from the eighteenth century showing that the cost of a cartouche could be from 25 to 65 percent of the cost of engraving the plate for a map.[49] This amount is a telling indication of the importance of the cartouche both to the cartographer and to consumers of maps; at the same time, it is easy to imagine cartographers being unhappy about paying out such a large amount of money, and the market found another solution, as we shall see momentarily.

Given that the cartouche could be such a high percentage of the total cost of the map, one imagines that the specialized artists who designed cartouches would want

to take credit for their work and assert their authorship by signing them.[50] It is difficult to be certain when this first happened, but one unusual early case may be found in a map by the English publisher of heraldic books and maps Richard Blome (1635–1705). In 1669 Blome copied a map of North America by the French cartographer Nicolas Sanson, translating it into English and replacing Sanson's rather austere cartouche with a more elaborate one, and in his title he declares that his map, though designed by Sanson, had been "Rendred into English, and Illustrated by Richard Blome"—thus taking credit for the cartouche (we will return to this map later).[51] There was a clearly established vocabulary for signing cartouches: the engraver would write his or her name and the Latin word *sculpsit* ("s/he engraved [it]") or *fecit* ("s/he made [it]"), while the designer would write his or her name and *invenit* ("s/he invented [it]") or *delineavit* ("s/he designed [it]").[52] On rare occasions the roles are specified in a bit more detail: on a 1694 world map by the French cartographer Nicolas de Fer,[53] inscriptions at the bottom of the

and B. Van 't Hoff (Leiden: Brill, 1961); and Peter H. Meurer, *Die Manuskriptatlanten Christian Sgrootens* (Alphen aan den Rijn: Canaletto/Repro-Holland, 2007).

47   Several examples of surviving cartouche sketches are compared with the resultant cartouches on printed maps in Cassandra Bosters, J.F. Heijbroek, and M. Schapelhouman, "Ontwerptekeningen voor kaartdecoraties in de zeventiende eeuw," in Cassandra Bosters, J.F. Heijbroek, and M. Schapelhouman, eds., *Kunst in kaart: decoratieve aspecten van de cartografie* (Utrecht: H & S, HES uitgevers, 1989), pp. 65–94.

48   Marijn Schapelhouman, "Tekeningen van Pieter Jansz., 'Konstig Glasschrijver'," *Bulletin van het Rijksmuseum* 33 (1985), pp. 71–92. On Netherlandish cartographers hiring artists to decorate their maps see Shirley K. Bennett, "Art on Netherlandish Maps, 1585–1685: Themes and Sources," Ph.D. Dissertation, University of Maryland, College Park, 1990, who has also shed light on the connection between Jansz. and Joan Blaeu, though her focus is on art "placed outside the map proper, either in the corners, the spandrels between hemispheres, or in ample borders" (p. 281) rather than on cartouches. However, she does focus on cartouches in her article "Nine Religious Drawings by Nicolaes Berchem: Designs to Ornament Maps in a 1669 Bible," *Hoogst-eder Mercury* 13–14 (1992), pp. 60–73. Also, the National Library of Australia recently acquired a design for a map cartouche by Pieter Jansz, which Joan Blaeu used in his wall map titled *Archipelagus Orientalis, sive Asiaticus*, first printed in 1659. The drawing has the call number MAP RM 4981, and a high-resolution image of it is available at http://nla.gov.au/nla.obj-698612586.

49   Mary Sponberg Pedley, *The Commerce of Cartography: Making and Marketing Maps in Eighteenth-Century France and England* (Chicago: University of Chicago Press, 2005), p. 63.

50   The miniaturist and cartographer Joris Hoefnagel (1542–1601) used cartouche decoration, specifically the frames of two cartouches, to signal his identity, but he was not a separate artist hired to make a cartouche. The map in question is his *Mirabilium sulphureorum motium apud Puteolos (Campos Flegreos Plin. Vulcani forum Strabo Vulgo nunc Solsataria vocant Neapolitani) genuina accuratissimaq[ue] ad viuum depcita representatio*, in Georg Braun and Frans Hogenberg's *Civitates orbis terrarum* (Cologne, 1572–1617), vol. 3, map 58. Hoefnagel's name means "horseshoe nail," and the two cartouches are framed by horseshoes with the nails rising prominently from the page in *trompe-l'oeil*. See Lucia Nuti, "The Mapped Views by Georg Hoefnagel: The Merchant's Eye, the Humanist's Eye," *Word & Image* 4.2 (1988), pp. 545–570; esp. 553–554; and Lubomir Konečný, "Joris Hoefnagel's 'Emblematic' Signature Reconsidered," *Journal of the Warburg and Courtald Institutes* 61 (1998), pp. 267–272, esp. 269.

51   The full title of Blome's map is *A New Mapp of America Septentrionale Designed by Mousieur Sanson Geographer to the French King, and Rendred into English, and Illustrated by Richard Blome by His Majesties Especiall Command* (London: Printed for Richard Blome, 1669). It was printed for inclusion in his book *A Geographical Description of the Four Parts of the World* (London: Printed by T.N. for R. Blome, 1670). On Blome see Thompson Cooper, "Blome, Richard," in Leslie Stephen, ed., *Dictionary of National Biography* (New York: Macmillan; London: Smith, Elder, 1885–1901), vol. 2, pp. 687–688; on his map see Philip D. Burden, *The Mapping of North America: A List of Printed Maps* (Rickmansworth: Raleigh Publications, 1996–2007), vol. 1, p. 397.

52   For the vocabulary of engravers and artists signing maps see Peter van der Krogt, "Latin Texts on Old Maps: Elementary Latin Grammar and Cartographic Word Lists," *The Portolan* 70 (Winter, 2007), pp. 10–26, esp. 17–18.

53   Nicolas de Fer, *Mappe-monde ou carte générale de la terre, divisée en deux hémisphères suivant la projection la plus commune* (Paris: chez l'auteur, 1694). A zoomable image of the map is available at https://gallica.bnf.fr.

map read *la Carte est Gravée par H. van Loon*, "the map was engraved by H[erman] Van Loon," and *les Ornemens Inventé et Gravé par N. Guerard*, "the ornaments were designed and engraved by N[icolas] Guérard."[54] Usually, though, the designer of a cartouche is not indicated, and we are left to surmise, without any certainty, that the engraver also designed the cartouche. There is ample reason to wish that more of the designers of cartouches had signed their works, but even when they do, sometimes we know nothing about them aside from their names.

With regard to a less expensive source of cartouches, beginning in 1543 with the work of Cornelis Bos, the Flemish engraver and publisher, artists created bound series of cartouche designs which are now called pattern books or model books.[55] These model books of cartouches are part of a much wider tradition of model books that served artists in various media; many medieval model books survive, and the earliest printed model book, published by Johann Schönsperger in Augsburg in 1523, was of designs for embroidery and weaving.[56] These model books of cartouches served the artists of their day, but over time their cartouches went out of fashion, and as a result the model books do not survive well;[57] in addition, their bibli-

ography is challenging, as they often do not bear a year of publication or the author's name. But it is well worth listing some of them whose titles are revealing in terms of the names applied to cartouches, or that include indications about the contexts in which they would be used.[58]

The Dutch painter, architect, and engineer Hans Vredeman de Vries (1527–c.1607) published a book of cartouches titled *Multarum variarumque protractionum (compartimenta vulgus pictorum vocat) libellus vtilissumus, iam recens delineatus* (Antwerp: Gerardus Iudaeus, 1555); the title translates as "A Most Useful Book of Many and Varied Drawings, Popularly Called Compartments of Pictures, Recently Sketched Out."[59] The title is noteworthy for its use of the word *compartimenta*, "compartments," for cartouches. The publisher of this model book was the cartographer, engraver, and printer Gerard de Jode (1509–1591), who in the same year printed a world map by Giacomo Gastaldi,[60] the cartouches on which however are simple rectangular frames, and bear no connection with those in the model book. James Welu has shown that Abraham Ortelius borrowed cartouches from Vredeman de Vries' book for the maps in his *Theatrum orbis terrarum*, first printed in 1570.[61] For example, the fifth cartouche in Vredeman de Vries' book (Fig. 16) was copied by Ortelius in his map of New Spain, which was first printed in the 1579 edition of the *Theatrum* (Fig. 17).[62] Welu's analysis

54 For discussion of the different roles of the artists responsible for John Mitchell's famous map of North America see Matthew H. Edney, "John Mitchell's Map of North America (1755): A Study of the Use and Publication of Official Maps in Eighteenth-Century Britain," *Imago Mundi* 60.1 (2008), pp. 63–85, at 81.

55 H.A.M. van der Heijden, *The Oldest Maps of the Netherlands: An Illustrated and Annotated Carto-Bibliography of the 16th Century Maps of the XVII Provinces* (Utrecht: HES, 1987), p. 71, citing Robert Hedicke, *Cornelis Floris und die Florisdekoration* (Berlin: J. Bard, 1913), vol. 1, pp. 295–299. On Bos's collections of cartouches see Marijnke de Jong and Irene de Groot, *Ornamentprenten in het Rijksprentenkabinet* (Amsterdam: Het Kabinet; 's-Gravenhage: Staatsuitgeverij, 1988), p. 29, nos. 23 and 24. On Bos also see Désiré Guilmard, *Les maîtres ornemanistes. Dessinateurs, peintres, architectes, sculpteurs et graveurs. Écoles française, italienne, allemande et des Pays-Bas (flammande & hollandaise)* (Paris: E. Plon, 1880–81), pp. 476–477; and Sune Schéle, *Cornelis Bos: A Study of the Origins of the Netherland Grotesque* (Stockholm: Almqvist & Wiksell, 1965), pp. 165–190 and plates 34–67.

56 On medieval model books see Robert W. Scheller, *Exemplum: Model-Book Drawings and the Practice of Artistic Transmission in the Middle Ages (ca. 900–ca. 1470)*, trans. Michael Hoyle (Amsterdam: Amsterdam University Press, 1995); on early printed model books for Artur Lotz, *Bibliographie der Modelbücher: beschreibendes Verzeichnis der Stick- und Spitzenmusterbücher des 16. und 17. Jahrhunderts* (Leipzig: Hiersemann, 1933); and Lena Dahrén, "Printed Pattern Books for Early Modern Bobbin-made Borders and Edgings," *Konsthistorisk Tidskrift* 82.3 (2013), pp. 169–190.

57 There was a model book titled *Cahier de cartouches pour contenir les titres des différentes Cartes, comme Cartes Militaires, de Marine, Géographie & Topographie, très-utile aux Ingénieurs & Arpenteurs* ("Notebook of Cartouches to Contain the Titles of

Different Maps, such as Military Maps, Marine Maps, Geographical and Topographical Maps, Very Useful for Engineers and Surveyors"), published in Paris by Panseron, probably in 1782, which does not survive, but there are notices of it in the *Journal de Litterature, des Sciences et des Arts* 1782, p. 288; *Affiches, annonces, et avis divers* 41 (October 9, 1782), p. 164; and *Gazette de France* 76 (September 20, 1782), p. 362.

58 The best works on these model books are Désiré Guilmard's *Les maîtres ornemanistes* (see note 55), and de Jong and de Groot, *Ornamentprenten* (see note 55).

59 On Vredeman de Vries' *Multarum variarumque protractionum* see F.W.H. Hollstein, *Dutch and Flemish Etchings, Engravings, and Woodcuts, ca. 1450–1700* (Amsterdam: M. Hertzberger, 1949–2010), vol. 47, nos. 1–13; and de Jong and de Groot, *Ornamentprenten* (see note 55), pp. 95–96, no. 161. On his printed collections of ornaments see Ilja Veldman, "Hans Vredeman de Vries und die Herausbildung des Antwerpener Graphikgewerbes," in Heiner Borggrefe, ed., *Hans Vredeman de Vries und die Renaissance im Norden* (Munich: Hirmer, 2002), pp. 50–58; and Peter Fuhring, "Hans Vredeman de Vries und das Ornament als Vorlage und Modell," in the same book, pp. 60–68.

60 Rodney W. Shirley, *The Mapping of the World: Early Printed World Maps 1472–1700* (London: Holland Press, 1983), p. 113, no. 100.

61 James A. Welu, "The Sources and Development of Cartographic Ornamentation in the Netherlands," in David Woodward, ed., *Art and Cartography: Six Historical Essays* (Chicago: University of Chicago Press, 1987), pp. 147–173 and 233–238, at 150–151.

62 Ortelius's map of New Spain is titled *Hispaniae novae sivae magnae, recens et vera descriptio*; for discussion of it see

FIGURE 16
Cartouche 5 in Hans
Vredeman de Vries,
*Multarum variarumque
protractionum
(compartimenta vulgus
pictorum vocat) libellus
vtilissumus* (Antwerp:
Gerard de Jode, 1555)
RIJKSMUSEUM
RP-P-1988-297-119.
COURTESY OF THE
RIJKSMUSEUM

FIGURE 17
Cartouche from Abraham
Ortelius, *Hispaniae novae
sivae magnae recens
et vera descriptio*, first
published in the 1579
edition of his *Theatrum
orbis terrarum*; this
exemplar is from the 1595
edition
STANFORD UNIVERSITY,
RARE BOOK
COLLECTION, G1006 .T5
1595 FF BB. COURTESY
OF STANFORD
UNIVERSITY LIBRARIES

of Ortelius's borrowing from other model books of cartouches is pioneering and excellent.

A model book of cartouches printed in Antwerp in 1556 and attributed to the Flemish painter printmaker Jacob Floris the Elder (1524–81) bears the title *Varii generis partitionum, seu (ut Italis placet) compartimentorum formae, iam recens, in pictorum, statuariorum, sculptorum, aurifabrorum, architectorum, reliquorumque, id genus artificum gratiam, excogitatae*, that is, "The Shapes of Various Types of Partitions, or, as the Italians Call Them, Compartments, Recently Devised for the Benefit of Painters, Statue-Makers, Sculptors, Goldsmiths, Architects, and Other Artists of this Sort."[63] Both the words "partition" and "compartment" emphasize the separation between cartouche space and cartographic space. and Presumably Floris would have included cartographers—if he was thinking about them—among the painters mentioned in the title.

Some years later Floris created a model book of fourteen cartouches titled *Compertimenta pictoriis flosculis manubissque bellicis variegata* (Antwerp: Hieronymus Cock, 1567); the title translates as "Compartments Decorated with Pictures, Little Flowers, and Armor."[64] Here Floris specifies not the variety of users who could use the book, but rather the variety of decoration in the cartouches.

There is an interesting case of a book by a cartographer which, though it is about the art of writing rather than being a sourcebook of cartouches, is laid out with a cartouche around each example of a different style of writing. This is Jodocus Hondius's *Theatrum artis scribendi: varia summorum nostri seculi artificum exemplaria complectens, novem diversis linguis exarata* (Amsterdam: J. Hondius, 1594);[65] the title translates as "The Theater of the Art of

Writing, Including Many Examples by the Greatest Artists of our Age, Inscribed in Nine Different Languages." The cartouches are not of any symbolic or interpretive interest, but the book does show the great Flemish cartographer (1563–1612) making use of cartouches in another medium. I do not find that Ortelius used any of the cartouches from this book in his maps, or vice versa, which testifies to the great variety of cartouches available.

The title of a model book that has been attributed to the Parisian printer and print seller Jean Messager (*c*.1572–1649) gives a good idea of intended users for the cartouches it contains: the model book is *Diferents conpartiments et chapiteaux, propres, pour tous sculpteurs, peintres, graveurs, macons et autr[e]s* (Paris: Melchior Tauernier, 1619),[66] that is, "Various Elegant Cartouches and Capitals for All Sculptors, Painters, Engravers, Masons, and Others." Messager perhaps thought of cartographers as either the engravers or the painters mentioned in his title.

The engraver Robert Pricke (fl. 1669–98) printed the earliest good collection of cartouches in English in *The Ornaments of Architecture: Containing Compartments, Shields, Mantlings, Foldige, Festones, Monuments for Tombs, Alphabets of Large Letters Plain and Enrich'd, with the Order of Making Them. With some New Designes for Carving and Painting of Eminent Coaches, Useful for Painters, Carvers, Stone-Cutters, Plaisterers. Containing Fifty Copper-Plate-Prints* (London: Printed for Rob. Pricke, 1674).[67] The inclusion of "Eminent Coaches" among the places Pricke

---

Howard F. Cline, "The Ortelius Maps of New Spain, 1579, and Related Contemporary Materials, 1560–1610," *Imago Mundi* 16 (1962), pp. 98–115; and Marcel P.R. van den Broecke, *Ortelius Atlas Maps: An Illustrated Guide* (Houten: HES & De Graaf, 2011), p. 53, no. 13.

63   There is an exemplar of this rare model book in the Provinsjale Biblioteek fan Fryslân, shelfmark 429 BH 1; it is described by de Jong and de Groot, *Ornamentprenten* (see note 55), pp. 75–76, no. 83. Welu, "The Sources and Development" (see note 61), p. 234, says that Ortelius borrowed many cartouches from this model book in his *Theatrum orbus terrarum*.

64   On Floris's *Compertimenta* see Guilmard's *Les maîtres ornemanistes* (see note 55), p. 478; de Jong and de Groot, *Ornamentprenten* (see note 55), pp. 73–74, no. 82; and F.W.H. Hollstein, *Dutch and Flemish Etchings, Engravings, and Woodcuts, ca. 1450–1700* (Amsterdam: M. Hertzberger, 1949–2010), vol. 4, p. 189, nos. 365–399; vol. 6, p. 256, nos. 1–35; and vol. 9, p. 31, nos. 70–104.

65   On Hondius's *Theatrum artis scribendi* see A.S. Osley, "A Man of Many Parts: Jodocus Hondius," in his *Scribes and Sources: Handbook of the Chancery Hand in the Sixteenth Century: Texts from the Writing-Masters Selected, Introduced and Translated* (Boston: D.R. Godine, 1980), pp. 204–212; and Ton Croiset Van Uchelen, "Jodocus Hondius's *Theatrum artis scribendi* Examined

Anew," *Quaerendo* 34.1–2 (2004), pp. 53–86. There is a facsimile edition of the book, Jodocus Hondius, *Theatrum artis scribendi varia summorum nostri seculi, artificiam exemplaria complectens, novem diversis linguis exarata* (Nieuwkoop: Miland, 1969).

66   Guilmard attributes this work to Messager in *Les maîtres ornemanistes* (see note 55), p. 42. On Messager see Vanessa Selbach, "L'activité de l'éditeur d'estampes parisien Jean Messager (vers 1572–1649): l'affirmation de la gravure française du premier quart du XVIIe siècle, au carrefour des influences flamandes et italiennes," *In Monte Artium* 3 (2010), pp. 35–51.

67   On Robert Pricke see Lionel Henry Cust, "Pricke, Robert," in Sidney Lee, ed., *Dictionary of National Biography* (New York: Macmillan; and London: Smith, Elder & Co., 1885–1900), vol. 46, p. 347. On Pricke's book see Eileen Harris, *British Architectural Books and Writers, 1556–1785* (Cambridge, England, and New York: Cambridge University Press, 1990), pp. 379–380; and Elizabeth McKellar, *The Birth of Modern London: The Development and Design of the City 1660–1720* (Manchester, England, and New York: Manchester University Press, 1999), pp. 140–141. In the eighteenth century Matthew Lock published collections of cartouches and other decorative elements in London: see Morrison Heckscher, "Lock and Copland: A Catalogue of the Engraved Ornament," *Furniture History* 15 (1979), pp. 1–23 and 67 plates. Another English model book of cartouches from this same period, a few years earlier than Pricke's, is Robert White, *A New Booke of Variety of Compartments* (London: sold by John Overton, 1671); this model book is available in electronic format at https://archive.org.

FIGURE 18   Cartouche for a map of the Assyrian Empire, designed by
            Johannes Gottfried Haidt and printed in 1745 as part of
            a pattern book of cartouches—it does not seem to have
            been used in a map
            AMSTERDAM, RIJKSMUSEUM, RP-P-1964-1024.
            COURTESY OF THE RIJKSMUSEUM

thought his cartouches belonged is interesting, and shows just how pervasive these decorations were in the seventeenth century. If Pricke was thinking about cartographers using his cartouches, he probably would have seen them as "Painters."

There is an anonymous and undated—but certainly eighteenth-century—bound collection of printed ornaments in Paris that is of particular interest here, as the cartouches in the collection, which were created by Johannes Gottfried Haidt (or Haid) (1714–1776), were designed not just for use on maps, but for specific maps, for historical maps of the Assyrian, Persian, Greek, and Roman empires (Fig. 18).[68] These cartouches come from an also untitled

collection of cartouches and other ornaments made by Haidt and printed in Augsburg by Johann Georg Hertel c.1750.[69] The cartouches show the makers of these model books seeking to make their products immediately useable by cartographers.

To mention another example of model books whose cartouches were used by cartographers, in the third quarter of the eighteenth century Pierre-Philippe Choffard (1730–1809) produced a series of model books titled *1e. cahier de cartouches* ("First Book of Cartouches"), and so forth.[70] The cartographer Jean Janvier (fl. 1746–1776) used the third cartouche from Choffard's first *Cahier* (Fig. 19) in his map *Les Couronnes du Nord comprenant les royaumes de Suede, Danemarck et Norwege* (Paris: Lattré & Delalain, 1762), where it appears reversed left to right (Fig. 20). Normally the engraver had to engrave elements on the printing plate reversing them left to right, so that they would come out correctly when reversed in the printing process. But directionality was not important in cartouche design (aside from words, such as the words of the title), and the engraver found it much easier to copy the cartouche frame directly (unreversed) onto the plate, and it was then reversed left to right when it was printed.[71]

Some of the cartouches from Choffard's model books also appear on maps he engraved, for example on Jean de Beaurain's *Carte topographique de l'isle de Minorque* (Paris: chez l'auteur, 1756),[72] where the cartouche is reversed right-to-left from the first cartouche in his third *Cahier*; and on Giovanni-Antonio Rizzi-Zannoni's *L'Allemagne divisée par cercles* (Paris: chez Lattré, 1782),[73] where the cartouche is

68   The anonymous volume of printed ornaments that contains
      Haidt's cartouches is in the Bibliothèque de l'Institut National
      d'Histoire de l'Art, collections Jacques Doucet, shelfmark NUM 4
      EST 296, and bears the assigned title [Ornements style rocaille:

      recueil factice.] The volume is available in digital format at http://
      bibliotheque-numerique.inha.fr/idurl/1/19097. The cartouche
      for the map of the Persian Empire is discussed and illustrated
      by Margery Corbett, "The Cartouche in English Engraving in the
      16th and 17th Centuries," *Motif* 10 (1962–63), pp. 61–76, at 76.

69   Haidt's collection of cartouches and other ornaments survives
      in just one exemplar in the Technische Informationsbibliothek
      in Hannover. This book is listed in Peter Jessen, *Katalog der
      Ornamentstich-Sammlung des Kunstgewerbe-Museums, mit 200
      Abbildungen* (Leipzig: E.A. Seemann, 1894), p. 31, no. 120.

70   Vera Salomons, *Choffard* (London: J. & E. Bumpus Ltd., 1912),
      addresses the books Choffard illustrated, rather than his cartographic
      work. There is an untitled volume of Choffard's cartouches
      that includes all six *cahiers* in Paris at the Bibliothèque
      de l'Institut National d'Histoire de l'Art, Collections Jacques
      Doucet, NUM FOL RES 103, which is available in digital format.

71   For discussion of engravers reversing or not reversing their
      designs see Ad Stijnman, *Engraving and Etching, 1400–2000:
      A History of the Development of Manual Intaglio Printmaking
      Processes* (London: Archetype Publications, 2012), pp. 160–162.

72   Good images of Beaurain's *Carte topographique de l'isle de
      Minorque* can be consulted at http://www5.kb.dk and https://
      gallica.bnf.fr.

73   A zoomable image of Rizzi-Zannoni's *L'Allemagne divisée par
      cercles* is available at https://gallica.bnf.fr.

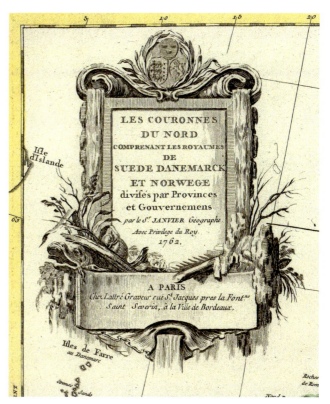

FIGURE 19   The first cartouche from Pierre-Philippe Choffard's
             1ᵉ. cahier de cartouches from the third quarter of the
             eighteenth century
             BIBLIOTHÈQUE NUMÉRIQUE DE L'INSTITUT
             NATIONAL D'HISTOIRE DE L'ART, COLLECTIONS
             JACQUES DOUCET, NUM FOL RES 103. COURTESY OF
             THE INHA

FIGURE 20   The cartouche from Jean Janvier's *Les Couronnes du
             Nord comprenant les royaumes de Suede, Danemarck
             et Norwege* (Paris: Lattre & Delalain, 1762), borrowed
             from Choffard (see fig. 19). The map is in Janvier's *Atlas
             Moderne* (Paris: Lattre & Delalain, 1791)
             STANFORD UNIVERSITY, DAVID RUMSEY MAP
             COLLECTION, G1015 .B6 1791 F. COURTESY OF THE
             DAVID RUMSEY MAP COLLECTION

reversed right-to-left from the sixth cartouche in his third *Cahier*. Given that the *cahiers* are not dated, it is possible that Choffard was collecting in them cartouches he had already created for maps, rather than using them as sources, but the matter is not certain.

In addition to these model books, cartographers had another ready source of cartouches available to them: they could simply copy cartouches from other maps. For example, the Milanese nobleman Urbano Monte (1544–1613), in making his huge 60-sheet manuscript world map of 1587,[74] copied decorations and textual descriptions from

various printed maps, and in particular, he copied the design for the cartouche in which he addresses the reader (Fig. 21) from an anonymous map of Scandinavia titled *Septemtrionalium regionum Suetiae Gothiae Norvegiae Daniae et terrarum adiacentium recens exactaq. descriptio*, printed in Venice by Michele Tramezzino in 1558 (Fig. 22).[75] Copying a cartouche design from an earlier map was quite common.[76]

---

74   Some other examples of cartographers borrowing cartouches from other maps are discussed in Emanuel Chetcuti, "The Cartographic Cartouche in Maps," *Journal of the Malta Map Society* 2.2 (2021), pp. 52–59. On Urbano Monte see Annalisa d'Ascenzo, "Monti, Urbano (Monte dall'Angelo)," in Alberto M. Ghisalberti, ed., *Dizionario Biografico degli Italiani* (Rome: Istituto della Enciclopedia Italiana, 1960-), vol. 76, pp. 298–300; and Chet Van Duzer, "Urbano Monte's World Maps: Sources and Development," *Imago temporis* 14 (2020), pp. 415–435. Monte's 1587 world map is at the David Rumsey Map Center at Stanford University, call number G1015 .M6 1587 F. High-resolution images of all of the sheets of the map, as well as an image of the whole map with

the sheets digitally assembled, are available at https://search works.stanford.edu. The cartouche to the reader, which is the only artistically elaborate cartouche on the map, is on sheet 42.

75   On Tramezzino's 1558 map of Scandinavia see R.V. Tooley, "Maps in Italian Atlases of the Sixteenth Century, Being a Comparative List of the Italian Maps Issued by Lafreri, Forlani, Duchetti, Bertelli and Others, Found in Atlases," *Imago Mundi* 3 (1939), pp. 12–47, at 19, no. 40; and William B. Ginsberg, *Printed Maps of Scandinavia and the Arctic, 1482–1601* (New York: Septentrionalium Press, 2006), pp. 70–73. A high-resolution image of the map may be consulted in the digital version of a composite atlas with the assigned title [Geografia tavole moderne di geografia] at the Library of Congress; the direct link to the map is https://www.loc.gov/item/2006629142/.

76   Just to mention briefly another case of a cartographer copying a cartouche from an earlier map, Johannes van Keulen borrowed

FIGURE 21   Decorative cartouche with Urbano Monte's address to
             the viewer of the map on sheet 42 of his manuscript wall
             map of the world of 1587
             STANFORD UNIVERSITY, DAVID RUMSEY MAP
             COLLECTION, G1015 .M6 1587 F. COURTESY OF THE
             DAVID RUMSEY MAP COLLECTION

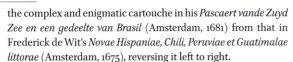

FIGURE 22   Detail of a cartouche on the map *Septemtrionalium
             regionum Suetiae Gothiae Norvegiae Daniae et terrarum
             adiacentium recens exactaq. descriptio*, printed by
             Michele Tramezzino in 1558. In [Geografia tavole
             moderne di geografia] (Rome: Antoine Lafréry, *c.*1575)
             LIBRARY OF CONGRESS, GEOGRAPHY AND MAP
             DIVISION, G1015 .L25 1575B. COURTESY OF THE
             LIBRARY OF CONGRESS

Beginning in the seventeenth century, cartouches often illustrate the flora, fauna, or people indigenous to the region depicted on the map they decorate, but careless copying of cartouches from one geographic context to another can result in striking mismatches between the decoration and the region. James Welu has noted that the Dutch cartographer Justus Danckerts (1635–1701)[77] copied cartouches from earlier maps with great freedom, particularly from Joan Blaeu (1596–1673).[78] For example, for his map of Europe (*Paskaarte vertonende alle de Zekusten van Europa*) of about 1660,[79] Danckerts borrowed one cartouche from Blaeu's map of China (*Imperii Sinarum nova descriptio*) in his *Novus atlas sinensis* (Amsterdam, 1655), and part of a decorative cartouche frame with three naked figures in South America from Willem Jansz. Blaeu's *West*

Indische paskaert of *c.*1630.[80] Danckerts thus relocated Chinese people to the Atlantic, and naked indigenous peoples of South America to the frigid waters north of Iceland.[81]

---

80   There are three surviving exemplars of Blaeu's *West Indische paskaert* in Brussels, Royal Library of Belgium, III 9359; Karlsruhe, Badische Landesbibliothek, D 4 [R]; and Portland, Maine, Osher Map Library, 44362. For discussion of the map see Marcel Destombes and Désiré Gernez, "La 'West Indische paskaert de Willem Jansz. Blaeu' de la Bibliothèque Royale," *Mededeelingen, Academie van Marine van België Communications, Académie de Marine de Belgique* 4 (1947–49), pp. 35–50, reprinted in *Marcel Destombes, 1905–1983: contributions sélectionnées à l'histoire de la cartographie et des instruments scientifiques*, ed. Günter Schilder, Peter van der Krogt, and Steven de Clercq (Utrecht: HES Publishers; Paris: A.G. Nizet, 1987), pp. 23–40; and Günter Schilder, *Monumenta cartographica Neerlandica* (Alphen aan den Rijn: Canaletto, 1986–2013), vol. 4, pp. 114–117.

81   Another example of the copying of cartouche decoration without concern for context is the appearance of a llama in a map of Virginia, the *Nova Virginiae tabula*, included by Arnoldus Montanus in his *De nieuwe en onbekende Weereld* (Amsterdam: Jacob Meurs, 1671) and John Ogilby in his *America* (London: the author, 1671): the engraver of this map, Jacob van Meurs, had included a llama in the cartouche of his map titled simply *Peru* for these same two works, and simply copied it into his cartouche on his map of Virginia. On this type of contextual misplacing of exotica see Benjamin Schmidt, "Collecting Global Icons: The Case of the Exotic Parasol," in Daniela Bleichmar and Peter C. Mancall, eds., *Collecting across Cultures: Material Exchanges in the Early Modern Atlantic World* (Philadelphia: University of Pennsylvania Press, 2011), pp. 31–57 and 292–296, esp. 292 and 296.

---

      the complex and enigmatic cartouche in his *Pascaert vande Zuyd Zee en een gedeelte van Brasil* (Amsterdam, 1681) from that in Frederick de Wit's *Novae Hispaniae, Chili, Peruviae et Guatimalae littorae* (Amsterdam, 1675), reversing it left to right.

77   For discussion of the maps and atlases made by members of the Danckerts family see Cornelis Koeman, *Atlantes Neerlandici: Bibliography of Terrestrial, Maritime and Celestial Atlases and Pilot Books, Published in the Netherlands up to 1880* (Amsterdam: Theatrum Orbis Terrarum, 1967–71), vol. 2, pp. 88–97; and Gyuri Danku and Zoltán Sümeghy, "The Danckerts Atlas: The Production and Chronology of its Maps," *Imago Mundi* 59.1 (2007), pp. 43–77.

78   See Welu, "The Sources and Development" (see note 61), pp. 166–167, and also the remarks on p. 3 of the book in which his article appears, *Art and Cartography*.

79   There is an exemplar of Danckerts' *Paskaarte vertonende alle de Zekusten van Europa* in the British Library, Maps *1040.(2.).

FIGURE 23   The cartouche on Rupert Carl's *Hispania Benedictina seu Monasteria* (Nuremberg: Impensis Homannianorum Heredum 1750)
COURTESY OF COLECCIÓN DE CARTOGRAFÍA ANTIGUA GM

Cartographers also drew material for cartouches from prints and from the title pages, frontispieces, and illustrations in books.[82] For example, the Benedictine cartographer Rupert Carl (1682–1751) made a map titled *Hispania Benedictina seu Monasteria et alia pia loca Ord. S. Benedicti quae in Regni Hispaniae et Portugalliae nec non America*

in hodiernum usque diem florent ("Benedictine Spain, or the Monasteries and Other Holy Places of the Order of St. Benedict that now Flourish in Spain and Portugal and also in America") which was published in Nuremberg by the heirs of Johann Homann in 1750.[83] The cartouche in the lower right corner (Fig. 23) shows a scene in which Benedictine monks are boarding a ship sailing for the missions in the New World. On the ship's mainsail is the text *Unus non sufficit orbis*, "One world is not enough," indicating that the ship is sailing to a destination beyond the "Old World" consisting of Europe, Africa and Asia. In the background we see the monastery from which the monks came, and above it, the Virgin enthroned with Christ on her lap, and above her, a banner with the text *Mater Dei monstrante viam*, "The Mother of God showing the way."

The cartographer borrowed the ship from the frontispiece of a book published about 90 years earlier,[84] namely

82   See Cassandra Bosters et al., *Kunst in kaart: decoratieve aspecten van de cartografie* (Utrecht: H & S, HES uitgevers, 1989), particularly the chapter "Prenten als bron voor het decoreren van kaarten" ("Prints as a Source for Decorating Maps"), pp. 16–64. The book is reviewed by Ralph Hyde in "Review: The Art of the Dutch Map," *Print Quarterly* 7.2 (1990), pp. 189–191. See note 19 above on the cartouche illustration in the map *Guinea propria* (1743) which was borrowed from a book. We will examine several examples of cartouche artists borrowing from book illustrations below, but I will cite here an instance identified by Benjamin Schmidt, *Inventing Exoticism: Geography, Globalism, and Europe's Early Modern World* (Philadelphia: University of Pennsylvania Press, 2015), pp. 233–235, in which the heirs of J.B. Homann based the cartouche in their map *Peninsula Indiae citra Gangem hoc est orae celeberrimae Malabar et Coromandel* (Nuremberg: Homann Heirs, 1733) on the frontispiece from Philippus Baldaeus's *Naauwkeurige beschryvinge van Malabar en Choromandel* (Amsterdam: Johannes Janssonius van Waesberge and Johannes van Someren, 1672).

83   Carl's map is listed by Christian Sandler, *Johann Baptista Homann, Matthäus Seutter und ihre Landkarten: ein Beitrag zur Geschichte der Kartographie* (Amsterdam: Meridian Publishing, 1964), p. 123, no. 7.

84   I owe the observation that the cartouche in Rupert Carl's *Hispania Benedictina* was copied from Vasconcellos' frontispiece to

and removed Vasconcellos's Jesuit symbols to make it a
Benedictine ship, but the cartographer's debt is clear. And
his adaptation of this image to a map, a context where the
idea of travel is implicit, is inspired.

6   The Development of the Cartouche, Sixteenth
to Nineteenth Centuries

As we have seen, the earliest surviving cartouches in the
fourteenth century are simple frames around text, without any decoration; in the fifteenth century some cartographers, including Fra Mauro and Henricus Martellus,
used scroll cartouches. The sixteenth century saw an
explosive development in the decoration of cartouches,
which parallels a great increase in the elaboration of the
decoration of another element containing metadata, the
title pages of books.[86] By the third quarter of the century
complex decoration involving strapwork and grotesques
was common and pervades the work of the leading Dutch
and Flemish cartographers of the period such as Abraham
Ortelius and Gerard Mercator. The elaborateness of Dutch
and Flemish cartouches was part of the unique combination of art and science in these maps from about 1570 to
1670, when they led the world.[87]

During this same period an entirely different style of
cartouche decoration emerged, namely a representational style that we saw for example in the scene of the
Resurrection in Christian Sgrooten's *Peregrinatio filiorum
Dei* of 1572 (see Fig. 15), in which the artist depicts people, monuments, events, animals, or vegetation relevant
to the map. These two styles of cartouche co-existed for
some decades, as indeed they do in Sgrooten's map (also
see Fig. 3), and were sometimes combined in the same

Simão de Vasconcellos' *Chronica da Companhia de Jesu do
estado do Brasil* ("Chronicle of the Company of Jesus of
the state of Brazil") (Lisbon: Henrique Valente de Oliueira,
1663) (Fig. 24).[85] He changed the orientation of the ship
and various details, including which sail bears the motto,

the editor of the page for this map in https://coleccioncartogra
fiagm.com.

85   On Vasconcellos' book see Zulmira Coelho dos Santos, "Em
busca do paraíso perdido: a *Chronica da Companhia de Jesus do
Estado do Brasil* de Simão de Vasconcelos, s.j.," in José Adriano
de Freitas Carvalho, ed., *Quando os frades faziam História* (Porto:
Centro Universitário de História da Espiritualidade, 2001),
pp. 145–178; on the frontispiece see Domingo Ledezma and Luis
Millones Figueroa, "Introducción: los jesuitas y el conocimiento
de la naturaleza americana," in Domingo Ledezma and Luis
Millones Figueroa, eds., *El saber de los jesuitas, historias natu-
rales y el Nuevo Mundo* (Frankfurt am Main: Vervuert, 2005),
pp. 9–26, at 11–12; and José Luis Betrán Moya, "*Unus non sufficit*

orbis: La literatura misional jesuita del Nuevo Mundo," *Historia
Social* 65 (2009), pp. 167–185, at 170–172.

86   On the development of the title page see Sigfrid H. Steinberg,
Five Hundred Years of Printing (New York: Criterion Books,
1959), pp. 105–114; Margaret M. Smith, *The Title-Page, its Early
Development, 1460–1510* (London: British Library; New Castle,
DE: Oak Knoll Press, 2000), esp. pp. 123–142; and Margery
Corbett, "The Architectural Title-Page: An Attempt to Trace Its
Development from its Humanist Origins up to the Sixteenth and
Seventeenth Centuries, the Heyday of the Complex Engraved
Title-page," *Motif* 12 (1964), pp. 49–62. On the title pages of
atlases see Rodney W. Shirley, *Courtiers and Cannibals, Angels
and Amazons: The Art of the Decorative Cartographic Titlepage*
(Houten: Hes & De Graaf, 2009); and Agustín Hernando,
"Retórica iconográfica e imaginación geográfica: los frontispi-
cios de los atlas como proclamaciones ideológicas," *Boletín de la
Asociación de Geógrafos Españoles* 51 (2009), pp. 353–369.

87   Welu, "The Sources and Development" (see note 61), p. 147,
among many other sources that might be cited.

FIGURE 25   The cartouche from Abraham Ortelius's map *Terra Sancta, a Petro Laicstain perlustrata* from the 1595 edition of his atlas
STANFORD UNIVERSITY, RARE BOOK COLLECTION, G1006 .T5 1595 FF BB. COURTESY OF STANFORD UNIVERSITY LIBRARIES

cartouche, as Ortelius did in the cartouche of his map of the Holy Land titled *Terra Sancta, a Petro Laicstain perlustrata* (Fig. 25), first printed in the 1584 German and Latin editions of his atlas.[88] This cartouche has the strapwork, garlands, and a grotesque mask typical of Ortelius's other cartouches, but it also has medallions depicting the crucifixion, nativity, and resurrection of Christ, scenes very relevant to the area depicted on the map. Representational elements are included within the strapwork structure.

In the early seventeenth century the elaborateness of cartouche strapwork-and-grotesque decoration began to decline, while representational elements became more prominent.[89] The cartouche in Fig. 2, from North America

on Pieter van den Keere's world map of 1611, offers a good example of this change: the lower half of the cartouche is still framed by a combination of plants and monstrous animals, but here the animals, rather than invented composites, are realistically rendered creatures indigenous to the Americas (an alligator, crocodile, and birds). There is some strapwork, and the horse's legs and bull's skull at the bottom are grotesques, but these elements have a subsidiary role, and the focus of the cartouche is the three explorers, Vespucci, Magellan, and Columbus, who discuss a map of South America at the top of the cartouche. All three of them, of course, played a role in exploring the New World, which is the part of the world where the cartouche appears, so the decoration is appropriate to the region in which they are depicted.

Important evidence regarding the illustrative materials cartographers wanted for their cartouches around the middle of the seventeenth century is supplied by a letter from the Dutch cartographer Joan Blaeu (1596–1673) to Sir John Scot of Scotstarvet (1585–1670) regarding maps for an atlas of Scotland. The letter is dated March 10, 1642, and Blaeu published the atlas of Scotland in 1654 as volume 5 of his *Theatrum orbis terrarum sive atlas novus* ("Theater of

88   On Ortelius's map of the Holy Land see Kenneth Nebenzahl, *Maps of the Holy Land: Images of Terra Sancta through Two Millennia* (New York: Abbeville Press, 1986), pp. 84–86; Peter van der Krogt, *Koeman's Atlantes Neerlandici* ('t Goy-Houten: HES & De Graaf Publishers, 1997–2010), vol. 3B, p. 871, 8150:31D; and van den Broecke, *Ortelius Atlas Maps* (see note 62), p. 224, no. 173. A digital version of the hand-colored copy of the 1595 edition of Ortelius's *Theatrum orbis terrarum* at Stanford, which is that illustrated in Fig. 25, is available at https://searchworks.stanford.edu/view/201273.

89   Welu, "The Sources and Development" (see note 61), p. 157.

the World or New Atlas").[90] Blaeu writes that the proofs of the maps that he has seen were:[91]

"still lacking for completion the ornament, titles, mile scales and some other details; to the adornment of which many things would help me—notices of the graces of each region, the fruits which it bears, the metals it produces, the animals it begets or nourishes, and such things; and most immediately necessary are the arms or insignia, with the names, whether of dukes or counts or barons or other notable men which you judge fit to be inserted singly. Inasmuch as all these things contribute to the splendour of the maps, let them add no less the descriptions of the genealogy of those men, if they may be had from them."

In addition to indicating the types of material that were of interest for cartouche decoration in the mid seventeenth century, the passage shows the cartographer himself taking an active role in the gathering of that material, rather than leaving the task to an artist hired to design the cartouches: see the discussion above of Blaeu's hiring of Pieter Jansz. to design cartouches for him between 1635 and 1654.

A telling example of the decreasing elaborateness of strapwork-and-grotesque decoration in the course of the seventeenth century,[92] and also of the different tastes in cartouches among different cartographers, is supplied by the maps in two editions of Ptolemy's *Geography*, those of 1578 and 1695. The maps in the 1578 Cologne edition of Ptolemy, which are the most skillfully engraved and elegant that illustrate any edition of Ptolemy, were designed by Gerard Mercator (1512–1594).[93] Many of the cartouches

contain the elaborate strapwork and grotesques typical of Dutch and Flemish cartography of the latter part of the sixteenth century. The copper printing plates for the maps of this edition were reused in the editions of 1584 (Cologne), 1605 (Amsterdam), and 1618 (Leiden),[94] and in each of these, no alteration to the cartouches was thought necessary. Indeed, altering the cartouches on the copperplates would have been a time-consuming and thus expensive undertaking. The plates were re-used again for the maps in the 1695 edition of the *Geography*,[95] but after the passage of almost 120 years since the original 1578 edition, the cartouches were evidently felt to be hopelessly old-fashioned, so much so that they would have reduced sales of the book, and the plates were laboriously revised, and all of the cartouches replaced with less elaborate ones, a truly remarkable change.[96]

In Fig. 26 we see the cartouche on the sixth map of Asia in the 1618 edition of the *Geography*, the last printed with the plates before their revision, and in Fig. 27, the same map in the 1695 edition. The latter image shows a radical revision of the cartouche. It is much smaller, less than half the size of the earlier cartouche, and much more modestly decorated, abandoning the extravagant strapwork and grotesques of its predecessor. The area around the new cartouche is blank rather than filled with the dots

90   Blaeu's atlas of Scotland has been published in facsimile, with commentary, as Joan Blaeu, *The Blaeu Atlas of Scotland* (Edinburgh: Birlinn in association with National Library of Scotland, 2006).

91   Blaeu's letter is preserved in Edinburgh, National Library of Scotland, Adv. MS 17.1.9, f. 5r, and the text is translated in D.G. Moir and R.A. Skelton, "New Light on the First Atlas of Scotland," *Scottish Geographical Magazine* 84.3 (1968), pp. 149–159, at 155; and more recently in Ian Campbell Cunningham, "The Blaeu-Scott Correspondence," in Joan Blaeu, *The Blaeu Atlas of Scotland* (see note 90), letter 8. Part of this passage is quoted by J.H. Andrews, *Maps in Those Days: Cartographic Methods before 1850* (Dublin: Four Courts Press, 2009), p. 442.

92   On the aesthetic changes in cartouches from the sixteenth to the seventeenth centuries see the remarks by H.A.M. van der Heijden, *The Oldest Maps of the Netherlands: An Illustrated and Annotated Carto-Bibliography of the 16th Century Maps of the XVII Provinces* (Utrecht: HES, 1987), pp. 71–72.

93   The 1578 edition of Ptolemy's *Geography* is titled *Tabulae Geographicae Cl. Ptolemaei* (Cologne: Typis Godefridi Kempensis, 1578); a digital version of the book is available at http://daten.digitale-sammlungen.de/bsb00093632/image_1. On this edition see Wilberforce Eames, *A List of Editions of Ptolemy's Geography*

1475–1730 (New York, 1886), pp. 24–25; Carlos Sanz, *La Geographia de Ptolomeo* (Madrid: Librería General V. Suárez, 1959), pp. 227–228; Józef Babicz, "Die Kugelgestalt der Erde als Grundlage des Modells der Kartenzeichnung von Gerhard Mercator bei der Redaktion der Ptolemäischen Geographie, 1578," *Der Globusfreund* 43–44 (1995–96), pp. 55–58; and Peter van der Krogt, *Koeman's Atlantes Neerlandici* ('t Goy-Houten: HES & De Graaf Publishers, 1997–2003), vol. 1, pp. 479–481, with bibliography.

94   On the 1584, 1605, and 1618 editions of Ptolemy see Eames, *A List of Editions of Ptolemy's Geography* (see note 93), pp. 25–26, 28–29, and 31–33, respectively; Sanz, *La Geographia de Ptolomeo* (see note 93), pp. 229–232, 239–240, and 242, respectively; and van der Krogt, *Koeman's Atlantes Neerlandici* (see note 93), pp. 481–486, with bibliography.

95   On the 1695 edition of the *Geography* see Eames, *A List of Editions of Ptolemy's Geography* (see note 93), p. 33; and van der Krogt, *Koeman's Atlantes Neerlandici* (see note 93), pp. 491–493.

96   A similar fate befell the cartouches on some maps in Mercator's *Atlas sive cosmographicae meditationes* (Duisburg, 1595) when Johannes Janssonius and Henricus Hondius revised his maps for their 1633 atlas: see Gerard Mercator, *Atlas; or, A Geographicke Description of the World, Amsterdam 1636*, with an introduction by R.A. Skelton (Amsterdam: Theatrum Orbis Terrarum, 1968), pp. xii and xxv. Compare for example Mercator's map *Forum Iulium Karstia, Carniola Histria et Windorum Marchia* of c.1619 with the Hondius-Janssonius map *Eboracum Lincolnia, Derbia, Staffordia, Notinghamia, Lecestria, Rutlandia, et Norfolcia* of c.1630. On the history of these atlases see J. Keuning, "The History of an Atlas: Mercator-Hondius," *Imago Mundi* 4 (1947), pp. 37–62.

FIGURE 26   The elaborate cartouche on the sixth map of Asia from
the 1618 edition of Ptolemy's *Geography*, Petrus Bertius's
Theatrum geographiae veteris (Amsterdam: Isaacus
Elzevirius and Iudoci Hondii, 1618)
STANFORD UNIVERSITY, DAVID RUMSEY MAP
COLLECTION, G1033 .B4 1618. COURTESY OF THE
DAVID RUMSEY MAP COLLECTION

FIGURE 27   The revised, smaller, and much simplified cartouche on
the sixth map of Asia from the 1695 edition of Ptolemy's
Geography, i.e. *Claudii Ptolemaei Tabulae geographicae orbis
terrarum veteribus cogniti* (Utrecht: François Halma, 1695)
COURTESY OF BARRY LAWRENCE RUDERMAN RARE
MAPS

representing the ocean, and this blank area shows the full
extent of the scrapping done to remove the old cartouche
from the plate. The 1695 edition of the *Geography* was
printed in Franeker, the Netherlands, by Leonardus Strick
(Leonard Strik) and in Utrecht by François Halma.[97] Over
the course of his career Halma published several books
with maps; in 1692 he had published Nicolas Sanson's
Introduction a la geographie, and would later publish
Sanson's *Description de tout l'univers, en plusieurs cartes*
(1700), and material from Sanson appeared in *Kanaän en
d'Omleggende Landen* (1717). The famous French cartographer Sanson (1600–67) is well known for making maps
with a more restrained aesthetic, reducing decoration and
being perfectly comfortable leaving blank spaces where
knowledge was lacking,[98] and it is tempting to think that

Sanson had a role in the decision to revise the cartouches
in the new edition of Ptolemy to make them smaller and
less elaborate.

In 1630 Louis XIII appointed Sanson royal geographer
("Géographe ordinaire du Roi"), a position he continued
to hold under Louis XIV, and through which he had an
immense influence on French cartography. The maps that
he and later his sons Guillaume (1633–1703) and Adrien
(1639–1718) made were instrumental in moving the
European center of map production from the Netherlands
to France,[99] and the cartographers Guillaume Delisle
(1675–1726) and Nicolas Bellin (1703–1772) continued his
tradition of placing more emphasis on the accuracy of
maps than on their decoration.

Despite Sanson's influence, more decorative styles of
cartography remained popular outside of France, and
good evidence of this continuation can be seen in a copy
made of one of Sanson's maps. Sanson made his 1650
map of North America, titled *Amerique Septentrionale,*

97   On Halma see G.A. Evers, "François Halma te Utrecht," *Het
Boek* 6 (1917), pp. 135–146.

98   A later French cartographer, Jean-Baptiste Bourguignon d'Anville
(1697–1782), is explicit about his willingness to leave blank
spaces in his *Éclaircissemens géographiques sur la carte de l'Inde*
(Paris: Imprimerie Royale, 1753), p. 134: *Ne convient-il pas que le
vuide d'une carte avertisse du défaut de connoissance? Un histo-
rien fidèle, qui trouve une lacune ou quelque interruption dans
une suite d'événemens, se permet-il d'y suppléer d'imagination,
lors même, qu'il pourroit juger le faire avec vrai-semblance?*, that
is, "Is it not appropriate that an empty space on a map should
indicate a lack of knowledge? Can a faithful historian, who finds

a lacuna or some interruption in a series of events, allow himself
to supply the gap from his imagination, even when he believes
he could do so with verisimilitude?"

99   On the movement of the center of map production from
the Netherlands to France see Mireille Pastoureau, "Guerre
cartographique sous Louis XIV: l'*Atlas Nouveau* de Jaillot,"
Mappemonde 1 (1987), pp. 31–34.

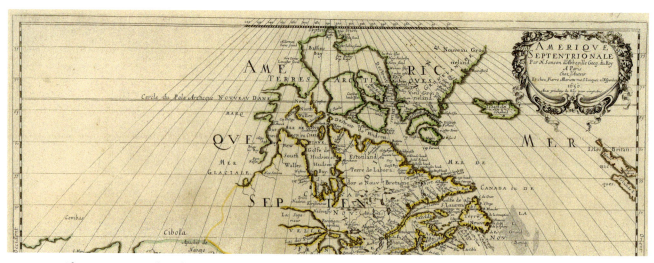

FIGURE 28   The upper portion of Nicolas Sanson's *Amerique Septentrionale* (Paris, 1650), showing a modest cartouche and ample blank space in northwestern North America

JOHN CARTER BROWN LIBRARY, CABINET C650 SAN. COURTESY OF THE JOHN CARTER BROWN LIBRARY

FIGURE 29   The upper portion of Richard Blome's version of Sanson's map, titled *A Geographical Description of the Four Parts of the World* (London, 1669), with a much larger and more elaborate cartouche than Sanson's, and also a coat of arms added

GLEN MCLAUGHLIN MAP COLLECTION, STANFORD UNIVERSITY. COURTESY OF THE GLEN MCLAUGHLIN MAP COLLECTION

using information from the latest narratives by French and Spanish explorers in North America, and it was the most influential map of the continent in the seventeenth century.[100] Its one cartouche in the upper right corner is modestly decorated with garlands and ribbons (Fig. 28). Richard Blome, the English publisher of heraldic books

and maps mentioned above, printed a map based on Sanson's map in 1669, acknowledging his source in the title.[101] But he was clearly unsatisfied with Sanson's austere cartouche, for he adorned his version of the map with a much larger and more elaborate cartouche, including drapery instead of ribbons, more showy vegetation, and two angels with trumpets (Fig. 29).

And the Sansons' influence in terms of favoring less decoration on maps was not even complete on their patron, Louis XIV.[102] Cardinal César d'Estrées (1628–1714),

---

100   On Sanson's map of North America see Burden, *The Mapping of North America* (see note 51), vol. 1, p. 294 (state 3); Mireille Pastoureau, *Les atlas français, XVIᵉ–XVIIᵉ siècles* (Paris: Bibliothèque nationale, Dép. des cartes et plans, 1984), pp. 387–389; Henry R. Wagner, *The Cartography of the Northwest Coast of America to the Year 1800* (Berkeley: University of California Press, 1937), vol. 2, pp. 130–132, no. 360; and Jennifer Turnham, "Mapping the New World: Nicolas Sanson's *Amérique Septentrionale* and French Cartography in the Seventeenth Century," *The Portolan* 45 (1999), pp. 25–40.

101   On Richard Blome and his map see note 51 above.

102   On Louis XIV's interest in maps see Monique Pelletier, "Cartographie et pouvoir sous les règnes de Louis XIV et Louis XV," in Danielle Lecoq and Antoine Chambard, eds., *Terre à découvrir, terres à parcourir: Exploration et connaissance du monde, XIIᵉ–XIXᵉ siècles* (Paris: L'Harmattan, 1998), pp. 112–127.

FIGURE 30   Cartouche on the line of demarcation between the overseas territories of Spain and Portugal, on Vincenzo Coronelli's terrestrial
globe made for Louis XIV 1681–83. Paris, BnF, GE A-500 (RES)
COURTESY OF THE BIBLIOTHÈQUE NATIONALE DE FRANCE

an adviser to Louis XIV, was impressed with globes that the Italian cartographer Vincenzo Coronelli (1650–1718) had made for the Duke of Parma, and commissioned him to make globes as a gift for the French king. Coronelli spent two years (1681–83) in Paris making a pair of colossal terrestrial and celestial globes, each 3.84 m (12.6 feet) in diameter,[103] and their elaborate decoration, and in par-

ticular the beautiful cartouches on the terrestrial globe, were totally at odds with the philosophy of the Sansons and their followers.

The globe was painted by Arnould de Vuez (1644–1720),[104] but Coronelli's later maps and globes—as we shall see below—are distinguished by their elaborate,

---

103   Coronelli's colossal globes are in Paris in the François Mitterrand branch of the Bibliothèque nationale de France. For discussion of the globes see Monique Pelletier, "Les globes de Louis XIV: les sources françaises de l'oeuvre de Coronelli," *Imago Mundi* 34 (1982), pp. 72–89; Catherine Hoffmann and Hélène Richard, eds., *Les globes de Louis XIV: étude artistique, historique et*

matérielle (Paris: Bibliothèque nationale de France, 2012); and Marica Milanesi, *Vincenzo Coronelli Cosmographer (1650–1718)* (Turnhout: Brepols, 2016), pp. 47–132.

104   Barbara Brejon de Lavergnée, "Arnould de Vuez peintre des globes de Louis XIV," in Catherine Hofmann and Hélène Richard, eds., *Les globes de Louis XIV: étude artistique, historique et matérielle* (Paris: Bibliothèque nationale de France, 2012), pp. 119–129.

FIGURE 31   One of the cartouches from a copy of Hendrick Doncker's *Pascaerte van Oost Indien* added to a copy of Pieter Goos's *Zee-atlas ofte*
                    waterwereld (Amsterdam: Albert Magnus, *c.* 1677)

fascinating cartouches, so it seems likely that he was involved in designing the cartouches on the globe for Louis XIV. For example, the cartouche in the South Atlantic about the *ligne de demarcacion* (line of demarcation) between the overseas possessions of Spain and Portugal, established by the Treaty of Tordesillas in 1494, is surrounded by a spectacular frame of sea shells, coral, and strings of jewels, and the emblem of the Order of the Golden Fleece (Fig. 30).[105] The dedicatory cartouche to Louis XIV, located on the hypothetical southern continent in the southern Indian Ocean, has the dedication inscribed on a monument which is surrounded by women who personify the arts and sciences, each holding an object that identifies her, as well as palm and laurel trees and military trophies; atop the monument is a bust of Louis XIV being crowned by Victory, and winged Fame blowing a trumpet.[106] The cartouche occupies a significant percent-

age of the globe's surface, and that fact combined with the globe's enormous size entails that it is one of the largest cartouches of the early modern period.

Thus at the same time that the Sansons and their followers offered of more "scientific" maps with modest cartouches, decorative maps with elaborate cartouches continued to be produced both in France and elsewhere in Europe. For example, a copy of Pieter Goos's *De Zee-atlas ofte water-wereld* (Amsterdam: Albert Magnus, *c.* 1677) in the Utrecht University Library was supplemented with three printed maps, one of Europe, one of the Atlantic, and another of the Indian Ocean.[107] The

---

105   The text of Coronelli's cartouche about the line of demarcation is transcribed in [François Le Large], *Recueil des inscriptions des remarques historiques et géographiques qui sont sur le globe terrestre de Marly*, Paris, Bibliothèque nationale de France, MS fr. 13365, pp. 179–181; a digital version of the manuscript is available at https://gallica.bnf.fr. For discussion of the manuscript see Gabrielle Duprat, "Deux manuscrits inédits, décrivant le globe terrestre de Marly, construit et dessiné par Coronelli (1681 à 1683)," *Der Globusfreund* 25–27 (1977–79), pp. 203–208.

106   The dedication to Louis XIV on Coronelli's globe is transcribed in Bibliothèque nationale de France, MS fr. 13365, p. 137 (see the

previous note), and the decoration of the cartouche is described in François Le Large, *Explication pour les figures qui accompagnent la dédicace du globe terrestre de Marly*, Paris, Bibliothèque nationale de France, MS fr. 13366, esp. pp. 1–3; a digital version of the manuscript is available at https://gallica.bnf.fr. For discussion of these allegorical figures on Coronelli's globe see Marica Milanesi, "The Dedication and Allegorical Figures," in her *Vincenzo Coronelli Cosmographer (1650–1718)* (Turnhout: Brepols, 2016), pp. 114–116.

107   This special copy of Goos's *De Zee-atlas* is in Utrecht UB, MAG: Utenhove fol 88 Lk Rariora. A digital version of the atlas is available at http://objects.library.uu.nl; the three added maps are on pp. 30 (Europe) 96 (Atlantic) and 108 (Indian Ocean) of the PDF. These three maps are reproduced in Günter Schilder and Hans Kok, *Sailing across the World's Oceans: History & Catalogue of Dutch Charts Printed on Vellum, 1580–1725* (Leiden and Boston: Brill and Hes & De Graaf, 2019), figs. 2.14–16.

hand-coloring on these maps is of a very high caliber and has been attributed to the famous colorist Dirk Jansz. van Santen (1637–1708).[108] In Fig. 31 we see a cartouche from the map of the Indian Ocean in this atlas, which is Hendrick Doncker's *Pascaerte van Oost Indien* from circa 1664.[109] Although the cartouche is in the lower left-hand corner of the map, south of Australia, it illustrates life in Africa, which is at the right-hand edge of the map: this is confirmed by the African animals, an elephant, cheetah, ostrich, and camels. The indigenous peoples in the foreground seem quite placid, while in the background an energetic deer hunt is underway. In the distance a European ship sails up the coast, and the headland supports what seems to be a European tower, but in general this elaborate cartouche displays remarkably little in the way of colonial discourse.

The amount of decoration, and the elaborateness of the cartouches, on a European map depended on the cartographer's taste and also the taste of map buyers, but while many European cartographers in the second half of the seventeenth century continued to make ornate cartouches like Goos's, there was another region (in addition to certain cartographic workshops in France) where more modest cartouches were the rule during this same period, which was the New World. This is to be expected, as the exigencies of daily life were paramount, artists were less numerous, and printing facilities were still being established.

As part of this brief history of cartouches, it is important to examine the first appearances of this art form in the New World. The earliest detailed map printed in the New World seems to have been an untitled map of Hispaniola, Tortuga, and part of Cuba made by the Spanish judge Juan Francisco de Montemayor y Córdova de Cuenca (1620–85) to illustrate his book *Discurso politico historico jurídico del derecho, y repartimiento de presas y despojos aprehendidos en justa guerra* (Mexico City: Juan Ruíz, 1658) (Fig. 32).[110] The simple cartouche, with modest strapwork,

FIGURE 32   The simple cartouche on an untitled map of Hispaniola, Tortuga, and part of Cuba made by the Juan Francisco de Montemayor y Córdova de Cuenca to illustrate his book *Discurso politico historico jurídico del derecho, y repartimiento de presas y despojos aprehendidos en justa guerra* (Mexico City: Juan Ruiz, 1658)
JOHN CARTER BROWN LIBRARY, B658 M777D.
COURTESY OF THE JOHN CARTER BROWN LIBRARY

contains the legend that identifies four features of the map which are indicated with the letters A to D.

The first map printed in what is now the United States is *A Map of New-England, being the First that Ever was Here Cut* (Boston, 1677), a woodcut made to illustrate William Hubbard's *A Narrative of the Troubles with the Indians in New England* (Boston: John Foster, 1677). The map has often been attributed to John Foster, but was probably designed by Hubbard;[111] it has an even plainer cartouche

108   On other works colored by van Santen see Herman de la Fontaine Verwey, "The Glory of the Blaeu Atlas and the Master Colourist," *Quaerendo* 11 (1981), pp. 197–229; and Truusje Goedings, "Dirk Jansz. van Santen and the Colouring of the Atlas of Laurens van der Hem," in Koert van der Horst, ed., *The Atlas Blaeu-van der Hem. The History of the Atlas and the Making of the Facsimile* (Houten: Hes & De Graaf, 2011), pp. 101–154.

109   Doncker's *Pascaerte van Oost Indien* is described in Schilder and Kok, *Sailing across the World's Oceans* (see note 107), pp. 629–636.

110   On Montemayor de Cuenca's map as the first printed in the New World see Louis C. Karpinski's review of Florian Cajori, *The Early Mathematical Sciences in North and South America*, in *Isis* 12.1 (1929), pp. 163–165, at 165. The map is listed by Luis Emilio Alemar, "Apuntes para la cartografía dominicana," *Boletín*

del *Archivo General de la Nación* (Santo Domingo) 4.17 (1941), pp. 218–222, at 222, no. 230; and in Emilio Cueto, *Cuba in Old Maps* (Miami: Historical Museum of Southern Florida, 1999), p. 253, note 282. A high-resolution image of the map is available on the website of the John Carter Brown Library, at https://jcb.lunaimaging.com. On Montemayor and his works see Javier Barrientos Grandón, *Juan Francisco Montemayor: Un jurista aragonés en las Indias* (Zaragoza: Diputación Provincial de Zaragoza, Área de Cultura, 2001); and Oscar Cruz Barney, "La bibliografía del Discurso político jurídico del derecho y repartimiento de presas y despojos aprehendidos en justa guerra. Premios y castigos de los soldados de don Juan Francisco de Montemayor y Córdoba de Cuenca," *Anuario Mexicano de Historia del Derecho*, México, UNAM, Instituto de Investigaciones Jurídicas 14 (2002), pp. 165–218.

111   After Hubbard's map was printed in Boston a new woodblock was cut in London and the map was printed again there to illustrate a London edition of his book, also published in 1677; the two versions of the map may be distinguished by the fact that on the first, the hills north of Lake Winnipesaukee are labeled

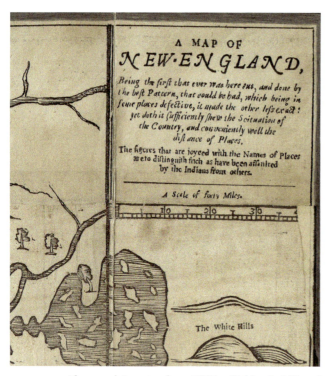

than that on the map by Montemayor de Cuenca—a simple linear frame around the title (Fig. 33). But elaborate cartouches were soon being made in the New World. The earliest printed map of Boston was made in 1722 by John Bonner and is titled *The Town of Boston in New England*; it has no cartouche, and its title is written in the upper left without any frame.[112] In 1728 the Boston publisher

William Burgis printed an engraved map of his city that was based closely on Bonner's, titled it a *Plan of Boston in New England*, and dedicated it to William Burnet, then acting governor of the Province of Massachusetts Bay.[113] Burgis placed a large cartouche on the map that has the legend below, the coat of arms and motto of Burnet above (*Virescit vulnere virtus*, "Courage grows strong through a wound"), the god Mercury on the left, representing the commerce of the city, and on the right, the goddess of agriculture Ceres who is looking at Mars, the god of war (Fig. 34). Thus the cartouche represents the agricultural abundance, military power, and commerce of Boston. The cartouche is no masterpiece, but it does show that by the first quarter of the eighteenth century elaborate cartouches were being produced in the New World.[114]

The earliest map printed in South America was made by the Jesuit evangelist Samuel Fritz (1654–1724), and was printed in 1707 in Quito, for Jesuit officials in that province. It shows the course of the Amazon and the areas where the Jesuits were active in the river's upper basin.[115] Perhaps in part because it is later than the two earliest maps printed in North America, its cartouches are more elaborate (Fig. 35). The map's title is in a banner at the top center, while the dedication to Philip V of Spain (r. 1700–1724 and 1724–1746) is in the upper right corner, framed by native birds and fruits typical of the region such as pineapple and bananas. In the lower right there is a large cartouche with text about the Amazon and the history of the Jesuits in the region near the river. This frame

the White Hills, and on the latter the Wine Hills. See David Woodward, "The Foster Woodcut Map Controversy: A Further Examination of the Evidence," *Imago Mundi* 21 (1967), pp. 50–61. For additional discussion of the map see James Clements Wheat and Christian F. Brun, *Maps and Charts Published in America before 1800: A Bibliography* (New Haven: Yale University Press, 1969), pp. 144–145; and Barbara Backus McCorkle, *New England in Early Printed Maps, 1513 to 1800: An Illustrated Carto-Bibliography* (Providence, RI: John Carter Brown Library, 2001), p. 41, no. 677.2. Matthew H. Edney and Susan Cimburek argue that the map was made by Hubbard in "Telling the Traumatic Truth: William Hubbard's *Narrative* of King Philip's War and his 'Map of New-England'," *William & Mary Quarterly* 61.2 (2004), pp. 317–348. A high-resolution image of Hubbard's map may be consulted at https://www.digitalcommonwealth.org/search.

112   On Bonner's map of Boston see John W. Reps, "Boston by Bostonians: The Printed Plans and Views of the Colonial City by its Artists, Cartographers, Engravers, and Publishers," in *Boston Prints and Printmakers 1670–1775* (Boston: The Colonial Society of Massachusetts, 1973), pp. 3–56, at 8–14; and Alex Krieger and David Cobb, eds., *Mapping Boston* (Cambridge, MA: MIT Press,

1999), pp. 174–175. A good digital image of Bonner's map may be consulted at https://www.digitalcommonwealth.org/search.

113   A high-resolution image of Burgis's map of Boston is available at https://loc.gov. On Burgis's works see Richard B. Holman, "William Burgis," in *Boston Prints and Printmakers, 1670–1775* (Boston: Colonial Society of Massachusetts, 1973), pp. 57–81; on his map see Reps, "Boston by Bostonians" (see note 112), pp. 14–32; and Krieger and Cobb, eds., *Mapping Boston* (see note 112), pp. 176–177.

114   An interesting demonstration of how taste regarding cartouches changes over time is supplied by the facsimile edition of Burgis's map published by the Bostonian Society in 1885, on which the cartouche has been removed. For an image of this facsimile see https://collections.leventhalmap.org/search/commonwealth:9s161951b.

115   Fritz's map is titled *El gran rio Marañon o Amazonas con la Mission de la Compañia de Iesus* (Quito: J.N. Iesu quondam in hoc Marañone Missionarius Sculpebat, 1707). For discussion of it see André Ferrand de Almeida, "Samuel Fritz and the Mapping of the Amazon," *Imago Mundi* 55 (2003), pp. 113–119; and Camila Loureiro Dias, "Jesuit Maps and Political Discourse: The Amazon River of Father Samuel Fritz," *The Americas* 69.1 (2012), pp. 95–116. On Fritz see David Graham Sweet, "Samuel Fritz, S.J. and the Founding of the Portuguese Carmelite Mission to the Solimões," chapter 6 of "A Rich Realm of Nature Destroyed: The Middle Amazon Valley, 1640–1750," Ph.D. Dissertation, University of Wisconsin, 1974.

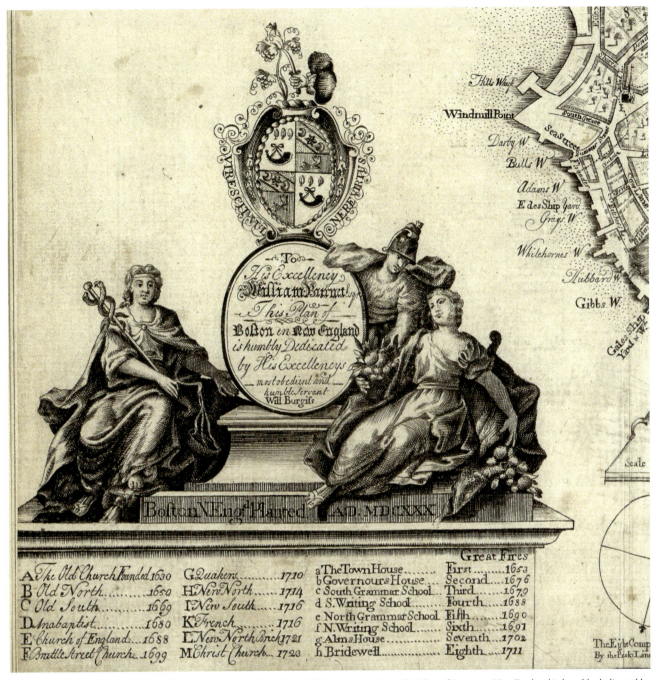

FIGURE 34   The cartouche from William Burgis, *To his Excellency William Burnet, Esqr., this Plan of Boston in New England is humbly dedicated by his Excellencys most obedient and humble servant Will Burgiss* (Boston: s.n., 1728)

of this cartouche is decorated with a crocodile, a serpent, pineapples, melons, and native peoples.[116]

But returning to developments in Europe, the second half of the seventeenth century and first half of the

---

116   Carolina Martínez in her article "Patagones en el mapa del Amazonas de Samuel Fritz (1707)," *Terra Brasilis* 14 (2020), online at http://journals.openedition.org/terrabrasilis/6883, shows that the native peoples on Fritz's map are copied from images of Patagonians on earlier maps. Incidentally, Fritz includes a relatively simple cartouche on his 1691 manuscript map of the river titled *Mapa geographica del rio Marañon o Amazonas*, BnF, Cartes et plans, GE C-5037 (RES), viewable at https://gallica

.bnf.fr. A later version of Fritz's map, printed in Edward Cooke's *A Voyage to the South Sea, and Round the World* (London: H.M. for B. Lintot and R. Gosling in Fleet-Street, 1712), and titled *The Great River Marañon or of ye Amazons with the Mission of the Society of Jesus*, gives up all of the elaborate cartouche decoration of Fritz's original, an interesting change. The map in Cooke's volume is not much smaller than Fritz's, so it was not smaller dimensions that made such a change necessary.

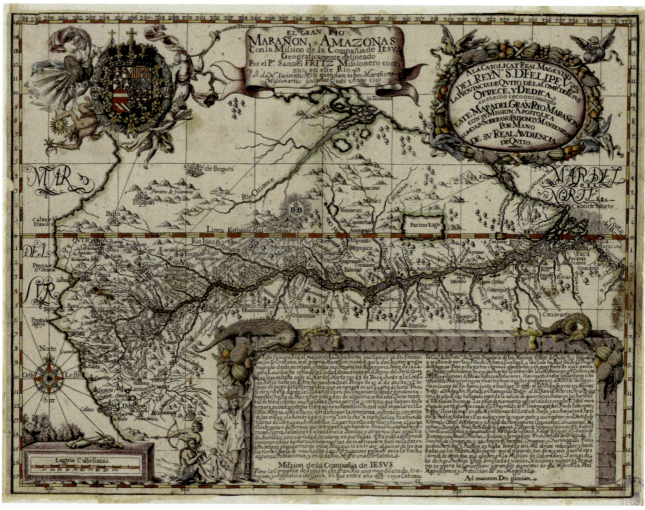

FIGURE 35   Samuel Fritz, *El gran rio Marañon o Amazonas con la Mission de la Compañia de Iesus* (Quito, Equador: J.N. Iesu quondam in hoc
Marañone Missionarius Sculpebat, 1707)

eighteenth century were the heyday of the decorative cartouche. We will see many examples of these cartouches in the chapters below, and it will perhaps suffice here to cite two pieces of evidence of cartographers' interest in cartouches during this period. The first piece of evidence is visual. The German cartographer Matthäus Seutter (1678–1757) and the artists who worked with him were very creative in designing his cartouches, and he declares his interest in these decorations on the title page of his *Atlas novus sive tabulae geographicae totius orbis faciem, partes, imperia, regna et provincias exhibentes* (Augsburg: Matthäus Seutter, 1730).[117] In the upper register

of the title page (Fig. 36) we have personifications of the parts of the world (the continents), with Europe sitting in a commanding position atop the globe, and Asia, Africa, and America in front of the globe. In the foreground are the Roman gods Minerva, Mercury, and Mars—representing European industry, trade and war—each holding a map, indicating the importance of maps in those enterprises, and on two of the three maps there is a clear schematic representation of a cartouche (Fig. 37). Seutter felt cartouches were so important that he included them even in small images of maps on his title page, although few of the geographical features in the maps are visible.[118]

117   On Seutter's atlas production see Markus Heinz, "Die Atlanten der süddeutschen Verlage Homann und Seutter (18. Jahrhundert)," in Hans Wolff, ed., *Vierhundert Jahre Mercator, vierhundert Jahre Atlas: die ganze Welt zwischen zwei Buchdeckeln: eine Geschichte der Atlanten* (Weissenhorn: A.H. Konrad, 1995), pp. 81–94.

118   The title page of an identically-titled atlas produced in about 1740 by Seutter's son-in-law Tobias Conrad Lotter does not have cartouches on the decorative maps on its title page: for bibliographic details and a high-resolution image see https://search works.stanford.edu/view/fm936sm7554. Two other atlases that

The second piece of evidence of cartographers' particular interest in cartouches in the late seventeenth and early eighteenth centuries is textual. By the middle of the eighteenth century the custom of decorating cartouches with the symbols of the person to whom it was dedicated, or with animals, people, plants, and other products of the region depicted, was so entrenched that Diderot declared these decorations to be characteristic of cartouches in his *Encyclopédie*:[119]

"That design is also called a cartouche which is placed at the bottom of plans or geographical maps, and which serves to enclose the title or the coat of arms of the person to whom it is to be presented. These cartouches are susceptible of attributes or allegories which must be relative to the person to whom these maps are presented, or to their subject."

This characterization should be contrasted with William Folkingham's early seventeenth-century instructions (quoted above) on what to include in the decoration of a cartouche, where he emphasized simple decoration such as vegetal motifs and grotesques.

An important but brief fashion in the design of cartouches, particularly in France, was the rocaille or rococo cartouche, which lasted from about 1740 to about 1770.[120] Rocaille, from the French for "rock," was an initially French style of exuberant, undulating, asymmetric decoration incorporating shell motifs; the term rococo, a variation on "rocaille," does not necessarily imply the presence of rocks or shells.[121] Rococo has been called "the eighteenth

century's most original contribution to the European decorative vocabulary,"[122] but in terms of the development of cartographic cartouches, the style's focus on textures and shapes tended to exclude the more elaborate allegories of earlier cartouches (some examples are illustrated in Chapter 27 below). Contemporary critics objected to the perceived excesses of rococo,[123] and in 1759 the architect and teacher Friedrich August Krubsacius (1718–1789) published a satirical rococo cartouche engraved by J.D. Philipp that was composed of sixteen disparate elements. Krubsacius' goal was to highlight the lack of unity in rococo compositions, and in fact his satirical cartouche does not look so different from un-ironic rococo cartouches.[124] In any case, the exuberance of rococo soon gave way to more austere Neoclassicism in many artistic media, including cartouche design.

---

have depictions of maps with cartouches on their title pages are Johannes van Keulen, *De nieuwe groote lichtende zee-fackel, 't tweede deel* (Amsterdam: Johannes van Keulen, 1685), and later editions, with discussion in Rodney Shirley, *Courtiers and Cannibals, Angels and Amazons: The Art of the Decorative Cartographic Titlepage* (Houten, Netherlands: Hes & De Graaf, 2009), pp. 176–177; and Gerard Valck (or Valk), *Nova totius geographica telluris projectio* (Amsterdam: Gerardus Valk, c.1720).

119   See Diderot, *Encyclopédie* (see note 3), vol. 2, p. 731. Volume 2 of the *Encyclopédie* was published in 1751.

120   This duration of the fashion for rococo cartouches is asserted by J.H. Andrews, *Maps in Those Days: Cartographic Methods before 1850* (Dublin: Four Courts Press, 2009), pp. 458–459. The term rocaille was first used in the title of a model book for furniture design and ornaments by François-Thomas Mondon, *Premier livre de forme rocquaille et cartel* (s.l, 1736).

121   For discussion of rococo see Alastair Laing, "French Ornamental Engravings and the Diffusion of the Rococo," in Henri Zerner, ed., *Le stampe e la diffusione delle immagini e degli stili* (Bologna: CLUEB, 1983), pp. 109–127; Bruno Pons, "The Rocaille," in Alain Gruber, ed., *The History of Decorative Arts: Classicism and the Baroque*, trans. John Goodman (New York: Abbeville Press

Publishers, 1996), pp. 325–432; and Günther Irmscher, "Style rocaille," *Barockberichte* 51–52 (2009), pp. 339–414. A model book not of rocaille cartouches, but of rocaille design elements that might have been used in cartouches, may be found in Jacques de Lajoue, *Nouveaux tableaux d'ornements et rocailles* (Paris: Huquier, c.1738–39), an incomplete copy of which is in Paris at the Bibliothèque de l'Institut National d'Histoire de l'Art, shelfmark NUM 4 EST 287, and is available in digital format. Princeton University Library has a complete copy of this model book.

122   Alain Gruber, *The History of Decorative Arts: Classicism and the Baroque*, trans. John Goodman (New York: Abbeville Press Publishers, 1996), p. 21.

123   Indeed, as early as 1737 Jacques-François Blondel had objected to decoration consisting of *un amas ridicule de coquilles, de dragons, de roseaux, de palmiers & de plantes*, "a ridiculous jumble of shells, dragons, reeds, palm trees and plants," in his *De la distribution des maisons de plaisance, et de la decoration des edifices en general* (Paris: Charles-Antoine Jombert, 1737), vol. 2, p. 67. The English translation is from Svend Eriksen, *Early Neo-Classicism in France* (London: Faber, 1974), p. 25. On other criticisms of rococo see Christian Michel, "*Le goût contre le caprice*: les enjeux des débats sur l'ornement au milieu du XVIIIe siècle," in Patrice Ceccarini, Jean Loup Charvet, Frédéric Cousinié, and Christophe Leribault, eds., *Histoires d'ornement, actes du colloque de l'Académie de France à Rome, Villa Médicis, 27–28 juin 1996, Paris-Rome, 2000* (Paris: Klincksieck; Rome: Académie de France à Rome, 2000), pp. 203–214.

124   Laing, "French Ornamental Engravings" (see note 121); Friedrich August Krubsacius, "Kurze Untersuchung des Ursprungs der Verzierungen, der Veränderung und des Wachstums derselben, bis zu ihrem itzigen Verfalle; nebst einigen wohlgemeynten Vorschlägen zur Verbesserung und Richtschnur aller Zierrathen," *Das Neueste aus der anmuthigen Gelehrsamkeit* (1759), pp. 22–38, 93–104, 175–185, and 262–268, esp. 177–179, with the satirical cartouche following p. 240.

FIGURE 36   The allegorical title page of Matthäus Seutter's *Atlas novus sive tabulae geographicae totius orbis faciem,*
partes, imperia, regna et provincias exhibentes (Augsburg: Matthäus Seutter, 1730)

FIGURE 37   Detail of Seutter's title page in Figure 36, showing the schematic cartouche on the map held by Minerva
COURTESY OF THE DAVID RUMSEY MAP COLLECTION

7   The Decline of Cartouches

In the late eighteenth and early nineteenth centuries the use of decorative cartouches underwent a rapid decline. George Kish asserted that this decline occurred following the Napoleonic Wars, which took place between 1803 and 1815—that after those conflicts the "'decorative map' was replaced by a severe, utilitarian product constantly improved as surveying, mapmaking, and printing processes continued to evolve towards greater and greater accuracy."[125] Mary Pedley, on the other hand, has argued that the French Revolution (1789–99) was the

decisive factor in the decline of decorative ornament on maps, as it spelled the end of the *géographes du roi* (royal geographers) in France and other forms of kingly and noble support for cartographers.[126] Matthew Edney sees the "increasing plainness of formal maps" as the fruit of the Enlightenment, rather than a product of the French Revolution, and a change that had already been underway during the eighteenth century.[127] More precisely,

125   Kish, "Cartouches: Notes on Decorative Maps" (see note 10), p. 9.

126   Mary Pedley, "The Map Trade in Paris, 1650–1825," *Imago Mundi* 33 (1981), pp. 33–45.

127   Matthew H. Edney, "Reconsidering Enlightenment Geography and Map Making: Reconnaissance, Mapping, Archive," in David N. Livingstone and Charles W.J. Withers, eds., *Geography*

Peter Barber attributes the change in maps towards a "distinctively austere appearance" beginning around 1770 to the rise of Neoclassicism and the associated preference for simplicity of style.[128] Ascribing the changes in maps to the rise of Neoclassicism fits well with the cartouche evidence, for there were indeed very plain cartouches on some French maps prior to the French Revolution.

It is possible to find maps without cartouches at any period, including before the arrival of Neoclassicism—for example, in Nicolas Sanson's *Creta insula, plerumque Deum natalibus, Iovis incunabulis, sepulchroque inclyta* (Paris, 1676) there is no frame of any type around the title and author information in the map's upper left-hand corner.[129] There are always some cartographers who favor a minimalist aesthetic, and the use of more elaborate or less elaborate cartouches depends on context and audience. We can see this in the maps of Gerard van Keulen (1678–1726) in his *Groote nieuwe vermeerderde zee-atlas* (Amsterdam: van Keulen, 1720).[130] Many of the maps have elaborate cartouches, but quite a number have very plain cartouches whose frames are simple ovals.[131] The explanation here is not that Gerard was anticipating Neoclassicism but simply that he borrowed this plain style of cartouches from his manuscript nautical charts,[132] where evidently he felt that a basic, unornamented style of cartouche was more appropriate given the maps' practical function and audience.

We can see some of the disruption of the transition to Neoclassical cartouches in the *Hydrographie françoise* by Jacques Nicolas Bellin (1703–1772), the finest marine atlas of its day, first published in 1756, with many subsequent editions.[133] Some of the maps have traditional, elaborately decorated title cartouches, others have plain title cartouches, framed by simple rectangles or circles, and others have the title information unframed. Bellin himself made a map with unframed title information in 1737,[134] and another with a plain cartouche in 1765[135] (both of which appear in his *Hydrographie françoise*) as well as many maps with elaborate cartouches. The maps by other cartographers that Bellin includes in his atlas show this same variety in their cartouches.

It is worth emphasizing that it is not difficult to find plain cartouches before the French Revolution. For example, in Edme Mentelle's rare *Atlas nouveau* printed in Paris in 1779, the cartouches are unadorned rectangular frames, and the same is true in his *Cosmographie élémentaire, divisée en parties astronomique et géographique* (Paris: chez l'auteur; Paris: Imprimerie de Stoupe, 1781).[136] And one can see the change from decorative cartouches to plain cartouches continuing to take place in the early nineteenth century. Specifically, one can see this change in the maps that Pierre Lapie (1779–1850) made for an

and Enlightenment (Chicago: University of Chicago Press, 1999), pp. 165–198, esp. 169.

128   Peter Barber, "Enlightened Mapping? Maps in the Europe of the Enlightenment," *Cartographic Journal* 57.4 (2020), pp. 379–399, at 381.

129   A high-resolution image of Sanson's cartoucheless map *Creta insula* of 1676 is available at https://gallica.bnf.fr.

130   On Gerard van Keulen's *Zee-Atlas* of 1720 see Philip Lee Phillips, *A List of Geographical Atlases in the Library of Congress: with Bibliographical Notes* (Washington: Government Printing Office, 1909–1992), vol. 5, no. 5693; and Cornelis Koeman, *Atlantes Neerlandici: Bibliography of Terrestrial, Maritime and Celestial Atlases and Pilot Books, Published in the Netherlands up to 1880* (Amsterdam: Theatrum Orbis Terrarum, 1967–1985), vol. 4, p. 301, Keu 31.

131   Maps in Gerard van Keulen's 1720 *Zee-Atlas* that have plain oval cartouche frames include his *Nieuwe afteekening van de haven en stad Wismar*, his *Nieuwe aftekening van het Eyland Rugen*, and his *Nieuwe afteekening van Het Eyland Spits-Bergen*. Good images of these maps are available at https://gallica.bnf.fr.

132   On Gerard van Keulen's manuscript nautical charts, which consistently have plain oval cartouches, see Maria Antonietta Guiso and Nicoletta Muratore, *Ad usum navigantium: carte nautiche manoscritte di Gerard van Keulen 1709–1713* (Rome: Istituto Poligrafico e Zecca della Stato, 1992); Dirk de Vries, "The Manuscript Charts," in Dirk de Vries, Günter Schilder, Willem Mörzer Bruyns, Peter van Iterson, and Irene Jacobs, *The Van Keulen Cartography: Amsterdam, 1680–1885* (Alphen aan den Rijn: Canaletto/Repro-Holland, 2005), pp. 91–113.

133   On Bellin's works see Mireille Pastoureau, *Les atlas français: XVIᵉ–XVIIᵉ siècles: Répertoire bibliographique et étude* (Paris: Bibliothèque Nationale de France, 1984), pp. 351–356; and Olivier Chapuis, *A la mer comme au ciel: Beautemps-Beaupré & la naissance de l'hydrographie moderne, 1700–1850: l'émergence de la précision en navigation et dans la cartographie marine* (Paris: Presses de l'Université de Paris-Sorbonne, 1999), pp. 161–167. On Bellin's atlas see Jean-Marc Garant, "Jacques-Nicolas Bellin et son oeuvre en Amérique," *Proceedings of the Meeting of the French Colonial Historical Society* 11 (1987), pp. 59–66; and Mireille Pastoureau, "Jacques-Nicolas Bellin, French Hydrographer, and the Royal Society in the Eighteenth Century," *Yale University Library Gazette* 68.1–2 (1993), pp. 65–69.

134   Bellin's 1737 map with unframed title information is his three-sheet *Carte reduite de la Mer Mediterranee*; high-resolution images of the sheets are available at https://searchworks.stanford.edu. On this map see Chapuis, *A la mer comme au ciel* (see note 133), pp. 170–171.

135   Bellin's 1765 map with a very simple rectilinear frame for its title cartouche is his *Carte de l'Isle de Madagascar dressée au Dépôt des Cartes et Plans et Journaux de la Marine pour le service des vaisseaux du roi*; a good image of this map is available at https://gallica.bnf.fr.

136   On Mentelle see Anne Godlewska, "Geography under Napoleon and Napoleonic Geography," *Proceedings, Consortium on Revolutionary Europe 1750–1850* 19.1 (1989), pp. 281–302; and Michael Heffernan, "Edme Mentelle's Geographies and the French Revolution," in David N. Livingstone and Charles W.J. Withers, eds., *Geography and Revolution* (Chicago: University of Chicago Press, 2005), pp. 273–303.

atlas by Conrad Malte-Brun that was printed in 1812, and in the maps that Lapie made for his own atlas that was printed four years later, in 1816.[137] Lapie's map of Africa in Malte-Brun's *Atlas complet du précis de la géographie universelle* (Paris: S. Buisson, 1812) has a cartouche embellished with a sphinx and some palm trees (Fig. 38), while his map of the same continent in his own atlas printed four years later, titled *Atlas classique et universel de géographie ancienne et moderne* (Paris: Magimel, Anselin, et Pochard, 1816), has the map's title and cartographer's name in a thin and unadorned oval frame (Fig. 39). Similar differences, symptomatic of the decline that elaborately decorated cartouches were experiencing at this time, are observable in comparing the maps throughout the two atlases.[138]

An intriguing stage in the decline of elaborate cartouches is illustrated by *The Atlantic Neptune*, a four-volume atlas of the British colonies in North America made by Joseph F.W. Des Barres (1722–1824) for the British Admiralty, and first published in 1777.[139] Most of the cartouches in *The Atlantic Neptune* are very plain, simple ovals or rectangles, and thus provide additional evidence of the movement towards unadorned cartouches in the latter part of the eighteenth century. But Des Barres often places his cartouches at an angle with respect to the frame of the map—sometimes of just a few degrees—and many of them impinge upon the neatlines of the map.[140] His intention seems to have been to create a *trompe-l'oeil* effect, as if the cartouches are separate pieces of paper lying on top of the maps, which is to say, his intention was to emphasize the distinctness of cartouche space from the surrounding cartographic space. Des Barres does not offer any explanation of this practice, but evidently he felt that plain cartouches did not offer the same clear demarcation between these two spaces that elaborately decorated cartouches did, unless the plain cartouche was rotated.

A design possibility that might have generated movement away from title cartouches—but seems not to have done so—is the recognition that the title information could be placed in the upper or lower margin of the map. Titles in the margins of maps would seem to render superfluous the title cartouche, the most common and usually the most elaborate type of cartouche. The great French cartographer Guillaume Delisle (1675–1726) has marginal titles on several of his maps, for example his map of Sicily, titled *Carte de l'Isle et royaume de Sicile* (Amsterdam: Jean Cóvens et Corneille Mortier, c.1717).[141] The map has its title in the upper margin, and no title cartouche, even though the shape of the island left plenty of room for such a cartouche—and indeed, two later maps based on Delisle's include title cartouches.[142] These reactions to Delisle's experiments suggest that he was ahead of his time in his use of marginal titles, but even Matthäus Seutter (1678–1757), who was very fond of cartouches, resorted to marginal titles when other cartouches left no room for a title cartouche, for example in his map *Imperium Japonicum*

137   On Lapie see Joseph Fr. Michaud and Louis Gabriel Michaud, eds., *Biographie universelle, ancienne et moderne* (Paris: Michaud frères, 1811–62), vol. 23, pp. 228–229; and Alphonse Rabbe, Claude Augustin Vieilh de Boisjolin, and Charles Claude Binet de Sainte-Preuve, eds., *Biographie universelle et portative des contemporains* (Paris: chez l'éditeur, 1836), vol. 3, p. 149. For discussion of some of his historical maps see Richard Talbert, "A Forgotten Masterpiece of Cartography for Roman Historians: Pierre Lapie's *Orbis Romanus ad Illustranda Itineraria* (1845)," in Hans Michael Schellenberg, Vera-Elisabeth Hirschmann, and Andreas Krieckhaus, eds., *A Roman Miscellany: Essays in Honour of Anthony R. Birley on his Seventieth Birthday* (Gdansk: Foundation for the Development of Gdansk University, 2008), pp. 149–156.

138   A dramatic case of the reduction of ornamentation of cartouches in late eighteenth-century maps may be seen in the atlases of William Guthrie (1708–1770), titled *A New Geographical, Historical, and Commercial Grammar*: the cartouche ornamentation was reduced in the 1783 edition, and again in 1787. See Barbara Backus McCorkle, *A Carto-Bibliography of the Maps in Eighteenth-Century British and American Geography Books* (Kansas City: Digital Publishing Services, University of Kansas Library, 2009), nos. 165 and 167. On Guthrie see Robert Mayhew, "William Guthrie's Geographical Grammar, the Scottish Enlightenment and the Politics of British Geography," *Scottish Geographical Journal* 115.1 (1999), pp. 19–34.

139   On *The Atlantic Neptune* see Philip L. Phillips, *A List of Geographical Atlases in the Library of Congress* (Washington, DC, 1909–1992), vol. 1, pp. 632–654; vol. 3, pp. 453–471; and vol. 4, pp. 253–257; Robert Lingel, "The Atlantic Neptune," *Bulletin of the York Public Library* 40 (1936), pp. 581–603; Henry Stevens, *Catalogue of the Henry Newton Stevens Collection of the Atlantic Neptune* (London, H. Stevens, Son & Stiles, 1937); and Stephen J. Hornsby, "The Atlantic Neptune," in his *Surveyors of Empire: Samuel Holland, J.F.W. Des Barres, and the Making of The Atlantic Neptune* (Montreal, CA: McGill-Queen's University Press, 2011), pp. 163–198 and 245–248.

140   The Library of Congress has digitized multiple copies of *The Atlantic Neptune*, and high-resolution images of their maps can be readily viewed at https://loc.gov; their exemplar with the most maps is this one: https://www.loc.gov/item/75332508/.

141   A high-resolution image of Delisle's map of Sicily is available at https://catalog.princeton.edu.

142   The two later versions of Delisle's map of Sicily that include title cartouches are, first, John Senex's *A Map of the Island and Kingdom of Sicily from the Latest Observations* (London, 1721), which has that title in the upper margin, and in the cartouche, the title *A New Map of Sicily, most Humbly Inscrib'd to Montague Garrard Drake Esqr.*—a good image of the map is available at https://dlg.galileo.usg.edu. The second map is Paolo Santini's *Carte de l'Isle et Royaume de Sicile* (Venice: Remondini, 1779), a good image of which is available at https://searchworks.stanford.edu.

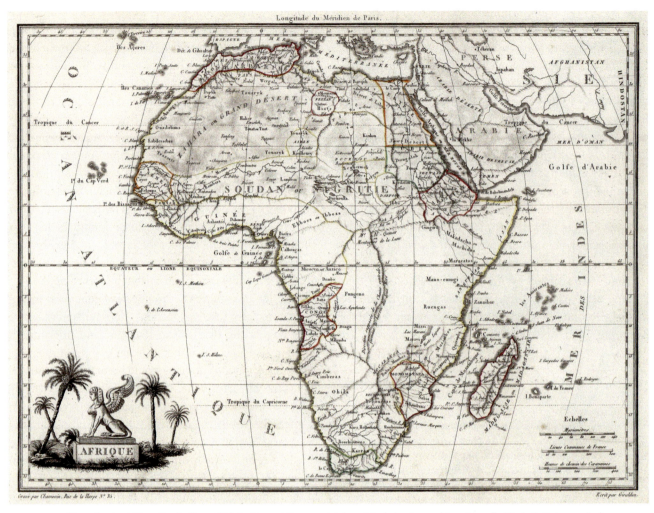

FIGURE 38   Pierre Lapie, *Africa*, 1812, in Conrad Malte-Brun, *Atlas complet du précis de la géographie universelle* (Paris: S. Buisson, 1812)
STANFORD UNIVERSITY, DAVID RUMSEY MAP COLLECTION, G1019 .M3 1812 F. COURTESY OF THE DAVID RUMSEY
MAP COLLECTION

per sexaginta et sex regiones digestum atque ex ipsorum Japonesium mappis descriptum (Augsburg, c.1730–60), illustrated in Fig. 126 below. The possibility of using marginal titles did not in and of itself displace elaborate title cartouches: the tradition of title cartouches was evidently too strong. The diminishment of title cartouches instead took place due to changes in aesthetic and intellectual tastes generated by the Enlightenment, specifically Neoclassicism.

The aesthetic impulse behind the generally decreasing interest in elaborate cartouches during the nineteenth century, and the judgment that undecorated maps were superior and more "scientific", found extreme expression at the hands of the Czech and Austrian architect Alfred Loos (1870–1933). In 1910 Loos wrote a lecture titled "Ornament und Verbrechen" ("Ornament and Crime") which was published in 1913,[143] in which he argued that "The evolution of

culture is synonymous with the removal of ornament from objects of daily use," that ornament is "a symptom of backwardness or degeneracy," and that "lack of ornamentation is a sign of intellectual strength."[144] Loos's view is dishearteningly narrow and even bigoted—as Kent Bloomer has noted in his recent exploration and defense of ornament, "humans have always demonstrated an

For discussion see Christopher Long, "Ornament, Crime, Myth, and Meaning," in Lawrence W. Speck, ed., *Architecture, Material and Imagined: Proceedings of the 85th ACSA Annual Meeting and Technology Conference* (Washington, DC: Association of Collegiate Schools of Architecture, 1997), pp. 440–445; and Long's "The Origins and Context of Adolf Loos's 'Ornament and Crime'," *Journal of the Society of Architectural Historians* 68.2 (2009), pp. 200–223.

144   Adolf Loos, *Ornament and Crime: Selected Essays*, ed. Adolf Opel, trans. Michael Mitchell (Riverside, CA: Ariadne Press, 1998), pp. 167–176, at 167, 170, and 175. For a more recent devaluing of decoration specifically in a cartographic context see Arthur H. Robinson, *The Look of Maps: An Examination of Cartographic Design* (Madison: University of Wisconsin Press, 1952), p. 17.

143   The earliest printing of Loos's essay is in Adolf Loos, "Ornement et crime," *Les cahiers d'aujourd'hui* 5 (1913), pp. 247–256.

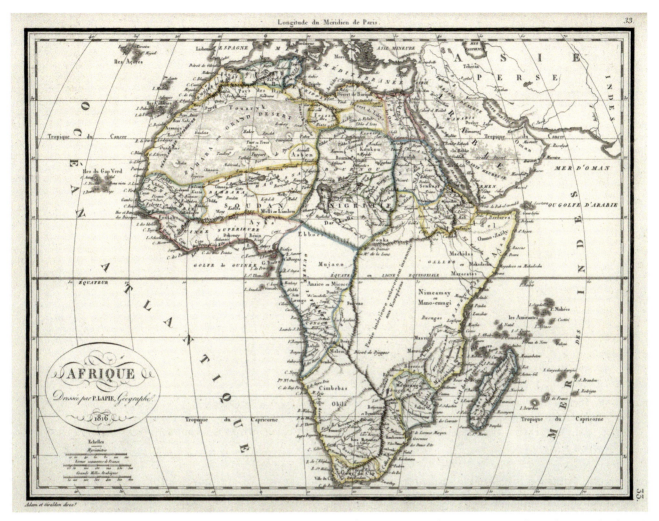

FIGURE 39   Pierre Lapie, *Afrique*, in his *Atlas classique et universel de geographie ancienne et moderne* (Paris: Magimel, Anselin, et Pochard, 1816)
STANFORD UNIVERSITY, DAVID RUMSEY MAP COLLECTION, G1033 .L3 1816 F. COURTESY OF THE DAVID RUMSEY
MAP COLLECTION

inclination to exceed the limits of utility"[145]—but it is also true that the attitude Loos signaled in such exaggerated terms is still with us in many ways. The digital maps that we now use to find our way in the world lack ornamentation, let alone cartouches, and most modern printed maps also lack ornament.

It is important to note that whatever the general aesthetic trends, the degrees of decoration in cartouches vary according to the taste of the individual cartographer, and it is possible to find elaborate cartouches when most cartographers were producing plain ones, and vice versa. There are some elaborate cartouches that were made in the nineteenth century, and the cartographers of some twentieth-century pictorial maps have revived

the cartouches of earlier centuries.[146] But the early nineteenth century seems like a good time to bring this history of the cartographic cartouche to a close.

8   The Ontology of Cartouches

One of the more interesting problems presented by cartouches is that of the relationship between the space they occupy and the cartographic space of the maps in which—on which?—they are located. The frame is a defining characteristic of a cartouche, and we might hope that that frame would create a pure and purely distinct meta-cartographic space for the cartouche, something entirely separate from the surrounding map, but this is not at all the case. We cannot think of cartouches as the

145   Kent Bloomer, *The Nature of Ornament: Rhythm and Metamorphosis in Architecture* (New York: W.W. Norton, 2000), p. 42. On pp. 206–230 Bloomer supplies a list of the arguments commonly alleged against ornament, and his responses to each of them.

146   See for example Stephen J. Hornsby, *Picturing America: The Golden Age of Pictorial Maps* (Chicago and London: University of Chicago Press, in association with the Library of Congress, 2017).

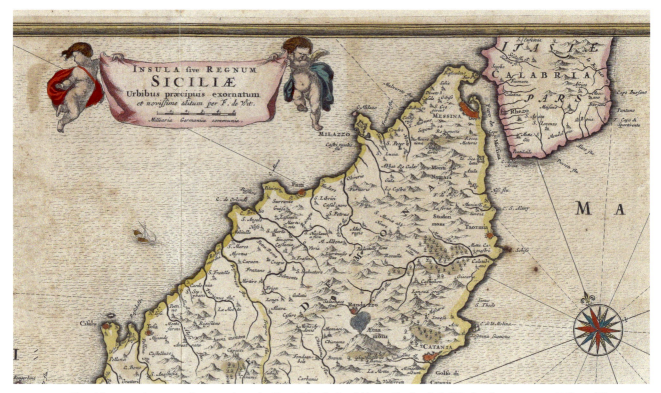

FIGURE 40   The title cartouche covers the area where the Lipari Islands should be on Frederick de Wit, *Insula sive regnum Sicilae urbibus*
praecipuis exornatum et novissime editum (Amsterdam, *c.* 1671–1676)
YALE UNIVERSITY, BEINECKE LIBRARY, 408 1680. COURTESY OF THE BEINECKE RARE BOOK AND MANUSCRIPT LIBRARY

cartographic equivalents of what are called "paratexts" in books, the texts "beside" the main text, such as the title pages, frontispieces, prefaces, dedications, publishers' jacket copy, etc.[147] For cartouches are not actually above (meta-) or beside (para-) the maps they embellish, but on them, part of them. David Woodward has appropriately included cartouches in the category "epicartographic elements," emphasizing the fact that are located on maps.[148]

That is to say, at the same time that cartouches pretend, via their frames, to be meta-cartographic or para-cartographic, beyond the realm of the map proper, and as much as they can supplement the map with additional descriptions, illustrations, instructions, and metadata, they are also inescapably anti-cartographic, in that they occupy part of the cartographic space and cloak it from our view. To place a cartouche on a map is to weigh the

advantages of the information or pleasure it conveys against the disadvantages of the information lost in the cartographic space it covers. We hope that the cartographer has placed the cartouche where it is not obscuring anything important to us, but the only way to know what it is covering is to consult another map. Thus, the presence of cartouches is a radical enough disruption of the map's cartography to render necessary a second map to achieve a full knowledge of the area depicted on a map.

In some maps the cartouches, though they still conceal geography, are located with care. For example, in Pieter Schenk's map of Asia, *Nova totius Asiae tabula* (Amsterdam, *c.*1710), the two cartouches are located in parts of Europe and Africa.[149] Since the person buying the map was interested in Asia, one might argue—and Schenk clearly decided—that covering parts of Europe and Africa would not interfere with the client's interests

147   The classic study of paratexts is Gérard Genette, *Paratexts: Thresholds of Interpretation*, trans. Jane E. Lewin (Cambridge and New York: Cambridge University Press, 1997).

148   For Woodward's proposal of the phrase "epicartographic elements" see David Woodward, "Cartography and the Renaissance: Continuity and Change," in J.B. Harley and David Woodward, eds., *The History of Cartography*, vol. 3, *Cartography in the European Renaissance* (Chicago and London: University of Chicago Press, 2007), part 1, pp. 3–24, at 16; and David Woodward, "Techniques of Map Engraving, Printing, and Coloring in the European Renaissance," in the same volume, part 1, pp. 591–610, at 603.

149   On Schenk's map of Asia see Günter Schilder, *Monumenta cartographica Neerlandica* (Alphen aan den Rijn: Canaletto, 1986–2013), vol. 3, p. 168. The same cartouche placement is found in a copy of Schenk's map by Henry Overton, *To the most Sacred Majesty Caroline, Queen of Great Britain France & Ireland This Mapp of Asia According to the Newest and most Exact Observations is most Humble Dedicated* (London, *c.*1730). A good image of Overton's map is available on the website of the State Library of Queensland.

FIGURE 41   The large cartouche with an inset map simultaneously conceals and depicts the Atlantic in John Senex's *A New Map of the English Empire in America* (London, 1719)
COURTESY OF BARRY LAWRENCE RUDERMAN RARE MAPS

too much. But in fact it is precisely the parts of Europe and Africa near Asia, which are the parts Schenk covers, that a client interested in Asia would most want to see. If a cartouche is within the map's neatlines, there is almost always a loss of geographical information.

It is not difficult to find cases where cartographers did a poor job in placing cartouches—and these cases are illuminating. For example, Frederick de Wit (1629/1630–1706), in a map of Sicily he published in the early 1670s, omits the Lipari Islands, which are north of Sicily, in favor of the title cartouche held aloft by two *putti* (Fig. 40); another map of the island he made years later corrects this error.[150] In

some cases a cartouche covers part of the cartographic space with an inset map that supplies some of the information thus obscured: for instance, in John Senex's *A New Map of the English Empire in America* (London, 1719), a complex of three cartouches—the title cartouche and two inset maps—occupies much of the Atlantic, obscuring Bermuda and parts of the Grand Banks (Fig. 41).[151]

150   De Wit's earlier map of Sicily in which he omits the Lipari Islands in favor of the title cartouche is *Insula sive regnum Sicilae urbibus praecipuis exornatum et novissime editum* (Amsterdam,

c. 1671–76); his later map that includes the Lipari Islands is *Regni et insulae Siciliae typus corectissimus ex auctoribus et relationibus novissimus excerptus* (Amsterdam, *c.* 1707–1710). A high-resolution image of the first map is available as part of the digital collections of the Beinecke Library; on both maps see George Carhart, *Frederick de Wit and the First Concise Reference Atlas* (Leiden and Boston: Brill and Hes & De Graaf, 2016), pp. 250–251.

151   On Senex's map of America see Louis Charles Karpinski, *Bibliography of the Printed Maps of Michigan, 1804–1880* (Lansing:

FIGURE 42   The boats sail smoothly from the cartouche into the map, making it difficult to distinguish between the two, in Johann Baptist
Homann's *Regnorum Hispaniae et Portugalliae tabula generalis de l'Isliana* (Nuremberg: Johann Baptist Homann, 1724), in Homann's
Grosser Atlas (Nuremberg, 1731), from the American Geographical Society Library, University of Wisconsin-Milwaukee Libraries,
At.050 A-1742
COURTESY OF THE AMERICAN GEOGRAPHICAL SOCIETY LIBRARY

The larger inset map is of the Atlantic, showing a wider view of the ocean than the main map, extending north to Greenland, south to South America, and east to the coasts of Europe and Africa. But even in this unusual case where the cartouche seems to supply and indeed supplement the information it obscures on the main map, it does so at a smaller scale, so the information supplied is not of the same detail as that which it obscures.[152] Moreover, we have seen and will see cases in which the cartographer deploys a cartouche to cover part of the map about whose geography he or she is unsure:[153] in this case the cartouche's anti-cartographic quality is deliberately exploited.

In addition, the distinction between cartouche space and cartographic space is often less clear than would be the case if cartouches were purely meta-cartographic or para-cartographic entities. As we have seen, cartouches include imagery outside the frame that defines them, which begins to complicate the question of defining the limit between cartouche and cartography. And there are numerous cartouches that complicate the matter further. In a map of Spain and Portugal by Johann Baptist Homann (1663–1724) titled *Regnorum Hispaniae et Portugalliae tabula generalis de l'Isliana* (Nuremberg: Johann Baptist Homann, 1724), the cartouche (Fig. 42) shows the King of Spain, Philip V (1683–1746), on horseback, ordering men and supplies onto boats on the shore below. The shore and the boats are certainly part of the cartouche, but when the boats are loaded they row out to join a large fleet of sailing

Michigan Historical Commission, 1931), p. 128, no. 46. A high-resolution image of the map is available at https://www.digital commonwealth.org/search.

152   A strategy similar to that in Senex's map, namely of filling the Atlantic with an inset map which includes the Atlantic at a smaller scale, is employed in the Society of Anti-Gallicans' map *A New and Accurate Map of the English Empire in North America* (London: William Herbert, 1755). A high-resolution image of the map is available at https://loc.gov.

153   The contributions of women to map production in the early modern period were all too often anonymous; see Alice Hudson

and Mary Ritzlin, "Preliminary Checklist of Pre-Twentieth Century Women in Cartography—Who are the Groundbreakers?" *Cartographica* 37.3 (2000), pp. 3–8; and Will C. van den Hoonaard, *Map Worlds: A History of Women in Cartography* (Waterloo, Canada: Wilfrid Laurier University Press, 2013), Chapter 3, "The Thirteenth to Seventeenth Centuries," pp. 29–44.

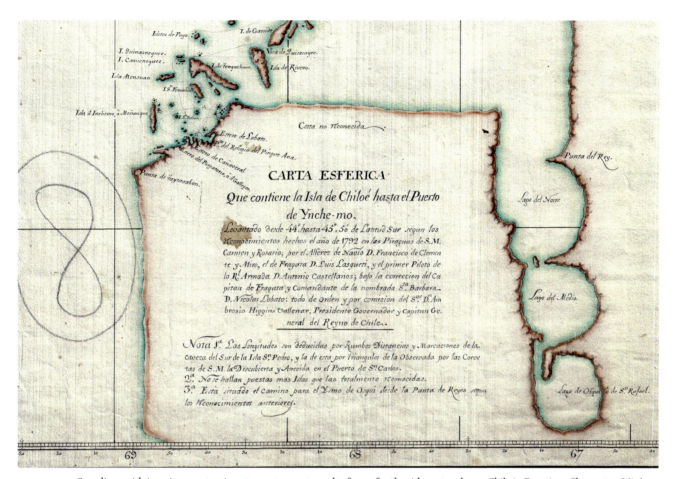

FIGURE 43 Coastlines with imaginary extensions to create a rectangular frame for the title cartouche on Chile in Francisco Clemente y Miró, *Carta esferica que contiene la Isla de Chiloé hasta el Puerto de Ynche-mo*, 1792

MADRID, MINISTERIO DE DEFENSA (MUSEO NAVAL), SHELFMARK MN-50-A-7. COURTESY OF THE MINISTERIO DE DEFENSA

vessels, and those vessels seem to be part of the decoration of the map proper, rather than part of the cartouche. It is not easy to know where the cartouche ends and the map begins.[154]

A remarkable case of interference between cartouche and cartography may be seen in a manuscript map of the coast of Chile made by the ensign Francisco Clemente y Miró in 1792.[155] The map shows the island of Chiloé in the north, and in the south, numerous small islands and the title cartouche (Fig. 43). To create the frame for the cartouche, the cartographer has joined some known coasts with long hypothetical coastlines, creating out of almost nothing a huge rectangular peninsula, so that the exigencies of framing the cartouche have overridden the cartographic imperative of depicting an accurate coastline. The cartographer indicates that the hypothetical coastlines are such by designating them with dotted lines, but the map's colors, both of land and sea, argue that the peninsula is real.

A somewhat similar case may be seen in an atlas by the French cartographer Christophe Tassin (d. 1660), who was

154 Another ontologically challenging cartouche appears on Matthäus Seutter's map *Novus orbis sive America Meridionalis et Septentrionalis*, first published in about 1720. The mythical landmass labeled *Terra Esonis incogn.* off the northwest coast of North America, which is much larger on other maps of this period, is subsumed into a large decorative cartouche, so that it is impossible to say where the geography ends and the cartouche begins. On the Terra Esonis see Frank Alfred Golder, "Terra de Jeso," in his *Russian Expansion on the Pacific, 1641–1850* (Cleveland: Arthur H. Clark Company, 1914), pp. 117–131; good images of Seutter's map are available at https://jcb.lunaimaging.com, https://www.digitalcommonwealth.org/search, and the Beinecke Digital Library.

155 The manuscript map of the coast of Chile is Francisco Clemente y Miró, *Carta esferica que contiene la Isla de Chiloé hasta el Puerto de Ynche-mo*, 1792, and is in Madrid at the Museo Naval, shelfmark MN-50-A-7. A high-resolution image of the map is available at http://bibliotecavirtualdefensa.es.

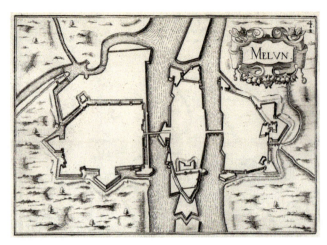

FIGURE 44   The map of Melun, with a typical cartouche, in
             Christophe Tassin's *Les plans et profils de toutes les
             principales villes et lieux considérables de France* (Paris:
             M. Tavernier, 1636)
             STANFORD UNIVERSITY, DAVID RUMSEY MAP
             COLLECTION, IN PROCESS. COURTESY OF THE DAVID
             RUMSEY MAP COLLECTION

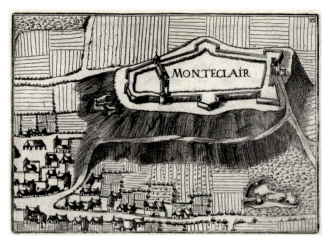

FIGURE 45   The map of Montclair (now Andelot-Blancheville)
             in Tassin's *Les plans et profils* (Paris, 1636), where the
             cartographer turns a cartographic element, the outline of
             the fortifications, into a cartouche frame, a remarkable
             instance of ontological ambiguity
             STANFORD UNIVERSITY, DAVID RUMSEY MAP
             COLLECTION, IN PROCESS. COURTESY OF THE DAVID
             RUMSEY MAP COLLECTION

the royal geographer to Louis XIV.[156] The atlas is his *Les
plans et profils de toutes les principales villes et lieux consi-
dérables de France* (Paris: M. Tavernier, 1636) ("Maps and
Views of All of the Principal Cities and Important Places
of France").[157] In most of the maps in this small-format
atlas he places the name of the city in a cartouche, which
may be plain or decorated, as in this map of Melun, southeast of Paris (Fig. 44). But in his map of Montclair (now
Andelot-Blancheville) he places the name of the city
within the outline of the fortifications of the city's acropo-
lis (Fig. 45), transforming a cartographic element into a
frame that is supposed to separate cartouche space from
cartographic space, a remarkable instance of ontological
ambiguity.

Just as cartouches can extend into cartographic space
in ways that make it difficult to distinguish between the
two, cartographic space can extend into cartouches. One
such case is presented by a map of the Principality of Jawor
in Silesia (Poland) made by Johann Wolfgang Wieland

(1673–1736), and finished by Matthaeus Schubarth
(1723–1758) after Wieland's premature death. The title of
the map is *Princip. Silesiae Iavoriensis in IV Circulos, Iaver,
Hirschberg, Lemberg und Buntzlau divisi* (Nuremberg:
Heredes Homanniani, 1736) ("The Silesian Principality
of Jawor Divided into Four Districts, Jawor, Hirschberg,
Lemberg and Buntzlau").[158] The title cartouche (Fig. 46)
has scenes of farming, wood-cutting, floating logs down-
river, and glassblowing, with Diana, goddess of the hunt,
on the right, and a personification of Spring on the left.
Also on the right is a bathhouse—and a chunk of cartography appears partly on the steps of the bathhouse,
and partly in the water. This is the town of Petschendorf
(now Pieszków), which, though it was some distance
from the Principality of Jawor proper, belonged to that
principality,[159] and so Wieland felt obliged to include it,
giving it the same outline color as the rest of the principality, even though it was well inside the cartouche.[160]

---

156   On Tassin see David Buisseret, "The Manuscript Sources of
      Christophe Tassin's Maps of France: The 'Military School,'" in
      Wouter Bracke, ed., *Margaritae cartographicae: studia Lisette
      Danckaert, 75um diem natalem agenti oblata* (Brussels: Archives
      et bibliothèques de Belgique, 2006), pp. 86–113.

157   Tassin's 1636 atlas is available in digital format at https://www
      .davidrumsey.com. Incidentally the publisher of Tassin's atlas,
      Melchior Tavernier, also published model books of cartouches,
      for example the anonymous *Diférents conpartiments et chapi-
      teaux, propres, pour tous sculpteurs, peintres, graveurs, macons
      et autr[e]* (Paris: Melchior Tavernier, 1619); and Daniel Rabel,
      *Cartouches de diferentes inventions: tres utilles a plussieurs sortes
      de personnes* (Paris: Melchior Tauernier, 1632).

158   On Wieland's maps of Silesia see Václav Novák, "Wielandovy
      mapy Slezska," *Slezský sborník* 49 (1951), pp. 289–299 and 484–503.

159   A less complicated depiction of the region around Petschendorf
      may be seen on another map made by Johann Wolfgang Wieland
      and finished by Matthaeus Schubarth, namely *Principatus Sile-
      siae Lignicensis in suos circulos, tres nempe Lignicenses Gold-
      bergensem, Haynavviensem et Lubenensem divisi* (Nuremberg:
      Hered. Homanniani, 1736).

160   A similar case of incursion of cartographic space into the car-
      touche may be seen in Pieter van der Aa's *La Norvegue, suiv-
      ant les nouvelles observations de Messrs. de l'Academie Royale
      des Sciences* (Leiden: chez Pierre van der Aa, 1714), where
      the *Isle de Santfless* appears well within the cartouche space.

FIGURE 46   The town of Petschendorf (now Pieszków) depicted well within the cartouche in Johann Wolfgang Wieland's *Princip. Silesiae*
Iavoriensis in IV Circulos, Iaver, Hirschberg, Lemberg und Buntzlau divisi (Nuremberg: Heredes Homanniani, 1736)
UNIV.- UND LANDESBIBLIOTHEK MÜNSTER, RK HAXT 1254. COURTESY OF THE UNIV.- UND LANDESBIBLIOTHEK MÜNSTER

Most of the paratexts in books exist on pages separate from the main text; even where main text and paratexts share book pages, as is the case with footnotes and commentary on the main text, the text and paratext generally co-exist amicably, one making space for the other. On maps, on the other hand, the cartouches compete for space with the cartography, the cartouche inevitably obscuring some of the map's geography. This competition entails that the one will sometimes encroach beyond what was supposed to be the boundary with the other, making it difficult to see them as being ontologically separate entities. Or perhaps as much as a competition we should understand a symbiotic commingling between cartouche and cartographic space, with the complementary function of cartouches—providing information and decoration that supplements the map—being reflected in the intermixture of their spaces.

A high-resolution image of the map is available at https://www.davidrumsey.com.

9   Cartouches and Emblems: Two Distinct Genres

Given that we have almost no record of how viewers interpreted complex cartouches in the seventeenth and eighteenth centuries, it might be tempting to try to gain some insight into their reactions by considering how viewers responded to similar images. Some superficially similar images that come to mind are emblems, the didactic combinations of illustration and text popular in the sixteenth and seventeenth centuries that were intended to challenge and instruct cultured viewers.[161] Emblems often

161   The literature on emblems is vast; useful starting points include Mario Praz, "A Bibliography of Emblem-Books," in his *Studies in Seventeenth-Century Imagery* (Rome: Edizioni di storia e letteratura, 1964–74), vol. 1, pp. 233–576; Arthur Henkel and Albrecht Schöne, eds., *Emblemata. Handbuch zur Sinnbildkunst des 16. und 17. Jahrhunderts* (Stuttgart: J.B. Metzler, 1967); C.W.R.D. Moseley, *A Century of Emblems: An Introductory Anthology* (Aldershot, England: Scolar Press; Brookfield, VT: Gower Pub. Co., 1989); Peter M. Daly and Mary V. Silcox, *The English Emblem:*

involve personifications and allegory, and a viewer experienced at interpreting emblems would be an able interpreter of cartouches.

But in all other respects emblems and cartouches are very different, so much so that it would be very misleading to try to understand how cartouches were interpreted based on how emblems were deciphered. The standard format of an emblem is very different from that of a cartouche, consisting of a brief motto (the *inscriptio*), an enigmatic picture (the *pictura*), and an epigram (the *subscriptio*), where both the *inscriptio* and *subscriptio* provide hints as to the interpretation of the *pictura*. No explanatory texts accompany cartouches. The function of emblems was moral edification, and in fact there is a rich tradition of Jesuit emblems,[162] and also Protestant emblem books,[163] whereas the function of cartouches is decorative and explanatory. This distinction is well illustrated by the differing roles of animals in emblems and cartouches: in emblems, animals always have an allegorical role and embody a moral character, whereas in cartouches, animals usually illustrate the wildlife or domesticated animals of a region depicted in the map.

Another difference between emblems and cartouches is that emblems were intended to be difficult to interpret, so that they would sharpen the interpretive skills of their viewers—this is related to their didactic function.[164] There certainly are cartouches that are challenging to interpret, but creating cartouches with this characteristic was never declared to be a goal inherent to the genre. Comparing cartouches and emblems quickly reveals that cartouches are an entirely distinct genre.

Moreover, while globes appear as symbols in a number of emblems,[165] we have little evidence of contact or interaction between cartographers and emblem artists. The knowledge of emblems by the cartographer, printmaker, and miniaturist Joris Hoefnagel (1542–1601) "was unrivaled among sixteenth-century artists," but his cartouches show almost no signs of this knowledge.[166] In 1597 the calligrapher and emblematist Paulus de Kempenaer (1554–1618) designed some emblems intended to be presented to the cartographer Petrus Plancius (1552–1622), but they never reached him;[167] and the cartographer Heinrich Scherer (1628–1704) wrote unpublished texts in which he describes emblematic decorations for religious dramas.[168] These are the only pieces of evidence of contact between the two spheres that I have found, though there were certainly opportunities for interaction at publishing houses that printed both maps and emblem books, such as the Plantin Press (founded in 1555) in Antwerp, Johann Theodor de Bry (active 1596–1623) in Frankfurt and Oppenheim, and

Bibliography of Secondary Literature (Munich and New York: K.G. Saur, 1990); G. Richard Dimler, "Jakob Masen's *Imago Figurata*: From Theory to Practice," *Emblematica* 6 (1992), pp. 283–306; Michael Bath, *Speaking Pictures: English Emblem Books and Renaissance Culture* (London: Longman, 1994); David Graham, "'Emblema multiplex': Towards a Typology of Emblematic Forms, Structures and Functions," in Peter M. Daly, ed., *Emblem Scholarship: Directions and Developments. A Tribute to Gabriel Hornstein* (Turnhout: Brepols, 2005), pp. 131–158; Peter M. Daly, ed., *Companion to Emblem Studies* (New York: AMS Press, 2008); and Pedro Germano Leal, ed., *Emblems in Colonial Ibero-America: To the New World on the Ship of Theseus* (Geneva: Droz, 2017). On how emblems were interpreted by contemporaries see Peter M. Daly, "How Were and How Are Emblems Read?" in his *The Emblem in Early Modern Europe: Contributions to the Theory of the Emblem* (Farnham, Surrey, and Burlington, VT: Ashgate, 2014), pp. 167–174.

162 G. Richard Dimler, "The Jesuit Emblem Book in 17th Century Protestant England," *Archivum Historicum Societatis Iesu.* 53.105 (1984), pp. 357–369; G. Richard Dimler, *The Jesuit Emblem: Bibliography of Secondary Literature with Select Commentary and Descriptions* (New York: AMS Press, 2005); Ralph Dekoninck, "The Jesuit *Ars* and *Scientia Symbolica*: From Richeome and Sandaeus to Masen and Ménestrier," in Karl Enenkel, Walter Melion, and Wietse De Boer, eds., *Jesuit Image Theory, 1540–1740* (Leiden: Brill, 2016), pp. 74–88.

163 Huston Diehl, "Graven Images: Protestant Emblem Books in England," *Renaissance Quarterly* 39 (1986), pp. 49–66.

164 On the goal of creating emblems that were challenging to interpret see Dimler, "Jakob Masen's *Imago Figurata*" (see note 161); also see Ayers Bagley, "Some Pedagogical Uses of the Emblem in Sixteenth and Seventeenth Century England," *Emblematica* 7.1 (1993), pp. 39–60.

165 Catherine Hofmann, "The Globe as Symbol in Emblem Books in the West, Sixteenth and Seventeenth Centuries," *Globe Studies* 49–50 (2001–2), pp. 81–120.

166 The quote about Hoefnagel is from Lubomir Konečný, "Joris Hoefnagel's 'Emblematic' Signature Reconsidered," *Journal of the Warburg and Courtald Institutes* 61 (1998), pp. 267–272, at 272. On Hoefnagel's knowledge of emblems see Thea Vignau-Wilberg, *Die emblematischen Elemente im Werke Joris Hoefnagels* (Leiden: Universitaire Pers, 1969); and Marisa Bass, "Patience Grows: The First Roots of Joris Hoefnagel's Emblematic Art," in Walter Melion, Bret Rothstein, and Michel Weemans, eds., *The Anthropomorphic Lens: Anthropomorphism, Microcosmism and Analogy in Early Modern Thought and Visual Arts* (Leiden: Brill, 2015), pp. 145–178. His manuscript book of emblems, titled *Traité de la Patience*, is in Rouen, Bibliothèque municipale de Rouen, Leber 2916 f° 00c.

167 Alastair Hamilton and Pieter Obbema, "Paulus de Kempenaer and Petrus Plancius," *Quaerendo* 21.1 (1991), pp. 38–54; on Kempenaer's life and work see Alastair Hamilton, "Paulus de Kempenaer, 'non moindre Philosophe que tresbon Escrivain'," *Quaerendo* 10 (1980), pp. 293–335.

168 On Scherer's manuscripts containing emblems see Barbara Bauer, "Das Bild als Argument: emblematische Kulissen in den Bühnenmeditationen Franciscus Langs," *Archiv für Kulturgeschichte* 64.1 (1982), pp. 79–170, esp. 81–82 and 97–99.

Daniel de La Feuille (active 1686–1706) in Amsterdam. It is a matter for future investigation whether there was any borrowing between the cartouches and emblem books printed by these publishers. The general lack of evidence of contact between emblem artists and cartouche artists may result from the fact that we have so little information about the latter: if we knew more about them, we might find that an emblematist also designed cartouches, or vice versa. But to judge from the evidence we have, the contact seems to have been scanty.

One additional remarkable difference between emblems and cartouches is the volume of scholarship devoted to each of the genres. Peter Daly has estimated that at least 6500 books either containing emblems or about emblems were published during the Renaissance, with each containing between 15 to 1500 emblems.[169] Philip Lee Phillips, *A List of Geographical Atlases in the Library of Congress*,[170] which covers only one (albeit very rich) collection, and does not address separately printed maps, has 18,435 entries, each atlas containing numerous maps. Not every atlas's maps include cartouches, and not all cartouches are of great interpretive interest, but it is nonetheless surprising—given these numbers—how much larger the literature about emblems is than that about cartouches. This is perhaps in part a consequence of the fact that emblems are a much more self-conscious genre: emblems were produced as exercises in interpretation, so producing emblems often entailed writing about emblems.

10   **The Cartouches in the Body of This Book**

This book consists of two main parts, a substantial introduction that outlines the history of cartouches, their sources, and their most important characteristics, and then a series of short chapters that examine individual cartouches or a group of closely related cartouches. It is worth saying a few words about the criteria of selection for the cartouches discussed in the chapters.

While every work of art can repay analysis, there are many decorative cartouches that are perfunctory, in which the cartographer simply places his patron's coat of arms above the frame that surrounds the title, or adorns it with some routine allegorical figures, or locates generic indigenous peoples on either side of it—or indeed copies the

cartouche from a model book or another map. My goal in the body of this book has been to seek out and discuss the most intriguing and elaborate cartouches, the ones that have symbolism that cries out for explanation, the ones that offer a particularly rich communication between the cartographer and viewer, or that show a particular consciousness of the possibilities of the genre. As such, the selection is inevitably subjective, and I make no pretense that it includes all of the most complex examples, but I do think the selection will prove engaging. One consequence of this choice is that the strapwork-heavy cartouches typical of the sixteenth century, where there is little in the way of symbolism, do not figure much in the body of the book; the emphasis is rather on the message-laden cartouches of the late sixteenth through the late eighteenth century.

It is worth illustrating the difference between a relatively uninteresting cartouche and the iconographically richer cartouches I will discuss in the body of the book. I will do so by means of two maps of the same region from the same period, specifically two late seventeenth-century maps of England. The one with the unremarkable cartouche is *Angliae regnum tam in septem antiqua Anglo-Saxonum regna* (Amsterdam: per Nicolaum Visscher, 1693) by Nicolaus Visscher (1649–1702),[171] whose cartouche is signed by the German artist Philippe Tideman (1657–1705) (Fig. 47).[172] At the top of the cartouche we have Apollo playing a lyre, surrounded not by the nine Muses, as he often is, but rather by personifications of the seven liberal arts, so that the cartouche praises the nation as a land of learning; below is the coat of arms of England. The suggestion that England was known for its learning is puzzling, as it was rather Ireland that had enjoyed that reputation

---

169   Peter M. Daly in the preface to Peter M. Daly, ed., *Companion to Emblem Studies* (New York: AMS Press, 2008), p. x.

170   Philip Lee Phillips, *A List of Geographical Atlases in the Library of Congress, with Bibliographical Notes* (Washington, DC: Govt. Print. Off., 1909–1992).

171   Nicolaus Visscher, son of Nicolaes Visscher (1618–1679), is sometime listed as Nicolaes Visscher II. On the son see Huigen Leeflang, "The Sign of Claes Jansz Visscher and his Progeny. The History and Significance of a Brand Name," *The Rijksmuseum Bulletin* 62 (2014), pp. 240–269, at 263. To mention another instance of an iconographically uninteresting cartouche, Rodney W. Shirley, *Printed Maps of the British Isles, 1650–1750* (Hertfordshire: Map Collector Publications; London: British Library, 1988), pp. 127–128, no. 78, singles out the cartouche on John Senex's *A New Map of England from the Latest Observations* (London, 1721) as "one of the finest examples of early Georgian decoration." The cartouche is beautifully executed, but offers little to interpret.

172   A preliminary study that Tideman made for the cartouche on Carel Allard's map *Recentissima novi orbis, sive Americae Septentrionalis et Meridionalis tabula*, c.1696, survives, and was sold at Sotheby's in 2014. It is described in *Old Master Drawings* (New York: Sotheby's, 2014), p. 150, lot 153. On Tideman see Cassandra Bosters et al., *Kunst in kaart: decoratieve aspecten van de cartografie* (Utrecht: H & S, HES uitgevers, 1989), pp. 85–94.

FIGURE 47   The cartouche on Nicolaus Visscher's map of England, *Angliae regnum tam in septem antiqua Anglo-Saxonum regna* (Amsterdam, 1693), in *Atlas maior* (Amsterdam: Viduam ac filios Ioachimi Ottens, 1719–1725)
ALLARD PIERSON, UNIVERSITY OF AMSTERDAM LIBRARY, HB-KZL 1808 A 6 (VOL. 1 OF 7), MAP 27

for centuries,[173] but perhaps the idea was to make the map appealing to buyers in England. In short, the cartouche is perfunctory and involves no careful reflection on or representation of the qualities of the English people, typical English animals or products, or the current state of affairs in the country.

A far richer and more engaging cartouche appears on Vincenzo Coronelli's map of England, *Le royaume d'Angleterre divisé en plusieurs parties* (Paris: I.B. Nolin, 1689) (Fig. 48). It is signed by Nicolas Guérard (d. 1719), who also published a short model book of cartouches,[174] and the framed text is backed by a huge harp. There was a close association between the harp and Ireland, but the

---

173   Michael W. Herren, "Classical and Secular Learning among the Irish before the Carolingian Renaissance," *Florilegium* 3 (1981), pp. 118–157.

174   Nicolas Guérard, *Livre de cartouches et supports d'ornemens pour les armories* (Paris: Nicolas Guerard, *c*.1715).

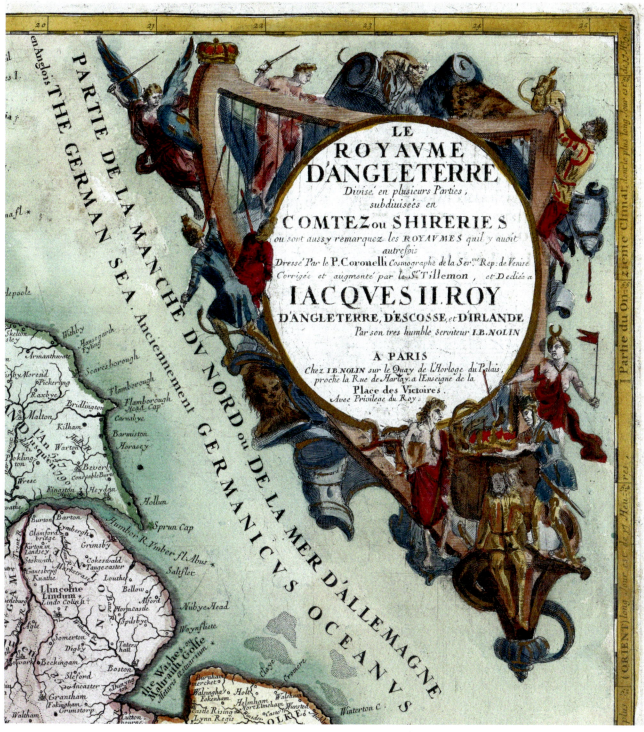

FIGURE 48   The cartouche on Vincenzo Coronelli's map of England, *Le royaume d'Angleterre divisé en plusieurs parties* (Paris: I.B. Nolin, 1689)
NEW YORK PUBLIC LIBRARY, MAP DIV. 96-7612. COURTESY OF THE NEW YORK PUBLIC LIBRARY

instrument was also popular in England. The focus of the cartouche is political power, for there is a crown on each corner of the harp. That at the upper left is being defended by a man and a winged woman bearing a shield with the French fleur-de-lis against two men approaching from below who have lions on their helmets. A man is stealing the crown at the upper right, while the crown at the bottom is about to be placed on a man's head. This latter scene is complicated: in the background is a hydra behind bars which are actually the strings of the harp, and the goddess Diana is about to cut one of these, freeing the hydra. Two men are in the process of crowning another man below. The one on the left has snakes for hair and holds a book and a torch, while the one on the right wears armor, carries a sword, and has a small lion on his head. The man being crowned has just removed a mask from his face, which is now dark, and holds a quill pen in his other hand.

The interpretation of the cartouche is as follows. The map, which was printed in Paris, is dedicated to James II, "King of England, Scotland, and Ireland." James was Roman Catholic, and had been forced from power during the Glorious Revolution of 1688, the year before the map was printed: Protestant nobles in England had invited the Protestant William of Orange, James's son-in-law, to invade and take the rule of the country. William did so, and James fled to France at the end of the year. The French, who were predominantly Catholic, remained sympathetic to and supportive of James. So the imminent coronation in the lower corner of the cartouche is that of William; he was crowned on April 11, 1689, by Henry Compton, Bishop of London (1632–1713), who was one of the nobles who had invited William to invade. It is Henry whom we see at the left crowning William, the book he holds representing his religious authority, and his serpentine hair representing his extreme and dangerous Protestantism; the hydra in the cage which is about to be loosed embodies a Protestant scourge that will be released when William takes power. The other man crowning William represents military power, which the artist fears the new Protestant king will use. Diana is presumably the one about to release the hydra because of her role as goddess of wild animals. William removing his mask suggests that once he has assumed power, he will reveal his true, more sinister identity.

The battle in the upper left corner of the harp, where the personification of France and a soldier defend a crown from attackers, represents French support of James II in the Williamite War in Ireland, while the two soldiers below, with lions on their helmets, represent English supporters of William. On March 12 James II had landed at Kinsale with 6000 French soldiers, determined to regain control of the country; in the cartouche this effort is optimistically portrayed as a defense of James's crown, rather than an attempt to regain rule. The crown in the upper right must be that of Scotland, but I do not know who would be portrayed as stealing the Scottish crown while no one is looking, not even the lion nearby. But it is clear that when Diana cuts one of the harp's strings, freeing the hydra and destroying the harp that supports the three realms, great cacophony will ensue. It is cartouches like this, with complex imagery that explores the possibilities of the genre, that will be my focus below.

In the body of the book I present the cartouches chronologically, so that the reader will be able to follow the historical development of the genre outlined above. In order to be able to include enough examples to show the variety of sophisticated cartouches that were created from the late sixteenth to the early nineteenth century, I have kept most of the chapters short, but the notes offer many avenues for further exploration.

11   The Hand-Coloring of Cartouches

Many of the cartouches on printed maps that are reproduced in this book are hand-colored. After maps were printed, colors could be applied with various levels of expertise. The cost of the hand-coloring of a printed map could vary considerably depending on the skill of the artist and on the types of pigments used.[175] I sought out exemplars of maps with hand-colored cartouches not only because they are more visually appealing than uncolored examples, but also because the colors make it easier for the eye to distinguish the elements of the scene and understand what is happening. But it bears mentioning that these maps with hand-colored cartouches are unusual. In many maps that are hand-colored, it is only the geographical features that bear pigment, while the cartouches are uncolored (Fig. 49).[176] The fact that on

175   For discussion of the cost of hand-coloring see David Woodward, "Techniques of Map Engraving, Printing, and Coloring in the European Renaissance," in David Woodward, ed., *The History of Cartography*, vol. 3, *Cartography in the European Renaissance* (Chicago: University of Chicago Press, 2007), vol. 1, pp. 591–610, at 603, who says that coloring added 50% to the cost of a map. Ulla Ehrensvärd, "Color in Cartography: A Historical Survey," in David Woodward, ed., *Art and Cartography: Six Historical Essays* (Chicago and London: The University of Chicago Press, 1987), pp. 123–146, at 139, says that coloring "very seldom contributed more than a quarter of the cost of an uncolored map." Dirk Imhof, "The Production of Ortelius Atlases by Christopher Plantin," in Marcel van den Broecke, Peter van der Krogt, and Peter Meurer, eds., *Abraham Ortelius and the First Atlas: Essays Commemorating the Quadricentennial of his Death, 1598–1998* (Houten: HES, 1998), pp. 79–92, at 82, cites evidence that hand-coloring could double the cost of an atlas; Catherine Hofmann, "L'enluminure des cartes et des atlas imprimés, XVIᵉ–XVIIIᵉ siècle," *Bulletin du Comité Français de Cartographie* 159 (1999), pp. 35–47, esp. 42–43, indicates an increase in price of 50% to 100%; while Truusje Goedings, *'Afsetters en meester-afsetters': De kunst van het kleuren 1480–1720* (Nijmegen: Vantilt, 2015), p. 71, cites evidence that it could quadruple the cost. On coloring by the famous colorist Dirk Jansz. van Santen see note 108 above.
176   On the coloring of cartouches see the remarks in Hofmann, "L'enluminure des cartes et des atlas imprimés" (see note 175), pp. 39, 40, and 43. In contrast to this tendency to leave cartouches uncolored, Henri Gautier emphasizes the importance of coloring cartouches in his *L'Art de laver, ou Nouvelle manière de peindre sur le papier* (Lyon: chez Thomas Amaulry, 1687),

FIGURE 49   An exemplar of Johann Baptiste Homann's *Totius Americae Septentrionalis et Meridionalis Novissima Representatio* (Nuremberg, 1710) on which the geographical features are hand-colored, but the cartouches are not
COURTESY OF BARRY LAWRENCE RUDERMAN RARE MAPS

many maps the geography is hand-colored but the cartouches are not complicates our understanding of the importance assigned to cartouches by those involved in a map's creation. In some cases the publisher spent a large portion of the map's total price commissioning the

creation of a cartouche for it, while in others he copied the cartouche from a model book or from another map with little concern for its context. The cartouche is often the most visually engaging element on a map, but some colorists applied their brushes only to the geography, and not the cartouches, evidently with an eye to how color could enhance the map's ease of use, rather than its decoration.

Thus, many of the maps illustrated in this book are atypical in two regards: they were chosen for their particularly engaging or elaborate or abstruse cartouches, and also for the fact that those cartouches are, somewhat unusually, hand-colored.

It is worth illustrating the difference between an uncolored cartouche, a perfunctorily colored cartouche, and a well colored cartouche to show the extra life, interest, and

pp. 129–131. And specific instructions on how to color cartouches are supplied by John Smith, *The Art of Painting in Oyl* (London: Printed for Samuel Crouch, 1705), pp. 105–106; this very interesting passage is quoted in Raymond Lister, *How to Identify Old Maps and Globes* (Hamden, CT: Archon Books, 1965), p. 58; and discussed by Nancy Purinton, "Materials and Techniques Used for Eighteenth-Century English Printed Maps," in Craigen Bowen, Susan Dackerman, and Elizabeth Mansfield, eds., *Dear Print Fan: A Festschrift for Marjorie B. Cohn* (Cambridge: Harvard University Art Museums, 2001), pp. 257–261.

FIGURE 50
The cartouche showing the bombardment of
Gdánsk on a largely uncolored exemplar of the
map *Das belagerte Danzig eine Weltberühmte
Haupt- und Handelstatt des Polnischen
Preussens*, by the heirs of Johann Baptist
Homann (Nuremberg, 1739)
BIBLIOTEKA NARODOWA ZZK 1 189.
COURTESY OF BIBLIOTEKA NARODOWA

FIGURE 51
The cartouche on a poorly colored exemplar of
the map of the bombardment of Gdánsk
BIBLIOTEKA NARODOWA, ZZK 1 189.
COURTESY OF THE BIBLIOTEKA NARODOWA

FIGURE 52
The cartouche on a spectacularly hand-colored
exemplar of the map of Gdánsk in Homann's
*Grosser atlas uber die gantze Welt wie diese
sowel* (Nuremberg, 1731)
FROM THE AMERICAN GEOGRAPHICAL
SOCIETY LIBRARY, UNIVERSITY OF
WISCONSIN-MILWAUKEE LIBRARIES, RARE
OVERSIZE ATLAS, AT.050 A-1742. COURTESY
OF THE AMERICAN GEOGRAPHICAL SOCIETY
LIBRARY

intelligibility that skillful coloring can bring to these decorative features. I do so by way of a map of Gdańsk, Poland, by the heirs of Johann Baptist Homann (1664–1724), titled *Das belagerte Danzig eine Weltberühmte Haupt- und Handelstatt des Polnischen Preussens: mit ihren Vorstaedten und der Weichselmünder Schanz, wie solche vom 14. Febr. 1734 von denen Russen eingeschlossen, von 20. Mart. aber biß zu den 7. ten Jul. erfolgten Ubergabe, förmlich belagert worden* ("Gdańsk Besieged, a World-Famous Important Trading Center of Polish Prussia, with its Suburbs and the Fortress Schanz on the Vistula, which from Feb. 14, 1734, was Blockaded by the Russians, and from March 20 until the July 7 Surrender, was Formally Besieged") (Nuremberg, 1739).[177] The map depicts the Russian Siege of Danzig (Gdańsk) in 1734, during the War of the Polish Succession. At the left the Russian fleet arrives on the Baltic; the Russian encampments are depicted below the city, and the Polish encampments below and to the left.

In the lower right corner of the map is a spectacular cartouche illustrating the Russian bombardment of the city. Fig. 50 shows the cartouche on an almost uncolored exemplar of the map, Fig. 51 on a poorly colored exemplar, and Fig. 52 on an exemplar that was expertly colored. In the uncolored cartouche the eyes have to work to distinguish the different parts of the scene, and it takes time to understand what is where and what is happening. In the poorly colored cartouche the scene has more life to it and the eyes assimilate it more quickly, and in the expertly colored image the artist has done the work for the viewer's eyes, which are not only freed from the expenditure of effort but also enjoy the sensual stimulation of bright colors, while the mind revels in immediate comprehension of the scene.

12   The Theatricality of Cartouches

A number of authors have written about Abraham Ortelius's title for the collection of maps he first published in 1570, which is generally regarded as the first atlas in the modern sense of the word, the *Theatrum orbis terrarum* or "Theater of the Lands of the World," and have tried to find a theatrical element in the work, but with little success.[178]

Ann Blair has noted that in the sixteenth and seventeenth centuries, books whose authors call them "theaters" are often collections of objects "arranged according to a more or less carefully conceived plan."[179] Ortelius in his introductory epistle seems to offer at least one reason for his title:[180]

"For, that I may speake that which is the trueth, those great and large Geographicall Maps or Chartes, which are folded or rowl'd up, are not so commodious: nor, when any thing is peradventure read in them, so easie to be look'd upon. And he that will in order hang them all along upon a wall, had need have not only a very large & wide house, but even a Princes gallery or spacious Theatre. This I having oft made triall of, I began to bethink my selfe, what meanes might be found to redresse these discommodities, which I have spoken of, and either to make them somewhat lesse, or, if possibly it might bee, to take them all cleane away. And at length me thought it might be done by that meanes which we have observed and set downe in this our booke."

That is, the atlas format that he developed, presenting a detailed image of the world by means of a collection of consistently designed maps bound together, was an alternative to presenting one large, detailed map in a theater-sized space. The cartouches in Ortelius's maps are decorated mostly with strapwork, ropework, vegetal motifs, and grotesques, with almost no people or personifications. But I would suggest that later maps whose cartouches were decorated with images of sovereigns, indigenous peoples, *putti*, historical figures, Roman gods, and personifications, thus acquired the theatrical quality that has been sought in Ortelius's maps.[181] The map becomes the stage, the frame of the cartouche becomes the backdrop, and the human figures and animals that populate the cartouche become the actors who enliven

177   On the map of Gdańsk see Antonius Jammers and Egon Klemp, *Historische Pläne und Grundrisse von Städten und Ortschaften in Polen: ein deutsch-polnischer Katalog* (Wiesbaden: SBB PK, 2000), p. 78, no. 633.

178   See Tom Conley, "Pierre Boaistuau's Cosmographic Stage: Theater, Text, and Map," *Renaissance Drama* 23 (1992), pp. 59–86, at 62; John Gillies, *Shakespeare and the Geography of Difference* (Cambridge, England, and New York: Cambridge University Press, 1994), esp. pp. 71–72 (an unsatisfactory account).

179   Ann Blair, *The Theater of Nature: Jean Bodin and Renaissance Science* (Princeton: Princeton University Press, 1997), p. 176.

180   Abraham Ortelius, *Theatrum orbis terrarum—The Theatre of the Whole World* (London: I. Norton, 1606), on the first page of the epistle of the reader.

181   For remarks on the theatricality of cartouches see Benjamin Schmidt, "On the Impulse of Mapping, or How a Flat Earth Theory of Dutch Maps Distorts the Thickness and Pictorial Proclivities of Early Modern Dutch Cartography (and Misses Its Picturing Impulse)," *Art History* 35.5 (2012), pp. 1036–1049, esp. 1038 and 1042, in his discussion of the cartouches on Nicolaes Visscher, *Novissima et accuratissima totius Americae descriptio* (Amsterdam, 1658). On the theatricality of maps also see Álvaro Alonso, "Cervantes y los mapas: la cartografía como metáfora," *Lectura y signo* 1 (2006), pp. 75–88, esp. 78–79.

that theater with their gestures, their poses, their antics, their battles, and their daily tasks.

Cartouches, as mentioned earlier, are ineluctably anti-cartographic insofar as they obscure part of the cartographic space, and are thus entangled with that space, but it is perhaps in their theatricality that they feel the most distinct from cartographic space. The theatricality of cartouches places in relief the vast differences in scale, perspective, subject matter, and susceptibility to interpretation of symbolism from the surrounding geography. That is to say, their theatricality emphasizes the characteristics that make cartouches such striking, strange, wonderful, and engaging additions to maps.

Covering Emptiness with a Hope for Peace

Gerard Mercator, Nova et aucta orbis terrae descriptio ad usum navigantium, *1569*

The Flemish cartographer Gerard Mercator's famous world map of 1569, which he both designed and engraved himself, was printed on eighteen sheets that when assembled measure 132.5 × 195 cm, or 52 × 76.7 inches.[1] It is titled *Nova et aucta orbis terrae descriptio ad usum navigantium emendate accomodata*, that is, "New and Augmented Map of the World Perfectly Adapted to the Use of Navigators," and is known for being the first to make practical use of a projection that came to bear Mercator's name, wherein a course on a constant compass heading is a straight line on the map.[2] Mercator indicates in the title that it was intended for use by navigators, but in many ways the map seems more appropriate to a scholarly audience, with its extensive texts in Latin, rather than a vernacular language,[3] which contain accounts of the Nile River and the mythical Christian king Prester John, things of little relevance to navigators.[4] And indeed neither the map nor its projection proved popular with navigators in the first decades following its publication.

The map has numerous cartouches, most containing descriptive text and decorated with strapwork; there is also a cartouche containing a map of the northern polar regions in the lower left-hand corner, and a cartouche with a diagram for calculating distances along courses in the lower right-hand corner.[5] By far the largest cartouche on the map is the multi-part example that occupies much of the interior of North America (Fig. 53). The largest frame, decorated with strapwork, contains Mercator's address to the reader in which he takes up three subjects. First he explains his new projection; second he expresses his desire for geographical accuracy in the map, and his use of Spanish and Portuguese charts as sources; and third he explains that he hopes his map distinguishes between the part of the world known to the ancients (Europe, Africa, and Asia), indicating the limits of that part, and the New World and southern continent, which are recent discoveries.[6]

Above this long two-column text is Mercator's dedication of the map to William of Jülich-Cleves-Berge (1516–1592), the tolerant and peace-loving ruler of the lands where Mercator lived,[7] which are now divided by the border between the Netherlands and Germany. Above the dedication are William's coat of arms and personifications of Peace, Justice, and Piety, and to the left and right of the dedication are scroll cartouches containing a poem

1 Three copies of Mercator's 1569 map survive, one in Paris at the Bibliothèque nationale de France, Rés Ge. A 1064; another in Basel at the Universitätsbibliothek, Kartenslg AA 3–5; and a third at Maritiem Museum in Rotterdam, Atlas51. Zoomable images of the sheets of the first are available at https://gallica.bnf.fr/. The Rotterdam exemplar is hand-colored and has been reproduced at a reduced scale in *Gerard Mercator's Map of the World (1569) in the Form of an Atlas in the Maritiem Museum 'Prins Hendrik' at Rotterdam* (Rotterdam: Maritiem Museum, 1961); and more recently at full scale in *Atlas of the World: Gerard Mercator's Map of the World (1569)* (Zutphen: Walburg Pers, 2011). On the surviving copies of the map see Patricia Seed, "Unpasted: A Guide to Surviving Prints of Mercator's Nautical Chart of 1569," in Gerhard Holzer, Valerie Newby, Petra Svatek, and Georg Zotti, eds., *A World of Innovations: Cartography in the Time of Gerhard Mercator* (Newcastle upon Tyne: Cambridge Scholars, 2015), pp. 146–157. For good short discussions of the map see Robert W. Karrow, *Mapmakers of the Sixteenth Century and Their Maps: Bio-Bibliographies of the Cartographers of Abraham Ortelius, 1570* (Chicago: Speculum Orbis Press, 1993), pp. 389–390; and Rodney W. Shirley, *The Mapping of the World: Early Printed World Maps 1472–1700* (Riverside, CT: Early World Press, 2001), pp. 137–142.
2 For discussion of Mercator's projection see Michele D. Abee, "The Mercator Projection: Its Uses, Misuses, and Its Association with Scientific Information and the Rise of Scientific Societies," Ph.D. Dissertation, The University of North Carolina at Greensboro, 2019; and the same author's "The Spread of the Mercator Projection in Western European and United States Cartography," *Cartographica* 56.2 (2021), pp. 151–165.
3 So Andrew Taylor, *The World of Gerard Mercator: The Mapmaker Who Revolutionized Geography* (New York: Walker & Co., 2004), p. 225.
4 Walter Ghim in his biography of Mercator in the prefatory material to Mercator's *Atlas* of 1595 says that Mercator placed the 1569 map "before the eyes and gaze of learned men and travelers and sailors," indicating a lower priority for sailors. See Gerard Mercator, *Atlas sive cosmographicae meditationes de fabrica mundi et fabricate figura*, trans. David Sullivan (Oakland: Octavo, 2000) (CD-ROM), p. 8 of the PDF.
5 The legends on the map are transcribed and translated into English in A. Wedermeyer, "Text and Translation of the Legends of the Original Chart of the World by Gerhard Mercator, Issued in 1569," *Hydrographic Review* 9.2 (1932), pp. 7–45.
6 See Wedermeyer, "Text and Translation" (see note 5), pp. 9–15.
7 For the dedication see Wedermeyer, "Text and Translation" (see note 5), pp. 8–9. On William of Jülich-Cleves-Berge see Guido von Büren, Ralf-Peter Fuchs, and Georg Mölich, eds., *Herrschaft, Hof und Humanismus: Wilhelm V. von Jülich-Kleve-Berg und seine Zeit* (Bielefeld: Verlag für Regionalgeschichte, 2018).

© CHET VAN DUZER, 2023 | DOI:10.1163/9789004523838_003

FIGURE 53
A detail of North America and of the cartouche that
covers much of its interior in Gerard Mercator's world
map of 1569, *Nova et aucta orbis terrae descriptio ad usum
navigantium*
PARIS, BNF, GE A-1064 (RES). COURTESY OF THE
BIBLIOTHÈQUE NATIONALE DE FRANCE

by Mercator in which he sets forth his views about how a state can be well governed, and he ends by asserting that his region enjoys just such a government.[8] The poem is not only of philosophical importance, but is also an encomium of William and his government more thoughtful and profound than any that appears on other maps. On the one hand, it seems remarkable that a cartographer would set forth his political philosophy in a cartouche, rather than in a separate treatise; on the other, it makes perfect sense that he should do this on a world map: implicit is the hope that other parts of the world will also enjoy enlightened governance.

In this cartouche Mercator follows Waldseemüller's example in his *Carta marina* (see above) of making the cartouche with the address to the reader the largest and most elaborate on the map.[9] The cartouche is also unusual in that it includes an account of the allegorical figures:[10] Mercator explains that the combination of Peace, Justice, and Piety makes being governed pleasant and easy, and even increases happiness, and that moreover the sisters Piety and Peace "hinder or discover all malevolent deeds." The cartographer identifies the personifications as divine by giving them halos,[11] and the symbolism of the fact that the three personifications sit around William's coat of arms is clear.

The cartouche occupies much of the interior of North America, and Mercator is certainly using this decoration to conceal his ignorance of the geography of the continent's hinterlands. Mercator was the first cartographer to use a cartouche this way in the interior of North America, and this practice was adopted by numerous other cartographers after him. Mercator also uses the cartouche to avoid

committing to an answer to the much-discussed question of whether there was a passage west to Asia to the north of North America, the so-called Northwest Passage.[12] He shows part of an east-west channel to the west of the cartouche and also to its east, but the personifications of Peace and Piety, together with William's coat of arms, cover the part of the map that would reveal whether these two channels connect, or whether intervening land renders a passage impossible.[13]

In 1587 Mercator's son Rumold made a world map based on his father's 1569 map that has no cartouche here and indicates the existence of a Northwest Passage, a striking change. But while Mercator's son chose not to reprise his father's cartouche, a later cartographer imitated it as a sign of respect to the great Flemish mapmaker. This was the English astronomer, mathematician, physicist, and meteorologist Edmond Halley (1656–1742). Sometime between 1702 and 1708 Halley made a world map on Mercator's projection, which like Mercator's was designed for use by navigators, as it shows the declination of the compass—the difference between the direction a compass points and true north—everywhere except in the Pacific, the one ocean for which Halley did not have data.[14] In the South Pacific on his map Mercator places an inset map of the northern polar regions, and in the South

8   For Mercator's poem see Wedermeyer, "Text and Translation" (see note 5), pp. 8–9. On Mercator's belief in the value of peace and concord see Rienk Vermij, "Mercator and the Reformation," in Manfred Bütner and René Dirven, eds., *Mercator und Wandlungen der Wissenschaften im 16. und 17. Jahrhundert* (Bochum: Brockmeyer, 1993), pp. 77–90.

9   We have no explicit evidence that Mercator saw Waldseemüller's *Carta marina*, but this is rendered likely by the fact that his friend Abraham Ortelius consulted it: Ortelius cites the *Carta marina* as a source in his *Theatrum orbis terrarum* (Antwerp: apud Aegid. Coppenium Diesth, 1570), in his *Catalogus auctorum tabularum geographicarum* (Catalog of mapmakers), on sig. Cii[r].

10   It is worth remarking that Ortelius's *Theatrum* of 1570 includes a poem by Adolphus Mekerchus that explains the personifications of the continents on the book's title page: see Werner Waterschoot, "The Title-Page of Ortelius's *Theatrum Orbis Terrarum*," *Quaerendo* 9 (1979), pp. 43–68.

11   On the use of halos on personifications see Ernst H. Kantorowicz, *The King's Two Bodies: A Study in Mediaeval Political Theology* (Princeton: Princeton University Press, 1957), pp. 78–79.

12   On ideas about and maps of a possible Northwest Passage see R.A. Skelton, "The North-West Passage, 16th to 18th Centuries," in his *Explorers' Maps: Chapters in the Cartographic Record of Geographical Discovery* (London: Routledge & Paul, 1958), pp. 118–136; and Theodore E. Layng, "Early Geographical Concepts of the Northwest Passage," *Cartographer* 2.2 (1965), pp. 81–91.

13   Rumold Mercator's 1587 map is titled *Orbis terrae compendiosa descriptio*; high-resolution images of it are available in https://catalog.princeton.edu. On Rumold's map see Rodney W. Shirley, *The Mapping of the World: Early Printed World Maps 1472–1700* (Riverside, CT: Early World Press, 2001), pp. 178–179, no. 157; and Robert W. Karrow, *Mapmakers of the Sixteenth Century and Their Maps: Bio-Bibliographies of the Cartographers of Abraham Ortelius, 1570* (Chicago: Speculum Orbis Press, 1993), p. 392, 56/17.10.

14   Halley's map has titles in both Latin and English, *Nova & accuratissima totius terrarum orbis tabula nautica variationum magneticarum index juxta observationes anno. 1700 habitas constructa per Edm. Halley = A New and Correct Chart of the Whole World Shewing the Variations of the Compass as They Were Found in the Year M.D.CC*. A high-resolution image of a hand-colored copy of the map is available at https://jcb.lunaimaging.com; for discussion of it see Norman J.W. Thrower, "Edmond Halley as a Thematic Geo-Cartographer," *Annals of the Association of American Geographers* 59 (1969), pp. 652–676, at 667–669; and Lori L. Murray and David R. Bellhouse, "How Was Edmond Halley's Map of Magnetic Declination (1701) Constructed?" *Imago Mundi* 69.1 (2017), pp. 72–84.

FIGURE 54   Detail of the cartouche in North America on Edmond Halley, *Nova & accuratissima totius terrarum orbis tabula nautica variationum magneticarum index* (London, c.1702–08)

Pacific on his map Halley includes an inset map of the western half of the northern polar regions.

And just as Mercator has a large cartouche topped by three allegorical figures that occupies much of North America, so does Halley (Fig. 54), but in place of Peace, Justice, and Piety, Halley has personifications of Astronomy, Navigation, and Geography. That is to say, Halley has replaced symbols of Mercator's humanistic concerns with symbols of the Enlightenment.[15] Many cartographers copied cartouche designs from their colleagues as acts of appropriation, with no thought of giving credit to the source, but something different is happening on Halley's map. Halley did not need to borrow a cartouche design. In his world map based on Mercator's projection he seems to be using this cartouche and the north polar inset to signal to the knowledgeable viewer his admiration for and debt to Mercator.[16]

---

15   Halley had placed very similar personifications of Astronomy, Navigation, and Geography on a cartouche in Africa on an earlier map of his, but this earlier map is focused on the Atlantic and is not a world map—this earlier use of these same personifications does not diminish their allusion to Mercator on Halley's world map. The earlier map is *A New and Correct Chart Shewing the Variations of the Compass in the Western & Southern Oceans as Observed in ye year 1700 by his Maties. Command* (London, c.1701). Digital images of this map are available at https://catalog.princeton.edu   and   https://digitalcollections.nypl.org; for discussion of it see Thrower, "Edmond Halley" (see note 14), pp. 664–667.

16   Halley speaks of the utility of maps based on Mercator's projection in his preface "To the Reader" in the *Atlas maritimus & commercialis* (London, 1728), much of which has been attributed to Daniel Defoe.

CHAPTER 2

The Gaze of the Sea Monster

Ignazio Danti's map of Sardinia in the Galleria delle carte geografiche, *1580–82*

The Gallery of Maps (*Galleria delle carte geografiche*) in the Vatican, commissioned by Pope Gregory XIII in 1580 and measuring 120 meters (394 feet) long, contains a series of frescoed maps, beginning with two general maps of Italy and then forty detailed topographical maps of the peninsula. The maps were designed by the priest and cartographer Ignazio Danti (1536–86), and are arranged as though the axis of the Gallery is the Apennine Mountains that run down the center of Italy, with the regions to the east on one side, and the regions to the west on the other, and above on the ceiling, frescoes of the most important miracles to have taken place in each of those regions.[1] The maps were the first large-scale maps of all of Italy, and were painted by Danti and a team of artists from 1580 to 1583.[2] It seems likely that the idea of the Gallery was that by contemplating the maps, Pope Gregory would best understand how to govern Italy, for the Pope at this time was as much the temporal ruler of Italy as the spiritual leader of Christianity.[3]

All of the maps in the gallery are embellished with cartouches, and often there are multiple cartouches decorating a single map. As one might expect from maps made in the late sixteenth century, many of these cartouches have elaborate strapwork, vegetal motifs, and grotesques; we know that Danti composed the descriptive texts in the cartouches, but it is not certain that he designed them.[4] In addition to the more elaborate cartouches containing descriptive texts there are also many less elaborate cartouches with inset views of the most important city or cities in the region depicted.

Towards the end of the gallery on the right is the map of Sardinia.[5] To the left of the island there is an elaborate title cartouche with text about the history of the island,[6] while to the right there is a spectacular and very original cartouche that displays the map's scale of miles and indicates in latitude and longitude the part of the earth's surface that the map covers (Fig. 55). This information is on the sail of a ship, but the ship is foundering under the attack of a sea monster that churns the sea with its forelimbs while it raises its fishy tail high in front of the sail. The monster bares its sharp teeth and looks toward the viewer, breaking the fourth wall, as it were, and the perspective on the foundering ship and sea monster is different than that in the rest of the map: the image is three-dimensional and stands out of the plane of the map.

And the monster breaks the fourth wall in another way. It is not just sinking a ship, as sea monsters do on other maps;[7] in sinking this ship that has the scale of miles on its sail it is imperiling the conveyance of cartographic knowledge to the viewer, and thus interfering with the cartographic project of the Gallery of Maps. This dynamic cartouche is thus an excellent example of the meta-cartographic communication that is possible in

---

1   For discussion of the Gallery of Maps in the Vatican see Lucio Gambi, "Egnazio Danti e la Galleria delle Carte geografiche—Egnazio Danti and the Gallery of Maps," in Lucio Gambi and Antonio Pinelli, eds., *La Galleria delle Carte geografiche in Vaticano = The Gallery of Maps in the Vatican* (Modena: F.C. Panini, 1994), vol. 2, pp. 83–96; Marica Milanesi, "Le ragioni del ciclo delle carte geografiche—The Historical Background to the Cycle in the Gallery of Maps," in the same volume, pp. 97–123; Gianni Guadalupi, "The Pope's Atlas: The Vatican Map Gallery," *FMR* 86 (June 1997), pp. 105–128; Francesca Fiorani, *The Marvel of Maps: Art, Cartography and Politics in Renaissance Italy* (New Haven: Yale University Press, 2005), "The Gallery of Maps," pp. 171–207, and "Appendix B, The Gallery of Maps," pp. 266–272; and Alvise Chiggiato, *La Galleria delle Carte geografiche in Vaticano = The Gallery of Maps in the Vatican*, ed. Lucio Gambi and Antonio Pinelli, trans. Barbara Fisher et al. (Modena: Franco Cosimo Panini, 2008).

2   On the artists who painted the maps in the Gallery see Fiorani, *The Marvel of Maps* (see note 1), pp. 176–181.

3   Milanesi, "Le ragioni del ciclo delle carte geografiche" (see note 1), pp. 104 and 106–107; and Rolando Ferri, "Una 'passeggiata in Italia': L'anonima *Ambulatio gregoriana*—A 'Walk through Italy': The Anonymous *Ambulatio gregoriana*," in Lucio Gambi and Antonio Pinelli, eds., *La Galleria delle Carte geografiche in Vaticano = The Gallery of Maps in the Vatican* (Modena: F.C. Panini, 1994), vol. 2, pp. 73–81, at 78. On maps as an administrative tool in the sixteenth century see David Buisseret, ed., *Monarchs, Ministers and Maps: The Emergence of Cartography as a Tool of Government in Early Modern Europe* (Chicago: University of Chicago Press, 1992).

4   See Fiorani, *The Marvel of Maps* (see note 1), pp. 186–187.

5   Danti's map of Sardinia is discussed by Chiggiato, *La Galleria delle Carte geografiche in Vaticano* (see note 1), no. 15.

6   The text about Sardinia on the map is transcribed by Agostino Taja, *Descrizione del Palazzo Apostolico Vaticano* (Vatican City: Appresso Niccolò e Marco Pagliarini, 1750), p. 328; and Erasmo Pistolesi, *Il Vaticano descritto ed illustrato* (Rome: Tipografia della Società editrice, 1829), vol. 6, p. 182.

7   See Chet Van Duzer, *Sea Monsters on Medieval and Renaissance Maps* (London: British Library, 2013), pp. 38–39.

---

cartouches, whether it is the imparting of metadata about the map, the cartographer signaling his or her interests, or as we see here, an image that both connects directly with the viewer by means of the monster's gaze and suggests the possibility of failure in Danti's project for the Pope. We will see several cartouches in which cartographers depict the tools of their trade or even include self-portraits—that is, they allude to the process of making maps, and identify themselves as the makers—but here Danti seems playfully to suggest that cartographic projects like his ambitious Gallery of Maps cannot always be brought to completion.

FIGURE 55   A detail of the cartouche of Ignazio Danti's map of Sardinia from the Galleria delle carte geografiche in the Vatican Palace

CHAPTER 3

An Exotic Medicine from the Tombs of Egypt

Daniel Cellarius, Asiae nova descriptio, *c.1590*

The cartographer of our next map, Daniel Cellarius, was from Wildberg in Württemberg, Germany, and was active in the second half of the sixteenth century, but we have little documentary evidence about him, not even the dates of his birth and death. He collaborated with Gerard de Jode (1509–1591) in creating the atlas titled *Speculum orbis terrarum* that was printed in Antwerp in 1578,[1] which came to market several years after Abraham Ortelius's pioneering *Theatrum orbis terrarum* in 1570. In his epistle to the reader in that work Cellarius writes about the value and importance of adding images and texts to maps—a type of statement about map decoration that we rarely encounter in the sixteenth century. He remarks:[2]

"I do not ignore the fact that a terrestrial map joined with a picture is not only strengthened and invigorated, but in addition to its general usefulness, also produces great pleasure for the reader. Lest I be found wanting in this matter as well by those learned in geography, I thought it would not be inappropriate if I filled the remainder with text, which when brought together with the maps themselves, would supply fuller information about places to everyone."

He is no doubt referring to images of ships and sea monsters, as well as some city views, that he included in maps in the *Speculum orbis terrarum*, for the cartouches in this atlas are not particularly elaborate. But later in his career he made more complex cartouches. In about 1590 Cellarius made a new map of Asia (*Asiae nova descriptio*) on eight sheets that together measure 126 × 96 cm (more than 4 × 3 feet); it survives in only one copy, in Göttingen, at the Lower Saxony State and University Library.[3] The map has numerous cartouches, most of which contain descriptive text, but there are two with images. In the upper right-hand corner of the map there is a cartouche containing a bird's-eye view of the Chinese city of Quinsay (Hangzhou), with a description of the city from Marco Polo in another cartouche just below.[4] Cellarius borrowed the image, with some modifications, from *La cosmographie uniuerselle* by the French explorer and cartographer André Thevet, which was printed in 1575.[5]

At the lower left-hand edge of the map, in Africa, there is another double cartouche with an image above and a text below (Fig. 56). These cartouches address an intriguing subject: the use of pieces of human flesh from Egyptian mummies as medicine in Europe, and specifically the question of the source of the flesh.[6] For some held that the flesh did indeed come from Egyptian

---

1 On De Jode's atlas see Fernand Gratien van Ortroy, *L'oeuvre cartographique de Gérhard et de Corneille de Jode* (Ghent: E. van Goethem & cie, 1914), pp. 43–82; R.A. Skelton's introduction in the facsimile edition, Gerard de Jode, *Speculum orbis terrarum, Antwerpen, 1578,* (Amsterdam: Theatrum Orbis Terrarum, 1965); and Peter van der Krogt, *Koeman's Atlantes Neerlandici* ('t Goy-Houten: Hes & De Graaf, 1997–2003), vol. 3, pp. 255–260.

2 Cellarius's original Latin is on the second page of his epistle to the reader in De Jode's *Speculum orbis terrarum,* and it reads: … *nec ignorarem, Graphicam terrarum descriptionem cum pictura conjunctam non solum confirmari, ac nervos adipisci, sed & praeter haud vulgarem utilitatem, ingentem quoque voluptatem lectori ciere: ne hac quoque parte Geographiae studiosis deesem, putavi non abs re fore, si alteram scriptis implerem, quae cum ipsis tabulis collatae, pleniorem locorum notitiam omnibus suppeditarent.*

3 It was Gerard de Jode, with whom Cellarius had collaborated on the atlas *Speculum orbis terrarum,* who printed Cellarius's map of Asia. For discussion of the map see Günter Schilder, *Monumenta cartographica Neerlandica* (Alphen aan den Rijn: Canaletto, 1986–2013), vol. 2, pp. 80–82.

4 On Quinsay see Ivar Hallberg, *L'Extrême Orient dans la littérature et la cartographie de l'Occident des XIIIᵉ, XIVᵉ, et XVᵉ siècles* (Gothenburg: W. Zachrissons boktryckeri a.-b., 1907), pp. 425–429; and A.C. Moule, "Marco Polo's Description of Quinsai," *T'oung Pao* 33 (1937), pp. 105–128.

5 Cellarius's text about Quinsay comes from Marco Polo, but at the end he refers the reader to Thevet. He borrowed the image of the city from André Thevet, *La cosmographie uniuerselle* (Paris: Pierre L'Huillier, 1575), vol. 1, f. 454v; a high-resolution image of Thevet's view of Quinsay is available at https://jcb.lunaimaging.com. This same image of the city was copied by Matthaus Merian in his view of *Xuntien alias Quinzay* in Pierre d'Avity's *Neuwe Archontologia cosmica* (Frankfurt, 1638), following p. 680; and in Jan Jansson's *Theatrum urbium celebriorum* (Amsterdam, 1657), vol. 8.

6 On the use of mummy as medicine see Warren R. Dawson, "Mummy as a Drug," *Proceedings of the Royal Society of Medicine* 21.1 (1927), pp. 34–39; Karl H. Dannenfeldt, "Egyptian Mumia: The Sixteenth Century Experience and Debate," *The Sixteenth Century Journal* 16.2 (1985), pp. 163–180; Richard Sugg, *Mummies, Cannibals, and Vampires: The History of Corpse Medicine from the Renaissance to the Victorians* (London and New York: Routledge, 2011), esp. pp. 14–26 and 67–77; and Louise Noble, *Medicinal Cannibalism in Early Modern English Literature and Culture* (New York: Palgrave Macmillan, 2011), esp. pp. 17–34.

FIGURE 56
Detail of the pair of cartouches in
Africa about the source of mummy in
Daniel Cellarius's *Asiae nova descriptio*
(Frankfurt, *c.*1590)
GÖTTINGEN, NIEDERSÄCHSISCHE
STAATS- UND UNIVERSITÄTSBIBLIOTHEK,
MAPP 1334. BY PERMISSION OF THE
NIEDERSÄCHSISCHE STAATS- UND
UNIVERSITÄTSBIBLIOTHEK

mummies, while others believed that it came from the bodies of people much more recently killed and desiccated in North African sandstorms.

Cellarius asserts both by image and by text that the medicine called mummy was indeed from Egyptian mummies. The scene above is located in Egypt by the presence of the pyramids (which are depicted far too small, as was common at this period) and also by the river flowing in the background, which we are to understand is the Nile.

Cellarius shows three scenes of men breaking into tombs, in the lower left, in the middle ground on the right, and again in the distance just above the last-mentioned scene. In the lower right he shows mummies being carried out of a tomb, with two mummies displayed in the foreground so that the viewer can see the details of their appearance. In the center of the scene we see mummies being loaded onto the backs of camels to begin the journey to Europe. The text below translates into English as follows:

"By means of this image, gentle reader, André Thevet tries to show the origin of true mummy, since the opinions of many people on this subject differ. "Mummy" is an Arabic word meaning a thing formed of hardened precious spices. Of this type were those bodies of heroes found in the very ancient tombs of the Egyptians, which were usually formed of a mixture of all different spices, such as balsam, myrrh, and aloe, all put together. For among all the nations in the whole world there was no people so scrupulous in the burial and preservation of the bodies of the dead as the Egyptians. This is demonstrated by those most ancient and wonderful monuments, the pyramids, whose structures are so tightly built and encrusted with strong solid plaster that even with the greatest effort they can barely be broken open. Inside them, bodies are found to be so undamaged and firm as though they have been preserved for only four days, rather than for about two thousand years. For which reason they seem to be mistaken who think that this kind of mummy is found in the deserts of Arabia, from bodies of those suffocated in the sand there and were dried by the sun, which this evidence shows to be far from the truth: everyone knows that men or beasts who die from hunger or thirst rot and disintegrate with a very foul stench."

Cellarius again cites the French explorer and cartographer André Thevet; Thevet discusses mummies, with an illustration, in his *Cosmographie de Levant* (Lyon: Jean Tournes et Guil. Gazeau, 1556), chapt. 42, pp. 155–159, esp. 157–158, but what Thevet says is not similar to the legend on Cellarius's map, and Thevet's image of a mummy is not at all similar to Cellarius's complex scene.[7] One possible source for Cellarius's text about the distinction between true Egyptian mummy and mummy from more

recent cadavers is one of the most influential works of the Renaissance, Girolamo Cardano's *De subtilitate*.[8] But the wonderful image that accompanies the text is Cellarius's own composition, despite his attempt to give it greater authority by ascribing it to Thevet. I know of no other map that evinces such a strong interest in mummy, so the subject must have piqued Cellarius's curiosity. This example well illustrates the tremendous variety of subjects that cartographers address in their cartouches; in this case, Cellarius reassures the reader about the genuineness of an exotic medicine.

Cellarius's scene of gathering mummies in Egypt evidently inspired a scene in the upper margin of an untitled double-hemisphere world map made by Claes Jansz Visscher in about 1617.[9] In the upper margin there is the scene of mummy collection at the left, in the center, from left to right, personifications of Asia, Africa, Europe (in the middle, the position of honor), then the New World personifications of Magallanica, Mexicana, and Peruviana, and to their right, a scene of New World cannibalism. Remarkably, the cartographer silently suggests a comparison between the gathering and consumption of mummy in Europe, on the one hand, and Brazilian cannibalism, on the other.

---

7   For discussion of Thevet's passage on mummies see André Thevet, *Cosmographie de Levant*, ed. Frank Lestringant (Geneva: Droz, 1985), pp. lxviii and lxxi–lxxii and 311.

8   For Cardano's discussion of mummy see Girolamo Cardano, *De subtilitate libri XXI* (Lyon: Guillaume Rouillé, 1559), Book 18, p. 645. The passage is translated into English in John M. Forrester, trans., *The 'De Subtilitate' of Girolamo Cardano* (Tempe: ACMRS, 2013), vol. 2, p. 912. For a later discussion of the difference between true and fake mummy see Pierre Pomet, *Histoire generale des drogues* (Paris: Jean-Baptiste Loyson & Augustin Pillon, 1694), part 2, chapter 1, pp. 1–7.

9   The unique surviving copy of Claes Jansz Visscher's world map of *c.*1617 is in Vienna, Österreichische Nationalbibliothek FKB 282–2,I,1 KAR MAG; for discussion see Günter Schilder, *Monumenta cartographica Neerlandica* (Alphen aan den Rijn, Holland: Canaletto, 1986–2013), vol. 3, pp. 172–173 and 176; and Rodney W. Shirley, *The Mapping of the World: Early Printed World Maps, 1472–1700* (London: Holland Press, 1983), pp. 317–319, no. 294.

CHAPTER 4

New Personifications of the Continents

Jodocus Hondius, Nova et exacta totius orbis terrarum descriptio, *1608*

Before the European discovery of the New World there was a medieval system of personifications for the three traditional parts or divisions of the world, Europe, Asia, and Africa—for which I will use the modern designation of "continents" here. In Genesis 9:18–19 following Noah's Flood we read that Noah's three sons Shem, Ham, and Japheth were the progenitors of the peoples who repopulated the earth, and over time this idea was elaborated into a belief that the people of Asia were descended from Shem, the peoples of Africa from Ham, and the peoples of Europe from Japhet.[1] This association between the three sons of Noah and the three continents that were known in antiquity is common on medieval maps, and Noah's sons came to represent those continents (Fig. 57).

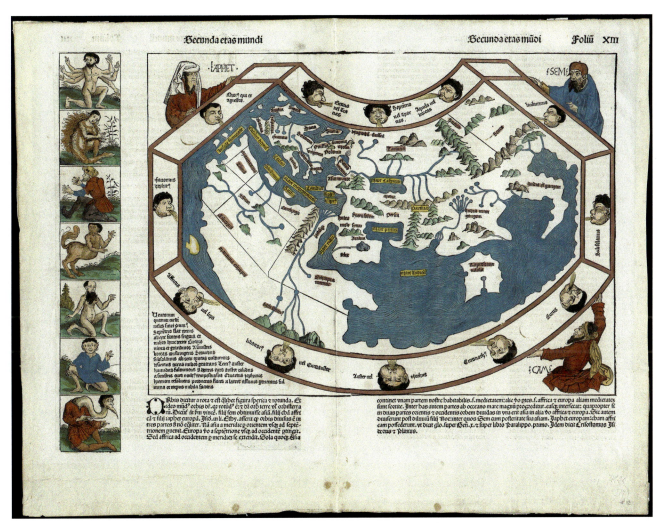

FIGURE 57   World map in Hartmann Schedel's *Liber chronicarum*, 1493, with the three sons of Noah representing Europe, Asia, and Africa
COURTESY OF THE SYDNEY R. KNAFEL MAP COLLECTION, PHILLIPS ACADEMY, AND THE NORMAN B. LEVENTHAL MAP & EDUCATION CENTER AT THE BOSTON PUBLIC LIBRARY

1   For discussion see Benjamin Braude, "The Sons of Noah and the Construction of Ethnic and Geographical Identities in the Medieval and Early Modern Periods," *The William and Mary Quarterly* 54.1 (1997), pp. 103–142, esp. 108–115.

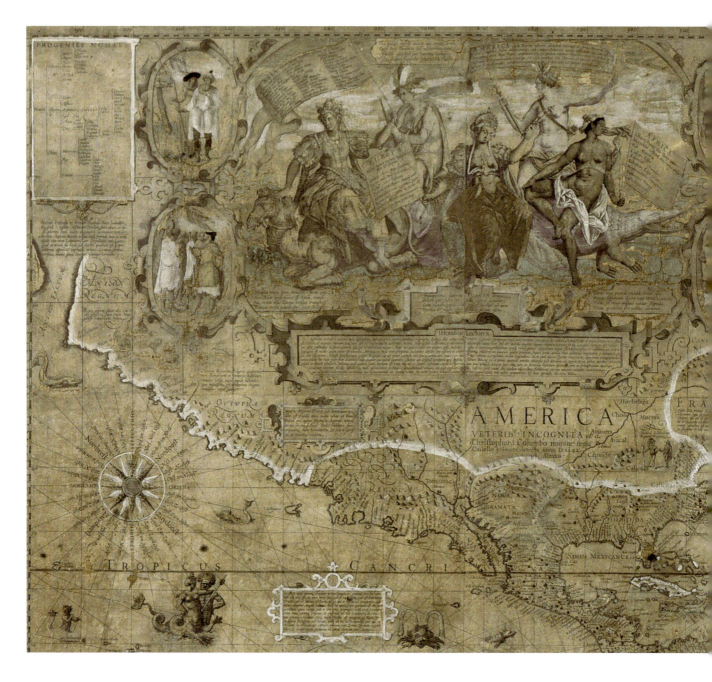

The European discovery of America, which Europeans called the fourth part of the world, necessitated a new system of personifications for the continents, for Noah only had three sons. In the title page of his *Theatrum orbis terrarum*, first published in 1570, Abraham Ortelius personified Europe, Asia, Africa, and America as women, and this image was instrumental in disseminating personifications of the continents as women, both in prints and in maps.[2]

In Amsterdam in 1608 the Flemish cartographer Jodocus Hondius (1563–1612) printed a wall map of the world titled *Nova et exacta totius orbis terrarum descriptio geographica et hydrographica* ("New and Exact Geographical and Hydrographical Map of the Whole World") that retrospectively represents—in a spectacular cartouche—the

---

2   Images of Ortelius's title page are available in digitized copies of his *Theatrum*, for example of the 1570 and 1595 editions available at https://searchworks.stanford.edu. For discussion of his title page see Werner Waterschoot, "The Title-Page of Ortelius's *Theatrum Orbis Terrarum*," *Quaerendo* 9 (1979): 43–68, esp. 43; on other sixteenth- and seventeenth-century personifications of the continents as

women see Elizabeth McGrath, "Humanism, Allegorical Invention, and the Personification of the Continents," in Hans Vlieghe, Arnout Balis, and Carl Van de Velde, eds., *Concept, Design & Execution in Flemish Painting 1550–1700* (Turnhout: Brepols, 2000), pp. 43–71. For discussions of personifications of the continents on world maps see Alex Zukas, "Class, Imperial Space, and Allegorical Figures of the Continents on Early-Modern World Maps," *Environment, Space, Place* 10.2 (2018), pp. 29–62.

FIGURE 58
Detail of the cartouche in North America in Jodocus Hondius, *Nova et exacta totius orbis terrarum descriptio geographica et hydrographica*, 1608. London, Royal Geographical Society
© ROYAL GEOGRAPHICAL SOCIETY (WITH IBG)

passing of the torch from the sons of Noah as representatives of Europe, Asia, and Africa, to this new humanist system of representation.³

We saw that Mercator in his 1569 world map filled the interior of North America with an elaborate, multi-part cartouche, one of whose multiple roles was to conceal his ignorance of the interior of the continent. Hondius adopts this same strategy in his 1608 world map with a stupendously large and rich cartouche (Fig. 58).⁴ At the

3 My discussion of Hondius's cartouche here is based on that in my chapter "The Pre-History of the Personification of Continents on Maps: Earth, Ocean, and the Sons of Noah," in Maryanne Cline Horowitz and Louise Arizzoli, eds., *Bodies and Maps: Early Modern Personifications of the Continents* (Leiden and Boston: Brill, 2020), pp. 101–129, at 121–124. In that chapter I discuss the different cartouche on Hondius's earlier version of this world map, published in 1603, which includes the sons of Noah and shows how the peoples descended from his sons populated the world, but not the personifications of the continents. The unique surviving exemplar of Hondius's 1603 world map is in Libertyville, Illinois, MacLean Collection no. 3648. For discussion of that map, in addition to

my chapter, see Paul E. Cohen and Robert T. Augustyn, "A Newly Discovered Hondius Map," *The Magazine Antiques* 155, no. 1 (1999), pp. 214–217; and see Günter Schilder, *Monumenta cartographica Neerlandica* (Alphen aan den Rijn: Canaletto, 1986–2013), vol. 8, pp. 307–312.

4 The unique surviving exemplar of Hondius's 1608 world map is in London at the Royal Geographical Society, on display in the East Ambulatory. For discussion of the map see Edward Heawood,

far left there is a table of Noah's descendants, and in the huge strapwork frame around the central scene there are four roundels containing images of Noah (in the upper left) and his three sons, each bearing a flag indicating his name, and surrounded by his descendants. Thus, the old program of personifying the continents is placed around the edges of the cartouche, while in the central part there are five women, personifications of Europe, Asia, Africa, and America, and another woman without a flag but wearing a feathered headdress, no doubt representing North America. Africa sits on the back of a crocodile, representative of her continent, and Asia on a similarly representative camel; America rides a giant armadillo, a New World creature, whose head is visible to the left of Europe; Europe, unsurprisingly, is at the center, seated on a globe that symbolizes her power.[5] Each of the four personified continents—but not North America—is described by four lines of hexameter verse in a small cartouche, and each of the four women holds a banner that describes the peopling of her continent by the sons of Noah, so that the passing of the torch from the sons of Noah as representatives of the continents to these women could not be clearer. For example, the banner held by America has text which translated into English runs:[6]

"What father America may have had, is very uncertain. Arias Montanus and other learned men identify Ophir, whence gold was brought in the time of Solomon, with Peru. And so they make Ophir [and/or] his grandson Sem the father [of America], and that from some play upon the name. But it is more credible that this region began to be peopled from the northern parts of Europe and Asia (with which America is contiguous or separated only by a narrow strait); but by whom or when is altogether uncertain."

The confinement of Noah and his sons in roundels at the edges of the cartouche, together with their relatively small size, indicates their lesser importance, while the strapwork frame around the central female personifications is open at the top, and they are both larger and more dynamic than Noah and his sons. By means of this cartouche Hondius has turned the unknown interior of North America into a venue for meta-cartographic reflection on the discovery of the New World, which increased the number of continents known to Europe, on the history of the personification of the continents, and on changes in how the world is presented on maps.[7]

The framed text below the cartouche is Hondius's address to the reader,[8] so this cartouche, the largest and richest on the map, is the one that includes the cartographer's most direct communication with the viewer. The cartographer includes in this address a reference to his cartouche in North America:[9]

"And that no space should be left vacant, we have appended the distribution of the Sons of Noah, that it may be manifest how the world began to be settled after the flood, and from what centres colonies were first sent out into other shores: and this both from the testimony of the sacred writings and on the authority of the most approved authors."

"Hondius and His Newly-Found Map of 1608," *Geographical Journal* 54.3 (1919), pp. 178–184; and Schilder, *Monumenta cartographica Neerlandica* (see note 3), vol. 8, pp. 312–314. The map has been reproduced in facsimile as Edward Heawood, *The Map of the World on Mercator's Projection by Jodocus Hondius: Amsterdam 1608* (London: Royal Geographical Society, 1927).

5   The personifications are based on those engraved by Adriaen Collaert in about 1585; for discussion and illustration of Collaert's images see Edmond Smith, "De-Personifying Collaert's Four Continents: European Descriptions of Continental Diversity, 1585–1625," *European Review of History—Revue européenne d'histoire* 21.6 (2014), pp. 817–835. On the European tendency to place the personification of Europe in a superior position see Ernst van den Boogaart, "The Empress Europe and her Three Sisters. The Symbolic Representation of Europe's Superiority Claim in the Low Countries 1570–1655," in *America, Bride of the Sun: 500 Years Latin America and the Low Countries* (Gent: Imschoot, 1991), pp. 121–128; Michael J. Wintle, "Renaissance Maps and the Construction of the Idea of Europe," *Journal of Historical Geography* 25.2 (1999), pp. 137–165; and Sabine Poeschel, "Europa: Herrscherin der Welt? Die Erdteilallegorie im 17. Jahrhundert," in Klaus Bussmann and Elke A. Werner, eds., *Europa im 17. Jahrhundert: Ein politischer Mythos und seine Bilder* (Stuttgart: F. Steiner, 2004), pp. 269–287.

6   The translation is from Heawood, *The Map of the World on Mercator's Projection* (see note 4), p. 19.

7   Curiously, while Hondius represents this transition on his 1608 world map, he represents the continents by means of the sons of Noah, rather than personifications, in the corners of his 1611 world map titled *Novissima ac exactissima totius orbis terrarum descriptio*. This map is illustrated and discussed below.

8   Hondius's address to the reader is translated by Heawood, *The Map of the World on Mercator's Projection* (see note 4), p. 16. Hondius discusses the technical virtues of his map, particularly a system for drawing rhumb lines that he invented; says that he made use of the latest sources, and mentions his inclusion of information about the peopling of the world by the sons of Noah (this last passage quoted momentarily).

9   The first phrase in this quotation indicates that Hondius was influenced by *horror vacui*, the hesitancy to leave blank spaces in a work of graphic art, in this case a map. I will address this subject further in the following chapter.

Hondius does not explicitly mention the new personifications of the continents or the change in the representation of the continents, but the banners held by the new personifications of the continents do discuss the populating of the continents by the descendants of Noah. It is important to note, however, that Hondius has copied his address to the reader here verbatim from that on his 1603 world map, where the cartouche decoration in North America was different.[10] One cannot help but wish that the cartographer had changed the text to give us a comment on this specific cartouche and the change in personifications that it illustrates.

10   On Hondius's 1603 world map see note 3 above.

CHAPTER 5

Cosmographers in the Southern Ocean

Pieter van den Keere, Nova totius orbis mappa, *c.1611*

Pieter van den Keere's spectacular double-hemisphere wall map of *c.*1611, which survives in just one exemplar at the Sutro Library in San Francisco, is titled *Nova totius orbis mappa ex optimus auctoribus desumta*, "New Map of the Whole World Compiled from the Best Authorities."[1] In Fig. 2 in the Introduction we saw the cartouche in North America from this map, and there—just as in Mercator's 1569 map and Hondius's 1608 map—a large cartouche conceals the cartographer's ignorance of the geography of that part of the world. In Van den Keere's case, the cartouche shows three explorers of the New World, Vespucci, Magellan, and Columbus, consulting a map of South America, and the central text gives an account of the early European exploration of North America.

Van den Keere seems to have been influenced by *horror vacui*, a fear of leaving spaces blank, when making maps, or if not this fear, then certainly a desire to fill with decoration every part of the map that open ocean or a lack of geographical knowledge had left empty.[2] For he fills most of the spaces that would otherwise have been blank on his map with decorations, and in particular, fills the Southern Ocean with two huge cartouches, one in the western hemisphere, and the other in the eastern. The cartouche in the Western Hemisphere shows Peace, enthroned at the center, being crowned by Victory, with Mars (the Roman god of war) kneeling with his arms and legs in shackles—with Justice holding those chains on the right. To the left, three figures bring offerings to Peace: "Cornucopia," which we can translate as "Abundance," and a couple representing Prosperity. The cartouche alludes to the Twelve Years' Truce (1609–1621) in the Eighty Years' War (1568–1648) with Spain,[3] and the cartographer's hope that the peace and the United Provinces of the Netherlands would endure.

In the eastern hemisphere the Southern Ocean is occupied by a huge cartouche consisting of a gallery of famous mathematicians, cartographers, and astronomers (Fig. 59). The small frame that qualifies the scene as a cartouche is at the bottom, and contains a brief text that identifies the scene as an "Academy of ancient and recent astronomers, cartographers, and mathematicians." Just above that banner the Greek titan Atlas, famous for supporting the heavens, rises out of the earth, bearing a celestial sphere on his right shoulder. Curiously, the image of the celestial globe is reversed: along the ecliptic it shows Leo, Cancer, and Gemini from left to right, but the order should be the opposite. Above the sphere a figure who seems to be Astronomy rendered as an angel uses a cross staff to measure the angle between two stars, while the Danish astronomer Tycho Brahe (1546–1601) uses dividers to take a measurement on the sphere.[4] Perhaps they are measuring the distance between the same stars, the angel in the sky, and Brahe on the sphere?

To the right of the sphere the famous cartographer Abraham Ortelius consults a book, probably intended to be a copy of his own *Theatrum orbis terrarum*. Ortelius had passed away in 1598, some years before Van den Keere made his map, but in later years when Van den Keere made maps based on Ortelius's, he gave him credit by adding the phrase *ex conatibus geographicis Abrahami Ortelii*,

---

1   Van den Keere's *c.*1611 world map measures 197 × 126 cm, or 6.5 × 4.1 feet. For discussion of the map see Rodney W. Shirley, *The Mapping of the World: Early Printed World Maps 1472–1700* (Riverside, CT: Early World Press, 2001), pp. 296–299, no. 274; and Rodney Shirley, "The World Map by Pieter van den Keere in the Sutro Library, San Francisco," *IMCoS Journal* 63 (1995), pp. 41–44. There is also a facsimile of the map, but with minimal commentary: Günter Schilder and James Welu, *The World Map of 1611 by Pieter van den Keere* (Amsterdam: Nico Israel, 1980).

2   Some scholars have doubted whether *horror vacui* was an important factor in the design of maps, for example Marion Schmid, "Der weiße Fleck auf der Landkarte," in Karl-Heinz Kohl, ed., *Mythen der Neuen Welt: Zur Entdeckungsgeschichte Lateinamerikas* (Berlin: Frölich & Kaufmann, 1982), pp. 264–271; and Catherine Delano-Smith, "Smoothed Lines and Empty Spaces: The Changing Face of the Exegetical Map before 1600," in Isabelle Laboulais-Lesage, ed., *Combler les blancs de la carte* (Strasbourg: Presses Universitaires de Strasbourg, 2004), pp. 17–34. I present strong evidence, in the form of statements by the cartographer Urbano Monte (1544–1613), that *horror vacui* was a factor in the creation of maps in my article "Urbano Monte's World Maps: Sources and Development," *Imago Temporis* 14 (2020), pp. 415–435, esp. 419–420.

3   On the Twelve Years' Truce see for example Alicia Esteban Estríngana, "Preparing the Ground: The Cession of the Netherland's Sovereignty in 1598 and the Failure of its Peace-Making Objective, 1607–1609," in Randall Lesaffer, ed., *The Twelve Years Truce (1609): Peace, Truce, War, and Law in the Low Countries at the Turn of the 17th Century* (Leiden: Brill Nijhoff, 2014), pp. 15–47. I thank Günter Schilder for his help interpreting this cartouche.

4   The portrait of Brahe seems to depend on that on the title page of Brahe's *Astronomiae instauratae mechanica* (Nuremberg: Leuinum Hulsium, 1602). A digital version of the book is available on https://archive.org.

FIGURE 59   The cartouche in the Southern Ocean from Pieter van den Keere, *Nova totius orbis mappa, ex optimis auctoribus desumta*, Amsterdam, *c*.1611

"based on the cartographical works of Abraham Ortelius," to the title.[5] Behind Ortelius is the Greek Neoplatonist philosopher Proclus, who lived in the fifth century, no doubt depicted here because of his commentary on Euclid's *Elements of Geometry*.[6]

To the left of the sphere the Greek cartographer and astronomer Claudius Ptolemy takes a measurement from a terrestrial globe while the Greek mathematician Archimedes looks over his shoulder. Further to the left is Alfonso X the Learned of Castile, who ruled in the thirteenth century and was famous for his patronage of astronomy;[7] he is surveying using a theodolite. Below are

the Greek mathematician and geographer Euclid and the Flemish cartographer Gerard Mercator (1512–1594), the latter clearly the focus of the composition, writing in a book that is probably intended to represent his *Atlas* of 1595.[8] Ptolemy seems to be looking at Mercator, which is appropriate, as Mercator had published an edition of Ptolemy's maps in 1578.[9] Later in his life Van den Keere

---

5   For example, Van den Keere gave Ortelius this credit in his map *Belgii veteris typus* (Amsterdam: apud Johannem Janssonium, 1645), and in his map *Insularum Britannicarum acurata Delineatio* (Amsterdam: apud Joannem Janssonium, *c*.1646).

6   John Dee attributed a work titled *On the Divisions of Surfaces* to Euclid: see the preface to Muhammad Baghdadi, *De superficierum divisionibus liber Machometo Bagdedino ascriptus* (Pisauri: apud Hieronymum Concordiam, 1570), and Raymond Clare Archibald, *Euclid's Book On Divisions of Figures* (Cambridge, England: The University Press, 1915), pp. 1–7.

7   On Alfonso X as a patron of astronomy see Owen Gingerich, "Alfonso the Tenth as a Patron of Astronomy," in Francisco Márquez

Villanueva and Carlos Alberto Vega, eds., *Alfonso X of Castile, the Learned King, 1221–1284: An International Symposium, Harvard University, 17 November 1984* (Cambridge, MA: Dept. of Romance Languages and Literatures of Harvard University, 1990), pp. 30–45; and Julio Samsó, "Alfonso X and Arabic Astronomy," in Mercè Comes, Roser Puig, and Julio Samsó, eds., *De astronomia alphonsi regis. Actas del Simposio sobre Astronomía Alfonsí celebrado en Berkeley (agosto 1985) y otros trabajos sobre el mismo tema* (Barcelona: Universidad de Barcelona, 1987), pp. 23–38.

8   Mercator wears a similar hat in many of his portraits, including that by Frans Hogenberg printed in Mercator's *Atlas sive cosmographicae meditationes* (Duisburg, 1595). A digital version of this atlas is available at https://loc.gov.

9   On Mercator's 1578 edition of Ptolemy's *Geography* see Wilberforce Eames, *A List of Editions of Ptolemy's Geography 1475–1730* (New York, 1886), pp. 24–25; Carlos Sanz, *La Geographia de Ptolomeo* (Madrid: Librería General V. Suárez, 1959), pp. 227–228; and Józef Babicz, "Die Kugelgestalt der Erde als Grundlage des Modells

re-engraved many of Mercator's maps for the 1628 edition of his *Atlas minor* and for the 1632 edition of his *Atlas sive cosmographicae meditationes*.[10]

In the title of his map Van den Keere declares that it is "compiled from the best authorities," and in this huge cartouche he depicts some of those very authorities—that is, he shows the viewers of his map the solid foundations of research on which he built it. Other cartographers such as Martin Waldseemüller in his *Carta marina* of 1516 and Urbano Monte on his world map of 1587 listed their sources in cartouches.[11] Van den Keere follows a dif-

ferent tradition and presents his sources graphically in a cartouche, a visual strategy that goes back to Martin Waldseemüller's world map of 1507, on which he includes portraits of Ptolemy and Amerigo Vespucci, his two most important sources, in the map's upper margin.[12] Van den Keere's design choice allows him to fill the Southern Ocean, which otherwise would be empty, with decoration that informs the viewer about how he had gone about making the map.

---

der Kartenzeichnung von Gerhard Mercator bei der Redaktion der Ptolemäischen Geographie, 1578," *Der Globusfreund* 43–44 (1995–96), pp. 55–58.

10   A digital version of Van den Keere's *Atlas minor* of 1628 is available at https://archive.org.

11   For a transcription and translation of Waldseemüller's cartouche about his sources on his *Carta marina* see Chet Van Duzer, *Martin Waldseemüller's Carta marina of 1516: Study and Transcription of the Long Legends* (New York: Springer, 2020),

pp. 10–19 and 128–130. Urbano Monte lists some of his cartographic and textual sources on sheet 25 of his 1587 manuscript world map, which is in the Rumsey Map Center at Stanford University. The text of this cartouche on his 1590 manuscript is transcribed by Annalisa d'Ascenzo, *Cultura geografica e cartografia in Italia alla fine del Cinquecento: Il Trattato universale di Urbano Monte* (Rome: Viella, 2012), p. 29.

12   A high-resolution image of Martin Waldseemüller's 1507 world map, with the portraits of two of his most important sources, is available at https://www.loc.gov/item/2003626426.

Ingratitude Bites Kindness

Jodocus Hondius, Novissima ac exactissima totius orbis terrarum descriptio, *1611 / 1634*

Dutch and Flemish cartography, which led the Western world from about 1570 to 1670, was largely a secular commercial enterprise. The focus was on selling maps, and the imagery on the maps centered on exploration, trade, and commerce, as well as information about the peoples and animals of the world, while religious imagery was largely absent. This is in contrast to medieval world maps, whose very form, with a "T" of waters separating Asia, Europe, and Africa, seems to allude to the cross,[1] and in which religious imagery is abundant.[2] Thus we have an outlier in a world map made by Jodocus Hondius in 1611, and published in new editions in 1618 and 1634, whose cartouches and other imagery are strikingly religious.[3] In his voluminous production of maps, Hondius had made just one earlier world map with religious imagery, which includes an allegory of a Christian knight fighting the Rulers of Darkness, evidently an effort by Hondius to rally Protestants against the Catholic powers in Europe.[4] But this was his only other religious map aside from his 1611 world map. There are some inset maps of Biblical history on his 1603 wall map of the world,[5] but these do not have the same moralistic tenor present on his 1611 map, and religious imagery is essentially absent from his other earlier maps.[6]

Hondius's focus on religion on his 1611 double-hemisphere world map is immediately evident in a notable difference between it and his 1608 world map which was discussed in Chapter 4: on his earlier map he illustrates a transition from representing the continents using the sons of Noah to using secular female personifications, but in his 1611 map he returns to the biblical

1 Jonathan T. Lanman, "The Religious Symbolism of the T in T-O Maps," *Cartographica* 18 (1981), pp. 18–22; reprinted in a slightly expanded version in his *Glimpses of History from Old Maps: A Collector's View* (Tring, England: Map Collector Publications, 1989), pp. 32–37; and Christoph Mauntel, "The T-O Diagram and its Religious Connotations: A Circumstantial Case," in Christoph Mauntel, ed., *Geography and Religious Knowledge in the Medieval World* (Berlin: De Gruyter, 2021), pp. 57–84.

2 See for example Andrew Gow, "Gog and Magog on *Mappaemundi* and Early Printed World Maps: Orientalizing Ethnography in the Apocalyptic Tradition," *Journal of Early Modern History* 2.1 (1998), pp. 61–88; Anna-Dorothee von den Brincken, "Jerusalem on Medieval Mappaemundi: A Site both Historical and Eschatological," in P.D.A. Harvey, ed., *The Hereford World Map: Medieval World Maps and their Context* (London: British Library, 2006), pp. 355–379; reprinted in Anna-Dorothee von den Brincken, *Studien zur Universalkartographie des Mittelalters*, ed. Thomas Szabo (Göttingen: Vandenhoeck & Ruprecht, 2008), pp. 683–703; Chet Van Duzer and Ilya Dines, *Apocalyptic Cartography: Thematic Maps and the End of the World in a Fifteenth-Century Manuscript* (Leiden: Brill, 2016); and Jeffrey Jaynes, *Christianity beyond Christendom: The Global Christian Experience on Medieval Mappaemundi and Early Modern World Maps* (Wiesbaden: Harrassowitz Verlag in Kommission, 2018).

3 On Hondius's 1611 world map, titled *Novissima ac exactissima totius orbis terrarum descriptio*, and its states see Günter Schilder, *Monumenta cartographica Neerlandica* (Alphen aan den Rijn: Canaletto, 1986–2013), vol. 8, pp. 314–322; the 1618 state is reproduced in facsimile in Edward Luther Stevenson and Joseph Fischer, *Map of the World by Jodocus Hondius, 1611* (New York: American Geographical Society and the Hispanic Society of America, 1907). On the map's imagery see James A. Welu, "Vermeer and Cartography," Ph.D. Dissertation, Boston University, 1977, pp. 100–101; James A. Welu, "The Sources and Development of Cartographic Ornamentation in the Netherlands," in David Woodward, ed., *Art and Cartography: Six Historical Essays* (Chicago: University of Chicago Press, 1987), pp. 147–173 and 233–238, at 160; and Shirley K. Bennett, "Art on

Netherlandish Maps, 1585–1685: Themes and Sources," Ph.D. Dissertation, University of Maryland College Park, 1990, pp. 94–95.

4 Hondius's "Christian Knight map" of *c.*1597 is titled *Typus Totius Orbis Terrarum, In Quo & Christiani militis ceramem super terram (in pietatis studiosi gratiam) graphice designatur;* for discussion of it see Peter Barber, "The Christian Knight, the Most Christian King and the Rulers of Darkness," *The Map Collector* 48 (1989), pp. 2–8; and Günter Schilder, *Monumenta cartographica Neerlandica* (Alphen aan den Rijn, Holland: Canaletto, 1986–2013), vol. 7, pp. 241–251.

5 Hondius's 1603 world map is titled *Nova et Exacta Totius Orbis Terrarum Descriptio Geographica et Hydrographica* and survives in just one exemplar which is in the MacLean Collection in Libertyville, IL. For discussion of the map see Paul E. Cohen and Robert T. Augustyn, "A Newly Discovered Hondius Map," *The Magazine Antiques* 155.1 (1999), pp. 214–217; and Schilder, *Monumenta Cartographica Neerlandica* (see note 3), vol. 8, pp. 307–312.

6 One other Dutch world map with substantial religious content preceded this map by Hondius, namely Nicolaes van Geelkercken's double-hemispheric *Universi orbis tabula de-integro delineata* (Amsterdam: David de Meyne, 1610), on which the cartographer depicts the Last Judgment between the hemispheres above, and Adam and Eve in Eden below. This map may have inspired Hondius, but does not include religious elements in cartouches within the map proper. On van Geelkercken's map see Johannes Keuning, "Nicolaas Geelkerken," *Imago Mundi* 11 (1954), pp. 174–177, at 174; and Rodney W. Shirley, *The Mapping of the World: Early Printed World Maps 1472–1700* (Riverside, CT: Early World Press, 2001), pp. 288–290, no. 269. A 1618 state of the map, titled *Orbis terrarum descriptio duobis planis hemisphaeriis comprehensa*, has the Fall of Adam and Eve above and the Last Judgment below; a high-resolution image of this map is available at https://loc.gov.

© CHET VAN DUZER, 2023 | DOI:10.1163/9789004523838_008

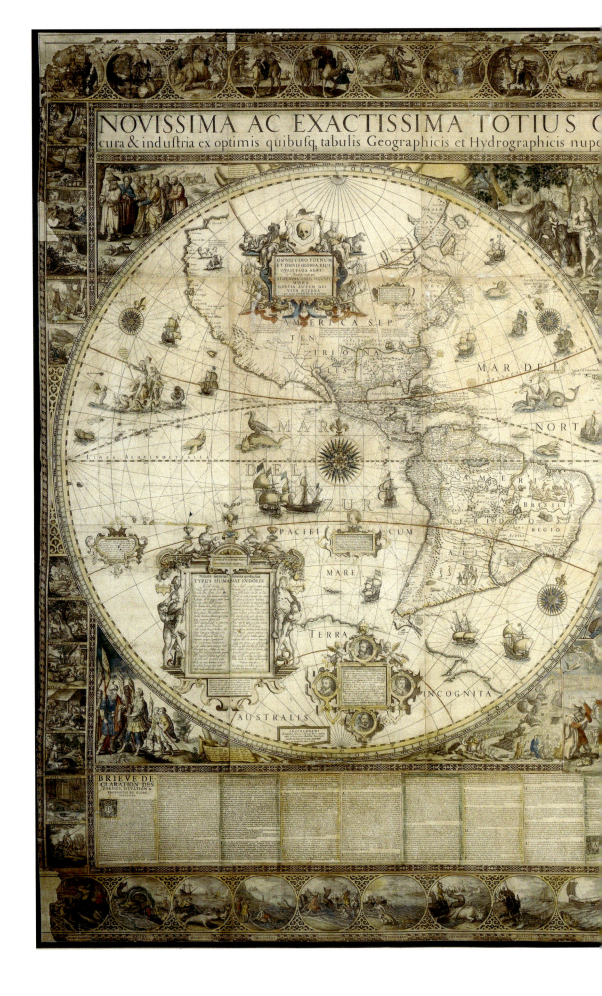

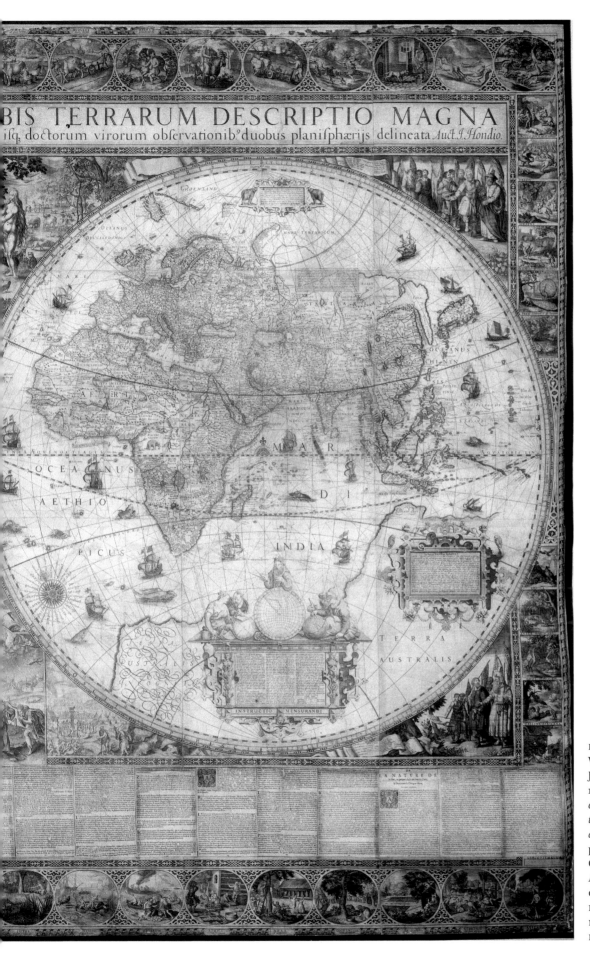

FIGURE 60
World map by
Jodocus Hondius,
1611, titled *Novissima
ac exactissima
totius orbis terrarum
descriptio*, in the 1634
printing, Paris, BnF,
Cartes et plans, GE
A-34 (RES)
COURTESY OF THE
BIBLIOTHÈQUE
NATIONALE DE
FRANCE

FIGURE 61   Detail of the cartouche in North America on Hondius's world map of 1611 / 1634
PARIS, BNF, CARTES ET PLANS, GE A-34 (RES). COURTESY OF THE BIBLIOTHÈQUE NATIONALE DE FRANCE

patriarch Noah and his three sons, who occupy the four corners of the map (Fig. 60). In the upper margin between the two hemispheres there is a representation of the Fall of Adam and Eve, and below there are three scenes: on the left, Moses receiving the Ten Commandments on Mount Sinai (Exodus 20:1–26); on the right, the Israelites worshipping the golden calf while Moses returns with the Ten Commandments (Exodus 32); and in the middle, the Last Judgment.[7] Christ is above astride a globe that is supported by a rainbow, surrounded by saints and angels blowing trumpets, while shooting stars rain down on the earth. Below, a wealthy man, a noble, a scholar, and a king all cower in terror, reacting to both the shooting stars and the coming of Christ.

And two of the cartouches on the map also show a strong interest in religion. The cartouche in North America is macabre (Fig. 61), with skeletons on either side and a skull occupying the coat of arms above, while the hourglass below warns the viewer that time is passing, and life is short. James Welu identified the source of this cartouche as a print by Jan Sadeler that forms the title page of his book *Bonorum et malorum consensio & horum praemia, illorum poena* ("The Agreement of the Good and the Evil, and the Rewards of the Former, and the Punishments of the Latter") (Fig. 62).[8] Thus the source of the cartouche is of a stern and moralistic nature,[9] and further, Hondius has replaced the coat of arms on the original (those of Ferdinand II of Austria) with the skull. The text in the cartouche reads "All flesh is as grass, and all glory is as the flower in the field. Isaiah 40. For the wages of sin are death; but the gift of God [is] eternal life in Jesus

---

7   The Last Judgment is depicted at the top of the Hereford *mappamundi* of *c.*1300; for discussion see Alessandro Scafi, "Mapping the End: The Apocalypse in Medieval Cartography," *Literature & Theology* 26.4 (2012), pp. 400–416. The Hereford *mappamundi* has been reproduced in facsimile as *The Hereford World Map: Mappa Mundi* (London: The Folio Society, 2010).

8   Welu, "The Sources and Development" (see note 3), p. 160. The book is Jan Sadeler, *Bonorum et malorum consensio & horum praemia, illorum poena* (Antwerp: Moguntiae, 1586).

9   On Sadeler's title page the skeleton on the right holds a piece of paper that reads *Cinis es et in cinerem reverteris*, "You are ashes, and to ashes you will return," a phrase based on Genesis 3:19 which was pronounced at the imposition of ashes on Ash Wednesday.

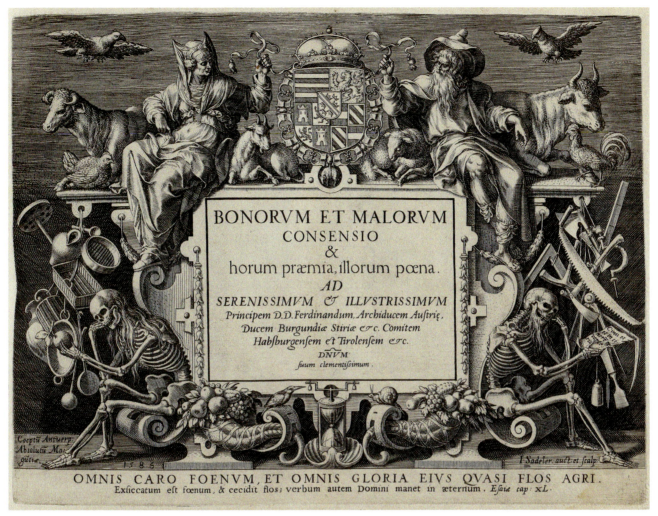

FIGURE 62   Hondius's source for the cartouche in North America, the title page of Jan Sadeler, *Bonorum et malorum consensio & horum praemia, illorum poena* (Antwerp: Moguntiae, 1586)
UNIVERSITÄTBIBLIOTHEK FRANKFURT, WF 418 NR. 2. COURTESY OF THE UNIVERSITÄTBIBLIOTHEK FRANKFURT

Christ our Lord."[10] Hondius took the first phrase, which originally is from Isaiah 40:6, from the bottom of Sadeler's title page, while the second is from Romans 6:23. James Welu has suggested that the cartouche illustrates the theme of *vanitas*,[11] the idea that the pleasures of life are in vain and death is inevitable, but the religious element is stronger than that.

Religious themes also dominate the cartouche in the South Pacific (Fig. 63). It bears the title "It is a sin to serve the ungrateful; what is done for good men does not go to waste,"[12] and below that, "Everyone follows the seed of his own nature; A picture of human nature." On the left and right of the mirror are two multi-breasted women who have just given birth, and male figures blow breath into the mouths of the newborns. The idea is that the man on the left represents the influence of evil nature and the man on the right the influence of good nature, and this is confirmed both by the iconographical source of the image, and by the text in the cartouche. James Welu identified the iconographical source as a print made by Jan Saenredam around 1600 that bears the same title as Hondius's cartouche (Fig. 64),[13] where the men are identified as *Bona*

---

10   The original Latin text reads *Omnis caro foenum, et omnis gloria eius quasi flos agri. Esaiae cap. 40. Stipendia enim peccati mors. Gratia autem Dei vita aeterna in Jesu Christo D. nostro.* Schilder, *Monumenta cartographica Neerlandica* (see note 3), vol. 8, p. 318, translates this text into English a bit differently than I do.

11   Welu, "Vermeer and Cartography" (see note 3), pp. 100–101; and Welu, "The Sources and Development (see note 3), p. 160.

12   The original Latin of the title of Hondius's cartouche in the South Pacific reads *Ingratis servire nefas. Non perit bonis quod fit bene.*

13   On Saenredam's print see K.G. Boon, *Netherlandish Drawings of the Fifteenth and Sixteenth Centuries*, trans. Margot Murtz (The Hague: Govt. Pub. Off., 1978), p. 117, no. 328; and Henk van Os, Jan

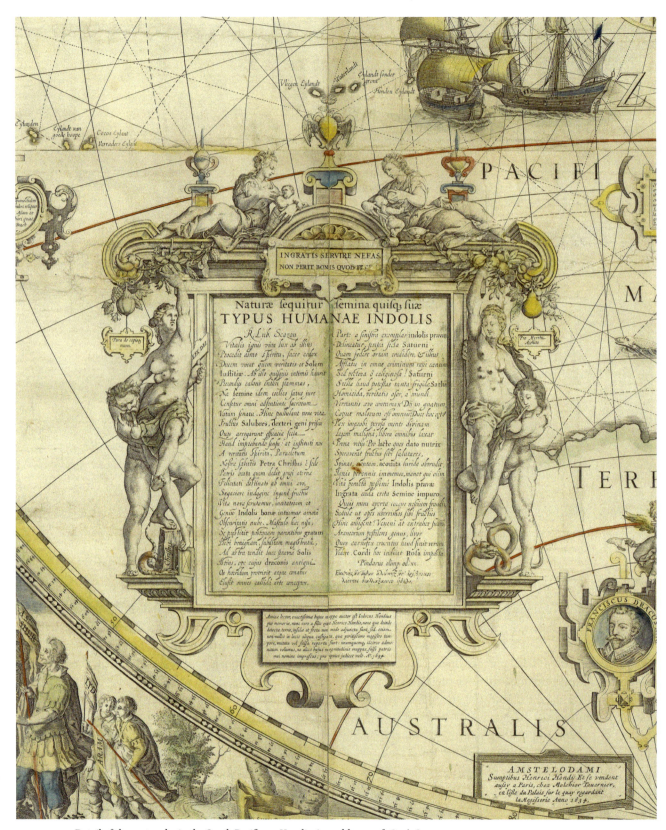

FIGURE 63   Detail of the cartouche in the South Pacific on Hondius's world map of 1611 / 1634

PARIS, BNF, CARTES ET PLANS, GE A-34 (RES). COURTESY OF THE BIBLIOTHÈQUE NATIONALE DE FRANCE

FIGURE 64   Hondius's source for his cartouche in the South Pacific, a print by Jan Saenredam titled *Naturae sequitur semina quisque suae* (Amsterdam, c.1610–1648)

AMSTERDAM, RIJKSMUSEUM, RP-P-OB-10.654. COURTESY OF THE RIJKSMUSEUM

indoles (Good character) and *Malignitas* (Evil), and the central scene shows *Beneficentia* (Kindness) being bitten by Ingratitude, and respected by Gratitude. Above we see the two children being fed, one from a spoon and the other, the good one, directly from the breast.

The text in the cartouche, far from being about *vanitas*, is a meditation on differences in the lives of those born with a good nature and those born with a bad nature. Part of the latter section runs:[14]

"The dregs of a wicked man, hating divine law in his evil mind, gives free rein to all the vices. Instead of the wholesome fruit the nurse had expected from the milk she gave him, he puts forth thorns, a needle, and ghastly wolf's bane, and forgetful of the everlasting fire, he remains the same person who in the future, after leading his life terribly, [has] the ungrateful heart of a depraved nature that grew from impure seed."

This map thus stands apart from other Dutch and Flemish world maps of its time, which were much more secular in their texts and imagery. Hondius evidently recognized that some buyers wanted a map in which religion was prominent, and he created a program of religious texts and imagery in the cartouches on his 1611 map. The fact that the map was reprinted in 1618 and 1634 shows that there was indeed a market for such a map, though, on the other hand, when Claes Jansz Visscher published a version of the map in 1669, he changed the religious cartouches to secular ones, replacing the one in North America with one about the European discovery of the continent, and the one in the South Pacific with his address to the viewer.[15]

Piet Filedt Kok, Ger Luijten, and Frits Scholten, *Netherlandish Art in the Rijksmuseum 1400–1600* (Amsterdam: Rijksmuseum, 2000), vol. 1, pp. 205–206.

14   I thank Catherine Akeroyd for her discussion of this map and this passage with me. She discusses the map in her soon-to-be-completed Ph.D. Dissertation at the Australian National University titled "Terra Australis as a Framework for Knowledge: A Cartographic/Iconological Study."

---

15   The map is Claes Jansz Visscher, *Novissima ac exactissima totius orbis terrarum descriptio magna cura & industria ex optimis quibusq. tabulis geographicis et hydrographicis nupperimisq. doctorum virorum observationib. duobus planisphaeriis delineata* (Amsterdam: apud Nicolaum Joannis Visscher, 1669). There is an exemplar in the Bibliothèque nationale de France, GE DD-5163 (1–20RES), which is viewable in its separate sheets at https://gallica.bnf.fr. There is a facsimile of this map, published as Jodocus Hondius and Nicolaes Visscher, *The World Map of 1669*, ed. Günter Schilder (Amsterdam: N. Israel, 1978).

Eurocentrism on Display

Arnold Floris van Langren, terrestrial globe, 1630–32

As a general rule, elaborate cartouches are less common on globes than on maps, though the Italian cartographer Vincenzo Coronelli would demonstrate that this need not be the case. Jacob Floris van Langren (*c*.1525–1610) and his son Arnold Floris van Langren (*c*.1571–1644) were the first makers of globes in the Low Countries, and in 1592 obtained from the States General of the Netherlands a monopoly on the production of globes.[1] Following some financial difficulties in 1607 or 1608 Arnold fled from his creditors in Amsterdam and was forced to leave behind most of his materials for making globes. After settling in Brussels he was able to obtain some of his father's globe gores from Amsterdam, but not the printing plates that would have enabled him to generate more of those gores. As Peter van der Krogt has demonstrated, he was able to make some globes from the gores he had; at the same time, he set about designing new, updated gores, and made some globes using combinations of the old and new gores, and finally made globes using just the new gores, so that his globes show considerable variation.[2]

The gores of Arnold's father Jacob had a cartouche in the form of a scroll in the hypothetical southern continent titled *Mercium aliquot peregrinarum, et locorum unde ad nos adderunt, catalogus* ("A List of Some Exotic Products and of the Places Whence They are Brought to Us"). Under this title are listed the places from which gold, silver, diamonds, rubies, turquoise, pearls, ivory, sugar, pepper, ginger, mace, cloves, cinnamon, dates, rhubarb, brazilwood, and a few other rare commodities were brought to Europe.[3] He borrowed this list from Abraham Ortelius's eight-sheet 1564 world map, specifically a cartouche in the lower left corner of that map.[4] On his revised gores,

visible on his globe of 1630–32 in Grenoble, Arnold made the text longer and added elaborate decoration to this cartouche (Fig. 65).[5] The additional text comes from the same cartouche that his father had used as a source, namely from the cartouche in the lower left-hand corner of Ortelius's 1564 world map.[6] Arnold's cartouche now has the shape of an altar, and around the altar grow exotic trees and plants, a few of which are listed in the text: there are rose apple, pepper, the coconut palm, pineapple, ginger, the West-Indian fig, and durians.[7] On top of the altar there is a personification of Europe, enthroned and crowned, who receives riches from representatives of several non-European peoples.[8] On the right there are the

---

traditiones descriptio. These are in London, British Library, Maps c2.A.6; and Basel, Offentliche Bibliothek der Universität Basel, Ziegler Collection. The map is discussed in Günter Schilder, *Monumenta cartographica Neerlandica* (Alphen aan den Rijn: Canaletto, 1986–2013), vol. 2, pp. 3–58, and reproduced in facsimile in vol. 2, maps, facsimile 1. For additional discussion of the map see Günter Schilder, "The Wall Maps by Abraham Ortelius," in M.P.R. van den Broecke, Peter van der Krogt, and Peter H. Meurer, eds., *Abraham Ortelius and the First Atlas: Essays Commemorating the Quadricentennial of His Death, 1598–1998* ('t Goy-Houten: HES, 1998), pp. 93–123, esp. 95–106.

5   The globe is in the Bibliothèque municipale de Grenoble, and does not have a shelfmark. On this globe see van der Krogt, *Globi Neerlandici* (see note 1), pp. 450 and 454; Monique Pelletier, "Permanence des globes, de la Renaissance au siècle des Lumières," in Monique Pelletier, ed., *Couleurs de la Terre: des mappemondes médiévales aux images satellitales* (Paris: Seuil and Bibliothèque nationale de France, 1998), pp. 92–99, at 97; Yves Jocteur Monrozier and Marie-Françoise Bois-Delatte, *Mille ans d'écrits: trésors de la Bibliothèque municipale de Grenoble* (Grenoble: Glénat, 2000), pp. 82–83; and Monique Pelletier, "Les globes dans les collections françaises aux XVIIe et XVIIIe siècles," in *Cartographie de la France et du monde de la Renaissance au siècle des Lumières* (Paris: Bibliothèque nationale de France, 2001), pp. 30–44, at 33–34 and 72. A digital model of a similar globe by van Langren at the BnF, shelfmark GE A-275 (RES), can be rotated and zoomed in on at https://gallica.bnf.fr/ark:/12148/btv1b55008713v/f1.medres3d.

6   Schilder, "The Wall Maps by Abraham Ortelius" (see note 4) notes van Langren's use of the text from Ortelius on p. 98.

7   One thinks of the spice plants depicted in the borders of Sebastian Münster's *Typus cosmographicus universalis* (Basel, 1532). A good image of the map is available on the Luna site of the John Carter Brown Library, at https://jcb.lunaimaging.com.

8   On personifications of the continents and the tendency of European artists to depict Europe as superior see Ernst van den Boogaart, "The Empress Europe and her Three Sisters. The Symbolic

---

1   Johannes Keuning, "The Van Langren Family," *Imago Mundi* 13 (1956), pp. 101–109, esp. 103; Peter van der Krogt, *Globi Neerlandici: The Production of Globes in the Low Countries* (Utrecht: HES Press, 1993), p. 259; and Peter van der Krogt, "Three Generations of Van Langrens: Globe Makers, Engravers and a Cosmographer," *Journal of the International Map Collectors' Society* 91 (2002), pp. 25–39.

2   Van der Krogt, *Globi Neerlandici* (see note 1), p. 261; and van der Krogt, "Three Generations" (see note 1), p. 35.

3   For an illustration of this cartouche on Jacob's gores see van der Krogt, *Globi Neerlandici* (see note 1), p. 433, fig. 2.1.18, and see the description of the cartouche on pp. 431–432.

4   There are just two surviving copies of Ortelius's 1564 wall map of the world, which is titled *Nova totius terrarum orbis iuxta neotericorum*

representatives from Peru, Mexico, Java, Asia, and Guinea; and on the left, people from the Congo, China, Senegal, Persia, and Guiana.[9]

The scene on top of the altar is a visual interpretation of the title of the cartouche, which is about the places from which exotic goods are brought to Europe. To modern eyes, the image is distressingly Eurocentric, in effect representing the non-European world as nothing but the source of goods to be servilely offered up to Europe for consumption.[10] We saw some Eurocentrism earlier in the cartouche in North America in Hondius's 1608 world map, where Europe was portrayed as the richest, most powerful, and central of the personifications of the

continents, but van Langren has taken things much further. Maps usually emphasize the economic interests and political ambitions of the region in which they are produced, or of the ruler for whom they were produced, and Eurocentrism on European maps is common.[11]

This is an interesting case where we can trace the influence of a specific cartouche over time. Martin Waldseemüller included in the lower right-hand corner of his *Carta marina* of 1516 a large cartouche that lists the spices available in Calicut, India, the regions from which the various spices were brought to that city, their prices, and the systems of weights and money used in selling them.[12] We know that Abraham Ortelius was familiar with Waldseemüller's *Carta marina*, for he cites it as a source in his *Theatrum orbis terrarum* of 1570,[13] so it seems very likely that he used Waldseemüller's cartouche as inspiration for his cartouche about the sources of exotic goods on his 1564 world map. Jacob Floris van Langren borrowed text from Ortelius's cartouche for the cartouche on his globe, and then his son Arnold Floris van Langren returned to Ortelius's cartouche to borrow more text for his new globe gores, and also developed an elaborate artistic program to illustrate the flow of goods described in the text.

Representation of Europe's Superiority Claim in the Low Countries 1570–1655," in *America, Bride of the Sun: 500 Years Latin America and the Low Countries* (Gent: Imschoot, 1991), pp. 121–128; Michael J. Wintle, "Renaissance Maps and the Construction of the Idea of Europe," *Journal of Historical Geography* 25.2 (1999), pp. 137–165; and Sabine Poeschel, "Europa: Herrscherin der Welt? Die Erdteilallegorie im 17. Jahrhundert," in Klaus Bussmann and Elke A. Werner, eds., *Europa im 17. Jahrhundert: Ein politischer Mythos und seine Bilder* (Stuttgart: F. Steiner, 2004), pp. 269–287.

9   It is worth remarking that no native peoples of North America are represented.

10   There is a somewhat similar Eurocentric decorative program on a manuscript world map made in 1610 by Harmen and Marten Jansz. titled *Nova orbis terrarum geografica ac hydrogra[phica] tabula ex optimis in hoc opere auctoribus desumpta*, Paris, BnF, Cartes et plans, GE A-1048 (RES). An image of the map is available at https://gallica.bnf.fr, and the Eurocentric decoration of the map is discussed by Catherine Hofmann, "'Paincture & imaige de la Terre': l'enluminure des cartes aux Pays-Bas," in Monique Pelletier, ed., *Couleurs de la terre: des mappemondes médiévales aux images satellitales* (Paris: Seuil and Bibliothèque nationale de France, 1998), pp. 68–85, at 82–83; and Günter Schilder, *Early Dutch Maritime Cartography: The North Holland School of Cartography (c.1580–c.1620)* (Leiden: Brill, Hes & De Graaf, 2017), chapter 13.1.1. See further the references cited in note 8 above.

11   On cartographic ethnocentrism see Yi-Fu Tuan, *Topophilia: A Study of Environmental Perception, Attitudes, and Values* (Englewood Cliffs, NJ: Prentice-Hall, 1974), pp. 30–44.

12   For a transcription and translation of the text in Waldseemüller's cartouche see Chet Van Duzer, *Martin Waldseemüller's Carta marina of 1516: Study and Transcription of the Long Legends* (New York: Springer, 2020), Legend 12.11. Waldseemüller took this information from the *Paesi nouamente retrovati* (Vicenza: Henrico Vicentino, 1507), chapters 82 and 83.

13   See Abraham Ortelius, *Catalogus auctorum tabularum geographicarum* (Catalog of mapmakers), in his *Theatrum orbis terrarium* (Antwerp: Aegid. Coppenius Diesth, 1570), signature Cii[r].

FIGURE 65   Detail of a cartouche on a terrestrial globe by Arnold Floris van Langren, 1630–32
BIBLIOTHÈQUE MUNICIPALE DE GRENOBLE. COURTESY OF THE BIBLIOTHÈQUE MUNICIPALE DE GRENOBLE

CHAPTER 8

The Giddy Pleasures of *Mise en Abyme*

Willem Hondius, Nova totius Brasiliae et locorum a Societate Indiae Occidentalis captorum descriptio, *1635*

In heraldry a miniature coat of arms is sometimes placed within the main coat of arms to commemorate a victory, indicate a marriage, or mark the acquisition of territory. The French term describing this situation is *mise en abyme*, meaning "placed in the abyss" (Fig. 66—also see Fig. 118 below). This term was adopted by André Gide (1869–1951) and later used by Lucien Dällenbach (1940–) to describe situations where a work of art appears within a work of art of the same type, a painting within a painting, for example, a play within a play, or a film within a film.[1] There is often a special self-consciousness in artworks of this type, and there can also be a pleasing philosophic vertigo in contemplating a thing-within-a-thing.

Maps on maps, that is, maps in cartouches on maps, are another example of *mise en abyme*, and a map by Willem Hondius (*c*.1598–*c*.1658), a Dutch engraver and cartographer who spent most of his life in Poland, is particularly rich in this regard. Willem was the son of the printmaker and publisher Hendrik Hondius the Elder; there is no clear connection between this family at that of the cartographer Jodocus Hondius discussed above.[2] In 1635 Willem published a large map of Brazil titled *Nova totius Brasiliae et locorum a Societate Indiae Occidentalis captorum descriptio* ("New Map of all of Brazil and of the Places Captured by the West India Company"), referring to the Dutch West India Company (Geoctroyeerde Westindische Compagnie) (Fig. 67).[3] It measures 4.7 × 3.2 feet (144 ×

100 cm), and is dedicated to Cardinal Richelieu of France (1585–1642). Beginning in 1624 the Company had been taking over lands in Brazil that had been controlled by the Portuguese, and in 1634, the year before the map was made, the Dutch had taken over the island of Curaçao from the Spanish. The long text at the bottom of the map discusses the history of Brazil, and the second half of it is devoted to the Dutch conquests.

Hondius has covered more than half of the surface of the map with cartouches containing inset maps, a very clear demonstration of the anti-cartographic nature of cartouches discussed in the Introduction. He designed the main map with this layout in mind, for he includes in it great swaths of the Atlantic that would have remained blank without these many cartouches. At the top center of the map there are two cartouches side by side, that on the left containing the dedication, and that on the right an inset map of the Ilha de Itamaracá, with only slightly more information about the depth of the water than appears in the main map just below.

The five larger inset maps in the lower half of the main map are all based on separately published maps, so in effect Hondius was assembling much of his map from components that already existed or that he produced at the same time as the main map. Against the right-hand edge of the map is an inset map of Paraiba, Brazil, made by Willem, and though I have not found a surviving example of this map, there is a record of the sale of a later state of it at auction.[4] In the lower right there is an inset map

---

1 See André Gide, *Journals 1889–1949*, trans. Justin O'Brien (London: Penguin, 1967), pp. 30–31, a passage Gide wrote in 1893; and Lucien Dällenbach, *The Mirror in the Text*, trans. Jeremy Whiteley with Emma Hughes (Cambridge, MA: Polity in association with Blackwell, 1989) (original French edition *Le récit spéculaire: essai sur la mise en abyme*, Paris, 1977); and for example Arthur Brown, "The Play Within a Play: An Elizabethan Dramatic Device," *Essays and Studies* 13 (1960), pp. 36–48.

2 On Willem see J.C. Block, *Das Kupferstich-Werk des Wilhelm Hondius* (Gdańsk: Kafemann, 1891); Irena Fabiani-Madeyska, "Willem Hondius en zijn Poolse oeuvre 1636–1652," *Jaarverslag van de Fundatio Hondius* 14 (1965), pp. 5–38; and Nadine M. Orenstein, *Hendrick Hondius and the Business of Prints in Seventeenth-Century Holland* (Rotterdam: Sound & Vision Interactive, 1996), esp. pp. 83–85.

3 On Hondius's map see Günter Schilder, *Monumenta cartographica Neerlandica* (Alphen aan den Rijn: Canaletto, 1986–2013), vol. 9, pp. 505 and 510–511; Kees Zandvliet, *Mapping for Money: Maps, Plans, and Topographic Paintings and their Role in Dutch Overseas*

Expansion during the 16th and 17th Centuries (Amsterdam: Batavian Lion International, 1998), pp. 248–249; and Bea Brommer, Henk den Heijer, Jaap Jacobs, Alexander Bick, and Martin van Wallenburg, *Grote atlas van de West-Indische Compagnie = Comprehensive Atlas of the Dutch West India Company*, vol. 1, *De oude WIC 1621–1674 = The Old WIC 1621–1674* (Voorburg: Asia Maior/Atlas Maior, 2011), pp. 162–163. A zoomable image of the map is available at https://gallica.bnf.fr.

4 The inset map at the right is titled in both Dutch and French, *Afbeeldinge der Stadt, Fortressen, en Ryviere, van Parayba = Figure de la Ville Fortesses et Riviere de Pariba*, and the text at the right indicates that it was made by Willem Hondius in 1635. The auction catalog that records a sale of a later copy of this map is listed is *Bibliotheca brasiliensis: Histoire, géographie, voyages, missions indiennes, linguistique, anthropologie, ethnographie, histoire naturelle, commerce, émigration* (Paris: Libr. Ch. Chadenat, 1907) (= *Bibliophile américaine*, no. 38), p. 101, no. 1658.

FIGURE 66 Coat of arms with *mise en abyme* on the title page of Paul Pambst, *Loossbuch, zu ehren der Römischen, Ungerischen unnd Böhemischen Künigin* (Strasbourg: Balthassar Beck, 1546)

of Curaçao, commemorating the recent Dutch victory there, which was also made by Willem.[5] The middle map along the lower margin shows the area around Recife, and was also made by Willem in 1635.[6] In the lower left corner is a map of Cabo de Santo Agostinho, evidently made by Willem, showing Dutch ships attacking; Willem's map was copied by Jan Janssonius made in 1656.[7] These

5 Digital images of Willem's separate map of Curaçao, also made in 1635, may be consulted at https://gallica.bnf.fr.

6 Willem Hondius, *Le plan de l'Isle Anthony Vaaz. Le Réciff, et terre ferme au havre de Pernambuco en Braesil, avec toutes ses fortifications—Grondt-Teyckening van het Eylandt Anthony Vaaz het Reciff ende vaste landt aen de haven van Pernambuco in Brasil, met alle de schansen, redouten, en andere wercken aldaer gemaeckt* (s.l:

s.n., 1635). A digital image of the 1635 state of Willem's map of Recife may be consulted at https://gallica.bnf.fr; a high-resolution image of a hand-colored copy of the 1640 state is available at https://searchworks.stanford.edu.

7 Willem's map of Cabo de Santo Agostinho is titled *Representation du Cabo de St. Augustijn*; the only other record of it is in a composite atlas in the Huntington Library (call number 109496) consisting of manuscript and printed maps from between 1616 and the 1720s:

FIGURE 67

Willem Hondius, *Nova totius Brasiliae et locorum a Societate Indiae Occidentalis captorum description* (The Hague, 1635)

FIGURE 68   Detail of the cartouche at the left on Willem Hondius's 1635 map of Brazil
PARIS, BNF, GE A-835 (RES). COURTESY OF THE BIBLIOTHÈQUE NATIONALE DE FRANCE

four maps all have their own title cartouches, so that they are not only maps on a map, but have cartouches within cartouches.

The cartouche at the left edge of the main map merits special attention (Fig. 68). It is closely based on a map by Henricus Hondius[8] published in 1633 (Fig. 69),[9] but Willem gave the map the appearance of a piece of leather that has been hung on posts to dry, an interesting way to frame it. The map in this cartouche itself has a cartouche in the lower left that gives its title as *Accuratissima Brasiliae Tabula*, "Very Accurate Map of Brazil," and it supplies the broader geographical context for the map that contains

see the list of maps in the atlas at an earlier stage of its existence in *Bibliotheca Americana: Histoire, géographie, voyages, archéologie et linguistique des deux Amériques* (Paris: Maisonneuve, 1878–1887), Supplément no. 1, Novembre 1881, no. 2, Issue 2, pp. 8–10, at p. 10. Jan Janssonius printed a version of this map in 1656 titled *Afbeeldinge van de Cabo St. Augustin Met haer forten*, to illustrate Isaac Commelin's *Histoire de la vie & actes memorables de Frederic Henry de Nassau Prince d'Orange* (Amsterdam: chez la vefue & les heritiers de Iudocus Ianssonius, 1656). A high-resolution image of this map is available at https://searchworks.stanford.edu.

8   This Henricus Hondius, sometimes called Henricus Hondius II (1597–1651), was not related to Hendrik Hondius (1573–1650) mentioned earlier in this chapter.

9   The map that served as the basis for Willem's map of Brazil was Henricus Hondius's *Accuratissima Brasiliae tabula*, printed in 1633 for Gerhard Mercator and Jodocus Hondius, *Gerardi Mercatoris et I. Hondii Atlas, ou, Représentation du monde universel, et des parties d'icelui faicte en tables et descriptions tresamples, et exactes* (Amsterdam: H. Hondius, 1633).

FIGURE 69   Henricus Hondius, *Accuratissima Brasiliae tabula* (Amsterdam, 1633)
WESLEYAN UNIVERSITY LIBRARY, SPECIAL COLLECTIONS CUTTER ++G M55. COURTESY OF WESLEYAN UNIVERSITY LIBRARY

it; it is the only one of the inset maps that includes a grid of latitude and longitude. And the map in the cartouche itself has two cartouches at the top that contain detail maps of Baya de Todos os Sanctos and Pernambuco. These are maps in a map in a map, and cartouches in a cartouche, as is the title cartouche.

Moreover, the layout of this map at the left edge of the main map, with two side-by-side cartouches at its top, echoes the layout of the larger map, with two side-by-side cartouches at its top that contain the dedication to Cardinal Richelieu and a detail map of the Ilha de Itamaracá.[10] This strongly suggests that Willem was con-

scious of the *mise en abyme* nature of his cartographic composition, and that he appreciated the possibilities that cartouches offered for recursive, self-reflexive structures on maps.[11]

10   Given that Henricus Hondius's *Accuratissima Brasiliae tabula*, the map that Willem was copying, already had two inset maps at its top, in order to create the similarity between the main map and the inset map, Willem had to add the two cartouches to the top of the main map.

11   There is a spectacular example of *mise en abyme* in a cartouche in Joseph Daniel von Huber's huge map of Vienna titled *Scenographie, oder, Geometrisch perspect. Abbildung der kaÿl. königl. Haupt u. Residenz Stadt Wien in Oesterreich* (Vienna, 1777). The cartouche in the lower right corner includes a small image of the whole map that illustrates how the 24 sheets are to be assembled; this small image is detailed enough that it shows the cartouche in the lower right corner, and a small image of the map that shows how the 24 sheets are to be assembled. So there is an image of the map in an image of the map in an image of the map. A high-resolution image of Huber's map is available at https://loc.gov; on Huber's map see Markus Heinz and Jan Mokre, "Über Joseph Daniel von Huber (1730/31–1788) und seinen Vogelschauplan von Wien," *Jahrbuch des Vereins für Geschichte der Stadt Wien* 47–48 (1991–92), pp. 93–122.

CHAPTER 9

The Cartographer's Self-Portrait

Georg Vischer, Archiducatus Austriae inferioris, *1670 / 1697*

Georg Matthäus Vischer (1628–1696) was the leading surveyor, topographer, and cartographer in Austria in the second half of the seventeenth century, and was known for the many engraved views he made of cities and castles.[1] In 1667 the Archduchy of Austria commissioned him to make a map of Upper Austria, which he did on the basis of his own survey, not relying on any previous sources, and this map was printed in 1669 to great acclaim.[2] It is particularly engaging for Vischer's fine rendering of landscape and his bird's-eye views of the principle buildings of cities. In fact, the cartographer proclaims his interest in these features in a cartouche at the bottom of the map that is decorated with some of the surveying tools he had used in making the map: in the center there is a miner's compass flanked by a pillar sundial and a small zenith sector for determining vertical angles; then an armillary sphere and a terrestrial globe, and then instruments to help artists in rendering landscapes. In the foreground, the *putto* on the left holds a geometrical circle, and the one on the right a geometric quadrant.[3] Vischer writes:[4]

"George Vischer, of Wenns in the Tyrol, who was then the parish priest at Leonstian in Upper Austria, traveled through every part of this province and delineated the mountains, valleys, cities, monasteries, and castles having seen them firsthand, and arranged them together as you see here."

So Vischer is telling us how he made the map and showing us the tools he used to do so. The map is decorated with six other cartouches that supply views of local castles, lakes, and both mining and metal-working operations, which were important parts of the archduchy's economy.

The remarkable quality of his map of Upper Austria persuaded the Archduchy to commission from Vischer a map of Lower Austria which was printed in 1670.[5] This map also has a cartouche at the lower edge that relates to surveying (Fig. 70). Two men and three horses stand on a ridge; the man on the right is surveying the surrounding countryside using a plane table with a compass and alidade (a tool for measuring angles). On the ground by his feet there is a view of a city,[6] some books, and other instruments, specifically dividers, an angle meter, and a measuring chain. The other man holds a banner with the map's legend, that is, the definitions of the symbols used on the map in both Latin and German, and it is this banner, this framed text, that makes the scene a cartouche. Below there is a "wind-head," a personification representing the wind that blows from the south-southwest.

The two men have the same features, and in fact, both are images of Vischer himself, as we can confirm

---

1 On Vischer see Josef Feil, "Über das Leben und Wirken des Geographen Georg Matthaeus Vischer," *Berichte und Mittheilungen des Alterthums-Vereines in Wien* 2 (1857), pp. 7–86; P. Altmarm Altinger, "Des österreichischen Geographen Georg Matthäus Vischer letztes Lebensjahr," *Mitteilungen der Kaiserlich-Königlichen Geographischen Gesellschaft* 41 (1898), pp. 380–393; Rainer Puschnig, "Beiträge zur Biographie Georg Matthäus Vischers," *Mitteilungen des Steiermärkischen Landesarchives* 19–20 (1970), pp. 145–163; and Franz Daxecker, "Ein neuer Brief des Wenner Kartographen Georg Matthäus Vischer," *Tiroler Heimatblätter* 3 (1997), pp. 81–84.

2 Georg Matthäus Vischer, *Archiducatus Austriae Superioris geographica descriptio* (Augsburg: Melchior Küsell, 1669). A good zoomable image of the map is available at https://gallica.bnf.fr.

3 I thank Jan de Graeve and Jan Mokre for their help in identifying the instruments. Surveying instruments also decorate a cartouche on another of Vischer's maps, his *Styriae Ducatus fertilissimi nova geographica descriptio* (Augsburg, 1678). A high-resolution image of the map is available from the Digital Library of Slovenia under the reference number 9VYD6XR6. For other maps with illustrations of surveying instruments see David Smith, "The Cartographic Illustration of Land Surveying Instruments and Methods," *Bulletin of the Society of Cartographers* 26.1 (1992), pp. 11–20; for discussion of surveying instruments see Uta Lindgren, "Land Surveys, Instruments, and Practitioners in the Renaissance," in J.B. Harley and David Woodward, eds., *The History of Cartography*, vol. 3, *Cartography in the European Renaissance* (Chicago and London: University of Chicago Press, 2007), part 1, pp. 477–508, esp. 489–499.

4 The Latin text in Vischer's cartouche on his 1669 map of Upper Austria runs *Provinciam hanc peragravit, delineavit, et montes valles civitates monasteria et arces ad vivum quantum proportio permisit in hunc modum concinnavit Georgius Visscher Tyryoensis e Wenns, tunc temporis, parochus in Leonstian Austriae superioris.*

5 Vischer's map of Lower Austria is titled *Archiducatus Austriae inferioris geographica et noviter emendata accuratissima descriptio* and was published in Vienna in 1670. High-resolution images of the individual sheets of the 1697 reprint of the map are available at https://searchworks.stanford.edu.

6 The city view is very similar to Vischer's own view of Diernstain in his *Topographia ducatus Stiriae* (Grätz: Bitsch, 1681). A digital copy of the book is available on Google Books, and the plates are arranged alphabetically.

FIGURE 70   Detail of a cartouche depicting the cartographer surveying and showing the viewer the map's legend on Georg Matthäus Vischer,
Archiducatus Austriae inferioris, 1670 / 1697
STANFORD UNIVERSITY, DAVID RUMSEY MAP COLLECTION, G6491.C28 1697 .V5. COURTESY OF THE DAVID RUMSEY
MAP COLLECTION

by comparing a portrait of Vischer (Fig. 71).[7] This scene on the knoll is a great demonstration of how cartouches can be venues of privileged communication between the cartographer and the viewer. In this case the cartographer not only shows us how he made his map by depicting himself surveying the territory,[8] but he also portrays him-

self conveying cartographical information directly to the viewer by holding aloft the banner with the map's legend. By looking directly at the viewer he reaches outside the cartographic space to connect with the viewer in an

---

7   For discussion of other maps that include self-portraits by cartographers see James A. Welu, "Cartographic Self-Portraits," in Carla Clivio Marzoli, Giacomo Corna Pellegrini, and Gaetano Ferro, eds., *Imago et mensura mundi: Atti del IX Congresso internazionale di storia della cartografia* (Rome: Istituto della Enciclopedia italiana, 1985), vol. 2, pp. 525–539; also see Rodney Shirley, "The Face of the Maker: Portraits of Cartographers Concealed in Maps and Title Pages," *Mercator's World* 1.4 (1996), pp. 14–19. There is also an appealing case of cartographic self-portraiture on Philipp Johann von Strahlenberg and Johan Anton von Matern's map *Nova descriptio geographica Tattariae Magnae* (Stockholm, 1730); high-resolution images of the map are available on the websites of the Biblioteka Narodowa in Poland and the Kungliga biblioteket in Sweden.

8   Comparative material on self-portraits of medieval illuminators at work may be found in Jonathan J.G. Alexander, *Medieval*

Illuminators and Their Methods of Work (New Haven: Yale University Press, 1992), pp. 4–35; and for other artists Peter Cornelius Claussen, "Nachrichten von den Antipoden oder mittelalterliche Künstler über sich selbst," in Matthias Winner, ed., *Der Künstler über sich in seinem Werk* (Weinheim: VCH, Acta Humaniora, 1992), pp. 19–54. On early modern painters' representations of themselves see Hans-Joachim Raupp, "Der Maler präsentiert sein Work," *Untersuchungen zu Künstlerbildnis und Künstlerdarstellung in den Niederlanden im 17. Jahrhundert* (Hildesheim and New York: Olms, 1984), pp. 329–350; Victor Stoichita, *The Self-Aware Image: An Insight into Early Modern Meta-Painting*, trans. Anne-Marie Glasheen (Cambridge and New York: Cambridge University Press, 1997), pp. 200–247. On the self-portrait as signature by an artist see Hermann Ulrich Asemissen and Gunter Schweikhart, *Malerei als Thema der Malerei* (Berlin: Akademie Verlag, 1994), pp. 67–70.

of two of his horses. Landowners were often hostile to cartographers in the field, since their work might bring about unfavorable changes to their lot sizes, or tax increases.[10] Measuring and mapping land is never without its consequences, never without winners and losers,[11] and Vischer's pistols are a striking visual reminder of that fact.

additional way, breaking the fourth wall, to use an expression from film.[9]

It is important to note that Vischer was armed when he went out surveying: he has pistols attached to the saddles

10   I thank Jan Mokre for pointing out the importance of the pistols in this cartouche, and for the references related to Peter Anich in this note. For descriptions of cases of violence against surveyors see Ignatius Weinhart, *Elogium rustici Tyrolensis celeberrimi Petri Anich Oberperfussensis coloni, tornatoris, chalcographi, mechanicarum artium magistri, geodetae, geographi et astrophili ad prodigium excellentis* (Innsbruck, 1768), p. 25; Andreas Alois di Pauli, *Lebensgeschichte des Landmessers Blasius Hueber: mit umständlichen Nachrichten von den Arbeiten der Geodeten von Oberperfus* (Innsbruck: Wagner'sche Universitäts-Buchhandlung, 1815), pp. 29–32; Charles J. Hoadly, ed., *Records of the Colony and Plantation of New-Haven, from 1638 to 1649* (Hartford: Printed by Case, Tiffany and Company, 1857), pp. 261–265; Clements R. Markham, *Major James Rennel and the Rise of Modern English Geography* (New York: Macmillan, 1895), pp. 48–49; Franz Heinz Hye, "Peter Anich und Blasius Hueber. Die Geschichte des 'Atlas Tyrolensis' (1759–1774)," in Hans Kinzl, ed., *Peter Anich: 1723–1766. Der erste 'Bauernkartograph' von Tirol. Beiträge zur Kenntnis seines Lebenswerkes* (Innsbruck: Universitätsverlag Wagner, 1976), pp. 7–50, at 24; Sarah Hughes, *Surveyors and Statesmen: Land Measuring in Colonial Virginia* (Richmond, VA: Virginia Surveyors Foundation, 1979), esp. pp. 2, 26, 35–36, and 121–122; and Peter Progress the Younger (R. Yorke Clarke), *The Rail, its Origin and Progress* (London: R.Y. Clarke, 1847), pp. 34–38.

11   Indeed, Louis XIV is said to have complained that a new survey of France by Jean Picard, Jean-Dominique Cassini, and Philippe de La Hire, presented in a map in 1683, had made the territory of France much smaller than it had been; this map was published as *Carte de France corrigee par ordre du Roy sur les observations de Mss. de l'Academie des Sciences* (Paris, 1693); for the remark by Louis XIV see Bernard Le Bovier de Fontenelle, "Eloge de M. de La Hire," in his *Oeuvres diverses* (The Hague: Gosse & Neaulme, 1728–29), vol. 3, pp. 266–276, at 268. The change in the coast of France can been seen in John Senex's map, *A New Map of France: Shewing the Roads & Post Stages Thro-out That Kingdom, as Also the Errors of Sanson's Map Compard with ye Survey Made by Order of ye Late French King* (London: J. Senex, 1719).

9   For theoretical discussions of actors directly addressing the audience in film see Pascal Bonitzer, "Les deux regards," *Cahiers du cinéma* 275 (April 1977), pp. 40–46; Marc Vernet, "The Look at the Camera," *Cinema Journal* 28.2 (1989), pp. 48–63; and Tom Brown, *Breaking the Fourth Wall: Direct Address in the Cinema* (Edinburgh: Edinburgh University Press, 2012).

Scheming for Control in the New World

Claude Bernou, Carte de l'Amerique septentrionale et partie de la meridionale, *c.1682*

A manuscript map of North America and the northern part of South America, which lacks a date and indication of author but has been attributed to the French Abbé Claude Bernou (*c.*1636–*c.*1701) and dated to 1682, has been called the most beautiful map of America (Fig. 72).[1] Much of that beauty is due to its large and spectacular cartouche in the Atlantic.[2]

The title of the map, which is indicated in the cartouche (Fig. 73), is *Carte de l'Amerique septentrionale et partie de la meridionale depuis l'embouchure de la Riviere St Laurens jusqu'à l'isle de Cayenne avec les nouvelles découvertes de la Riviere de Mississipi ou Colbert* ("Map of North America and part of South America from the Mouth of the Saint Lawrence River to Cayenne Island with the new discoveries of the Mississippi River or Colbert River"). Claude Bernou was a court official who was active in promoting new French settlement in North America, particularly as a way to secure his own objectives: he hoped to be consecrated bishop in such a new settlement.[3] The map is perhaps the earliest that survives that uses the name

Louisiana (*La Louisiane*), which was named in honor of the French King Louis XIV.[4]

In his correspondence Bernou speaks of making maps of Peru, New Mexico,[5] and North America,[6] and he had made a map of Beijing,[7] so he had experience as a cartographer, but the fact that none of the surviving maps attributed to him have elaborately decorated cartouches[8] confirms that the cartouche on the map considered here was made by a specialized artist.

The cartouche surrounding the title of the map consists of three registers, a heavenly, a terrestrial, and an aquatic.[9] At the top of the heavenly register there is an unfinished zodiac with a head radiating light located at the front, representing Louis XIV, the Sun King. Below there are two young angels who seem to be trying to wrest a cross from each other, and a bishop's miter has fallen to the ground; the banner below them reads *In hoc signo vinces,* "In this sign you shall conquer," referring to the cross. On the left there are personifications of the four Cardinal Virtues:

---

1   Bernou's map is in the Bibliothèque nationale de France, Cartes et plans, CPL SH 18E PF 122 DIV 2 P 0 RES, and measures 163 × 147 cm; a zoomable image of it is available at https://gallica.bnf.fr. On the dating of the map to 1682 see Jean Delanglez, *Hennepin's Description of Louisiana: A Critical Essay* (Chicago: Institute of Jesuit History, 1941), pp. 111–119. It was called the most beautiful map of America by Henry Harrisse, *Notes pour servir à l'histoire, à la bibliographie et à la cartographie de la Nouvelle-France et des pays adjacents 1545–1700* (Paris: Tross, 1872), p. 200: "Cette carte est sans contredit la plus belle qu'on ait faite de l'Amérique." For discussion of the map see Lauren Beck's essay in Chet Van Duzer and Lauren Beck, *Canada Before Confederation: Maps at the Exhibition* (Wilmington, DE: Vernon Press, 2017), pp. 155–168.

2   On the attribution of the map to Bernou see Jean Delanglez, *Some La Salle Journeys* (Chicago: Institute of Jesuit History, 1938), pp. 10–12 and 32–39; the same author's *Hennepin's Description of Louisiana: A Critical Essay* (Chicago: Institute of Jesuit History, 1941), pp. 111–119; and Conrad E. Heidenreich, "Seventeenth-Century Maps of the Great Lakes: An Overview and Procedures for Analysis," *Archivaria* 6 (1978), pp. 83–112, at 92.

3   Delanglez, *Some La Salle Journeys* (see note 2), pp. 11 and 66–68, with Pierre Margry, *Découvertes et établissements des Français dans l'ouest et dans le sud de l'Amérique Septentrionale, 1614–1698* (Paris: Maisonneuve, 1879–88), vol. 3, pp. 44–48 and 82; Jean Delanglez, "The Cartography of the Mississippi," *Mid-America* 30 (1948), pp. 257–284, and 31 (1949), pp. 29–52, at p. 38; Edmund Boyd Osler, *La Salle* (Don Mills, Ontario: Longmans Canada, 1967), pp. 160–164; and Raphael Hamilton, "Who wrote *Premier Etablissement de la Foy*

dans la Nouvelle France?" *Canadian Historical Review* 57.3 (1976), pp. 265–288, at 269, 271, 273, and 274.

4   The earliest surviving use of the name *Louisiane* is in a grant of an island from La Salle to one François Daupin dated June 10, 1679, transcribed in in Pierre Margry, *Découvertes et établissements des Français dans l'ouest et dans le sud de l'Amérique Septentrionale, 1614–1698* (Paris: Maisonneuve, 1879–88), vol. 2, pp. 20–22, at 21. Louis Hennepin claims to have given the name to the territory in his *Description de la Louisiane, nouvellement decouverte au sud'oüest de la Nouvelle France, par ordre du roy* (Paris: chez la veuve Sebastien Huré, 1683), in the Epistre, signature aiii^v; and La Salle used it later when he claimed the territory for Louis XIV on April 9, 1682: see Margry, vol. 2, p. 191.

5   On Bernou's maps of Peru and New Mexico see John P. Wilson, Robert H. Leslie, and A.H. Warren, "Tabira: Outpost on the East," in *Collected Papers in Honor of Charlie R. Steen, Jr.* (Albuquerque, NM: Archaeological Society of New Mexico 1983), pp. 87–158, at 101, citing BnF, MS fr. n. a. 7497, ff. 18–19.

6   On Bernou's mention of his map of North America see Delanglez, *Some La Salle Journeys* (see note 2), p. 36, citing BnF MS fr. n. a. 7497, f. 19r; and p. 38, citing BnF MS fr. n. a., 7497, ff. 89v, 92r, and 98v.

7   On Bernou's map of Beijing, which appears in Gabriel de Magalhães' *Nouvelle Relation de la Chine* (Paris, 1688), see David E. Mungello, *Curious Land: Jesuit Accommodation and the Origins of Sinology* (Stuttgart: F. Steiner Verlag Wiesbaden, 1985), pp. 95–96.

8   On the other maps attributed to Bernou see Delanglez, *Some La Salle Journeys* (see note 2), pp. 34–36.

9   I thank Pedro Germano Leal for his essential help in interpreting this cartouche.

FIGURE 72   Manuscript map of North America attributed to Claude Bernou, *c.*1682
BIBLIOTHÈQUE NATIONALE DE FRANCE, CARTES ET PLANS, CPL SH 18E PF 122 DIV 2 P 0 RES. COURTESY OF THE
BIBLIOTHÈQUE NATIONALE DE FRANCE

Fortitude (wearing armor), Prudence (holding a shield), Temperance (holding a bridle and reins) and Justice (with a sword); they all watch the action unfolding on the right. There we see the three Theological Virtues: Faith, holding a chalice, seems unperturbed by the movement just below her, where Hope and Charity, clothed and holding shields, a dagger and a spear, push a total of five naked men out of heaven.

In the terrestrial register, the earth seems to float in the ocean, and several human figures kneel and sit in the northern hemisphere, most of them looking to the

heavens and raising their arms in surprise or dismay at what is transpiring above. Three of these figures wear royal clothes: a woman by the palm tree at the far left, the figure in blue who is seated on North America, and the figure by the palm tree at the far right. These seem to be personifications of the continents: Asia on the far left, looking from the far side of the world, America holding a bow, and Africa on the right by the palm tree.

The figures in the aquatic register—a sea goddess, probably Venus Marina, riding a monster, together with her various attendants—were painted by a different hand

FIGURE 73   Detail of the cartouche on Bernou's map
COURTESY OF THE BIBLIOTHÈQUE NATIONALE DE FRANCE

than those in the heavenly and terrestrial registers, as may be seen in the artist's use of firm outlines and also of short black lines to lend the figures three-dimensionality, which is not done above. This probably indicates that an artist who specialized in aquatic imagery was hired to paint this part of the cartouche, rather than that it was a later addition. The puzzling thing about the aquatic register is that none of the figures pays any attention to the drama in heaven, which is a remarkable contrast with the terrestrial register, but then it is also true that there are no humans in the aquatic register, so perhaps only humans are affected by the change above. To the left, there is an unfinished image of Neptune and a female companion arriving on an aquatic chariot drawn by sea horses.

The questions are, who are the men being expelled from heaven, and what does the scene have to do with Bernou's political and religious ambitions regarding French settlement in North America? And if the map was prepared for Jean-Baptiste Colbert (1629–1683)[10]—it was formerly part of his collection, and the naming of the Mississippi River as the Colbert on the map[11] indicates a desire to flatter him—what message was it designed to send to the Minister of Finances, who himself had a strong interest in promoting French colonization in the New World?

The drama portrayed in the heavenly register is a religious one: there are no symbols of England or Spain, France's rivals in New World colonization. Instead there is a struggle over the cross, a bishop's miter has fallen to the ground, and the Theological Virtues are throwing men down from the empyrean. The scene is to be interpreted as an expression of a religious and political hope that the Jesuits, and perhaps specifically the ultramontaine Jesuits, would suffer a fall from power in their ambitions in the New World. The name "ultramontaine" referred to those who supported the authority of the Pope in France rather than that of the French Catholic Church, and Bernou was suspicious of the Jesuits, whom he called M.R.N., for "Monsieur Robe Noire," in his letters.[12] By means of this cartouche, then, Bernou was expressing his support of René-Robert Cavelier, Sieur de La Salle's claims of priority in discovering the upper Mississippi against those of the Jesuit Jacques Marquette (1637–1675), and a hope that French plans for further exploration and settlement in North America would proceed without the influence of the Jesuit order.

Bernou's map, including its cartouche, was used as a model by Louis Hennepin (1626–1704), a missionary of the Franciscan Recollect order, in the map that illustrates his *Description de la Louisiane, nouvellement*

decouverte au Sud'Oüest de la Nouvelle France (Paris: chez la veuve Sebastien Huré, 1683).[13] The map is titled *Carte de la Nouvelle France et de la Louisiane Nouvellement decouverte*,[14] and the debt its cartouche owes to Bernou is clear, even though it is far from being identical (see Fig. 74). It also has heavenly, terrestrial, and aquatic registers, an expulsion from heaven, concerned figures below (on the right), and marine creatures who pay no attention to what is happening above. However, the number of figures in each part is much reduced.

Here the cross is fixed in place, rather than being wrestled over; the motto reads *La triomphe de la Louisiane*; and it is Holy France personified (her shield bears the cross and the fleur-de-lis) who is expelling the figure to the left using a fiery sword. That figure holds a censer, indicating that Hennepin understood that the drama Bernou depicted was religious, but also serpents indicating his evil nature, which do not appear in Bernou's cartouche. The identity of the two figures on the right who are dismayed by the heavenly drama is not clear; below we have personifications of Victory on the left, and of Fame on the right, the latter pointing to a banner with the king's name (Louis) on it. At the bottom of the composition there are three men in the water who are supporting the cartouche, holding it up from the sea. Hennepin was certainly using Bernou's cartouche as a model, but it does not seem that he understood its message, or if he did, he did not wish to convey the same message.

The influence of Bernou's cartouche continued for some years, though by way of Hennepin's printed map rather than directly from Bernou's manuscript map. In 1691 Chrestien Le Clercq borrowed from Hennepin's cartouche the personification of Holy France with the flaming sword, but no other elements, for the cartouche on his map *Carte Generalle de la Nouvelle France ou est compris La Louisiane Gaspesie et le Nouveau Mexique avec les Isles Antilles* (Paris: Amable Auroy, 1691), which appears in two

10   On Colbert see Inès Murat, *Colbert*, trans. Robert Francis Cook and Jeannie Van Asselt (Charlottesville: University Press of Virginia, 1984); on his interest in colonizing in North America see Mathé Allain, "Colbert and the Colonies," in Glenn R. Conrad, ed., *The French Experience in Louisiana* (Lafayette: Center for Louisiana Studies, University of Southwestern Louisiana, 1995), pp. 5–30.

11   On the naming of the Mississippi as the Colbert see Lucien Campeau, "Les cartes relatives à la découverte du Mississipi par le P. Jacques Marquette et Louis Jolliet," *Les Cahiers des Dix* 47 (1992), pp. 41–90, at 63.

12   On Bernou's suspicion of the Jesuits see Delanglez, *Some La Salle Journeys* (see note 2), pp. 12, 53–54, and the footnote on p. 86; and Mathé Allain, *Not Worth a Straw: French Colonial Policy and the Early Years of Louisiana* (Lafayette: Center for Louisiana Studies, University of Southwestern Louisiana, 1988), p. 37; this passage is reprinted in Mathé Allain, "Colbert's Colony Crumbles: La Salle's Voyages," in Glenn R. Conrad, ed., *The French Experience in Louisiana* (Lafayette: Center for Louisiana Studies, University of Southwestern Louisiana, 1995), pp. 31–47, at 36.

13   On Hennepin see Catherine Broué, "Louis Hennepin," in *Francis in the Americas: Essays on the Franciscan Family in North and South America* (Berkeley: Academy of American Franciscan History, 2005), pp. 203–218. His *Description* has been translated into English as *Father Louis Hennepin's Description of Louisiana*, trans. Marion E. Cross (Minneapolis: Colonial Dames of America, and University of Minnesota Press, 1938). Hennepin's copying of Bernou's map is noted by Jean Delanglez, *Hennepin's Description of Louisiana: A Critical Essay* (Chicago: Institute of Jesuit History, 1941), p. 111.

14   On Hennepin's map see Philip D. Burden, *The Mapping of North America: A List of Printed Maps* (Rickmansworth: Raleigh Publications, 1996–2007), vol. 2, pp. 211–213, no. 556.

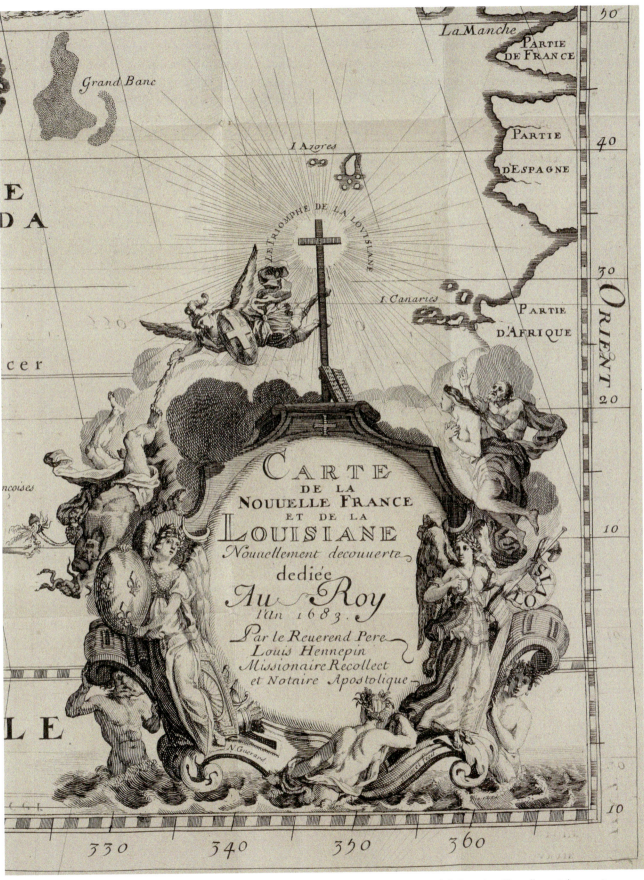

FIGURE 74   A cartouche inspired by Bernou's on Louis Hennepin's *Carte de la Nouvelle France et de la Louisiane Nouvellement decouverte*
(Paris: chez la veuve Sebastien Huré, 1683)
YALE UNIVERSITY, BEINECKE LIBRARY, CN 105. COURTESY OF THE BEINECKE RARE BOOK AND MANUSCRIPT LIBRARY

books of his printed that year.[15] And in 1698 there was printed an anonymous version of Hennepin's map that was dedicated to William III of England, and as a result the motto at the top of Hennepin's cartouche, together with the cross, was removed, leaving a strange void, and the personifications of France and Louisiana were replaced with angels holding the arms of Britain and a banner with William's name.[16] It is difficult to ascribe any significance to a cartouche in which two figures look up to, and one figure falls from an upper register that is missing. It is a strange and pointless type of cartouche copying in which the elements have lost all of their meaning, and a curious sequel to a cartouche (Bernou's) that was so full of meaning.

---

15   Le Clercq's map appears in some copies of his *Premier etablissement de la foy dans la Nouvelle France* (Paris: A. Auroy, 1691), and in some copies of his *Nouvelle relation de la Gaspesie* (Paris: A. Auroy, 1691). For discussion of the first of these works see Raphael Hamilton, "Who Wrote *Premier Etablissement de la Foy dans la Nouvelle France*?" *Canadian Historical Review* 57.3 (1976), pp. 265–288, who argues that Bernou was involved in the book's production; for discussion of the map see Burden, *The Mapping of North America* (see note 14), vol. 2, pp. 373–374, no. 676. A good image of the map is available on the Luna site of the John Carter Brown Library at https://jcb.lunaimaging.com.

---

16   This version of Hennepin's map is titled *Carte d'un nouveau monde. Entre le Nouueau Mexique et la Mer glacialle ... dedieé a sa Majesté Britanique le Roy Guilaume Troisieme* (Utrecht: Antoine Schouten, 1698); a good image of the map is available on the Luna site of the John Carter Brown Library at https://jcb.luna imaging.com.

Unveiling Text, Interpreting Allegory

Vincenzo Coronelli, terrestrial globe, 1688

In the Introduction I mentioned the colossal terrestrial globe 3.84 m (12.6 feet) in diameter that the Italian cartographer Vincenzo Coronelli completed in 1683 for Louis XIV of France. The cartouches on that globe are imaginative and artistically elaborate (see Fig. 30 above), but in general have little in the way of symbolism. Coronelli made use of all the geographical research he had done for the globe for Louis XIV in later maps and globes, and also became much more sophisticated in designing his cartouches, creating examples with complex symbolism.

In 1688 Coronelli produced printed globe gores—the printed sheets of paper that when cut and wrapped around a sphere of the right size produce a globe—designed for a sphere 108 cm (3.5 feet) in diameter.[1] One of the great intellectual questions that arose from the European discovery of the New World was whether those lands were part of, or connected to, Asia. Christopher Columbus believed that the lands he found were outlying regions of Asia, Amerigo Vespucci believed that the lands formed a separate landmass, and the matter was not definitively settled until the Finland-Swedish explorer Adolf Erik Nordenskiöld (1832–1901) sailed the northern coast of Siberia in 1878–79, demonstrating that eastern Asia and North America were not joined by land.[2]

But much earlier, in 1561, the Italian cartographer Giacomo Gastaldi had proposed that the two continents were separated by a strait that he called the Strait of Anian—that is, he made a guess about the world's geography, and he gave it a name that came from a mistaken reading of the name of a province of China in an Italian edition of Marco Polo's travel narrative.[3] The fact that this hypothesis happened to be correct is incidental to our purposes here; but it was very influential, and the Strait of Anian appears on numerous later maps and globes, including Coronelli's globe of 1688.

On the western side of the strait, in North America, Coronelli places a large cartouche with information about this feature (Fig. 75). Above there is a banner that reads *Dello Stretto d'Anian*, "Regarding the Strait of Anian" (difficult to read in our image because of excessively dark hand-coloring), and below there is a large monument with a long text about the strait written on the front.[4] A bird and two winged human figures are pulling away a curtain to reveal the text, implying that the information is about a recent discovery. In the lower left part of the scene, a woman with the sun shining on her forehead points to the text about the strait, the sun indicating the light of new knowledge. Below her another woman holds up a sundial in one hand and has a nautical chart in the other, with a compass behind her, while she, and particularly her long hair, dissolve into a river that flows off to the left. This woman with the trappings of nautical science who is disappearing represents earlier, incorrect knowledge, specifically the idea that North America and Asia were connected. Behind this woman a ship is sinking, which seems to be a reference to a failed English attempt to find the Strait of Anian that Coronelli mentions in the text (to be discussed momentarily).

---

1 On Coronelli's 1688 terrestrial globe see Nicolangelo Scianna, "Indagine sui grandi globi a stampa di Vincenzo Coronelli. Prima parte: il globo terrestre," *Nuncius: Journal of the History of Science* 13.1 (1998), pp. 151–168, which includes a census of surviving exemplars; and Marica Milanesi, *Vincenzo Coronelli Cosmographer (1650–1718)* (Turnhout: Brepols, 2016), pp. 169–173.

2 On the history of the idea that Asia and America were joined see Johann Georg Kohl, "Asia and America: An Historical Disquisition Concerning the Ideas which Former Geographers had about the Geographical Relation and Connection of the Old and New World," *Proceedings of the American Antiquarian Society* 21 (1911), pp. 284–338; J.H. Parry, "Asia-in-the-West," *Terrae Incognitae* 8.1 (1976), pp. 59–72; Errol Wayne Stevens, "The Asian-American Connection: The Rise and Fall of a Cartographic Idea," *Terrae Incognitae* 21.1 (1989), pp. 27–39; and Marica Milanesi, "Arsarot oder Anian? Identitat und Unterscheidung zwischen Asien und der Neuen Welt in der Kartographie des 16. Jahrhunderts (1500–1570)," in Adriano Prosperi and Wolfgang Reinhard, eds., *Die Neue Welt im Bewusstsein der Italiener und Deutschen des 16. Jahrhunderts* (Berlin: Duncker & Humblot, 1993), pp. 15–68.

3 Gastaldi shows the Strait of Anian on his world map of *c.*1561 which survives in just one exemplar in London, British Library, Maps C.18.n.1. The Italian edition of Marco Polo that led Gastaldi into this belief about the strait is that in the third volume of Giovanni Battista Ramusio's *Navigationi et viaggi* (Venice: Tommaso Giunti, 1550–1559). For discussion see George E. Nunn, *Origin of the Strait of Anian Concept* (Philadelphia: s.n., 1929).

4 There is a brief interpretation of this cartouche in Ana Isabel Seruya and Mário Pereira, eds., *Globos Coronelli: Sociedade de Geografia = Globes Coronelli: Sociedade de Geografia* (Portugal: Instituto Português de Conservação e Restauro, 2004), pp. 43–44, but they authors do not identify all of the figures, and not all of the identifications are correct.

FIGURE 75   Detail of the cartouche about the Strait of Anian on Coronelli's terrestrial globe of 1688
GENOA, MUSEO GALILEO. COURTESY OF THE MUSEO GALILEO

Further to the left is seated Father Time, identifiable from his scythe and the hourglass on the ground to his right,[5] while a winged human figure touches Father Time on the shoulder and gestures towards the woman who is disappearing. This part of the scene emphasizes that geographical knowledge changes and increases with time. Overall the cartouche accentuates Coronelli's authority by declaring his use of the very latest and most accurate information.

The text in the cartouche reads as follows:[6]

"Riferì alla Regina Elizabetta il General Fr[an]co Draco ritornato dall' Indie Orientali in Londra per il Sud, che internatosi 20 leghe nel STRETTO D'ANIAN, travaglio per le sue Navi poco adattate a questo viaggio, e per il grosso con voglio di 400000 scudi tolto a Spagnuoli. Facilito l'ingresso per il Sud, e lo difficultò per il Nord per il freddo, Stretti, Baie, e Golfi, per il quali soggiacque a mortalità, e pericoli, la Francia, Inghilterra, Suecia, Hollanda, e Danimarca, che ritornarono con la ruina dell'Equipaggio. Uscito nel 1609 un Vascello fabricato in Acapulco, e portato da borasca, entrò per sicurezza nel medemo stretto, creduto dai Naviganti, ch'erano Portughesi, una Rada, ma trovatisi nel mare del Sud, giunsero in doi Mesi a Dublin, e poi a Lisbona; dove presentate con i disegni del Viaggio le ragioni della loro navigazione, fece incendiar Filippo 3° le Carte, e confiscar il Navilio con le merci, affinche non pratticata questa strada, ignota ai Prencipi del Nort, restasse imperturbato il commercio del Mare del Sud. Quelli, che navigorno il Sud, dicono ch'il viaggio dell'Indie Orientali si

---

5   See Samuel Macey, "The Changing Iconography of Father Time," in J.T. Fraser, Nathaniel M. Lawrence, and David Park, eds., *The Study of Time III: Proceedings of the Third Conference of the International Society for the Study of Time, Alpbach, Austria* (New York: Springer, 1978), pp. 540–577; and Simona Cohen, "The Early Renaissance Personification of Time and Changing Concepts of Temporality," *Renaissance Studies* 14.3 (2000), pp. 301–328.

6   The text in Coronelli's cartouche about the Strait of Anian is transcribed, with some commentary, in "Alla Lettera antecedente comunicataci dal chiarissimo signor ab Amoretti dopo ch'era già stampata la lettera," *Giornale dell' Italiana letteratura* 38 (1814), pp. 321–322. The text about the Strait of Anian on Coronelli's earlier globe made for Louis XIV is transcribed by [François Le Large], *Recueil des inscriptions des remarques historiques et géographiques*

---

qui sont sur le globe terrestre de Marly, Paris, Bibliothèque nationale de France, MS fr. 13365, pp. 49–54; a digital version of the manuscript is available at https://gallica.bnf.fr.

possa far per questo Stretto in 40 giorni, in 30 per Panama, e 50 da Valdivia. Mosso con questi, et altri riflessi dalla Compagnia Reale d'Inghilterra il suo Re Carlo 2° destinò alla tracia del medemo Stretto Carlo Derque, il quale partito da Dunes li 26. Settemb. 1669 con 10000. doppie, et altre provisioni, morì per viaggio, et arenossi l'impresa.

General Francis Drake told Queen Elizabeth upon returning from the East Indies to London by the south, that he entered 20 leagues into the Strait of Anian, which was difficult for his ships, given that they were not suited to this voyage, and because the convoy was too heavy, as it carried 400,000 *scudi* taken from the Spanish. The entrance from the south was easier, but it was difficult in the north because of the cold, straits, bays, and gulfs, because of which it subjected to death and dangers France, England, Sweden, Holland, and Denmark, who returned with the destruction of their crews. In 1609 a ship, made in Acapulco, and carried by a storm, entered for safety in the same strait, believed by the sailors, who were Portuguese, to be a roadstead, but they found themselves in the Pacific, arrived in two months in Dublin, and then in Lisbon; where, together with the maps of the voyage, they presented the reasons for their route. This caused Philip III to burn the maps and confiscate the ship together with its goods, so that this route, unknown to the princes of the north, would not be taken, and the trade in the Pacific would remain unperturbed. Those who sail in the south say that the journey from the East Indies can be made by way of this strait in 40 days, in 30 days by way of Panama, and in 50 days from Valdivia. Moved by these and other considerations from the Royal Company of England, King Charles II sent Carlos Derque to explore this strait. He left from Dunes the 26 of September 1669 with 10,000 doubbloons and other provisions, but he died on the voyage, and the enterprise failed."

Coronelli thus tells the history of the Strait of Anian back to 1580, when Drake completed his circumnavigation, but does not mention Gastaldi or his map of c.1561.[7] Carlos

"Derque" in Coronelli's text is an error for Carlos Enriques Clerque, a mysterious figure who had been instrumental in proposing to Charles II that John Narborough make a voyage towards the Strait of Anian in 1669.[8]

One curious aspect of the history of this cartouche is that Coronelli reused it in his map of North America titled *America settentrionale colle nuove scoperte fin all'anno 1688*, which he first published in 1693.[9] Here, however, he removes the text about the Strait of Anian, replacing it with the map's title and additional bibliographic details, thus leaving the viewer who is unaware of the cartouche's earlier use on his globe unable to guess the significance of the allegorical scene. In the section "The Sources of Cartouches" in the Introduction I discussed some cases where a cartographer copies a cartouche into a different geographical context where its thematic decoration no longer matches the region, but the situation on Coronelli's map is different. Here the cartographer copies his own cartouche and keeps it in the same geographical location, in North America west of the Strait of Anian, but his removal of the text about the Strait renders the cartouche's symbolism incomprehensible. Although Coronelli was very interested in cartouches with rich allegory, his high rate of cartographic production entailed his re-use of some cartouches in ways that robbed them of the context necessary to understand them.

Map: Interdisciplinary Perspectives on Pieter van den Keere's Map, 'Nova totius terrarum orbis geographica ac hydrographica tabula' (Amsterdam, 1608/36) (Portland, ME: Osher Map Library and Smith Center for Cartographic Education, University of Southern Maine, 2001), pp. 4–8, at 6.

8   For a brief account of Narborough's voyage of 1669 see Peter T. Bradley, *British Maritime Enterprise in the New World: From the Late Fifteenth to the mid-Eighteenth Century* (Lewiston, NY: Edwin Mellen Press, 1999), pp. 436–442. On Clerque see Peter Bradley, "Narborough's Don Carlos," *The Mariner's Mirror* 72 (1986), pp. 465–475; Clayton McCarl, "Carlos Enriques Clerque as Crypto-Jewish Confidence Man in Francisco de Seyxas y Lovera's *Piratas y contrabandistas* (1693)," *Colonial Latin American Review* 24.3 (2015), pp. 406–420; and Richard J. Campbell, Peter T. Bradley, and Joyce Lorimer, *The Voyage of Captain John Narbrough to the Strait of Magellan and the South Sea in his Majesty's Ship Sweepstakes, 1669–1671* (Abingdon, Oxon, and New York, NY: Routledge for the Hakluyt Society, 2018), pp. 48–59.

9   High-resolution images of Coronelli's *America settentrionale* are available at https://loc.gov and https://searchworks.stanford.edu.

---

7   There is an earlier, much less detailed cartouche text about the Strait of Anian on Pieter van den Keere's world map of 1608: see Gloria Shaw Duclos, "The 'Classic Ground' of Van den Keere's Map," in Matthew H. Edney and Irwin D. Novak, eds., *Reading the World*

Concealing and Revealing the Source of the Nile

Vincenzo Coronelli, L'Africa divisa nelle sue parti, 1689

The same cartographer, Vincenzo Coronelli, deploys another elaborate allegorical cartouche in connection with another great geographical mystery on his map of Africa first printed in 1689, which is based closely—including this cartouche—on his terrestrial globe of 1688. It is titled *L'Africa divisa nelle sue parti secondo le più moderne relationi colle scoperte dell'origine, e corso del Nilo* ("Africa Divided into its Parts According to the Most Modern Accounts, with the Discovery of the Sources of the Nile, and its Course.")[1] The flooding of the Nile, which occurs in the summer when there is no rain in Egypt, rather than in the winter, was one of the great geographical mysteries of antiquity, and had generated exceptional curiosity about the river's sources. The Roman geographer Pomponius Mela, in trying to explain the river's flooding in the summer, went so far as to suggest that it had its source in the southern hemisphere, where the seasons are the opposite of those in the northern hemisphere,[2] and there were various other theories.

Coronelli's title for the map declares that he will reveal the sources of the river, raising expectations, but the way he handles the cartouche and the information about the sources of the Nile is entirely different from the way he handled the cartouche about the Strait of Anian on his 1688 globe. The cartouche here is centered on a text about the sources of the Nile (Fig. 76),[3] but paradoxically the cartouche covers precisely the area of the map where Coronelli might have depicted those sources—so that the cartouche seems to be used, like those of Johannes Ruysch, Martin Waldseemüller, and Gerard Mercator discussed above, to conceal geographical ignorance. In the cartouche about the Strait of Anian, a curtain was being pulled away to reveal the new information about the strait that was engraved on stone; here, in contrast, the text is being written on a curtain that covers the relevant part of the map. The writing of the text on fabric, rather than stone, seems to imply that the text is transitory and may be revised in the light of new knowledge. We also wonder why the curtain covers the geography: why does the cartographer favor a verbal description over a cartographic depiction? Is this Coronelli's way of indicating that he is not completely confident in his information about the river? The presence of personified Fame blowing a trumpet above the cartouche implies that new information is being revealed on the cartouche, even though that information may not be definitive.

On the left, the curtain hangs from a pyramid covered with esoteric symbols, which suggest Egyptian hieroglyphs, one of the most prominent features of ancient Egyptian culture. In the lower right-hand part of the cartouche is a personification of the river Nile who holds an urn from which the waters of the river flow;[4] the crocodile is a traditional symbol of the river. The man on the left is writing the text on the curtain, which indicates simultaneously that the information provided in the cartouche is new, and also that it may eventually need to be replaced.

---

1 On Coronelli's map of Africa see Oscar I. Norwich, Pam Kolbe, and Jeffrey C. Stone, *Norwich's Maps of Africa: An Illustrated and Annotated Carto-Bibliography*, 2nd edn. (Norwich, VT: Terra Nova Press, 1997), p. 69, map 56; and Richard L. Betz, *The Mapping of Africa: A Cartobibliography of Printed Maps of the African Continent to 1700* ('t Goy-Houten: Hes & de Graaf, 2007), pp. 447–448, no. 153. High-resolution images of the two sheets of the map are available at https://searchworks.stanford.edu.

2 On the idea that the Nile has its source in the southern hemisphere see Pomponius Mela, *De situ orbis*, 1.9.54; F.E. Romer, trans., *Pomponius Mela's Description of the World* (Ann Arbor: University of Michigan Press, 1998), p. 50; Chet Van Duzer, "The Cartography, Geography, and Hydrography of the Southern Ring Continent, 1515–1763," *Orbis Terrarum* 8 (2002), pp. 115–158, esp. 115–127; and also my updated discussion in "El Nilo que fluye desde otro mundo: El hipotético continente austral en el globo terráqueo de Johann Schöner de 1515," forthcoming in *Terra Brasilis* in 2023. The ancients did in fact know that the earth was a sphere: see William M. Calder, "The Spherical Earth in Plato's *Phaedo*," *Phronesis* 3.2 (1958), pp. 121–125; and Jeffrey Burton Russell, *Inventing the Flat Earth: Columbus and Modern Historians* (New York: Praeger, 1991).

3 The symbolism of this cartouche is discussed by Ana Isabel Seruya and Mário Pereira, eds., *Globos Coronelli: Sociedade de Geografia = Globes Coronelli: Sociedade de Geografia* (Portugal: Instituto Português de Conservação e Restauro, 2004), p. 43, but I am not in agreement with all of their identifications.

4 On Renaissance personifications of rivers see Ruth Olitsky Rubinstein, "The Renaissance Discovery of Antique River-God Personifications," in *Scritti di storia dell'arte in onore di Roberto Salvini* (Florence: Sansoni, 1984), pp. 257–264 and plates 72–73; and Claudia Lazzaro, "River Gods: Personifying Nature in Sixteenth-Century Italy," *Renaissance Studies* 25.1 (2011), pp. 70–94.

FIGURE 76   Detail of the cartouche about the sources of the Nile on Coronelli's map of Africa, titled *L'Africa divisa nelle sue parti*, this copy printed in 1691, in the Dr. Oscar I. Norwich Collection of Maps of Africa and its Islands, at the David Rumsey Map Center, Stanford University, G8200 [1691] .C67
COURTESY OF THE DR. OSCAR I. NORWICH COLLECTION OF MAPS

This man is kneeling on a globe with one leg while he stands on books with the other, giving a clinic in how not to treat these objects (it is important to remember here that Coronelli was a globe-maker); there is also a map protruding from beneath the right-hand part of the stand of the globe, in danger of falling into the Nile. The poor treatment of the globe, books, and maps indicates a rejection of earlier theories about the source of the Nile, something very similar to what we saw in Coronelli's cartouche about the Strait of Anian.

The text in the cartouche about the Nile reads:

"Il Nilo Fiume inondante fu chiamato dagli Abissini Abawi, cioè Padre dell'Acque. Rintracciarono la sua Fonte ignota li Re Sesastre e Tolomeo Filadelfo d'Egitto, Cambise di Persia, Alessandro il Grande, e replicatamente senza venire in chiaro Nerone. Lo creddero nato dalle Montagne della Lunai Geografi antichi, e diversi moderni. Riportarono poi li Portughesi la gloriosa distinta notitia, che ci servi per regolatione dell Abissinia, guista le relationi accreditate del P. Baldassar Tellez, e del Ladolfo.

The River Nile in flood was called Abawi by the Abyssinians, that is, Father of the Waters. King Sesostris, Ptolemy Philadelphus of Egypt, Cambyses of Persia, and Alexander the Great all tried to determine its unknown source, and Nero repeated their efforts without arriving at a clear solution. Ancient geographers, as well as several moderns, believed it was born in the Mountains of the Moon; the Portuguese then brought back glorious and distinguished news, which we use for the depiction of Abyssinia, namely the accredited accounts of Father Baltasar Tellez and of Hiob Ludolf."

Coronelli's list of early explorations seeking the source of the Nile reflects the long-standing interest in determining why the river floods in the summer.[5] The texts that Coronelli cites at the end of the cartouche are Baltasar Tellez's *Historia geral de Ethiopia a Alta, ou Preste Joam* (Coimbra: Manoel Dias, 1660), and Hiob Ludolf's *Historia Aethiopica* (Frankfurt: Joh. David Zunner, 1681).[6]

The cartouche is remarkably complex in the way it simultaneously proclaims its revelation of recent information about the source of the river while covering the exact part of the map where that new information might

be rendered cartographically, and also suggesting that new discoveries about the sources of the Nile are still to come.[7]

A preference for less elaborate cartouches is clearly reflected in a version of Coronelli's map by the geographer Jean Nicolas du Trallage, Sieur de Tillemont (1620–1698), and published by Jean-Baptiste Nolin beginning in 1689.[8] On this map (Fig. 77) the intricate symbolism of Coronelli's cartouche is replaced by a simple frame composed of two intertwining serpents that contains a longer text about European knowledge of the sources of the Nile, written by Coronelli,[9] still occupying the area where Coronelli and du Trallage might have depicted the sources of the Nile. This continued reluctance to depict the sources of the Nile is puzzling since in his longer text Coronelli cites a map he consulted that does show the sources, namely the map that appears in Hiob Ludolf's *Historia Aethiopica* (Frankfurt, 1681).[10]

Coronelli's decision to deploy a cartouche to cover exactly the part of his map where he might have depicted the sources of the Nile, while proclaiming in that same cartouche that he has recent information about the geography of the sources, becomes even more puzzling when we note that he himself made a map of the sources of the Nile one year after his map of Africa, using the same

---

5   On early explorations of the Nile see Harry Johnston, *The Nile Quest: A Record of the Exploration of the Nile and its Basin* (New York: F.A. Stokes Co., 1903); and Gosciwit Malinowski, "Alexander and the Beginning of the Greek Exploration in Nilotic Africa," in Volker Grieb, Krzysztof Nawotka, and Agnieszka Wojciechowska, eds., *Alexander the Great and Egypt* (Wiesbaden: Harrassowitz, 2014), pp. 273–286.

6   Tellez's work was translated into English as *The Travels of the Jesuits in Ethiopia* (London: Printed for J. Knapton, in St. Paul's Church-Yard, 1710); Ludolf's work was translated into English as *A New History of Ethiopia: Being a Full and Accurate Description of the Kingdom of Abessinia, Vulgarly, though Erroneously called the Empire of Prester John* (London: Printed for Samuel Smith, 1682). On Ludolf see Jürgen Tubach, "Ludolf, Hiob," in *Biographisch-Bibliographisches Kirchenlexikon* (Hamm in Westfalen: Verlag T. Bautz, 1970–2014), vol. 5, cols. 317–325.

7   Incidentally for a later map that purports to show the landscape of the source of the Nile in its cartouche see Johann Baptist Homann's *Totius Africae nova repraesentatio qua praeter diversos in ea Status et Regiones etiam Origo Nili* (Nuremberg, 1715), where just to the left of the man with the parasol there is a man poking a pole down in a hole which is labeled *Fontes nili*, the sources of the Nile. A good image of the map is available at https://search works.stanford.edu.

8   The first printing of this map is Vincenzo Coronelli and Jean Nicolas du Trallage, *Afrique selon les relations les plus nouvelles, dressée et dediée par de P. Coronelli Cosmographe de la Serenissime Republique de Venise, corrigée et augmentée par le Sr. Tillemon* (Paris: J.B. Nolin, 1689); in later printings the title varies slightly.

9   The longer text about the sources of the Nile on Coronelli's map of Africa published by Nolin is transcribed by Lucile Haguet, "La carte a-t-elle horreur du vide? Réexaminer les enjeux du tournant épistémologique du XVIIIᵉ siècle à la lumière de la cartographie occidentale de l'Égypte," *Cartes et Géomatique. Revue du comité français de cartographie* 210 (2011), pp. 95–106, at 101.

10   Coronelli writes: *M. Ludolf a recueilli encore divers mémoires sur lesquels il a dressé son Histoire d'Ethiopie, imprimée en latin a Francfort en 1681, il y a joint une carte de l'Abissinie dont je me suis servi comme étant la meilleure qui ait encore paru*, that is, "Mr. Ludolf has collected various accounts, based on which he composed his *Historia Aethiopica*, printed in Latin at Frankfurt in 1681. He included a map of Abyssinia which I used, since it is the best that has yet appeared." The map in question is titled *Jobi Ludolfi Habessinia seu Abassinia, Presbyteri Johannis Regio*, and a high-resolution image of it may be consulted at https:// searchworks.stanford.edu.

FIGURE 77   Detail of the cartouche in Vincenzo Coronelli and Jean Nicolas du Trallage, *Afrique selon les relations les plus nouvelles* (Paris: J.B. Nolin, 1689)
JERUSALEM, NATIONAL LIBRARY OF ISRAEL, AF 126.1. COURTESY OF THE NATIONAL LIBRARY OF ISRAEL

texts (and map) he cited in the cartouche. Coronelli's new map is titled *Abissinia, dove sono le fonti del Nilo: descritta secondo le relationi dè P.P. Mendez, Almeida, Païs, Lobo, e Lodulfo* ("Abyssinia, where the Sources of the Nile are Located, Depicted According to the Accounts of Fathers Mendez, Almeida, Païs, Lobo, and Lodulfo") (Venice: Domenico Padouani, 1690) (Fig. 78).[11] In an inset on the right, Coronelli shows the ancient conception of the

sources of the river, and in the map proper, the new conception according to the discoveries of Ludolf and others.

Why would Coronelli hide the sources of the Nile on one map only to reveal them on another, when he had the information necessary to depict the sources when he made the first map? The only likely motive that occurs to me is an economic one: it was a way for the cartographer to get the customer to buy two maps instead of one. Thus cartouches can be deployed not only to conceal geographical ignorance, and not only to attract the eye and thus encourage the purchase of a map, but also to render necessary the purchase of a second map.

---

11   Coronelli's map of the sources of the Nile is listed in Paulos Milkias, *Ethiopia: A Comprehensive Bibliography* (Boston: G.K. Hall, 1989), p. 210.

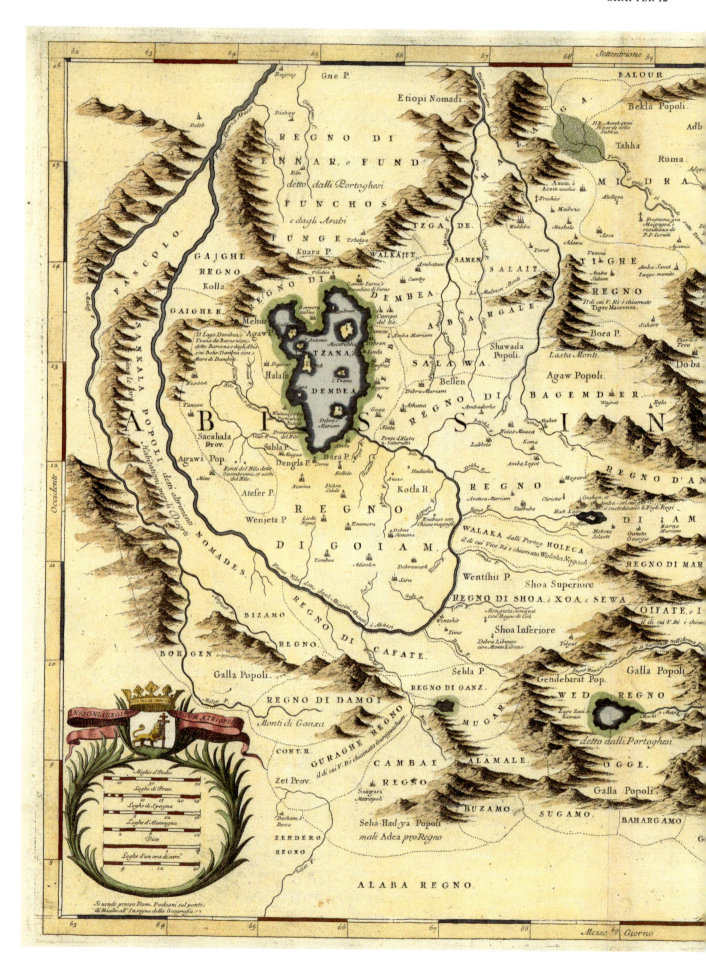

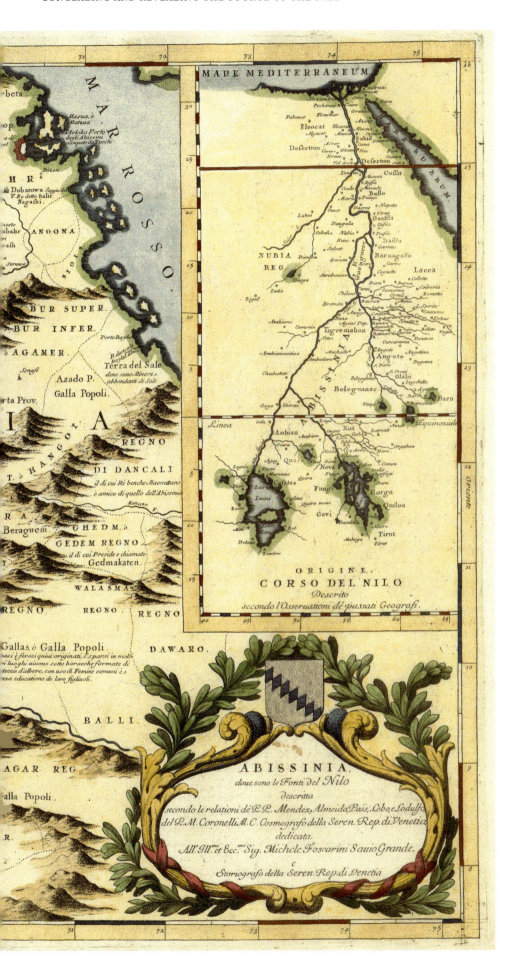

FIGURE 78
Vincenzo Coronelli, *Abissinia, dove sono le fonti del Nilo: descritta secondo le relationi dè P.P. Mendez, Almeida, Païs, Lobo, e Lodulfo* (Venice: Domenico Padouani, *c*.1695)

CHAPTER 13

Propaganda in a Cartouche

Vincenzo Coronelli, Paralello geografico dell'antico col moderno archipelago, *1692*

It is a commonplace in writings about the history of cartography that no map is a purely objective view of the earth or part of its surface, and maps often have a persuasive element, or express political desires or ambitions—and the decoration of cartouches is often part of these political programs. These programs can be subtle, but in the example we will examine here of a map by Vincenzo Coronelli, whose spectacular cartouches we have seen in the preceding two chapters, the cartouche is an undisguised and unapologetic piece of propaganda.[1]

The Republic of Venice and the Ottoman Empire had been intermittently at war since 1396. In 1683, the King of Poland broke the Ottoman siege of Vienna,[2] and in 1684 the Republic of Venice declared war on the Ottoman Empire, initiating what was later called the Sixth Ottoman-Venetian War or the Morean War, which lasted till 1699.[3] The goal was to take advantage of Ottoman weakness to push the Turks out of Morea (the Peloponnese in southern Greece), some of the Aegean islands, and Dalmatia. The people of Venice were very interested in following the progress of the war, which generally went well for Venice, and as a result there was a great demand for news about the campaign; in addition, the Republic wanted to maintain public enthusiasm for the war so that they could continue raising taxes to support it.[4]

In 1685 Coronelli was appointed Cosmographer of the Republic of Venice, and part of his job was to record Venetian victories cartographically, thus celebrating Venetian power and bearing witness to the greatness of the Republic.[5] In 1686 Coronelli published a book titled *Conquiste della Ser. Republica di Venezia nella Dalmazia, Epiro e Morea* ("Conquests of the Most Serene Republic of Venice in Dalmatia, Epirus, and Morea") that celebrates Venice's victories in the campaigns of 1684 and 1685.[6] The maps do not only show the theater of the war with plans of battles, but also some of the fighting: the view of Kalamata shows the Venetian army under Francesco Morosini,

---

1 On connections between maps, political power, and persuasion see L.B. Thomas, "Maps as Instruments of Propaganda," *Surveying and Mapping* 9 (1949), pp. 75–81; J.B. Harley, "Maps, Knowledge and Power," in Denis Cosgrove and Stephen Daniels, eds., *The Iconography of Landscape: Essays on the Symbolic Representation, Design and Use of Past Environments* (Cambridge: Cambridge University Press, 1988), pp. 277–312; John Pickles, "Texts, Hermeneutics and Propaganda Maps," in Trevor J. Barnes and James S. Duncan, eds., *Writing Worlds: Discourse, Text & Metaphor in the Representation of Landscape* (London: Routledge, 1992), pp. 193–230; Mark Monmonier, *Drawing the Line: Tales of Maps and Controversy* (New York: Henry Holt and Co., 1995); and Matthew Edney, "The Irony of Imperial Mapping," in James R. Akerman, ed., *The Imperial Map: Cartography and the Mastery of Empire* (Chicago: University of Chicago Press, 2009), pp. 11–45.

2 There is a cartouche that depicts the Habsburg army forcing the Turks to retreat from the siege of Vienna in a map made by Vincenzo Coronelli, *Le royaume de Hongrie, divisé en haute et basse Hongrie, avec l'Esclavonie* (Paris: Jean-Baptiste Nolin, 1687). A zoomable image of this map is available at https://gallica.bnf.fr. The human figures in the cartouche are very small, and thus the cartouche lacks the visual impact of Coronelli's cartouche that is the focus of this chapter.

3 On the Morean War see William Miller, "The Venetian Revival in Greece, 1684–1718," *English Historical Review* 35.139 (1920), pp. 343–366; Géraud Poumarède, *L'Empire de Venise et les Turcs: XVIᵉ–XVIIᵉ siècle* (Paris: Classiques Garnier, 2020); and Eric G.L. Pinzelli, *Vénise et l'Empire ottoman: les guerres de Morée (1684–1718)* (Athens: Eric G.L. Pinzelli, 2020).

4 On the importance of news and propaganda efforts during the Morean War see Mario Infelise, "The War, the News and the Curious: Military Gazettes in Italy," in Brendan Dooley and Sabrina Baron, eds., *The Politics of Information in Early Modern Europe* (London: Routledge, 2001), pp. 216–236; and Anastasia Stouraiti, "Printing Empire: Visual Culture and the Imperial Archive in Seventeenth-Century Venice," *The Historical Journal* 59.3 (2016), pp. 635–668.

5 On Coronelli's cartographic propaganda see Brendan Dooley, "The Wages of War: Battles, Prints and Entrepreneurs in Late Seventeenth-Century Venice," *Word & Image* 17.1–2 (2001), pp. 7–24, esp. 17–22; Anastasia Stouraiti, "Propaganda figurata: geometrie di dominio e ideologie veneziane nelle carte di Vincenzo Coronelli," *Studi veneziani* 44 (2002), pp. 129–155; and Laura Marasso, "Iconografia di guerra: immagini e informazione," in Anastasia Stouraiti and Mario Infelise, eds., *Venezia e la guerra di Morea: guerra, politica e cultura alla fine del '600* (Milan: F. Angeli, 2005), pp. 209–231, esp. 222–231. For a brief insightful account of Coronelli's career see Denis Cosgrove, "Global Illumination and Enlightenments in the Geographies of Vincenzo Coronelli and Athanasius Kircher," in David Livingstone and Charles Withers, eds., *Geography and Enlightenment* (Chicago: University of Chicago Press, 1999), pp. 33–66, esp. 34–50; the standard account of Coronelli's life and work is Marica Milanesi, *Vincenzo Coronelli Cosmographer (1650–1718)* (Turnhout: Brepols, 2016).

6 On Coronelli's *Conquiste* see Ermanno Armao, *Vincenzo Coronelli, cenni sull'uomo e la sua vita. Catalogo ragionato delle sue opere, lettere, fonti bibliografiche, indici* (Florence: Bibliopolis, 1944), no. 91; Leonora Navari, "Vincenzo Coronelli and the Iconography of the Venetian Conquest of the Morea: A Study in Illustrative Methods," *Annual of the British School at Athens* 90 (1995), pp. 505–519; and Stouraiti, "Propaganda figurata" (see note 5), pp. 144–150.

---

later the Doge of Venice, defeating Ottoman forces in a battle that took place on September 14, 1685. Later in 1686 Coronelli reused some of the material from this book in another, titled *Memorie istoriografiche de' Regni della Morea, Negroponte e littorali fin'a Salonichi* ("A Historical and Geographical Account of Morea, Negropont, and the Coasts as far as Thessalonica").[7] The book's title suggests that it will be an objective description of these regions, but the image on the title page makes clear its status as propaganda: it shows the Venetian lion leaping upon a fallen Turkish warrior and biting his face. The first plate shows a personification of Venice placidly enthroned while Neptune destroys the Turkish fleet in front of her.

Coronelli indicated Venetian victories in various maps he published. For example, sometime between 1688 and 1690 he made a map of the Isthmus of Corinth which curiously bears the title *Conquiste della serenissima republica di Venezia nella Morea sotto il comando del doge Francesco Morosini* ("Conquests of the Most Serene Republic of Venice in Morea under the Command of Doge Francesco Morosini"). The map bears this title because the floral border around the map contains roundels showing the forts of all of the cities in the Peloponnese that Venice had conquered.[8] Coronelli's map *Corso del Danubio da Vienna Sin à Nicopoli e paesi adiacenti* ("The Course of the Danube from Vienna to Nicopolis and Adjacent Countries"), made in about 1690, has an elaborate title cartouche in the lower left-hand corner in the form of a war trophy, that is, a battlefield monument composed of the captured arms of the enemy—in this case, Ottoman banners, armor, shields, cannons, and other weapons. And in the sea off the coast of Dalmatia there is a chronological list of the Venetian victories over the Turks in Dalmatia from 1683 to 1688.[9]

It is with this background and in this context that we must consider Coronelli's cartouche in his map of the Greek isles, titled *Paralello geografico dell'antico col moderno archipelago: per instruzione dell'Istoria dell'Isole contenute in esso* ("Geographical Parallel of the Ancient with the Modern Archipelago, for Instruction of the History of the Islands Contained in It"),[10] and included both in Coronelli's *Corso geografico universale* (Venice: the author, 1692), and his *Atlante Veneto* (Venice: Domenico Padouani, 1697). The map's title indicates that it is useful for comparing the ancient and modern circumstances of the Greek isles, and for teaching the history of the islands. And the map offers detailed notes about when each island was subject to Venice, and when it was under Ottoman control. For example, by the isle of Lemnos Coronelli writes:

"Stalimene, Lemnos de Veneti 1204, poi preso da Turchi, da Comin Corsaro 1464, da Ven. 1464, da Turchi 1573, da Ven. 1656, da Turchi 1657

Stalimene or Lemnos came under the power of the Venetians in 1204, then was taken by the Turks, by Comin Corsaro in 1464,[11] by the Venetians in 1464, by the Turks in 1573, by the Venetians in 1656, and by the Turks in 1657."

With regard to Euboea, Coronelli offers the comparison he alluded to in the map's title between the island's ancient

7 On Coronelli's *Memorie istoriografiche* see Armao, *Vincenzo Coronelli* (see note 6), no. 34, who found a total of fifteen editions and translations of the work; Navari, "Vincenzo Coronelli and the Iconography of the Venetian Conquest" (see note 6); Palmira Brummett, "'Turks' and 'Christians': The Iconography of Possession in the Depiction of the Ottoman-Venetian-Hapsburg Frontiers, 1550–1689," in Matthew Dimmock and Andrew Hadfield, eds., *The Religions of the Book: Christian Perceptions, 1400–1660* (Basingstoke, England, and New York: Palgrave Macmillan, 2008), pp. 110–139, at 127–132; Stouraiti, "Propaganda figurata" (see note 5), pp. 144–150; and Veronica della Dora, "Mapping 'Melancholy-Pleasing Remains': The Morea as a Renaissance Memory Theater," in Sharon E.J. Gerstel, ed., *Viewing the Morea: Land and People in the Late Medieval Peloponnese* (Washington, DC: Dumbarton Oaks Research Library and Collection, 2013), pp. 455–475. Coronelli's book was translated into English as *An Historical and Geographical Account of the Morea, Negropont, and the Maritime Places, as far as Thessalonica, Illustrated with 42 Maps of the Countries, Plains, and Draughts of the Cities, Towns and Fortifications* (London: Printed for Matth. Gillyflower ... and W. Canning ..., 1687).

8 Good images of Coronelli's map *Conquiste della serenissima republica di Venezia nella Morea* are available at https://gallica.bnf.fr and in vol. 2, p. 246, of the copy of Coronelli's *Corso Geografico Universale* (Venice, 1690) digitized in the Biblioteca Digital Hispánica at http://bdh.bne.es.

9 Good images of the two sheets of Coronelli's map *Corso del Danubio da Vienna Sin à Nicopoli e paesi* are available in vol. 2, pp. 331 and 333, of the copy of Coronelli's *Corso Geográfico Universale* (Venice, 1690) digitized in the Biblioteca Digital Hispánica at http://bdh.bne.es.

10 On Coronelli's map of the Greek archipelago see Ermanno Armao, "Le grandi carte geografiche di Vicenzo Coronelli," *Rivista geografica italiana* 57.3 (1950), pp. 158–180, at 170, no. 73; Palmira Brummett, *Mapping the Ottomans: Sovereignty, Territory, and Identity in the Early Modern Mediterranean* (New York: Cambridge University Press, 2015), pp. 15–18 and 230–232; and George Tolias and Leonora Navari, *Mapping Greece, 1420–1800: A History: Maps in the Margarita Samourkas Collection* (New Castle, DE: Oak Knoll Press; Houten, Netherlands: Hes & de Graaf Publishers, 2011), pp. 229 and 234.

11 It seems that Coronelli took the part about "Comin Corsaro" from one of the many editions of Luigi Contarini's *Il vago, e diletteuole giardino*; for example, in the 1590 edition titled *Aggiunta al vago, e diletteuole giardino del R. padre Luigi Contarini crucifero* (Vicenza: Per gli heredi di Perin libraro, 1590), the relevant passage is on f. 95v.

FIGURE 79   Cartouche on Vincenzo Coronelli's *Paralello geografico dell'antico col moderno arcipelago*, in Coronelli's *Corso geografico universale*
at the Biblioteca Nacional de España, GMM/128-GMM/129
COURTESY OF THE BIBLIOTECA NACIONAL DE ESPAÑA

and modern names, and also its recent political history. He writes:

"Negroponte Isola, e Regno, detto da Turchi Egribos, e dagli Antichi Euboea, Ettnia, Macra, Macris, Abantias, Chalois, Chalcadontis, Asopir, Ellopa, preso da Turchi a Veneti nel 1469.

The island and kingdom of Negroponte, which the Turks call Egribos, and which the ancients called Euboea, Ettnia, Macroa, Macris, Abantias, Calois, Chalcadontis, Asopir, and Ellopa, was taken from Venice by the Turks in 1469."

Taken together, Coronelli's notes on the map show that Venice's position in the Greek Isles was relatively weak, and in the cartouche the cartographer expresses not Venice's current strength in the islands, but rather a call for action and the result he hopes for as a Venetian propagandist.

The text of the cartouche (Fig. 79)[12] is presented as if written on the side of a building, and includes the title of the map, details about Coronelli and his post as Cosmographer of the Most Serene Republic of Venice, and the dedication to Giovanni Battista Donà (1627–99), then the *bailo* or Venetian ambassador to Constantinople.[13] At

the left, the winged lion of Venice breaks down the building and thrusts a large torch into it. At the right we see smoke billowing from the building, and three Turkish men (identifiable by their turbans), a noble woman, two children, and a dog flee the building, two of the men carrying goods with them, and the woman coughing from the smoke. In the background, faintly-rendered figures move more goods away from the danger. Coronelli's political message here is clear: he hopes that Venice will succeed in its efforts to push the Ottomans out of the Greek isles; the prominence of the word *ARCIPELAGO* on the edifice is probably to be seen as suggesting that the building stands for the archipelago. And the geography of Coronelli's wish is clear: the Venetian lion, coming from the west, forces the Turks to the east.

The cartouche with its aggressive Venetian lion visually dominates the map and makes the partisan nature of the document obvious. Coronelli made another map of Greece in 1687 without a propagandistic cartouche,[14]

---

12   Coronelli's cartouche on his map of Greece is discussed by Brummett, *Mapping the Ottomans* (see note 10), pp. 230–232.

13   Donà authored a book about Turkish literature, Giovanni Battista Donà, *Della letteratura de' Turchi* (Venice: Andrea

Poletti, 1688), and also a translation of various Turkish proverbs into Italian and Latin, *Raccolta curiosissima d'adaggi turcheschi trasportati dal proprio idioma nell'italiano, e latino dalli giovani di lingua sotto il bailaggio in Costantinopoli dell'illustriss. & Eccell. Sig. Gio. Battista Donado* (Venice: Andrea Poletti, 1688).

14   Coronelli's map of Greece without a propaganda cartouche is *La Grecia descritta dal P.M. Coronelli Cosmografo della Serenissima Republica di Venezia* (Venice, 1687). Good images of the map are available at https://gallica.bnf.fr and in vol. 2, p. 234, of the copy of Coronelli's *Corso Geografico Universale* (Venice, 1690) digitized in the Biblioteca Digital Hispánica at http://bdh.bne.es.

illustrating the fact that cartographers make different maps for different purposes and for different audiences.

Other European maps with cartouches that point towards a Venetian triumph over the Turks in the Greek Isles include Frederick De Wit, *Peloponnesus hodie Moreae Regnum distincte divisum in omnes suas provincias* (Amsterdam, *c.*1680), with a particularly dramatic cartouche;[15] Justus Danckerts, *Peloponnesus hodie Moreae regnum distincté divisum in omnes suas provincias* (Amsterdam, 1688);[16] Nicolas de Fer's *Peloponèse aujourd'hui la Morée et les Isles de Zante, Cefalonie, Sainte-Maure, Cerigo* (Paris: chez N. De Fer, 1688);[17] Jean-Baptiste Nolin's *La Grèce Ancienne et Moderne dédiée à son Altesse Royale Monseigneur le Duc de Bourgogne* (1699);[18] and Matthäus Seutter,

Peloponnesus hodie Morea (Augsburg: Matthäus Seutter, *c.*1727).[19] Meanwhile, Guillaume Delisle's *Carte de la Grece* (Paris, 1707) shows a Turkish man placing a yoke on the neck of a European woman,[20] and there is a more elaborate such scene in John Senex, *A Map of Greece with Part of Anatolia* (London: D. Browne, 1721).[21]

My purpose in listing other cartouches that depict the conflict between the Ottoman Empire and Europe is not only to show the broader context of Coronelli's cartouche, but also to suggest a future direction for cartouche studies: examining cartouches made by different cartographers on maps of the same region at different moments in history can be very revealing of the evolution of attitudes about and artistic reactions to events in politics, economics, and natural history.

---

15   High-resolution images of De Wit's map of the Peloponnese are available at https://loc.gov and https://www.digitalcommon wealth.org/search. On this map see George Carhart, *Frederick de Wit and the First Concise Reference Atlas* (Leiden and Boston: Brill and Hes & De Graaf, 2016), pp. 350–351, no. 100. The standard reference on maps of Greece is Christos G. Zacharakis, *A Catalogue of Printed Maps of Greece: 1477–1800* (Athens: S. Ioannou Foundation, 2009).

16   A good image of Danckert's map of the Peloponnese with a hand-colored cartouche is available from the Biblioteca comunale di Trento at https://commons.wikimedia.org.

17   High-resolution images of the 1705 printing of Nicolas de Fer's map of the Peloponnese are available at https://catalog.prince ton.edu and https://searchworks.stanford.edu.

18   A high-resolution image of Nolin's map of Greece is available from the Royal Danish Library at http://www.kb.dk.

19   A high-resolution image of Seutter's map of Greece is available at https://searchworks.stanford.edu. Stella Chrysochoou kindly points out to me that the shining cross in Seutter's cartouche celebrates the Venetian taking of the castle of Monemvasia in 1690, by which act all of the Peloponnese came back under Christian control.

20   A high-resolution image of Delisle's map of Greece is available at https://searchworks.stanford.edu.

21   A high-resolution image of Senex's map of Greece is available at https://searchworks.stanford.edu.

If It Bleeds, It Leads

David Funck, Infelicis regni Siciliae tabula, *c.1693*

In addition to their other roles, cartouches could be used to illustrate and record important current events, functioning in these cases like broadsides or newsreels. This role is played by a map of Sicily made in 1693 by the Nuremberg cartographer David Funck, and engraved by Johann Baptist Homann, titled *Infelicis Regni Siciliae Tabula in tres Valles divisa Demonae, Notae et Mazarae,* "A Map of the Unfortunate Kingdom of Sicily, Divided into Three Administrative Divisions, namely Demona, Noto, and Mazara."[1] Funck called the island—which at the time was a viceroyalty of Spain—unfortunate because on January 9 and 11 of 1693 it had suffered earthquakes and a tsunami; the earthquakes destroyed more than 70 towns and cities, particularly in the eastern part of the island, and killed about 54,000 people. This remains the most powerful (though not the most deadly) earthquake in the history of Italy, estimated at 7.4 on the moment magnitude scale, with its epicenter on the southeastern coast of the island near Syracuse.

In the lower right corner of the map Funck supplies a list of the cities destroyed by the earthquake, and he precedes and follows the list with this text:[2]

"Ruinae Urbium, Oppidorum et Pagorum, Quae Anno 1693. die 9. 10 et 11 Ianuarij in Regno Siciliae horribili Terrae Motu lapsae cum centum millibus hominum corruerunt .... Quatuordecim Urbes & Oppida ex his, sicut et octodecim diversa Praedia hic non nominata, terrae hiatu perierunt, nullo etiam vestigio remanente.

The ruins of cities, fortified cities, and villages which on the 9th, 10th, and 11th of January in the year 1693 in the kingdom of Sicily, hit by a dreadful earthquake, collapsed with over a hundred thousand men .... Fourteen of these cities and fortified cities, as well as eighteen different large estates not listed here, were lost into the gaping earth, without even a trace remaining."

The cities and towns swallowed by the earth are represented visually in the cartouche in the upper left-hand corner of the map (Fig. 80). Above the dramatically tilted rock on which the map's title and author information are inscribed, three women show their alarm at the calamity, two raising their hands, and the third pointing to an erupting volcano, certainly Mount Etna, in the distance. The woman on the left wears a crown but has dropped her scepter, and symbols of the Kingdom of Sicily lie at her feet. She personifies Sicily, and her dropping of her regal symbols indicates her shock at the severity of the disaster. The two women on the right wear mural crowns, identifying them as personifications of cities,[3] probably Catania and Syracuse, which were largely destroyed by the earthquake. The image of the volcano erupting is interesting: there is no geophysical evidence for lava flow during the earthquake, but contemporary accounts of the disaster do claim that Etna was erupting.[4] Below, five winged *putti*

---

1 On Funck's map of Sicily see Peter H. Meurer and Klaus Stopp, *Topographica des Nürnberger Verlages David Funck* (Alphen aan den Rijn: Canaletto, 2006), no. I.12A, who note that the plate for this map was recut in 1700 and the map was issued with a new title (*Regnorvm Siciliae et Sardiniae aova & accurata tabula*) and a different cartouche; Stefano Condorelli, "Le tremblement de terre de Sicile de 1693 et l'Europe: diffusion des nouvelles et retentissement," *Dimensioni e Problemi della Ricerca Storica,* 2013, Issue 2, pp. 139–169, at 154; and Antonio La Gumina, *Sikelia = Sicilia: l'isola a tre punte: repertorio cartografico della Sicilia* (Palermo: Ducezio edizioni, 2015), vol. 1, pp. 276–277, no. 109. For discussion of Funck's map in the context of cartouches on other maps of Sicily see Maria Ida Gulletta, "Mito e storia negli apparati decorativi della cartografia siciliana," in Vladimiro Valerio and Santo Spagnolo, eds., *Sicilia 1477–1861: La collezione Spagnolo-Patermo in quattro secoli di cartografia* (Naples: Paparo edizioni, 2013), pp. 29–36 and 83, at 30–31; and her article "Un caso di comunicazione non verbale nelle mappe antiche: la Sicilia 'rappresentata' = Nonverbal Communication in Ancient Maps: Portrait of Sicily (vel Sicily Portrayed)," *Bollettino dell'Associazione Italiana di Cartografia,* supplemento, 143 (2011), pp. 73–87, esp. 82 and 84. On the history of cartographic representations of Sicily see Paolo Militello, *L'isola delle carte: cartografia della Sicilia in età moderna* (Milan: F. Angeli, 2004).

2 The list of cities destroyed by the earthquake re-appears in a map of Sicily and Sardinia by Johann Baptist Homann titled *Regnorvm*

Siciliae et Sardiniae nova & accurata Tabula proposita (Nuremberg, c.1701–15).

3 On the mural crown as an attribute of personification cities see Fernand Allègre, *Étude sur la déesse grecque Tyché, sa signification religieuse et morale, son culte et ses représentations figurées* (Paris: Leroux, 1889), pp. 187–192; also see Dieter Metzler, "Mural Crowns in the Ancient Near East and Greece," in Susan B. Matheson, ed., *An Obsession with Fortune: Tyche in Greek and Roman Art* (New Haven: Yale University Art Gallery, 1994), pp. 76–85.

4 For assertions that Etna was erupting in 1693 see for example *An Account of the Late Terrible Earthquake in Sicily: with Most of its Particulars: Done from the Italian Copy Printed at Rome*

FIGURE 80   The cartouche from David Funck's *Infelicis Regni Siciliae Tabula in tres Valles divisa Demonae, Notae et Mazarae* (Nuremberg, 1693)
MUNICH, BAYERISCHE STAATSBIBLIOTHEK, 2 MAPP. 12#68. BY PERMISSION OF THE BAYERISCHE STAATSBIBLIOTHEK

also show their alarm and dismay as three large buildings, one domed, the second an obelisk, the third crenellated, are swallowed by the earth in front of them.[5]

The swallowing up of buildings is something mentioned frequently in the many accounts of the earthquake that circulated in Europe following the catastrophe.[6] The whole city of Catania was said to have been swallowed by the earth:[7]

"There happn'd some Fisher-boats to be at that time in the Bay that lyes south of the Town, and within a Leagues distance, who gave an Account, That they saw the City sink down with the noise as it were of some Thousand Pieces of Great Ordnance discharged all at once. After it was thus vanished out of their sight, the Fishermen say, That some Minutes thereafter, to the Eastward, near where the City stood, their rose up a little Mountain, which lifting itself

(London: Printed for Richard Baldwin, near the Oxford-Arms in Warwick-Lane, 1693), pp. 11 and 13. For scientific discussion of the earthquake see M.A. Gutscher, J. Roger, M.A. Baptista, J.M. Miranda, and S. Tinti, "Source of the 1693 Catania Earthquake and Tsunami (Southern Italy): New Evidence from Tsunami Modeling of a Locked Subduction Fault Plane," *Geophysical Research Letters* 33 (2006); and Stefano Branca, Raffaele Azzaro, Emanuela De Beni, David Chester, and Angus Duncan, "Impacts of the 1669 Eruption and the 1693 Earthquakes on the Etna Region (Eastern Sicily, Italy): An Example of Recovery and Response of a Small Area to Extreme Events," *Journal of Volcanology and Geothermal Research* 303 (2015), pp. 25–40.

5   It is at least possible that the domed structure is intended to represent the cathedral of Noto. For discussion of the collapse of the cathedral in the earthquake and its reconstruction see Stephen Tobriner, "Building the Cathedral of Noto: Earthquakes, Reconstruction and Building Practice in 18th-Century Sicily," *Construction and Building Materials* 17.8 (2003), pp. 521–532.

6   On accounts of the 1693 earthquake see Fernando Rodríguez de la Torre, "Spanish Sources Concerning the 1693 Earthquake in Sicily,"

Annali di geofisica 38.5 (1995), pp. 523–539; and Stefano Condorelli, "Le tremblement de terre de Sicile de 1693 et l'Europe: diffusion des nouvelles et retentissement," *Dimensioni e Problemi della Ricerca Storica*, 2013, Issue 2, pp. 139–169. An account by Alessandro Burgos, Bishop of Catania, was frequently reprinted and translated, including in the *Philosophical Transactions of the Royal Society* 17 (1693), pp. 830–838; an account by the Italian mathematician Domenico Guglielmini (1655–1710) has been edited by Ivan Nicosia as *La Catania destrutta di Domenico Guglielmini* (Barrafranca: Bonfirraro, 2018).

7   *An Account of the Late Terrible Earthquake in Sicily: with Most of its Particulars: Done from the Italian Copy Printed at Rome* (London: Printed for Richard Baldwin, near the Oxford-Arms in Warwick-Lane, 1693), p. 12.

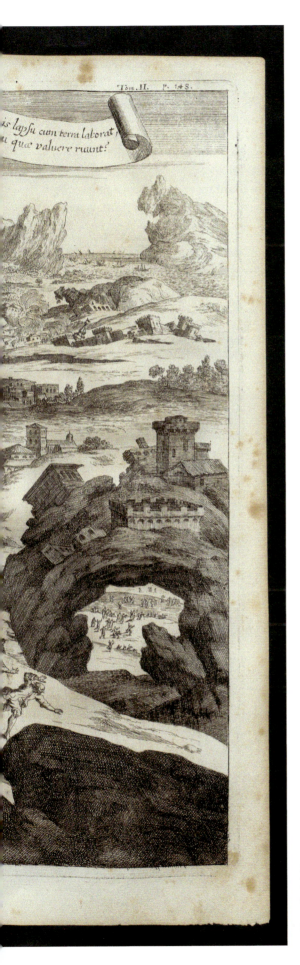

FIGURE 81

Image of the destruction caused by the 1693 Sicily earthquake in Johann Zahn, *Specula physico-mathematico-historica notabilium ac mirabilium sciendorum* (Nuremberg: Johann Christopher Lochner, 1696), vol. 2, Disquisitio 1, Chapter 13, following p. 148

up several times a considerable height, above the ground thereabout, sunk at last likewise out of their sight."

And in Ragusa, an inland city in southern Sicily:[8]

"One Street, the biggest of the Town, and Inhabited by the best Merchants and Tradesmen of the Place, was overwhelm'd in less than the Second of a Minute, the Earth sinking down, and leaving a vast Casma where the Street was. One of the Churches sunk after the manner the Street had done, but the other fell down."

There are few contemporary images of the earthquake's destruction,[9] which makes the cartouche on Funck's map

that much more important. One other representation of the destruction appears in Johann Zahn's collection of natural and historical marvels titled *Specula physico-mathematico-historica notabilium ac mirabilium sciendorum* (Nuremberg: Johann Christopher Lochner, 1696). In addition to a volcanic eruption, collapsed buildings, and people fleeing, Zahn depicts a long row of buildings that have sunk halfway into a large chasm, from which smoke rises in several spots (Fig. 81). So the image that Funck designed to illustrate the earthquake reflects both textual descriptions and contemporary iconography of the tragedy.

---

8 *An Account of the Late Terrible Earthquake in Sicily* (see note 7), p. 27.

9 Condorelli, "Le tremblement de terre de Sicile de 1693" (see note 6), p. 154. Another contemporary image of the eruption and the damage it caused in Catania (in addition to the one discussed and reproduced here) appeared in a news sheet titled *Das erschütterte Sicilien* printed in Germany in 1693, which is available online and is

reproduced in Paolo Militello, "'Un monumento di gloria della nostra Catania': Il monastero benedettino di San Nicolò l'Arena tra XVI e XIX secolo," in Francesco Mannino, ed., *Guida del monastero dei Benedettini di Catania* (Catania: Maimone Editore, 2015), pp. 35–43, at 37.

Celebrating a Triumph of Engineering

Jean-Baptiste Nolin, Le canal royal de Languedoc, *1697*

This beautiful map (Fig. 82) by the French cartographer Jean-Baptiste Nolin (*c.*1657–1708)[1] celebrates one of the most ambitious engineering projects of the seventeenth century in Europe, the Canal royal en Languedoc (Royal Canal in Languedoc). By means of this canal a ship could travel 150 miles (240 km) from Sète on the Mediterranean coast of France inland to Toulouse, which is on the Garonne River, and then down the Garonne to the Atlantic—without having to sail around the Iberian Peninsula. Initially the canal served to transport wine, wheat, and textiles. The entrepreneur Pierre-Paul Riquet (1609–1680) promoted, planed, and financed part of the construction of the canal, initially with the support of Louis XIV. The creation of the canal took fifteen years, from 1667 to 1681, and involved the construction of a multitude of locks and of a subsidiary canal from Montagne Noire to supply water to the main canal at its highest point, the watershed whence water drained either toward the Atlantic or toward Mediterranean. It was a triumph of French hydrological engineering. During the French Revolution in 1789 the canal was renamed the *Canal du Midi* ("Canal of Southern France") to remove the reference to royal patronage.[2]

The extravagant program of cartouches on Nolin's map is every bit up to the task of commemorating this extraordinary canal.[3] Around the edge of the map there are 53 diagrams and plans of the locks, aqueducts, and basins that form the canal, together with maps of its entrances on the Atlantic and the Mediterranean, and a map showing the whole route between the two bodies of water. Each of these is a cartouche, and some of these maps have title cartouches or descriptive cartouches, which are thus cartouches within cartouches.[4]

The title cartouche of the main map is a marvel of both size and elaboration, and rewards a detailed discussion (Fig. 83). The title reads *Le canal royal de Languedoc, pour la Ionction de l'ocean et de la mer Mediterranée, dedié et presenté à Mgrs. des Estats de Languedoc,* or "The Royal Canal of Languedoc, for the Joining of the Atlantic and the Mediterranean, Dedicated and Presented to their Lords of the Estates of Languedoc." The *États de Languedoc* were a provincial assembly that sat in judgment on royal taxes and organized their collection, who had been instrumental in the construction of the canal. Below the title we see one marine deity handing ships to another: this is Neptune (or a personification of the Atlantic) passing the ships to a personification of the Mediterranean, indicating the canal's function.

The strapwork tendrils that stretch left and right from the title frame across the top of the map bear (like fruit) the coats of arms of the numerous local nobles and members of the États de Languedoc who had supported the construction of the canal, each identified by name in a banner above or below. Most of these banners simply indicate the name of the noble, his titles, and his territory, but one of them, just to the right of center, indicates a more substantial role in the construction of the canal: *Mr. Nicolas de Lamoignon Sr. de Baville Conseiller d'Estat, Intendant de la Province de Languedoc, sous qui le Canal a esté achevé et mis en sa perfection* ("Monsieur Nicolas de Lamoignon, Seigneur de Baville, Counsilor of the State, and Intendant of the Province of Languedoc, under whom the canal was completed and brought to its perfection"). An Intendant served as the agent of the king in each of the

---

1   On Nolin see Numa Broc, "Une affaire de plagiat cartographique sous Louis XIV: le procès Delisle-Nolin," *Revue d'histoire des sciences et de leurs applications* 23 (1970), pp. 141–153.

2   On the history of the canal's construction see André Maistre, *Le Canal des deux mers, canal royal du Languedoc, 1666–1810* (Toulouse: E. Privat, 1968); Jeanne Hugon de Scoeux, *Le chemin qui marche: Pierre-Paul Riquet, créateur du Canal royal du Languedoc* (Portet-sur-Garonne: Loubatières, 1994); Chandra Mukerji, "Cartography, Entrepreneurialism, and Power in the Reign of Louis XIV: The Case of the Canal du Midi," in Pamela H. Smith and Paula Findlen, eds., *Merchants & Marvels: Commerce, Science, and Art in Early Modern Europe* (New York: Routledge, 2002), pp. 248–276; and Michael S. Mahoney, "Organizing Expertise: Engineering and Public Works under Jean-Baptiste Colbert, 1662–83," *Osiris* 25.1 (2010), pp. 149–170.

3   In the Introduction we saw that Nolin was connected with an elaborate cartouche through his publication of Vincenzo Coronelli's map of England, *Le royaume d'Angleterre divisé en plusieurs parties* (Paris: I.B. Nolin, 1689).

4   The maps with title cartouches or descriptive cartouches are, above, *Le Magazin ou Reservoir des Eaux de S. Farriol* and the *Carte de la riviere de Beziers, ou de l'Ore*; and below, (of the Bassin de Naurouze) *Ce Bassin a 200 Toises de Longeur sur 150 de Largeur, revêtu de Pierre de Taille,* the *Carte particuliere de l'entree de la Garonne,* the *Carte de la communication de l'Ocean et de la Mediteranee par le canal royal de Languedoc,* and *Le Port de Cette par ou le Canal Royal communique avec la Mer Mediterranée.*

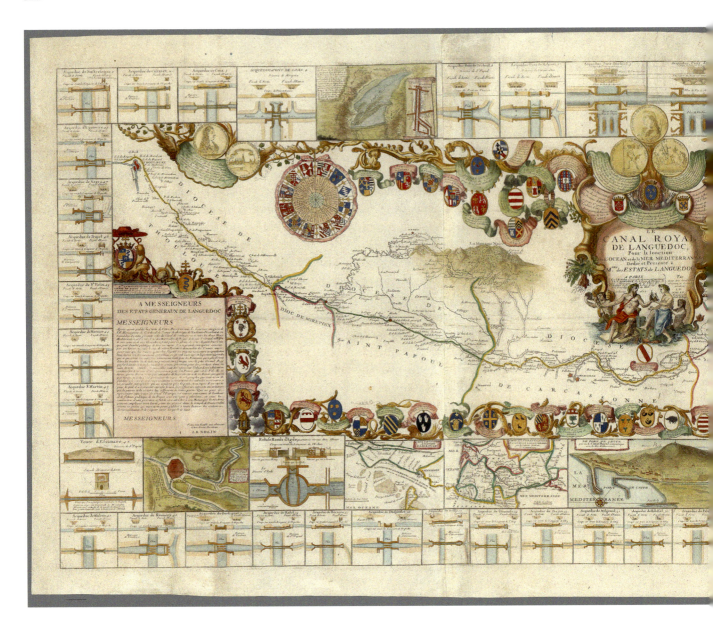

French provinces, and Nicolas de Lamoignon (1648–1724) held this role from 1685 to 1718.[5]

Of course it is the more important nobles who have their coats of arms near the center of this grand design. The central coat of arms is that of Louis-Auguste de Bourbon, duc du Maine (1670–1736), the illegitimate but favorite son of Louis XIV, who, as the banner below says, was Lieutenant General for the King in the province of Languedoc—but he took this role in 1682, after the canal had been completed.[6] To the left are the arms of the province of Languedoc itself (Fig. 84), through which the canal

flows, and to the right (Fig. 85), the arms of Victor-Maurice, comte de Broglie (1647–1727), who had been named Commandant of Languedoc in 1688, well after the canal's construction had been completed in 1681. His purely honorific place on the map is perhaps reflected in the fact that his name is erroneously indicated as "Victor Armand."

Above these coats of arms are images of two medals struck in 1677 and 1681, when the construction of the canal was about two thirds complete, to commemorate the joining of the Atlantic to the Mediterranean. The medal to the left shows Neptune using his trident to break the ground that separates two bodies of water, and the text above reads *Novum Decus Additur Orbi*, "A new ornament has been added to the world," and below *Maria Juncta, MDCLXVII*, "The seas have been joined, 1677." On the medal to the right, under the words *Iuncta Maria* ("The seas have been joined") there is a scene very similar to

---

5 On Nicolas de Lamoignon see Robert Poujol, *Basville, roi solitaire du Languedoc: intendant à Montpellier de 1685 à 1718* (Montpellier: Presses du Languedoc, 1992).

6 On Louis-Auguste de Bourbon see W.H. Lewis, *The Sunset of the Splendid Century: The Life and Times of Louis Auguste de Bourbon, duc du Maine, 1670–1736* (New York: W. Sloan Associates, 1955).

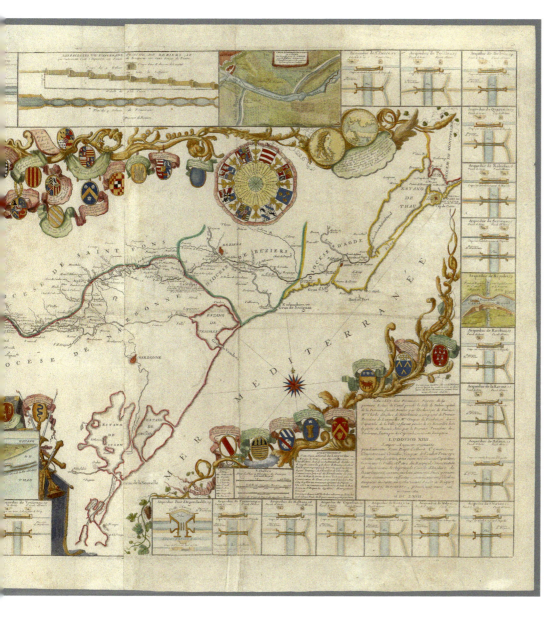

that in the lower part of the cartouche: one aquatic deity hands a ship to another, and below the text says that a canal was constructed from the Garonne to Mount Setium (now Mont Saint-Clair) in 1681.[7]

Beneath the medals are texts about the laying of the first stone of the canal on July 29, 1666, and the completion of the canal on May 15, 1681. Above the images of the two medals commemorating the completion of the canal,

at the very top of this elaborate cartouche, is an image depicting Louis XIV himself, copied from the obverse of the medal on the left just below.[8]

Out on the left and right branches of the cartouche are roundels that bring together several coats of arms in one unit. On the left there are the twelve coats of arms of the barons of the Vivarais in the Languedoc, while on the right there are the eight coats of arms of the barons of the Gévaudan, another region in the Languedoc. Towards the center of these two circles are indications of the year that each of the barons was a member of the États du Languedoc. The circular grouping of these coats of arms enables the cartographer to save space.

---

7   On the two medals see Claude-François Menestrier, *Histoire du roy Louis le Grand par les medailles, emblêmes, deuises, jettons, inscriptions, armoiries, et autres monumens publics* (Paris: chez I.B. Nolin graveur du Roy sur le Quay de l'Horloge du Palais, 1691), p. 15 and plate 15, and p. 26 and plate 26. Note that Nolin was the engraver of the plates in this book, so knew the medals well. Also see *Catalogue des poinçons, coins et médailles du Musée monétaire de la commission des monnaies et médailles* (Paris: A. Pihan de La Forest, 1833), p. 79, no. 146; and p. 183, no. 437.

---

8   See the second medal in Menestrier, *Histoire du roy Louis le Grand par les medailles* (see note 7), plate 15.

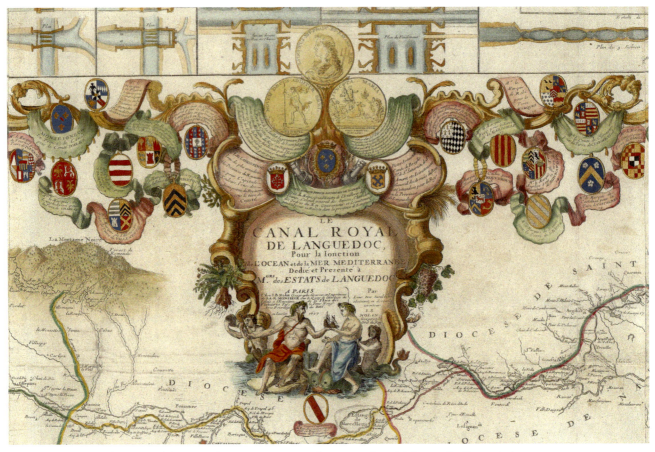

FIGURE 83   Detail of the center of the cartouche on Jean-Baptiste Nolin's *Le canal royal de Languedoc* (Paris, 1697)
COURTESY OF THE DAVID RUMSEY MAP COLLECTION

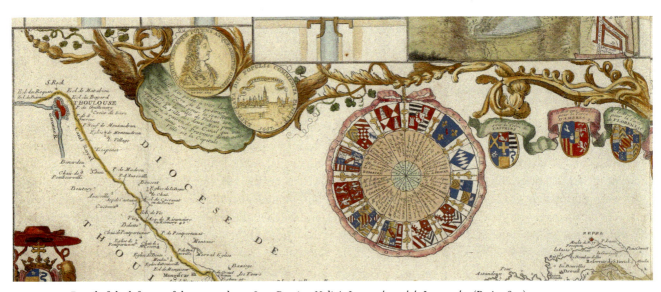

FIGURE 84   Detail of the left part of the cartouche on Jean-Baptiste Nolin's *Le canal royal de Languedoc* (Paris, 1697)
COURTESY OF THE DAVID RUMSEY MAP COLLECTION

At the far left of the title cartouche there are images of the obverse and reverse of a medal minted to commemorate the laying of the first stone of the canal, with a portrait of Louis XIV and an image of Toulouse, beneath a motto saying that the canal will make possible for the people the commerce they have long been awaiting.[9] Below these images is text about the minting of the medal which says that Toulouse is known as the "City of the Two Seas"

_____

9   See the third medal in Menestrier (see note 7), plate 15.

FIGURE 85   Detail of the right part of the cartouche on Jean-Baptiste Nolin's *Le canal royal de Languedoc* (Paris, 1697)
COURTESY OF THE DAVID RUMSEY MAP COLLECTION

because of the canal. And at the far right of the title cartouche is another medal with a portrait of Louis XIV and an image of the port at Sète; the text below explains that the first stone of the port was laid on July 29, 1666, and that the medal was struck to be a monument for posterity of the great project undertaken by Louis XIV.[10]

There are two other strings of coats of arms in the lower left-hand and right-hand corners of the map, which qualify as part of cartouche decoration because they are adjacent to framed text blocks. In the text block in the lower left Nolin gives an extended dedication of the map to the États de Languedoc, mentioning an earlier map he had made of the province of Languedoc that was dedicated to the Cardinal Pierre de Bonzi,[11] whose arms appear just above this text. He goes on to say that Louis's accomplishment in constructing the canal exceeds the accomplishments of the Romans:[12]

"Vous l'avez vu hereusement consommé ce grand ouvrage et la posterité apprendra que ce qui avoit été autrefois vainement tenté par les Romains, qui se glorifioient dêtre les maitres deu Monde, ne pouvoit être que sous le plus Grand Roy qui fut Iamais, et dont les moindres actions passeront pour des prodiges dans la suite de tous les siecles.

You have seen him successfully complete this great work, and posterity will learn that what had once been vainly attempted by the Romans, who boasted of being masters of the world, could only be accomplished under the greatest king who ever lived, whose smallest actions will pass for wonders in the following centuries."

All of the coats of arms associated with this text block, and which spill down from those of Pierre de Bonzi, are of bishops, and Nolin has arranged the coats of arms on the map according to the traditional "three estates" of French society: those of the nobles above, those of the clergy in the lower left, and those of commoners in the lower right.

In the lower right-hand part of the map Nolin placed a text about the laying of the first stone of the first lock of the canal near Toulouse, and transcribes the Latin inscription carved onto one of those stones. In a smaller text

---

10   See the first medal in Menestrier (see note 7), plate 15. The prominence of the canal project in French scientific culture of the time may be seen in a painting in Versailles by Henri Testelin titled *Etablissement de l'Academie des Sciences et fondation de l'Observatoire, 1666*, showing an imagined scene of Louis XIV presiding over the establishment of the French Academy of Science, where he is being shown a huge manuscript map of the canal. Evidently this map no longer exists. The painting is mentioned by Eudore Soulié, *Notice des peintures et sculptures composant le Musée Impérial de Versailles* (Versailles: Montalant-Bougleux, 1854–1855), vol. 2, p. 115, no. 1991.

11   Nolin's earlier map was Jean Baptiste Nolin, *Le gouvernement general de Languedoc divisé en trois Lieutenances generales* (Paris: I.B. Nolin, 1695).

---

12   On the idea that France under Louis XIV was the New Rome see Chandra Mukerji, "The New Rome: Infrastructure and National Identity on the Canal du Midi," *Osiris* 24.1 (2009), pp. 15–32.

block to the left he describes the earliest steps taken to set the construction of the canal in motion, including Paul Riquet's first proposal of the plan and the surveying of the route. The coats of arms attached to the tendrils that run along the upper edges of these cartouches are of civil officials such as mayors who assisted with the construction of the canal. Despite their lower status as members of the Third Estate, they were of great importance in the practical business of making the canal.

On Nolin's map the title cartouche that stretches most of the length of the map is certainly one of the longest of its century; taken together, the various cartouches occupy more than half the map's surface, and effectively place the cartographic depiction of the canal in the background. It is the cartouches that bring the map's commemorative

function to life, its celebration of the canal as a technical marvel and as a triumph of French science. It also celebrates the États de Languedoc who had been so instrumental in the canal's construction—and the status of the Languedoc as one of the *pays d'états* in France, which retained some independence in matters of taxation, versus the *pays de grande gabelle*, which were administered directly by the king.[13]

---

13   Nicolas de Fer in making his 1712 map of the canal relied heavily on Nolin's design: see his map *Le Gouvernement General de Languedoc* (Paris: Edme Mentelle and Malte Brun, chez Benard, 1712). A high-resolution image of the map is available at https://searchworks.stanford.edu.

CHAPTER 16

The Battle between Light and Darkness

Heinrich Scherer, Repraesentatio totius Africae, *1703*

We have seen that cartouches often reveal the cartographer's interests, wishes, and prejudices; in some cases these desires are merely hinted at, or are encoded in abstruse symbolism, while in others they are explicit. The latter is certainly the case in the cartouches on the maps of the devout German Jesuit Heinrich Scherer (1628–1704).[1] Scherer's maps stand out from the predominantly secular cartography of his day: many of his maps are about religion, decorated with elaborate Christian iconography, and devoted to showing the viewer the geography of Christianity, where his faith predominates or has recently been spread by Jesuit missionaries, and where heathenism still prevails. It is sometimes said that Scherer's maps are among the earliest thematic maps, that is, maps that concentrate "on showing the geographical occurrence and variation of a single phenomenon, or at most a very few,"[2] in the case of Scherer's maps, the geography of religion. In fact thematic mapping goes back well before the eighteenth century,[3] but Scherer was nonetheless an enthusiastic and important practitioner of the genre.

Scherer applied himself to cartography while he was working as a tutor to the princes of Bavaria, and in 1702 published his *Atlas novus exhibens orbem terraqueum per naturae opera, historiae novae ac veteris monumenta* ("New Atlas Showing the Whole Earth through the Works of Nature and Monuments of Ancient and Modern History") (Dillingen and Frankfurt: Bencard, 1702).[4] The atlas, which was reprinted a few times, was published in seven volumes which are usually cataloged separately. I will focus on a map of Africa in the volume of his atlas titled *Geographia hierarchica, sive, Status ecclesiastici Romanocatholici per orbem universum distributi succincta descriptio historico-geographica* ("Geography of Religious Power, or a Succinct Historical-Geographical Description of the State of the Roman Catholic Church as it is Distributed Across the Whole World") (Munich: Typis Mariae Magdalenae Rauchin, viduae, 1703).

The title of the map of Africa in question is *Repraesentatio totius Africae: cuius partes, quibus fides Catholica illuxit, umbra carent: reliquae omnes meris tenebris et umbra mortis involutae* ("Representation of the Whole of Africa: The Parts that the Christian Faith Shines Upon are Without Shadow, but the Rest are Enveloped in Complete Darkness and the Shadow of Death") (Fig. 86). And the map clearly shows Scherer's system of thematic cartography, of distinguishing between the Christian and non-Christian regions:[5] only four small parts of the continent are unshaded, namely the area around the Spanish enclaves of Ceuta and Melilla in northwestern Africa, Congo and Angola on the west coast, Amara (i.e. Amhara) between the Nile and Melinde, and a group of Portuguese settlements on the east coast that Scherer labels Zanguebar, i.e. Zanzibar.[6]

---

1 On Scherer see Christian Sandler, "Ein bayerischer Jesuitengeograph," *Mitteilungen der Geographischen Gesellschaft in München* 2.1 (1906), pp. 1–39; Adolf Layer, "Ein bedeutender Barockgeograph: P. Heinrich Scherer SJ (1628–1704)," *Jahrbuch des Historischen Vereins Dillingen an der Donau / Historischer Verein* 86 (1984), pp. 145–148; Franz Wawrik, *Berühmte Atlanten: kartographische Kunst aus fünf Jahrhunderten* (Dortmund: Harenberg, 1982), pp. 172–175; John Greene, "Maps with a Message: Categorizing the Works of Heinrich Scherer," *The Portolan* 52 (2002), pp. 34–44; and Hanspeter Fischer, "Eine mitteleuropäische Jesuitenkarte Heinrich Scherers (1628–1704) von 1703," *Jahrbuch / Verein für Augsburger Bistumsgeschichte e.V. Lindenberg* 47 (2013), pp. 313–323.

2 Arthur Howard Robinson, *Early Thematic Mapping in the History of Cartography* (Chicago: University of Chicago Press, 1982), p. 16.

3 See Chet Van Duzer and Ilya Dines, *Apocalyptic Cartography: Thematic Maps and the End of the World in a Fifteenth-Century Manuscript* (Leiden: Brill, 2016), pp. 80–93.

4 The atlas is described in Philip Lee Phillips, *A List of Geographical Atlases in the Library of Congress: with Bibliographical Notes*

(Washington: Government Printing Office, 1909–1992), vol. 3, pp. 243–246 and 259. Scherer describes his plan for the whole atlas (*totius operis geographici idea*) in part of the preface to vol. 4 of the atlas, titled *Geographia politica, sive historia geographica.*

5 Scherer explains his system of using light and shadow to distinguish between Christian and non-Christian regions in his *Geographia hierarchica*, p. 36. On the history of the identification of Africa as the "Dark Continent" see Lucy Jarosz, "Constructing the Dark Continent: Metaphor as Geographic Representation of Africa," *Geografiska Annaler*, Series B, *Human Geography* 74.2 (1992), pp. 105–115. As Adam Hochschild has written, the phrase "the Dark Continent" "says more about the seer than the seen": see *King Leopold's Ghost: A Story of Greed, Terror, and Heroism in Colonial Africa* (New York: Houghton Mifflin, 1998), p. 18. Another much later map that uses the same system of identifying the "heathen" regions of part of Africa as black is N. Landmark, *Missionskart over Madagaskar i Maalestok 1:1,826,000 samt overført paa samme Plade og efter samme Maalestok Zululand og Natal 1892* (Oslo, 1892).

6 Following an interesting passage in his *Geographia hierarchica* in which he explains the value of visual documents, in this case maps,

---

FIGURE 86
Detail of the title cartouche in Heinrich
Scherer, *Repraesentatio totius Africae*, c.1703
COURTESY OF ALEXANDRE ANTIQUE
PRINTS, MAPS, AND BOOKS, TORONTO

One of the reasons that I chose to discuss this cartouche is that it involves the same imagery and valences of light and

in clarifying things (p. 35), Scherer supplements the map with a textual description of the religion that prevails in every part of Africa, pp. 37–50. For his accounts of the parts that he marks as Christian on the map see p. 41 on Angola; p. 42 on Melilla, Oran, Pennon, and Ceuta; p. 40 on Amara / Amhara; pp. 42–43 on the Congo; and pp. 46–48 on Zanguebar. In this passage on Amhara, Scherer—strangely—does not mention the Christians there, but he does in vol. 6 of his *Atlas novus*, titled *Tabellae Geographicae: hoc est, regionum, provinciarum locorumque memorabilium in orbe ter-rarum succincta dispositio et ordo politico-geographicus* (Munich: Typis Mariae Magdalenae Rauchin, viduae, 1703), p. 259.

darkness that Scherer deploys elsewhere in this map and in other maps. As we just saw, the cartographer also mentions this system for indicating moral value in the title of the map, and he does the same in other maps in which he employs this system. The cartouche at the left-hand side is defined as such by the frame around the map's title, and its decoration continues below. Immediately beneath the frame is a cherub holding a banner with a quotation from Luke 1:79, "To give light to them that sit in darkness and in the shadow of death." Behind the cherub there is a thick pall of clouds that cast darkness on the tree below, and in the even deeper shadow of the tree, five Africans sit on the ground. The diversity of their clothing and head-wear indicates that they are from different tribes, and thus implicitly are representative of the many different native peoples of Africa.

Behind the tree stands Death personified as a skeleton,[7] and he swings not his traditional scythe, but rather an axe, with which he is chopping down the tree so that it will fall on the men. There is a rich iconographic tradition of Death chopping down trees;[8] usually in doing so Death demonstrates the precarious position of people up in the tree, but there is a branch (so to speak) of this tradition in which the danger is to people below the tree. These images seem to have their origin in a print by Hieronymus Wierix from the first quarter of the sixteenth century,[9] and Scherer was probably inspired by one of the images in this tradition. Here the presence of Death is to be understood in connection with the banner above which refers to those who "sit in darkness and in the shadow of death": the African men are in the shadow of the tree and Death is making the source of that shadow fall onto their heads.

While we have darkness in the cartouche on the left, there is light in the cartouche on the right—which qualifies as a cartouche because of the banner the cherub

holds. The text in the banner is from Psalm 112:4, "Unto the upright there ariseth light in the darkness," and below, two African women and two African men kneel and venerate the sun in which the less common singular form (Eloah) of the Hebrew name for God (Elohim) is written inside a triangle symbolizing the Trinity—and just as important for Scherer, the African people are illuminated by that sun. Also, one of the men has set aside his spear and shield, which lie in the foreground, an editorial remark by Scherer regarding the pacific influence of Christianity.

In the cartouches on this map, then, the cartographer sets forth his evangelizing hopes for the religious future of Africa, using the same imagery of darkness and light that informs his thematic cartography of the continent.

Scherer evidently had a particular interest in Africa: it was not by accident that he chose a map of that continent for a cartouche that employs the system of light and darkness that he uses in his thematic mapping. First he has a map titled *Mappa geographica exhibens religionem Catholicam alicubi per Africam sparsam* ("Geographical Map Showing the Catholic Religion Scattered in Various Places throughout Africa"), also printed in his *Atlas novus*.[10] On this map the legend sets forth specific symbols for places of Catholic power, archiepiscopal cities, episcopal cities, stable Catholic missions, temporary Catholic missions, places frequented and improved by Catholic missionaries, and places where the Catholic faith had been established but was later overthrown. The map thus contains much the same information that Scherer conveys in his other map using the imagery of darkness and light, but does so with a much less judgmental system of visual coding.

And finally Scherer also made a map that illustrates his own particular theory about the source of the Nile, titled *Utriusque Nili Albi et Atri fons et origo: ex veris relationibus geographice exhibetur* ("The Font and Origin of Both the White and the Black Nile, Depicted Cartographically from True Accounts").[11] In the cartouche he personifies the two sources of the White Nile and Black Nile—unsurprisingly, one as a white man, the other as Black.

---

7   For a general account of early personifications of death see Jill Bradley, "The Changing Face of Death: The Iconography of the Personification of Death in the Early Middle Ages," in Christian Krötzl and Katariina Mustakallio, eds., *On Old Age: Approaching Death in Antiquity and the Middle Ages* (Turnhout: Brepols, 2010), pp. 57–88.

8   On the iconography of Death cutting down a tree see Benito Navarrete Prieto, "Iconografía del árbol de la vida en la península Ibérica y América," in José Manuel Almansa, ed., *Actas del III Congreso Internacional del Barroco Americano: Territorio, arte, espacio y sociedad: Universidad Pablo de Olavide, Sevilla, 8 al 12 de octubre de 2001* (Seville: Departamento de Humanidades, Universidad Pablo de Olavide, 2001), pp. 349–358; Ewa Kubiak, "Grabados de los hermanos Wierix y la pintura barroca en el Perú y en Polonia," in Yobenj Aucardo Chicangana-Bayona, ed., *Caminos cruzados: cultura, imágenes e historia* (Medellín: Facultad de Ciencias Humanas y Económicas, Universidad Nacional de Colombia-Sede Medellín, 2010), pp. 73–87; and Didier Jugan, "L'arbre de la vie au péril de la mort (iconographie de l'arbre au miel, arbre sans fruit, arbre du pécheur, arbre vain)," in Marco Piccat and Laura Ramello, eds., *Memento mori: Il genere macabro in Europa dal Medioevo a oggi. Atti del Convegno internazionale, Torino, 16–18 ottobre 2014* (Alessandria: Edizioni dell'Orso, 2014), pp. 351–387.

9   The print by Hieronymus Wierix has been dated before 1619, and its inscription at the bottom begins *Fondeo frugis inops*: see L. Alvin, *Catalogue raisonné de l'oeuvre des trois frères, Jean, Jérôme & Antoine Wierix* (Brussels: T.J.I. Arnold, 1866), p. 231, no. 1182. On this image and those that derive from it see Jugan, "L'arbre de la vie" (see note 8), pp. 361–370.

10   An image of Scherer's *Mappa geographica* in the University of Cape Town Library may be consulted at https://digitalcollections.lib.uct.ac.za/collection/islandora-19661.

11   Digital images of Scherer's map of the sources of the Nile may be consulted at https://searchworks.stanford.edu and https://gallica.bnf.fr; for discussion of the map see Wulf Bodenstein, *Exploring Africa with Ancient Maps* (Tervuren, Belgium: Royal Museum for Central Africa, 2017), p. 135, map 34.

A Map in the Map as Prophesy

Nicolas Sanson and Antoine de Winter, Geographiae Sacrae Tabula, *1705*

The French cartographer Nicolas Sanson (1600–67) was recognized as the father of French cartography less than a hundred years after his death.[1] Louis XIII appointed him *Géographe Ordinaire du Roi* (Royal Geographer) in 1630, and his prolific production of maps was instrumental in moving the center of European map production from the Netherlands to France in the course of the seventeenth century.[2] The great influence he had is demonstrated by the copying of his maps by cartographers in Germany, England, and the Netherlands. As shown in the Introduction above, Sanson tended to use rather plain cartouches, but when his maps were adapted by other cartographers, they often replaced Sanson's restrained cartouches with more elaborate ones.

The cartouche we will consider in this chapter is one of this category: it decorates a map whose cartographic data comes from Sanson, but which was elaborated upon by a later artist. The base map is Sanson's map of the Holy Land which he printed in 1662, *Geographiae Sacrae ex Veteri et Novo Testamento desumptae, Tabula Secunda in qua Terra Promissa, sive Iudaea in suas Tribus partesque distincta* ("Second Map of Holy Geography Taken from the Old and New Testaments, in which the Promised Land, or Judaea, is Divided into its Tribes and Regions").[3] This map has a simple, generic cartouche, a wreath with a *putto* at the top and two small dolphins at the bottom:[4] there is no connection between the decorative program and the region depicted on the map, or the map's religious subject matter.

The Dutch publisher François Halma (1653–1722) obtained the plates of Sanson's maps for an atlas project and hired the Dutch engraver Antoine de Winter (c. 1652–1707) to make new versions of Sanson's maps. De Winter made few changes to the cartographic details of the maps, and retained the indication of Sanson's authorship, but replaced Sanson's cartouches with more elaborate ones on some of the maps. These new maps were first printed as part of an introduction to geography in 1692,[5] but we will examine a copy of the map in another introduction to geography, this one in Dutch, printed by the same printer in 1705.[6]

In reworking Sanson's plates de Winter added elaborate cartouches to only four of them: one of the Netherlands (unsurprising), one of Brandenburg, and two of the Holy Land; and the cartouche on one of the maps of the Holy Land, whose geography is based on Sanson's 1662 map, is by far the most interesting of these (Fig. 87). The map's title is very similar to that of Sanson's map, *Geographiae Sacrae Tabula, in qua terra promissa in suas Tribus*

---

1 Louis du Four de Longuerue, *Longueruana, ou Recueil de pensées, de discours et de conversations* (Berlin: s.n., 1754), p. 64: *Ses Cartes sont bien défectueuses, j'en conviens; mais c'est lui qui a commencé, & qui nous a mis en train & en goût de Géographie. Avant lui qu'avions nous?* that is, "His maps are very defective, I agree; but it was he who started, and who got us started and in love with geography. Before him what did we have?"

2 On Sanson and his maps see Jean-Pierre Niceron, "La vie de Nicolas Sanson," in *Mémoires pour servir à l'histoire des hommes illustres dans la République des Lettres* (Paris: Briasson, 1730), vol. 13, pp. 210–235; Mireille Pastoureau, "Le premier atlas mondial français: Les *Cartes générales de toutes les parties du monde* de Nicolas Sanson d'Abbeville (1658)," *Revue Française d'Histoire du Livre* 18 (1978), pp. 87–105; Mireille Pastoureau, "Les Sanson, un siècle de cartographie française (1630–1730)," thèse de doctorat, Université Paris IV, 1981; and Mireille Pastoureau's intrroduction to Sanson's *Atlas du monde* (Paris: Sand & Conti, 1988), pp. 11–46.

3 Sanson's map was first published in his book about the Holy Land, *Geographia sacra ex Veteri et Novo Testamento desumpta, et in tabulas duas distincta, quarum prima totius orbis partes continet, altera Terram promissam, sive Judaeam; tum et in utramque tabulam animadversiones, et index geographicus* (Paris: A. Vitré, 1662). On the

map see Eran Laor, *Maps of the Holy Land: Cartobibliography of Printed Maps, 1475–1900* (New York: A.R. Liss; Amsterdam: Meridian Pub. Co., 1986), p. 97, no. 688. A high-resolution image of a later, 1709 printing of the map is available at https://searchworks.stanford.edu.

4 It is possible that the two dolphins allude to Louis of France (1661–1711), the eldest son of Louis XIV, who was the Dauphin when the map was made, for the symbol of the Dauphin was the dolphin. But the map is not dedicated to Louis of France, so the matter is not clear.

5 Specifically Sanson's maps were printed in Jan Luyts, *Introductio ad geographiam novam et veterem* (Utrecht: Franciscus Halma, 1692). Luyts mentions Sanson's maps of the Holy Land on p. 498. A digital version of the book is available at https://archive.org.

6 The book is a revised and expanded Dutch translation of A. Phérotée La Croix's *Nouvelle méthode pour apprendre facilement la géographie universelle* (Lyon: Barbier, Jean-Baptiste, 1690). The Dutch translation is Simon de Vries, *Algemeene weereld-beschryving* (Amsterdam: F. Halma, 1705). The John Carter Brown Library owns a copy of this Dutch book in which all of the maps are hand-colored; high-resolution images of the maps in the book are available at https://jcb.lunaimaging.com.

© CHET VAN DUZER, 2023 | DOI:10.1163/9789004523838_019

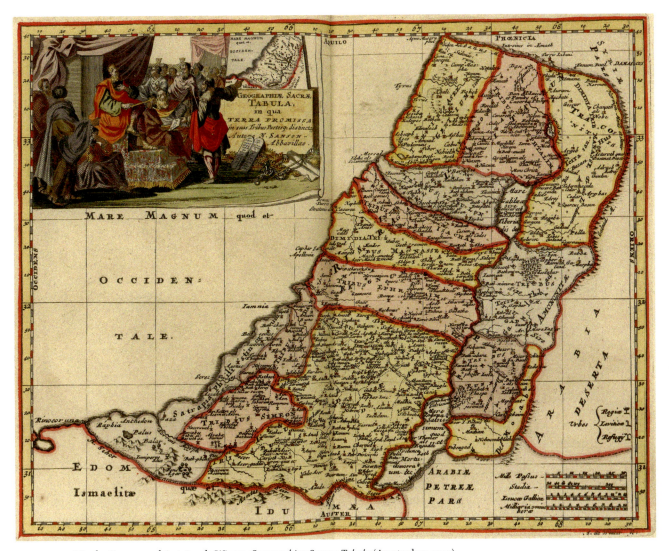

FIGURE 87   Nicolas Sanson and Antoine de Winter, *Geographiae Sacrae Tabula* (Amsterdam, 1705)
JOHN CARTER BROWN LIBRARY, E705 L147A /1-SIZE. COURTESY OF THE JOHN CARTER BROWN LIBRARY

Partesque distincta ("Map of the Holy Geography, in which the Promised Land is Divided into its Tribes and Parts"), but the cartouche is entirely different (Fig. 88).[7] It shows a bearded man holding a scepter and seated on a throne holding audience with men gathered around him in both the foreground and background; in front of him, a man holds a card that reads JUDA and points to a map of the Holy Land supported by a plinth. Engraved on the plinth is the title and author information for the main map, and below that on the ground, two stone tablets, a dozen crowns, some shackles, an olive branch, and a scroll.

The scene represented is the so-called "Blessing of Jacob" in Genesis 49, in which the patriarch prophesies what will happen to each of his twelve sons, and by extension, to

the twelve Tribes of Israel that would descend from them after their return from Egypt to Israel.[8] This scene is infrequently depicted, but one such depiction is in the Cologne Bible printed in that city by Heinrich Quentell in about 1478 (Fig. 89).[9] This illustration simply shows Jacob on his

---

7   On de Winter's map see the brief listing in Laor, *Maps of the Holy Land* (see note 3), p. 98, no. 693.

8   The identification of the sons with the Tribes of Israel is explicit in Genesis 49:28. For discussion of the text of the "Blessing of Jacob" see for example Kent Sparks, "Genesis 49 and the Tribal List Tradition in Ancient Israel," *Zeitschrift für die Alttestamentliche Wissenschaft* 115.3 (2003), pp. 327–347; and Geula Twersky, "Genesis 49: The Foundation of Israelite Monarchy and Priesthood," *Journal for the Study of the Old Testament* 43.3 (2019), pp. 317–333.

9   On the illustrations in this Bible see Hildegard Reitz, "Die Illustration der Kölner Bibel," in Rudolf Kautzsch, ed., *Die Kölner Bibel 1478/1479. Studien zur Entstehung und Illustrierung der ersten niederdeutschen Bibel. Kommentarband zum Faksimile 1979 der Kölner Bibel 1478/1479* (Hamburg, Friedrich Wittig Verlag, 1981), pp. 75–142; and Severin Corsten, "The Illustrated Cologne Bibles of *c*.1478: Corrections and

FIGURE 88   Detail of the cartouche on Nicolas Sanson and Antoine de Winter's *Geographiae Sacrae Tabula* (Amsterdam, 1705)
COURTESY OF THE JOHN CARTER BROWN LIBRARY

throne and his twelve sons kneeling before him to hear his predictions about their futures—it sets off by contrast the greater complexity and richness of de Winter's cartouche.

The cartouche is about the future of Jacob's sons and of the Tribes of Israel. The shackles on the ground allude to the sons later attaining their freedom from Pharaoh and returning to Israel; the tablets foreshadow Moses receiving the Ten Commandments on Mt. Sinai; and twelve crowns represent those the twelve sons will wear as founders of the Twelve Tribes. The piece of paper with JUDA written on it identifies the holder as Judah, the most favored and successful of Jacob's sons, whom his father praises highly in this scene.

The most original and striking element of the cartouche is the map of the Holy Land that Judah points

to, and de Winter was absolutely right to recognize the Blessing of Jacob as an episode full of cartographic significance. For in prophesying the fate of his sons, Jacob (who also bears the name Israel)[10] was to some extent assigning them places in their homeland, and thus in effect drawing the map of that territory. In the prophecy for one of his sons this cartographic element is very clear; he says: "Zebulun will live by the seashore and become a haven for ships; his border will extend toward Sidon."[11] He also says of Simeon and Levi, two of his violent sons, "I will scatter them in Jacob and disperse them in Israel."[12] And of his son Issachar, Jacob says: "When he sees how good is his resting place and how pleasant is his land, he will bend his shoulder to the burden and submit to forced labor,"[13] again referring to the geography of the sons' settlements. It also seems likely that the castigation of some of the sons was a way to explain how in the future, the territory of the tribes descended from those sons was smaller.

_____

Additions," in Martin Davies, ed., *Incunabula: Studies in Fifteenth-Century Printed Books Presented to Lotte Hellinga* (London: British Library, 1999), pp. 79–88. There is a representation of the Blessing of Jacob as a death-bed scene in a miniature by the Maître François in a manuscript of Augustine's *La Cité de Dieu*, The Hague, MMW, 10 A 11, f. 18r, *c*.1475; images of the manuscript are available at http://manuscripts.kb.nl/show/manuscript/10+A+11.

_____

10   On the renaming of Jacob as Israel see Genesis 32:28.
11   On Zebulum see Genesis 49:13.
12   On Simeon and Levi see Genesis 49:5–7.
13   On Issachar see Genesis 49:14–15.

FIGURE 89   Illustration of the Blessing of Jacob in the Cologne Bible of 1478
BOSTON PUBLIC LIBRARY, RARE BOOKS Q.401.26 FOLIO. COURTESY OF THE BOSTON PUBLIC LIBRARY

The map in the cartouche makes it clear that this was de Winter's interpretation of the scene, for the names of the sons are prominent, while few other geographical details are supplied.[14] In understanding the Blessing of Jacob and interpreting it visually as a cartographic event, de Winter is doing something very similar to what medieval scholars did with Noah's tripartition of the world among his sons Shem, Ham, and Japheth in Genesis 9–10. In the Bible it is not very clear which territories were assigned to which of Noah's sons, but medieval scholars settled on the idea that Noah assigned Asia to Shem, Africa to Ham, and Europe to Japheth.[15] This division was represented cartographically in medieval *mappaemundi*, where the names of the respective sons of Noah were often written in Asia, Africa, and Europe (see Fig. 57 above).[16] Medieval cartographers interpreted the division of the world among Noah's sons as one of seminal cartographic importance, and de Winter does the same with the Blessing of Jacob: the first relates to the map of the world, the second to the map of the Holy Land.

Most early European maps of the Holy Land, like this one, are oriented to the north so that the slanting coast of Israel leaves a large stretch of the Mediterranean empty in the upper left corner—perfect for decoration with a cartouche. Many cartographers took advantage of this opportunity, and as a result, maps of the Holy Land have

14   The name Simeon is missing from the map; this is probably just a mistake by de Winter, but could be a reflection of Jacob's negative opinion of that son of his.

15   Benjamin Braude, "The Sons of Noah and the Construction of Ethnic and Geographical Identities in the Medieval and Early Modern Periods," *William and Mary Quarterly* 54.1 (1997), pp. 103–142.

16   For discussion of medieval maps and texts associating the sons of Noah with the three "Old World" continents see Chet Van Duzer and Sandra Sáenz-López Pérez, "*Tres filii Noe diviserunt orbem post diluvium*: The World Map in British Library Add. MS 37049," *Word & Image* 26.1 (2010), pp. 21–39.

a large variety of interesting cartouches, and of course the great importance of the region in European history contributed as well. A number of these cartouches include inset maps of the Holy Land. But de Winter is the only artist who understood the cartographic significance of the Blessing of Jacob and placed his inset map in that historical context. Moreover, this is another case where the cartouche artist speaks to the viewer about how a map was created: by illustrating the Blessing of Jacob, de Winter visually cites the primordial mapping of the Holy Land, the historic source of the map that he is decorating with a cartouche.

CHAPTER 18

"One of the Most Singular Stories of Extreme Hardships"

Pieter van der Aa, Scheeps togt van Iamaica gedaan na Panuco en Rio de las Palmas, *1706*

It is not so often that the subject depicted in the decoration of a cartouche is reflected in the map's title, but such is the case with Pieter van der Aa's *Scheeps togt van Iamaica gedaan na Panuco en Rio de las Palmas Aan de Golf van Mexico gelegen* ("Ship Voyage from Jamaica to Pánuco and Río de las Palmas, Located on the Gulf of Mexico"), first printed in Leiden in 1706 (Fig. 90). It is appropriate that the subject of the cartouche figures in the title, for the image of the shipwreck dominates the map visually, turning the surrounding coasts of the Gulf of Mexico into a mere frame for this dramatic scene. The scene qualifies as a cartouche because of the framed title information on the stony island west of Florida, and the additional framing effect of the surrounding coastlines is rendered more striking by the fact that there are so few place names in the north.

Van der Aa (1659–1733), a Dutch publisher and mapmaker,[1] published several atlases and collections of travel narratives. He typically used texts that had already been printed elsewhere, had them translated into Dutch, organized them, and added a rich program of illustration with maps and engravings. The map in question here came from his *Naaukeurige versameling der gedenk-waardigste zee en land-reysen na Oost en West-Indiën* ("Accurate Collection of the Most Memorable Sea and Land Voyages to the East and West Indies"), covering voyages of exploration from 1246 to 1696 in 28 volumes with 107 engraved

maps and more than 500 engraved views.[2] The map is towards the end of volume 10, in the section on Hernán Cortés, and the text at the bottom of a smaller version of the map in van der Aa's *Atlas nouveau et curieux des plus celebres itineraires* (Leiden, 1714), map 106, says that it is based on the narrative of the Spanish-Basque explorer Francisco de Garay (1475–1523) and other authors.

Garay served as Governor of Jamaica from 1514 to 1523, and in that capacity in 1519 had sent an expedition under the leadership of Alonso Álvarez de Pineda to map the northern part of the Gulf of Mexico. The manuscript map of the Gulf that Pineda made on that voyage—which coincidentally covers much the same area as van der Aa's map—is the earliest to depict the Gulf that was based on actual exploration.[3]

The episode depicted in the cartouche was part of an expedition in which Garay himself participated a few years later, in 1523. It is easy to follow the sequence of events on van der Aa's map. In June of that year Garay set out from Jamaica with 16 ships, intending to establish a settlement on the Río Pánuco on the western coast of the Gulf of Mexico. The fleet stopped at Xagua (now Jagua), Cuba, and there Garay learned that Hernán Cortés had already established a colony named Villa de Santiesteban del Puerto on the Pánuco in 1522. Concerned about having political difficulties with the powerful Cortés, Garay sent one of his men, the lawyer Alonso Zuazo, who knew Cortés, to Mexico to discuss the situation with him. After waiting for Zuazo's return for some time, Garay gave up

---

1 On van der Aa's work as a publisher see Isabella Henriette van Eeghen, "Pieter van der Aa, boekverkoper Leiden (1677–1730) en de strijd om de privileges," in *De Amsterdamse boekhandel 1680–1725* (Amsterdam: Scheltema & Holkema, 1960–1978), vol. 5.1, *De boekhandel van de Republiek 1572–1795*, Appendix II, pp. 179–192; P.G. Hoftijzer, "The Leiden Bookseller Pieter van der Aa (1659–1733) and the International Book Trade," in Christiane Berkvens-Stevelinck, ed., *Le Magasin de l'univers: The Dutch Republic as the Centre of the European Book Trade: Papers Presented at the International Colloquium, Held at Wassenaar, 5–7 July 1990* (Leiden and New York: E.J. Brill, 1992), pp. 169–184; P.G. Hoftijzer, *Pieter van der Aa (1659–1733): Leids drukker en boekverkoper* (Hilversum: Verloren, 1999); and Chiara Piccoli, "Publishing in the Republic of Letters: Behind the Scenes of Pieter van der Aa's *Thesaurus antiquitatum et historiarum Italiae* (Leiden, 1704–25)," *Quaerendo* 43.1 (2013), pp. 61–82. I do not know a detailed study of van der Aa's work as a cartographer.

2 On the *Naaukeurige versameling* see P.A. Tiele, *Nederlandsche bibliographie van land- en volkenkunde* (Amsterdam: F. Muller en comp., 1884), pp. 2–3; the contents of the 127 parts of the 28 volumes of the work are listed in English in the Maggs auction catalog *Bibliotheca Americana*, Part VII (London: Maggs Bros., 1928), catalog no. 502, item 5226, pp. 281–284.

3 Pineda's manuscript map is in Seville at the Archivo General de Indias, MP-MEXICO,5, and may be viewed at http://pares.culturay deporte.gob.es/inicio.html. On Pineda's voyage of 1519 see Robert S. Weddle, *Spanish Sea: The Gulf of Mexico in North American Discovery, 1500–1685* (College Station: Texas A&M University Press, 1985), pp. 95–109; and Donald E. Chipman, "Alonso Alvarez de Pineda and the Río de las Palmas: Scholars and the Mislocation of a River," *The Southwestern Historical Quarterly* 98.3 (1995), pp. 369–385. On Pineda's map see John Farmer, "Piñeda's Sketch," *The Southwestern Historical Quarterly* 63.1 (1959), pp. 110–114.

Terlichichimechi

R. de la Madalena

Gaços

Culias

Vachus

R. de las Palmas

R. Montalto
Chila

PANUCO
Tancacana

Tameco
Tancuie St Estevan del Puerto
Panuco
S. Iago de los Valles
Nachapalan Tuzetuco
Tanquinitl

Puchca

Chuchica R.S.Pedro R.S. Paulo
Quastlavaca
Mexico
Almeria ó Villarica
Chalco Tlascala
Cuerna buça los Angeles

R. de Montanas

R. Panuco Tanuice

C. d'Arboledo

B. del Spirite Santo
C. de Hondo
C. de Cruz

de Spirito Santo
FLOR
Chicagua

C. Roxo
I. Lobos
R. de Tuspa
Chalechicoca

R. de Zempoal
Aquigaustiam
la Vera Crus
Jellin
de Sacrificios
de Ant Sardo
de Alvarado
la Partida

GOLFO
DE
MEXICO

la Bermeja
I. das Arenas

Triangulo

os Arcas

Negrillos
los
las Binoras
Baixo de Sisal

IUCA

Val
S. Franci
Campe
Lag

FIGURE 90
Pieter van der Aa's *Scheeps togt van Iamaica*, 1707
MAP AND IMAGERY
LIBRARY, SPECIAL
AND AREA STUDIES
COLLECTIONS, GEORGE
A. SMATHERS LIBRARIES,
UNIVERSITY OF FLORIDA,
F707 N111V. COURTESY
OF THE UNIVERSITY OF
FLORIDA

and sailed west, intending to establish a settlement on the Río Pánuco despite the possible difficulties with Cortés. He landed too far north, at what he called the Río de las Palmas (now Río Soto la Marina), marched south to Cortés's settlement, was routed by Cortés's lieutenants, and traveled to Mexico City to negotiate with Cortés for the rights to build a settlement on the Río de las Palmas.[4]

Alonso Zuazo had not reached Mexico as he had planned.[5] Instead, shortly after leaving Cuba his ship was overtaken by a storm, and on January 20, 1524, he was shipwrecked on *Isla de las Víboras* (Island of the Serpents), part of an atoll system now called Arrecife Alacranes (Scorpion Reef—on van der Aa's map it is *los Alcaranes*), just north of the tip of the Yucatan Peninsula. Van der Aa tells the story of this dramatic shipwreck in the text that the map illustrates, and he was drawing from the fuller account in Book 50 of Gonzalo Fernández de Oviedo's *Historia general y natural de las Indias*, first published in 1535;[6] that book of Oviedo's work is devoted to shipwrecks. Oviedo says that Zuazo's shipwreck is "one of the most singular stories of extreme hardships ever heard of or seen,"[7] and the account lives up to this billing.

The caravel had been torn open by the reef, and many on the ship were lost and drowned, but 47 or 48 adults and a few boys survived the first night, clinging desperately to the reef while the waves washed over them. When the

tide receded and the storm abated, by a remarkable stroke of good fortune they found a damaged old canoe mostly buried among the sands, which they were able to repair and to use to search for land. Under Zuazo's leadership a few of the men paddled to the east, instructing the other survivors to follow as best they could by clambering over the rocks and swimming. Eventually found a small island 10 paces wide and 150 paces long, and the other straggling survivors reached the island the next morning—this is the scene that van der Aa depicts. They were enormously grateful to have reached land, and the five large turtles they found on the island gave them their first food and drink in five days, by means of their meat, eggs, and blood.

But the island had no potable water anywhere, and the turtles fed them for just a few days. The survivors spied another island several miles distant, and Zuazo sent some men in the canoe to investigate. They reported that the other island had no water, but was very dense with nesting birds, so Zuazo set about ferrying all of the survivors there in the canoe. In addition to abundant birds the island had more turtles, so the survivors could eat again, but the diet of raw food, the lack of water, and the oppressive heat of the sun started killing them off. Zuazo had seen Indians rub sticks together to make fire, and succeeded in doing the same, so that their meat could be cooked, but the problem of water remained. One of the survivors, an eleven-year-old girl named Inés, had a vision of Saint Anne who declared that there was an island with water to the west, and the survivors, full of holy faith, ferried themselves west in the canoe, bringing as many eggs and birds as they could carry, and they did reach another island.

Despair quickly overtook them, however, for despite the presence of vegetation on this island, and despite digging in more than 2000 places, they could only find brackish water. Zuazo measured to determine the central and highest point of the small island, and digging there, he miraculously found fresh water that sustained them for the 135 days they would pass on that island. A sailor named Juan Sánchez suggested that they use the canoe to return to the site of the wreck and gather all of the wood and rigging and nails so they could and build a larger boat, and this task occupied them for three months. Finally they sent three men and a boy westward across the Gulf towards Villa Rica to get help, carrying with them a note that Zuazo had written using the purple blood of shellfish on a strip of parchment he had cut from a nautical chart, a remarkable reuse of a map.

It took the rescue ship 28 days to cross the Gulf and pick up the survivors. Of the 47 or 48 adults who had survived the shipwreck, only 17 were still alive to be rescued, including Zuazo. Francisco de Garay, on whose behalf Zuazo

4   Claudia Perodi, "La fundación de Santiesteban del Puerto y el arribo de Garay al Pánuco (comentarios históricos y lingüísticos)," *Historia Mexicana* 27.4 (1978), pp. 616–636; Rolena Adorno and Patrick Charles Pautz, "Francisco de Garay's Exploration of the Northern Coast of the Gulf of Mexico (1518 to 1519)," in *Álvar Núñez Cabeza de Vaca: His Account, His Life, and the Expedition de Pánfilo de Narváez* (Lincoln: University of Nebraska Press, 1999), vol. 3, pp. 227–245.

5   For a biography of Zuazo see Alberto A. García Menéndez, *Los jueces de apelación de la Española y su residencia* (Santo Domingo: Museo de las Casas Reales, 1981), pp. 135–155; for details on his explorations see Ana Gimeno Gómez, "Los proyectos de Alonso de Zuazo en búsqueda del Estrecho," *Congreso de Historia del Descubrimiento (1492–1556): actas (ponencias y communicaciones)* (Madrid: Real Academia de la Historia, and Confederación Española de Cajas de Ahorros, 1992), vol. 2, pp. 115–136.

6   Gonzalo Fernández de Oviedo, "How Licentiate Alonso Zuazo's Caravel was Wrecked on the Alacranes Islands with Almost Fifty-Five or Sixty Persons, of Whom Seventeen Miraculously Escaped with Him; and of Many Things that Happened on this Voyage and Shipwreck," in his *Misfortunes and Shipwrecks in the Seas of the Indies, Islands, and Mainland of the Ocean Sea (1513–1548): Book Fifty of the General and Natural History of the Indies*, trans. Glen F. Dille (Gainesville: University Press of Florida, 2011), pp. 33–79. For discussion see Pablo García Loaeza, "Comedia de un náufrago: Lectura anacrónica del capítulo x del libro L de la *Historia general y natural* de Gonzalo Fernández de Oviedo," *Revista de Estudios Hispánicos* 47.3 (2013), pp. 487–508.

7   Oviedo, "How Licentiate Alonzo Zuazo's Caravel was Wrecked" (see note 6), p. 33.

had been sent to negotiate with Cortés, had passed away in Mexico City during the months Zuazo was stranded. Afterwards Zuazo named the three islands *Insulae sepulchrorum*, "Islands of the Graves," for all of the shipmates he and his companions had had to bury in them.[8] The capable Zuazo became a member of all of the several triumvirates that governed New Spain (very approximately modern Mexico) from October of 1524 to May of 1525, while Cortés was away on a military expedition.

To return to the map, in designing his cartouche van der Aa was faced with the formidable task of condensing this long narrative into one scene, and he very reasonably chose to focus on the dramatic and happy moment when the survivors of the shipwreck first reached land. He also took some artistic liberties: the first island did not have any vegetation, Oviedo says nothing of horses or any other

animals having survived the shipwreck or reaching the island, and the storm had stripped the survivors of their clothing.

An interesting aspect of the cartouche, beyond the fact that it dominates the map visually and its subject figures in the map's title, is that it is in effect a zoomed-in detail of the map. That is to say, in the map proper Van der Aa depicts the islands (*los Alcaranes*) where the shipwreck took place, just north of the tip of the Yucatan. Just above them he places the cartouche decoration which consists of a large zoomed-in view of one of the islands, decorated with imagery from an important moment in its history. Normally the frame of a cartouche separates cartouche space from cartographic space, but in this case—similar to those discussed in the section "The Ontology of Cartouches" in the Introduction—the separation between the map and the matter depicted in the cartouche is not so clear, for the cartouche is showing a detail of part of the map.[9]

---

8   Zuazo also gave names to the individual islands (these names do not appear on van der Aa's map): the first he called *Sitis sanguinea turtucarum*, "Thirst for Turtle Blood"; the second *No penséis en la comida*, which means "Don't Think about Food," because of the abundance of birds on the island; and the third *Fontinalia Elisei*, "The Little Fountain of Elisha," alluding to Elisha's spring mentioned in 2 Kings 2:21, whose waters had been bad, but Elisha rendered them good with help from God. See Oviedo, "How Licentiate Alonzo Zuazo's Caravel was Wrecked" (see note 6), p. 61.

9   Incidentally the same island, Scorpion Reef / Arrecife Alacranes, was again the site of a shipwreck some 323 years later when the British postal steamer *Tweed* was wrecked on it in 1847; for a detailed account of the shipwreck see *Curiosities of Modern Travel: A Year Book of Adventure* (London: David Bogue, 1848), pp. 7–35.

Crimson Splendor

Nicolas Sanson, Téatre de la Guerre en Flandre & Brabant, *c.1710*

In November of 1700 Charles II of Spain died childless, and the question of who would be the next ruler of the Kingdom of Spain was a grave one for the balance of power in Europe. The anti-French Grand Alliance of England, the Dutch Republic and the Holy Roman Empire favored the Archduke Charles, son of the Holy Roman Emperor, but Charles II willed the kingdom to Louis XIV's grandson Philip of Anjou (1683–1746). The War of the Spanish Succession ensued, which dominated Western European political affairs from 1701 to 1714.

In 1702, John Churchill, 1st Duke of Marlborough (1650–1722) was given command of the Alliance's English, Dutch, and German mercenary forces, despite the fact that he was far less experienced than many of the Dutch and German commanders. Yet Marlborough proved himself a skilled diplomat in keeping the Alliance together, a courageous soldier, and a superb tactician: he was one of Britain's greatest generals.[1] At the same time, it bears emphasis that many of the army's officers and troops were Dutch and German, and in particular the Dutch played an essential role in keeping the army supplied.[2] Praise is heaped on successful leaders, but the Allies' victories were the products of wide collaborations. Late in 1702 the Allies had some initial successes in the Low Countries, taking the cities of Venlo, Roermond, Stevensweert and Liège, and early in 1703 captured Bonn, Huy, and Limbourg, victories that earned Marlborough the respect of allies and thus somewhat more latitude to direct the war as he saw fit.

In 1704, realizing that Vienna was threatened by both French and Bavarian forces, Marlborough undertook to relieve the city. Deceiving his foes as to his real destination in order to maintain the element of surprise, he marched his troops from the Low Countries to the Danube. There he was joined by reinforcements under Prince Eugene of Savoy (1663–1736), and on August 13 near the village of Blenheim (Blindheim) the Allies met the Franco-Bavarian army under Marshall Tallard (1652–1728). They crushed the opposing army with a carefully prepared late afternoon thrust through the center of the French line, resulting in a rout and the taking of Tallard and 15,000 other French soldiers prisoner. This was the first significant defeat of a French army during the long reign of Louis XIV, and a turning point in the war: the success strengthened the Grand Alliance, dashed Louis XIV's hopes for a quick victory, and made Marlborough's fortune.[3]

The cartouche on Sanson's map celebrates Marlborough's next important victory, that at the Battle of Ramillies, in modern-day Belgium, in 1706. The French went on the offensive that year, met with early success in Italy and Alsace, and Louis XIV urged the new commander of his forces, Marshal Villeroi (1644–1730), to strike a blow in the Spanish Netherlands. Marlborough too was eager for a pitched battle, and the armies soon met. On May 23 they formed battle lines in a plain north of the Mehaigne river, centered on the town of Ramillies, and Marlborough had an advantage before the fighting began, as he noticed that Villeroi had stretched his line too thin. The battle commenced at 1 pm. The Allies pushed forward in the north, which caused Villeroi to overcommit troops to that area. Later Marlborough ordered troops from the north to move to the center of the line around Ramillies, and they did so surreptitiously, leaving their regimental banners in place and taking advantage of the terrain to move unobserved by the French. Danish calvary under Marlborough's command broke through the French ranks in the center, the infantry followed, and the French retreat quickly turned into a rout and a staggering defeat.[4]

---

1 For general discussion of Marlborough's military career and skills see David G. Chandler, *Marlborough as Military Commander* (New York: Scribner, 1973); on the Allies' army see John Stapleton, "Marlborough, the Allies, and the Campaigns in the Low Countries, 1702–1706," in John B. Hattendorf, Augustus J. Veenendaal, Jr., and Rolof van Hövell tot Westerflier, eds., *Marlborough: Soldier and Diplomat* (Rotterdam: Karwansaray Publishers, 2012), pp. 145–171.

2 On the role of the Dutch in supplying the Allies' army see Olaf van Nimwegen, *De subsistentie van het leger: logistiek en strategie van het Geallieerde en met name het Staatse leger tijdens de Spaanse Successieoorlog in de Nederlanden en het Heilige Roomse Rijk (1701–1712)* (Amsterdam: De Bataafsche Leeuw, 1995), which includes a summary in English.

3 On the Battle of Blenheim see Jonas L. Goldstein, "Masterstroke at Blenheim," *Military Heritage* 9.5 (2008), pp. 28–36; and Charles Spencer, *Battle for Europe: How the Duke of Marlborough Masterminded the Defeat of France at Blenheim* (Hoboken, NJ: Wiley, 2004).

4 On the Battle of Ramillies see Jamel Ostwald, "The 'Decisive' Battle of Ramillies, 1706: Prerequisites for Decisiveness in Early Modern

The cartouche (Fig. 91) is large and spectacular,[5] showing Marlborough and his staff and a whole landscape stretching off to the horizon. Beneath the title banner held aloft by two *putti*, Marlborough commands both our attention and the battle, pointing towards the action with his baton, while his white steed, drooling with eagerness, rears and is about to trample two figures on the ground, a serpent-haired personification of Discord, and a masked demonic figure, already dead, probably a personification of Envy. Above him Fame blows her trumpet, and two *putti* prepare to crown Marlborough with the laurels of victory. We can identify the battle by the presence of the town of *Ramilie* (Ramillies), named on the horizon just below the title banner. This identification is confirmed by the presence of a river running across the field, representing the Mehaigne, and also by the fact that in the map proper, Ramillies is marked with crossed swords, indicating a place of battle, and indications of the opposing lines of the French and Grand Alliance armies. The representation of the battle in the cartouche compresses time, showing troops ranged and ready for action, the heat of the conflict with the explosion of shells, and the end of the battle, with the French soldiers fleeing the field towards the horizon.

This cartouche was part of a multimedia flood of enthusiasm for the Allies' victory at Ramillies: there were numerous other maps depicting the battle,[6] paintings and prints,[7] poems,[8] and even playing cards.[9] After this battle Marlborough's role in the war began to diminish, as siege warfare, in which he had no skill, became more and more important.[10] Nevertheless, his reputation was made.

Imagery of battles during this period was mostly generic, but one contemporary image has a detail that suggests it might have inspired the cartouche on Sanson's map. This is the view of the battle titled *Ordre de la bataille donnée à Ramellies le 23 May 1706 de la part des Alliez* ("The Order of the Battle at Ramillies on May 23, 1706, by the Allies") (Fig. 92), which appears as a cartouche accompanying a map of the battle by G.L. Mosburger, *Plan de la situation ou la bataille de Ramillis* (The Hague: Anna Beek, 1706). This cartouche also has Marlborough on a rearing horse at the left, holding his baton and surrounded by comrades, with the battlefield stretching out in front of him—and the name *Ramillis* helpfully written on the horizon, just as in the cartouche on Sanson's map. Mosburger placed the Dutch field commander Hendrik van Nassau-Ouwerkerk (Auverquerc) on the right opposite Marlborough, creating a symmetrical composition, while the artist who created the cartouche on Sanson's map chose to place the focus on the English general.

There is another image that the cartouche artist certainly used as a source. The other source is a portrait of Marlborough by Sir Godfrey Kneller (1646–1723) dated

---

Warfare," *Journal of Military History* 64.3 (2000), pp. 649–677; Demmy Verbeke, David Money, and Tom Deneire, eds., *Ramillies: A Commemoration in Prose and Verse of the 300th Anniversary of the Battle of Ramillies, 1706* (Cambridge, UK: Bringfield's Head Press, 2006); and Michael McNally, *Ramillies 1706: Marlborough's Tactical Masterpiece* (Oxford and New York: Osprey Publishing, 2014).

5   On Sanson's map *Téatre de la Guerre en Flandre & Brabant* see Marco van Egmond, *Covens & Mortier: A Map Publishing House in Amsterdam* (Houten: Hes & De Graaf, 2009), p. 334, nos. 10.3 and 10.4.

6   There are maps of the battle of Ramillies in the pamphlet *Das erlöste Braband und besiegte Spanische Flandern* (Frankfurt and Leipzig: Christoph Riegel, 1706), and in *The Glorious Campaign of His Grace the Duke of Marlborough, in the year 1706* (London: D. Mortier, 1707). Other maps include G.L. Mosburger, *Plan de la situation ou la bataille de Ramillis* (The Hague: Anna Beek, 1706); C. Hoppach, *Plan de la glorieuse bataille de Ramelis dans la plainne de Judoigne donnée le 23 may 1706* (The Hague: Pieter Husson, 1706); *Die siegreiche Erstlinge des 1706 Jahrs das ist Fürstellung des herrlichsten Siegs unserer Seiten welchen die combinirte Engel- und Holländische Armeen unter dem Herzog von Marlebourg* (Nuremberg: Felseker Erben, 1706). Several maps of the battle are listed in Claude Ponnou, *Champs de bataille du Grand Siècle: catalogue des cartes de l'Atlas historique jusqu'à la fin du règne de Louis XIV* (Paris: Archives & Culture, 2013), pp. 204–205.

7   See for example Louis Laguerre, *The Battle of Ramillies, 23 May 1706*, painting in Grimsthorpe Castle, with a copy in Plas Newydd; derivative print tiled *The Battle of Ramillies in the Year MDCCVI* (London: Tho. Bowles, 1735); and there is a view of the battle in Jean Dumont, *The Military History of His Serene Highness Prince Eugene of Savoy* (London: W. Rayner, 1736).

8   See for example Matthew Prior, *An Ode, Humbly Inscrib'd to the Queen, on the late Glorious Success of Her Majesty's Arms: written in Imitation of Spencer's Stile* (London: Jacob Tonson, 1706); John Paris, *Ramillies. A Poem, Humbly Inscrib'd to his Grace the Duke of Marlborough, Written in Imitation of Milton* (London: Jacob Tonson, 1706); *A Collection of Poems, Occasionally Written upon the Victories of Blenheim and Ramillies* (London: Jacob Tonson, 1708). The volume and low quality of the poems written about the victory generated complaints: see John Richardson, "Modern Warfare in Early-Eighteenth-Century Poetry," *Studies in English Literature, 1500–1900* 45.3 (2005), pp. 557–577, at 572. For more on writings celebrating Marlborough's victory see Robert D. Horn, *Marlborough, A Survey: Panegyrics, Satires and Biographical Writings, 1688–1788* (New York: Garland, 1975).

9   There are two sets of the playing cards at the British Museum, cataloged under the title *Marlborough and his Time* (London: s. n., 1710–25), reference numbers 1841,0508.4–55 and 1982,U.4619.1–52. Images of the cards are available at https://research.brit ishmuseum.org/research/collection_online/search.aspx.

10 See Stapleton, "Marlborough, the Allies, and the Campaigns in the Low Countries, 1702–1706" (see note 1), p. 171.

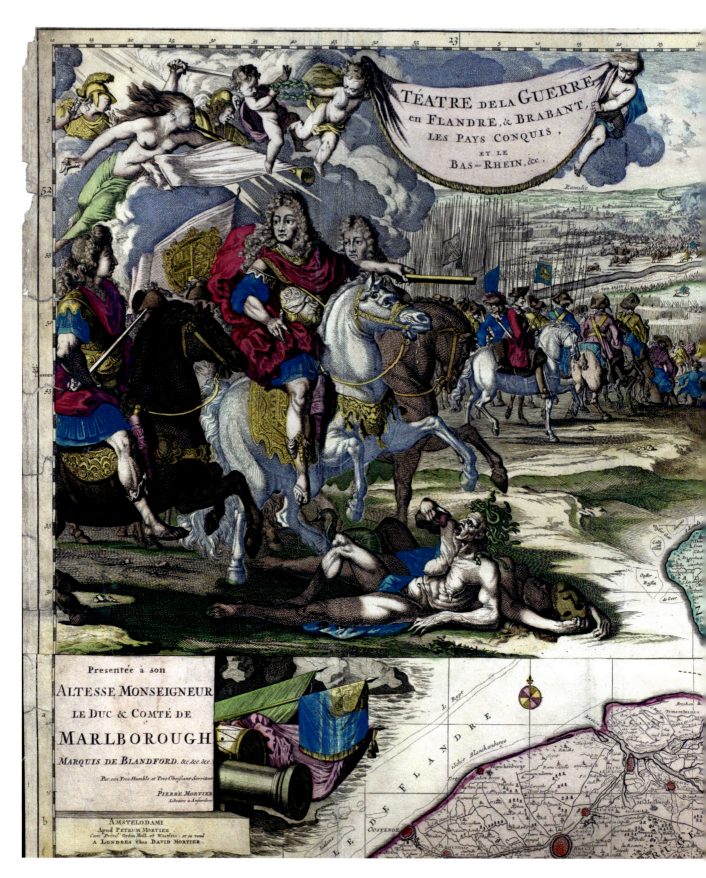

FIGURE 91

The cartouche celebrating Marlborough's victory in the Battle of Ramillies, in Nicolas Sanson, *Téatre de la Guerre en Flandre & Brabant* (Amsterdam: Petrus Mortier, *c.*1710)

FIGURE 92   Detail of *Ordre de la bataille donnee a Ramellies le 23 May 1706. de la part des Alliez*, on G.L. Mosburger, *Plan de la situation ou la bataille de Ramillis* (The Hague, 1706)
IN [A COLLECTION OF PLANS OF FORTIFICATIONS AND BATTLES, 1684–1709], LIBRARY OF CONGRESS, G&M, G1793 .B4 1709.
COURTESY OF THE LIBRARY OF CONGRESS

c.1706 in the National Portrait Gallery in London.[11] In this portrait (Fig. 93) Marlborough's rearing steed is about to trample two allegorical figures, Discord and a Dog of War,[12] much as in the cartouche the horse is about to trample Discord and Envy; and Fame is about to crown Marlborough with laurels, much as Fame blows a trumpet above the general while two *putti* are about to crown him with laurels in the cartouche. Perhaps it was a copy of the painting, rather than the painting itself, that served as an inspiration for the cartouche, but certainly there is a close relationship between the portrait and the map. It is a testament to the value placed on the cartouche that the artist would go to the trouble of combining and adapting details from two different models.

The cartouche appears on two versions of the map dedicated to different men. The first, illustrated here, is dedicated to Marlborough, the dedication appearing in a subsidiary cartouche decorated with a cannon, drum, and military banners, including the coat of arms of England,

below the main cartouche. In the later version the dedication was changed to Johan Willem Friso, Prince of Orange and Nassau (1687–1711), who served under Marlborough from 1707 till his death in 1711.[13] This later version was published by the firm Covens and Mortier, which was founded in 1721, so the dedication was not made to seek favor with the prince, who had passed away ten years earlier, but probably as a way to make the map more appealing to buyers in the Netherlands. The change in the dedication was executed with little care, for the firm neglected to change the coat of arms on the banner from those of England to those of Prince of Orange or of the Netherlands.

11   Kneller's portrait of Marlborough is NPG 902. For discussion of the painting see J. Douglas Stewart, *Sir Godfrey Kneller and the English Baroque Portrait* (Oxford: Clarendon Press; New York: Oxford University Press, 1983), pp. 62 and 117, no. 467, ill. no. 59; Desmond Shawe-Taylor, *The Georgians: Eighteenth-Century Portraiture & Society* (London: Barrie & Jenkins, 1990), pp. 33–34; and Tarnya Cooper, *National Portrait Gallery: A Portrait of Britain* (London: National Portrait Gallery, 2014), p. 96.

12   So Shawe-Taylor, *The Georgians* (see note 11), p. 33. Also about to be trampled is the sunburst shield of Louis XIV of France: see Cooper, *National Portrait Gallery* (see note 11), p. 96.

13   The title of the re-dedicated version of the map is *Teatre de la Guerre en Flandre & Brabant, les pays conquis et les Bas Rhein presentee a son altesse serenissime le Prince d'Orange et de Nassau*; a high-resolution image of this version of the map may be downloaded at https://www.archieven.nl.

FIGURE 93   Sir Godfrey Kneller, *John Churchill, 1st Duke of Marlborough, c.*1706
LONDON, NATIONAL PORTRAIT GALLERY 902. © NATIONAL PORTRAIT GALLERY, LONDON

CHAPTER 20

Generals Presenting Maps to the Emperor

Johann Baptist Homann, Leopoldi Magni Filio Iosepho I. Augusto Romanorum & Hungariae Regi ..., *c.1705–11*

The Duke of Marlborough also appears—in an interesting way—in the next cartouche we will consider, on a map by the famous German cartographer Johann Baptist Homann (1664–1724), who would become one of the most prolific map publishers of the seventeenth century.[1] The map is of Austria and southern Bavaria; the cartouche (Fig. 94) shows a scene in the court of the Holy Roman Emperor Leopold I (1640–1705), who had been one of the prime movers of the War of the Spanish Succession. Initially Leopold fought for his own claim to the Kingdom of Spain, but in 1703 he assigned that claim to his younger son the Archduke Charles (1685–1740). Leopold is seated on his throne at the left of the scene; behind him is a banner with the double-headed eagle of the Holy Roman Empire, and on a table, his crown and orb.

Homann made different versions of the map with different titles in the frame below. On the hand-colored copy of the map illustrated here, which was printed c.1705, the title, translating and omitting the long list of provinces that comes in the middle, reads: *To Joseph I, Son of Great Leopold and Venerable King of the Romans and Hungary, etc., the Cartographer and Engraver Johann Baptist Homann Very Submissively Offers this General Map of the*

Austrian Regions in Germany.[2] That is, he made the map as a gift for Leopold's son Joseph (1678–1711). The title on another of his versions of the map that bears no date is more revealing; it reads:[3]

"To Joseph I, Son of Great Leopold and Venerable King of the Romans and Hungary, as He Set Out to the Field to Take Command of the Army of the Rhine, the Most Humble Johann Baptist Homann Very Submissively Offered this General Map of Austria as a Token of his Solemn First Departure, with a Most Pious Prayer for His Perpetual Good Fortune, Victories, and Triumph."

That is, in this other title Homann specifies that he was giving the map to Joseph as he set off to take command of the Army of the Rhine, specifically the Siege of Landau in 1702, when he was 23 years old, which ended up being Joseph's only military experience.[4] The map includes Vienna towards its eastern edge, and Landau (here *Landow*) towards its northwest corner, so Joseph could easily have used it for his journey. This title indicates a

---

1 On Homann see Wilhelm Eberle, "Der Nürnberger Kartograph Johann Baptista Homann, zu seinem 200. Todestage. Ein Lebensbild," *Mitteilungen und Jahresberichte der Geographischen Gesellschaft in Nürnberg* 3 (1923–24), pp. 1–24; Christian Sandler, *Johann Baptista Homann, Matthäus Seutter und ihre Landkarten: ein Beitrag zur Geschichte der Kartographie* (Amsterdam: Meridian Publishing, 1964); Markus Heinz, "A Programme for Map Publishing: The Homann Firm in the Eighteenth Century," *Imago Mundi* 49 (1997), pp. 104–115; Michael Hochedlinger, "Die Ernennung von Johann Baptist Homann zum kaiserlichen Geographen im Jahre 1715," *Cartographica Helvetica* 24 (2001), pp. 37–40; and Steven M. Zahlaus, "Vom rechten Glauben und von guten Geschäften: der Kupferstecher, Kartograf und Verleger Johann Baptist Homann," in Michael Diefenbacher, Brigitte Korn, and Steven M. Zahlaus, eds., *Von nah und fern: Zuwanderer in die Reichsstadt Nürnberg; Begleitband zur gleichnamigen Ausstellung im Stadtmuseum Fembohaus vom 29. März bis 10. August 2014* (Petersberg: Michael Imhof Verlag, 2014), pp. 205–212. Markus Heinz proposes a stylistic chronology of Homann's cartouches in "Modell eines Werkskataloges des kartographischen Verlages Homann, Homanns Erben und Fembo in Nürnberg (1702–1848)," Ph.D. Dissertation, Universität Wien, 2002, on pp. 155–162 in its 2022 online publication.

2 The full title of Homann's 1705 map is *Leopoldi Magni Filio Iosepho I. Augusto Romanorum & Hungariae Regi etc. Hanc Austricarum Regionum in Germania Generalem Tabulam: In Qua Archiducatus Austriae, Ducatus Stiriae, Carinthiae, Carnioliae, Comitatus Tyrolis Cum Dependentiis Ortenaviae, Brisigaviae, Praefectura Sueviae &c. nec non Regnum Bohemiae cum parte Ducatus Silesiae & March. Moraviae continentur Submississime offert auctor et sculptor Ioannes Baptista Homannus.*

3 The full title of this other version of Homann's map, which must have been printed before Joseph's departure, is *Leopoldi magni filio Iosepho I. augusto romanorum et Hung. regi: ad capessendum Rhenanae militiae imperium in castra proficiscenti hanc Germaniae Austriacae generalem tabulam: primae profectionis Augustae indicem cum voto piissimo perpetuae felicitatis, victoriarum e triumphi submississime obtulit infimus* (Nuremberg: Johann Baptist Homann, c.1702).

4 On the 1702 Siege of Landau see Emil Heuser, *Die Belagerungen von Landau in den Jahren 1702 und 1703* (Landau: Kaußler, 1894), which includes a reproduction of a rare print showing the end of the siege, titled *Die von Ihro Römisch Königl: Maijestät Iosepho I. besiegte Vestung Landau und der darauf erfolgte Abzug der Französischen Besatzung* (Vienna, 1702); a high-resolution image of this print is available on the website of the Rijksmuseum, where it is cataloged under the title *Inname van Landau, 1702*. There is also a somewhat later map of the siege by Gabriel Bodenehr, *Die Belagerung Landau in A.o 1702* (Augsburg: G. Bodenehr, 1718).

© CHET VAN DUZER, 2023 | DOI:10.1163/9789004523838_022

FIGURE 94   Johann Baptist Homann, *Leopoldi Magni Filio Iosepho I. Augusto Romanorum & Hungariae Regi ...*, 1705
MUNICH, BAYERISCHE STAATSBIBLIOTHEK, 2 MAPP. 12–35. COURTESY OF THE BAYERISCHE STAATSBIBLIOTHEK

very specific context of the map's creation, suggesting the cartographer's desire to gain the favor of the young prince.

The cartouche shows Leopold receiving four men, three of them generals who, remarkably, hold maps showing the fields of action where they had been victorious. Thus on a map designed to be given to Leopold's son, we see generals offering maps to Leopold himself. The cartouche is very rich in terms of its consciousness of cartography, and specifically of the relationship between cartography and political power: maps are both tools to achieve military victory and symbols of those victories.[5] The first man, who is bowing before Leopold, is not identified and does not hold a map, but he is wearing armor, and this can only be Joseph taking leave of his father on his way to the battlefield. The emperor hands him a baton representing his authority to command.

Behind Joseph is a general holding a map; at the top of the map is the title *Expeditio Rhenana*, "The Campaign on the Rhine," and the text at the bottom reads *Linea ducitur ad Rhenum Duce Lud: Badense*, "The [battle] line on the Rhine was drawn under the leadership of Ludovicus Badensis," that is, Louis William, Margrave of

Baden-Baden (1655–1707), commander of the army of the Holy Roman Empire.[6] *Landau* is prominent in the upper left part of the map, and the campaign on the Rhine was the Siege of Landau, so when young Joseph departed from Vienna to take over the siege, he would be doing so with Louis William I (in fact Joseph would have the command in name only, Louis William would continue making the decisions). The city of *Baden*, marking the seat of Louis William's margravate, is just east of the Rhine in the upper left part of the map, northeast of Strasbourg.

The second general holds a map with the title *Expeditio Transalpina*, "The Campaign Across the Alps," and the text at the bottom of the maps reads *Exercitus per Alpes Italiam intrat Duce Eug. Sabaudo*, "The army crossed the Alps to enter Italy under the leadership of Eugenius Sabaudus," that is, Prince Eugene of Savoy (1663–1736). Eugene was a field marshal for the Holy Roman Empire, and like Marlborough, was one of the most successful generals of his time.[7] In 1701 he had led an army of 30,000

5   On cartouches symbolizing political victories see Christine M. Petto, "Semblance of Sovereignty: Cartographic Possession in Map Cartouches and Atlas Frontispieces of Early Modern Europe," in Gary Backhaus and John Murungi, eds., *Symbolic Landscapes* (Dordrecht: Springer, 2009), pp. 227–250.

6   On Louis William I see Manfred Kehrig, "Markgraf Ludwig Wilhelm von Baden-Baden, der Türkenlouis," *Acta Historica Academiae Scientiarum* 33.2–4 (1987), pp. 377–383; and Christian Greiner, "Der 'Türkenlouis' und Österreich-dynastische Interessenpolitik im militärischen Dienst des Hauses Habsburg," *Österreich in Geschichte und Literatur mit Geographie* 37.4–5a (1993), pp. 239–258.

7   On Eugene, in English see Derek McKay, *Prince Eugene of Savoy* (London: Thames and Hudson, 1977). Incidentally Eugene had a very large map collection, which included the Tabula Peutingeriana

men southward across the Alps to take the war into Italy.[8] The map shows the terrain he crossed, from Innsbruck, Austria, south to Mantua in Italy and the Po River.

In the background between Louis William and Prince Eugene is another noble: this is no doubt the Duke of Marlborough. Why is the commander of the military forces of the Grand Alliance in the background, without a map to proclaim his victories?[9] The answer is that Marlborough was not held in the same high level of respect in the court at Vienna, and by the cartographer, as he was in other circles.

The fourth man in the line before Emperor Leopold is younger and less elegantly dressed than the generals in front of him. The title of the map he holds is *Expeditio Adriatica*, "The Campaign in the Adriatic," and the text below reads *Alimentatur Exercitus Provisione maritima cura L. Bar. de Forsteren*, "The army was fed by supplies brought by sea under the direction of Baron Forstner." Little is known about the German Baron Forstner, more fully Wolfgang Jakob Baron von Forstner, but he was a close advisor of Louis William, Margrave of Baden-Baden,[10] so his presence before Leopold with Louis William is not

unexpected. The details of the supply voyages are difficult to see on the map that the Baron holds, but fortunately at the bottom of the large map the cartographer illustrates the Baron's ships and shows the routes they took, and writes that "Ships with provisions from the Gulfs of Trieste and Kvarner arrived at the mouth of the Po River for the Imperial army in 1702."[11] And the map shows the ships bringing supplies from *Zeng* (now Senj), Croatia; *S. Veit am Flaum* (Rijeka), Croatia; and Trieste, Italy; and taking them to the Po Delta. I do not find other records of this shipment of supplies, but Eugene was in desperate need of supplies after crossing the Alps and did not have the support from Vienna that he had hoped for.

And finally, behind the Baron there is an attendant holding the reins of a horse that is ready to carry Prince Joseph to Landau for his first experience of battle, guided by Louis William and checking his progress on the map that Homann had prepared for this journey. Joseph became emperor in 1705, but his reign was short, as he died in 1711.[12]

Interestingly, Homann sold another map of Austria that had a completely different and much less thoughtful or stimulating cartouche. The map is titled *Germania Austriaca*, "Austrian Germany"; some catalogers ascribe it a date as early as 1702, but it cannot have been printed before about 1711.[13] The cartouche (Fig. 95) shows a personification of a river, no doubt the Danube, pouring forth his waters, and beside him a globe showing Germany and Italy, above which there is an imperial eagle with the banner *Constantia et Fortitudine*, "By constancy and fortitude," which was the motto of the Holy Roman Emperor Charles VI—Joseph's younger brother, who took the throne following Joseph's death. The rest of the cartouche consists of *putti* holding the coats of arms of the various provinces on the map, a banal and commonplace type of cartouche decoration. It seems that Homann was more sympathetic to Joseph than he was to Charles.

Homann's cartouche for Joseph was copied, but with significant changes, by the German cartographer Petrus Schenk in a map he published in 1706 (Fig. 96),[14] and

and the Atlas Blaeu-van der Hem; on his death his map collection, together with the rest of his library, passed to his heiress, Princess Maria Anna Victoria of Savoy, who sold them to the Emperor, the maps now reside in the Österreichische Nationalbibliothek. The ÖNB has two manuscript catalogs of Eugene's library, including his maps, but these have not been studied; see Vittoria Feola, "Prince Eugene and his Library: A Preliminary Analysis," *Rivista Storica Italiana* 126.3 (2014), pp. 742–787, esp. 762. There are no doubt maps related to his military campaigns in the Kriegsarchiv in Vienna. I thank Jan Mokre for discussing Eugene's map collection with me.

8   There is a map with a spectacular scene of Eugene and his army crossing the Alps by Caspar Luyken, *Le Grand Teatre de la Guerre en Italie* (Amsterdam, *c*.1702), and a good image of a nicely hand-colored copy of the map is available on the website of the Rijksmuseum. On this map see Marco van Egmond, *Covens & Mortier: A Map Publishing House in Amsterdam* (Houten: Hes & De Graaf, 2009), pp. 376–377, no. 18.2.

9   Incidentally although Marlborough is shown without a map here, there is a portrait of him consulting a map. The portrait is cataloged under the assigned title *John Churchill, 1st Duke of Marlborough; John Armstrong* and has been attributed to Enoch Seeman, and assigned a date *c*.1720; it is in the National Portrait Gallery, London, NPG 5318. It shows Marlborough and his staff officer Colonel John Armstrong (1674–1742) discussing a map titled *Plan of the Siege of Bouchain*, which took place in 1711.

10   So William Coxe, *Memoirs of John, Duke of Marlborough with his Original Correspondence: Collected from the Family Records at Blenheim and Other Authentic Sources* (London: Longman, Hurst, Rees, Orme & Brown, 1818–1819), vol. 1, p. 384; there is a paragraph about Baron Forstner in Aloys Schulte, *Markgraf Ludwig Wilhelm von Baden und der Reichskrieg gegen Frankreich, 1693–1697* (Heidelberg: C. Winter's Universitätsbuchhandlung, 1901), p. 291.

11   Homann's original Latin text regarding Baron Forstner's resupply efforts reads: *Naves provisionariae ex Sinibus Tergesti et Flanatico ad Padi Ostium pro Cesareo Milite advehuntur 1702.*

12   On Joseph's rule see Charles W. Ingrao, *In Quest and Crisis: Emperor Joseph I and the Habsburg Monarchy* (West Lafayette, IN: Purdue University Press, 1979).

13   The full details of this map are Johann Baptist Homann, *Germania Austriaca complectens S.R.I. circulum Austriacum ut et reliquas in Germania augustissimae domui Austr. devotas terras haereditarias* (Nuremberg: Io. Bapt. Homann, *c*.1711).

14   On Schenk see I. van Eeghen, "Petrus Schenk en Zijn 'Afbeeldinge Der Voornaamste Gebouwen Van Amsterdam'," *Jaarboek van het*

FIGURE 95   Johann Baptist Homann, *Germania Austriaca* (Nuremberg, 1710)
UNIVERSITY OF CHICAGO LIBRARY, G6030 1710 .H6. COURTESY OF THE UNIVERSITY OF CHICAGO LIBRARY

FIGURE 96   Pieter Schenk, *Invictissimis Heroibus Duci Marleborough, Principibus Eugenio Sabaudo ...* (s.l., 1706)
ROTTERDAM MARITIME MUSEUM, KAART K7

those changes make for an interesting object lesson in the repurposing of a cartouche. Schenk changed the dedication of the map, the occasion the map celebrates, the identities of two of the people depicted in the cartouche, and also added a map within the cartouche.

Schenk does not dedicate his map to Joseph—despite the fact that Joseph had become Emperor the year before—and in fact he removes Joseph from the cartouche entirely,[15] re-identifying the first man in front of the Emperor as Marlborough. He instead dedicates the map to the generals, who now number four, and changes the identity of two of them. The title of his map, translated, reads:[16]

Genootschap Amstelodamum 66 (1974), pp. 117–136; and Peter van der Krogt, "Petrus Schenk I, overleden te Leipzig in 1711," *Caert-Thresoor* 4.2 (1985), pp. 37–38.

15   It is possible that Schenk intended the man on the throne to represent Joseph as Emperor, but if so, he should have made the sovereign look like Joseph, rather than leaving him with Leopold's distinctive mustache.

16   The full title of Schenk's map is *Invictissimis Heroibus Duci Marleborough, Principibus Eugenio Sabaudo, et Hassiae-Casselio, ut et Nobil. Do. Cuts; plurimis Victoriis atque Trophaeis, praecipue*

"For the Unconquered Heroes Duke Marlborough, Prince Eugene of Savoy, Hesse-Kassel, and the Noble Lord Cutts, Famous for So Many Victories and Trophies, Particularly the Most Glorious Victory over the French and the Bavarians Reported at Blenheim on August 13, 1704—[for Them] Petrus Schenck Most Humbly and Devotedly Made this General Map of Germany and Austria, with a Pure and Truly Loyal Prayer for Their Prosperity, Additional Victories, and Triumphs Most Worthy of Honor."

Schenk confirms the identity of the first general as Marlborough by having Leopold address him by name and also offer him the laurels of victory,[17] and Eugene of Savoy is still present, but Schenk has replaced Louis William, Margrave of Baden-Baden, with "Hesse-Kassel," that is, Charles I, Landgrave of Hesse-Kassel (1654–1730),[18] who supplied soldiers to the imperial army in the War of the Spanish Succession, but had nothing like the central role of Louis William. And he has replaced the admittedly obscure Baron Forstner with "Noble Lord Cutts," that is, Lieutenant-General John Cutts, 1st Baron Cutts, (1661–1707), a dashing poet and soldier who was the third in command at the Battle of Blenheim, which is mentioned in the map's title.[19]

The fourth commander depicted in Schenk's cartouche, who, if we follow the order in the map's title, must be Cutts, holds the map that shows Baron Forstner's exploits, which is awkward and confusing to the viewer. The third commander, who must be Charles I of Hesse-Kassel, is obliged to hold two maps, one largely covering the other, which are those that in those that in Homann's map show the exploits of Eugene of Savoy and Louis William of

Baden-Baden—again, an inelegant solution. The second commander, Eugene of Savoy, holds the new map, which has a different layout than the other three, lacking the title cartouche at the top. The text at the bottom of the map reads "Campaign on the Danube. The French and Bavarians were killed in a slaughter by the Dukes Marlborough and Eugene in the year 1704."[20] Near the top of the map we see *Plintheim*, one of the spellings of Blenheim, and also *Hocstetta*, for Höchstädt, the village from which the German name for the battle (Zweite Schlacht bei Höchstädt) derives. So Eugene holds a map of the Battle of Blenheim,[21] in which both he and Marlborough were active and victorious, and it seems that in Schenk's mind this makes up for the fact that Marlborough is not holding a map.

Schenk knew a good cartouche when he saw one, and it was natural that in changing the purpose of the map to celebrate the Alliance's military victories, he would bring Marlborough back to prominence. But by altering the identities of two of the commanders without changing their maps he made a muddle of the map's politics and image of history, and ruined its ability to win him favor: it is difficult to imagine Charles I of Hesse-Kassel or John Cutts being pleased with their confused depictions on the map. And for that matter neither Marlborough nor Eugene would be gratified that they have only one map to depict both of their victories.

The mess that Schenk made of the cartouche is aptly symbolized by the attendant standing off to the right with the horse, which in Homann's map had been ready to carry Joseph to his first command at the Siege of Landau. Here the attendant and the horse, though they look much the same as they did in Homann's cartouche, have been stripped of their purpose, and seem not only superfluous but also forlorn.

---

     vero Gloriosissima illa de Gallis Bavarisque reportata prope Hogstettam victoria XIII. Aug. 1704, inclytis Hanc Germaniae, Austriacae Generalem Tabulam: Cum candido et vere pio voto propriae prosperitatis certarum Victoriarum augustissimorumque Triumphorum humillime et devotissime sacram facit P. Schenck.

17   In Schenk's cartouche Leopold says to Marlborough, *Accipe Dux Marlborough Lauros Virtute, Trophaeis Dignos: aeternus queis tibi partus honor,* "Accept, Duke of Marlborough, these laurels which are worthy of your virtue and victories, by which you have won eternal honor."

18   For recent discussion of Charles I see Holger Th. Gräf, Christoph Kampmann, and Bernd Küster, eds., *Landgraf Carl (1654–1730): fürstliches Planen und Handeln zwischen Innovation und Tradition* (Marburg: Historische Kommission für Hessen, 2017).

19   On Cutts see Stanley Simpson Swartley, *The Life and Poetry of John Cutts* (Philadelphia: Press of Deputy Brothers Company, 1917).

---

20   The Latin text at the bottom of the map Eugene of Savoy is holding runs *Expeditio Danubiana, Galli et Bava[ri] occidione casei a Ducibus Marleburgo Eugenio Ao. 1704.*

21   I have not found a map of the Battle of Blenheim that is convincing as a model for the map that Eugene holds, and comparing with other maps, it seems that Schenk was rather vague in his depiction of the battle lines. Compare for example the map by Jan van Vianen, *Plan de la Glorieuse Bataille Donnée le 13. Aoust Prés de Hochstett sur le Danube* (The Hague: Anna Beek, 1704), a good image of which is available on the website of the Rijksmuseum.

How to Build a Giant Cartouche

Nicolas de Fer, Carte de la mer du Sud et de la mer du Nord, *1713*

The French cartographer Nicolas de Fer (1646–1720), known for his maps' elaborate decoration, was one of the most successful mapmakers of the late seventeenth and early eighteenth centuries, enjoying an appointment as royal cartographer for Louis XIV.[1] His 1713 map of the Pacific and Atlantic Oceans is his masterpiece, surpassing even his 1698 wall map of the Americas,[2] and yet very little has been written about it—in particular, there is nothing about its spectacular program of cartouches. The plates were engraved by Pieter Starckman; when the map's ten sheets are assembled, the resulting depiction of the oceans measures 3.5 × 6.8 feet (108 × 207 cm). Extravagantly, it bears two titles in its upper margin, one corresponding to each ocean: *Carte de la Mer du Sud et des costes d'Amerque* [*sic*] *et d'Asie, situées sur cette mer* ("Map of the Pacific Ocean and the Coasts of America and of Asia Situated on this Ocean"), and *Carte de la Mer du Nord et des costes d'Amerique, d'Europe et d'Afrique, situées sur cette mer* ("Map of the Atlantic Ocean and the Coasts of America, Europe, and Africa Situated on this Ocean") (Fig. 97).[3]

The map is remarkable for the centrality of the New World and for its emphasis on exploration, commerce, and the connectedness of the world. In the northern part of North America there are portraits of nine famous European explorers with banners summarizing their accomplishments,[4] and trade routes and the tracks of several explorers are indicated in the two oceans. In the North Pacific there is a cartouche depicting beavers engaged in various imagined industrious activities, which de Fer copied from the famous cartouche on his own 1698 map of the Americas;[5] and beside it, a cartouche showing the hunting of beavers, elk, and bears, inspired by a chapter in Nicolas Denys' *Description geographique et historique des costes de l'Amerique Septentrionale* ("Geographical and Historical Description of the Coasts of North America") of 1672.[6] In the North Atlantic there is a cartouche showing how cod is processed and salted, which is also copied from de Fer's own 1698 map of the Americas, and was inspired by chapters in Denys' *Description geographique*.[7] Of course the beaver pelts and salted cod were two important products of North America.

With regard to the cartographer's interest in showing the connectedness of the world, in the upper right corner of the map, in Europe, there is a cartouche with an inset

---

1 On de Fer see P.-S. Curville, "Fer, Nicolas de," in Roman d'Amat, ed., *Dictionnaire de biographie française* (Paris: Letouzey et Ané, 1933–2018), vol. 13, cols. 1001–1002; and Brian Kentish, "Nicolas de Fer (1646–1720): Geographer to the French King," *MapForum* 2 (2004), pp. 24–28.

2 On de Fer's 1698 wall map of the Americas see Edward H. Dahl, "The Original Beaver Map: De Fer's 1698 Wall Map of America," *The Map Collector* 29 (1984), pp. 22–26; Thomas Suárez, *Shedding the Veil: Mapping the European Discovery of America and the World, Based on Selected Works from the Sidney R. Knafel Collection of Early Maps, Atlases, and Globes 1434–1865* (Singapore: World Scientific, 1992), pp. 140–144, addressing the political aspects of the map; and Philip D. Burden, *The Mapping of North America* (Rickmansworth, UK: Raleigh Publications, 1996–2007), vol. 2, pp. 455–457. A high-resolution image of the 1705 state of the map is available at https://searchworks.stanford.edu.

3 On de Fer's 1713 map of the Pacific and Atlantic see Henry R. Wagner, *The Cartography of the Northwest Coast of America to the Year 1800* (Berkeley: University of California Press, 1937), vol. 2, no. 506; Thomas Suárez, *Early Mapping of the Pacific* (Singapore: Periplus Editions, 2004), pp. 104–105; and Jean-Marc Besse and Nicolas Verdier, "Iconography, Ornamentation, and Cartography," in Matthew H. Edney and Mary Sponberg Pedley, eds., *The History of Cartography*, vol. 4, *Cartography in the European Enlightenment* (Chicago and London: University of Chicago Press, 2019), pp. 651–658, at 652–655. A

high-resolution image of an un-colored exemplar of the map is available at https://searchworks.stanford.edu.

4 De Fer borrows the portraits of the explorers from his own world map titled *Mappe-monde ou carte générale de la terre* (Paris: N. de Fer, 1705), which appeared in his *Atlas curieux* of that year. A high-resolution image of this world map is available at https://loc.gov.

5 On the impressive cartouche depicting beavers on de Fer's 1698 map of the Americas see Dahl, "The Original Beaver Map" (see note 2); and for additional discussion see François-Marc Gagnon, "La première iconographie du castor," *Scientia Canadensis* 31.1–2 (2008), pp. 12–26.

6 The scene of hunting beavers, elk, and bears is inspired by Nicolas Denys' *Description geographique et historique des costes de l'Amerique Septentrionale* (Paris: Claude Barbin, 1672), vol. 2, chapter 25, pp. 419–441. Denys' book has been translated into English by William Francis Ganong as *The Description and Natural History of the Coasts of North America* (*Acadia*) (Toronto: The Champlain Society, 1908), where this passage in vol. 2, chapter 25, pp. 426–434. On Denys see Bernard Pothier, "Nicolas Denys: The Chronology and Historiography of an Acadian Hero," *Acadiensis* 1.1 (1971), pp. 54–70.

7 On the processing and salting of cod see Denys, *Description geographique*, vol. 2, chapters 10, 13, 14, and 15.

FIGURE 97   Nicolas de Fer, *Carte de la mer du Sud et de la mer du Nord* (Paris, 1713)
            COURTESY OF BARRY LAWRENCE RUDERMAN ANTIQUE MAPS

map showing the Strait of Gibraltar, which connects the Mediterranean with the Atlantic. It is telling that de Fer prioritizes showing the details of this passage over showing eastern France, Germany, and Italy. The left-hand part of the frame is a bust of Hercules with his pillars, the traditional western limit of the world as known to Europe, located at the Strait of Gibraltar;[8] at the bottom of the frame there are two human heads back-to-back, one European and the other a Berber, indicating the peoples on either side of the Strait. The cartographer could draw on two earlier maps of his own for depicting the Strait.[9]

In central North Africa de Fer placed a cartouche not about the sources of the Nile, but rather a view of the Cape of Good Hope, the point of passage between the South Atlantic and the Southern Indian Oceans, together with a detail of the fort the Dutch had established there.

The cartographer had included a more rudimentary view of the Cape, and also a plan of the fort, on his 1698 map of Africa,[10] but the image on his 1713 map is much closer to a separate view of the Cape he published in 1705.[11] Below at the Cape on the map proper de Fer has some text about the history of its discovery and about the establishment of the fort, and he shows the route around the Cape up to Europe, specifically to Port-Louis in France, which was the home of the French East India Company (Compagnie française pour le commerce des Indes orientales).

Given de Fer's interest in the connectedness of the oceans on this map, we might have expected a cartouche with an inset map of the Strait of Magellan—the passage between the two oceans the map depicts—but evidently he felt that his depiction of the Strait on the map proper,

---

8   For discussion of the early historical cartography of the Strait of Gibraltar and the Pillars of Hercules see Chet Van Duzer, "Rebasando los Pilares de Hércules: El Estrecho de Gibraltar en la cartografía histórica," in Virgilio Martínez Enamorado, ed., *I congreso internacional: Escenarios urbanos de al-Andalus y el Occidente Musulmán (Vélez-Málaga, 16–18 de junio de 2010)* (Malaga: Ayuntamiento de Vélez-Málaga and Fondo Europeo de Desarrollo Regional de la Unión Europea, 2011), pp. 257–292.

9   De Fer's two earlier maps of the Strait of Gibraltar are *Le Detroit de Gibraltar par lequel l'Ocean entre dans la Mer Mediterranée, et qui separe l'Europe de l'Afrique* (Paris: De Fer, 1696); and *Le Fameux Detroit de Gibraltar* (Paris: De Fer, 1699). Both appear in de Fer's *Atlas curieux* of 1705, in vol. 1.

10   Nicolas de Fer, *L'Afrique, où tous les points principaux sont placés sur les observations ... de l'Académie royale des sience [sic]* (Paris: De Fer, 1698); a zoomable image of the map may be consulted at https://gallica.bnf.fr. Incidentally Vincenzo Coronelli in his map *Route maritime de Brest à Siam, et de Siam à Brest, faite en 1685. et 1686. selon les remarques des six Peres Iesuites* (Paris: J.B. Nolin, 1687), includes a view of the Cape of Good Hope in a cartouche in North Africa; a high-resolution image of the map is available at https://searchworks.stanford.edu.

11   Nicolas de Fer, *Cap de Bonne Esperance; Baye de a Table; le Fort du Cap de Bonne Esperance aux Hollandois*, which appeared in his *Atlas curieux* (Paris, 1705), vol. 1, where he has some paragraphs of text about the Cape.

together with its central position on the map and also his remarks on its discovery, sufficed.[12]

In the lower left corner of the map he has a cartouche with an inset map of the Isthmus of Panama, apparently to show the spot where the Atlantic and Pacific are closest to each other. This map is based on an earlier map of the Isthmus that de Fer had created.[13] The same corner of the 1713 map has a cartouche with an inset map of the Mariana Islands, presumably featured because they were on the route of the Manila Galleon on its route across the Pacific—and indeed four of the Transpacific routes shown on the map go through or by the Marianas, suggesting that they are a sort of eastern gateway to the ocean. De Fer notes that he depicts the islands following the map of the Jesuit Charles Le Gobien in 1701.[14] In the right-hand part of the cartouche's frame there is a scene of some inhabitants of the Ladrones Islands, the "Islands of the Thieves," leaping off a European ship with some small items they have taken.[15]

The map also has two enormous cartouches that occupy much of the South Pacific and South Atlantic that combine multiple inset maps, ethnographic scenes, and images of plants and animals. Part of the function of these cartouches is certainly to conceal uncertainty about the existence of a large southern continent, and at the same time they give the map a spectacular graphic richness. The framing of these two cartouches consists in a thin string of conjoined baroque borders, which are difficult to follow because several scenes at the tops of the cartouches are outside the frames, and because they are sometimes extended to form frames within the larger frame.

I will now give a detailed account of the huge cartouche in the South Pacific (Fig. 98) to show how de Fer went about creating this complex composition by borrowing

images from several different sources.[16] Cartouche artists often thus borrow elements of their compositions from earlier sources, though most other cartouches are much smaller than de Fer's here.

The largest elements in the cartouche in the South Pacific are the inset maps, which from west to east are of the Mariana Islands and Isthmus of Panama, already mentioned; then the Port of Acapulco; the Gulf of Mexico and the Mississippi River; Callao and Lima (Peru); Valdivia (Chile); Mexico City; and La Concepción (Chile).[17] So there is some emphasis on ports, but space is also devoted to important features in the hinterlands of North America, namely the Mississippi River, which had been discovered for Europeans by the French, and Mexico City.[18]

Separating the inset maps along the map's bottom edge, that is, between the insets of Panama and Acapulco, between Acapulco and Lima, between Lima and Valdivia, and between Valdivia and La Concepción, are groups of local plants and animals. All of these images are copied from Charles de Rochefort's *Histoire naturelle et morale des iles Antilles de l'Amerique, enrichie de plusieurs belles figures des raretez les plus considerables qui y sont décrites* ("Natural and Moral History of the West Indies of America, Enriched by Several Beautiful Illustrations of the Most Important Rarities which are Described There") (Rotterdam: Arnould Leers, 1658), written to encourage

---

12   De Fer had printed a separate map of the Strait of Magellan titled *Le détroit de Magellan* (Paris: De Fer, 1705), which is included in vol. 1 of his *Atlas curieux*, accompanied by some paragraphs about the history of the Strait.

13   De Fer's earlier map of the Isthmus is titled *L'Istme et golfes de Panama et de Darien dressés pour l'intelligence des voyages de Lionnel Waffer* (s.l: s.n., 1708).

14   Charles Le Gobien's map of the Mariana Islands, titled *Archipel de St Lazare. Les Isles Marianes*, was printed in his *Histoire des isles Marianes, nouvellement converties à la religion chrestienne* (Paris: Nicolas Pepie, 1701). There is an English translation of his work: Charles Le Gobien, *History of the Mariana Islands*, trans. Yesenia Pumarada Cruz (Mangilao, Guam: University of Guam Press and Micronesian Area Research Center, 2016).

15   It was Magellan's men who had called the islands Islas de los Ladrones, Islands of the Thieves; the illustration was inspired by a passage in Le Gobien, *Histoire des isles Marianes* (see note 14), p. 4.

---

16   There is a recent book that similarly analyzes the many visual sources that the cartographer Rigas Velestinlis or Rigas Feraios (1757–1798) used in composing the title cartouche of his twelve-sheet 1797 map of Greece (Χάρτα της Ελλάδος), which is Εμμανουήλ Κωνσταντίνος Μιχαήλου, *Τα Εικονογραφικά Πρότυπα των Παραστάσεων που Περιβάλλουν τον Τίτλο της Χάρτας της Ελλάδος του Ρήγα Βελεστινλή* (Αθήνα: Μένανδρος, 2021), that is, Emmanouil Konstantinos Michailou, *The Pictorial Sources of the Depictions Surrounding the Title of the 'Charta of Greece' by Rigas Velestinlis* (Athens: Menandros, 2021) (ISBN 978-618-5447-11-3). For general discussion of the map see Evangelos Livieratos, "On the Cartography of Rigas *Charta*," e-*Perimetron* 3.3 (2008), pp. 120–145.

17   It is interesting to compare the selection of inset maps on de Fer's 1713 map—which in the South Atlantic includes inset maps of Río de la Plata, Havana, the Bay of Rio de Janeiro, and Vera Cruz—with those on an almost contemporary map by Herman Moll, *A New & Exact Map of the Coast, Countries and Islands within ye Limits of ye South Sea Company, from ye River Aranoca to Terra del Fuego ....* (London, c.1711). High-resolution images of Moll's map are available at https://loc.gov and https://jcb.luna imaging.com.

18   The map of Mexico City on de Fer's 1713 map is a precursor to his separate 1715 map of the city, titled *Plan de la fameuse et nouvelle ville de Mexique*. For discussion of that map see Manuel Carrera Stampa, "El plano de la ciudad de México en 1715 hecho por Nicolás de Fer," *Boletín de la Sociedad Mexicana de Geografía y Estadística* 65.2–3 (1948), pp. 413–433.

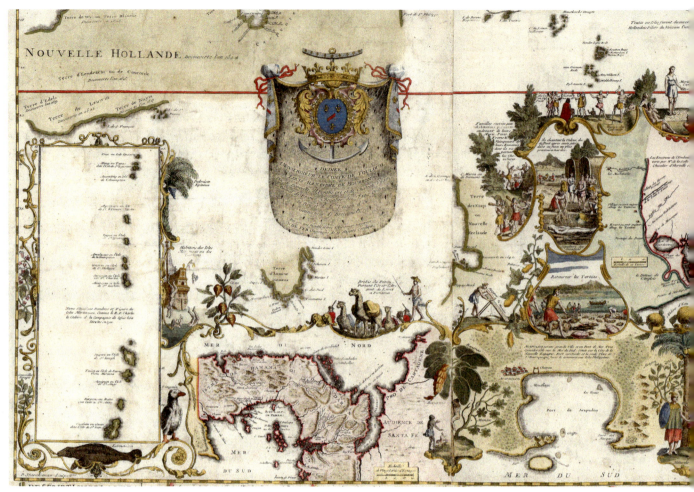

FIGURE 98   Detail of the huge cartouche in the South Pacific on de Fer's *Carte de la mer du Sud et de la mer du Nord*
COURTESY OF BARRY LAWRENCE RUDERMAN ANTIQUE MAPS

Huguenot emigration to the New World.[19] For example, the illustrations of banana and manioc trees between the insets of Panama and Acapulco come from pp. 91 and 88; and the watermelons, coco palm, cashew, and papaya come from pp. 116, 61 and 65, 55, and 50, respectively, in the book. The insets of Lima and Valdivia are separated by several birds (Fig. 99): an eagle attacking a parrot, a flamingo, a brown pelican (*Grand gozier*), a guineafowl, and a moorhen, and all of these birds come from one page in Rochefort's *Histoire* (Fig. 100). Similarly the cartographer

copied the animals between the insets of Valdivia and La Concepción—a muskrat, a peccary, an armadillo, and an opossum with its young (Fig. 101)—from one page in Rochefort (Fig. 102).

Most of the ethnographic scenes are located above the inset maps. Above the map of the Isthmus of Panama there is a scene depicting silver being transported from Lima to Panama on the backs of alpacas, which probably derives indirectly from a scene in Theodor de Bry's *America*.[20] Just to the right, the scene of processing manioc and the potato plant come from Rochefort's *Histoire*, pp. 88 and 100. Several of the ethnographic scenes above the inset maps of Acapulco and the Gulf of Mexico relate to Canada; the one that illustrates the marriage of

19   On Rochefort's *Histoire* see Everett C. Wilkie, Jr., "The Authorship and Purpose of the *Histoire naturelle et morale des îles Antilles*, an Early Huguenot Emigration Guide," *Harvard Library Bulletin* 2.3 (1991), pp. 27–84; Keith A. Sandiford, "Rochefort's 'History': The Poetics of Collusion in a Colonizing Narrative," *Papers on Language & Literature* 29.3 (1993), pp. 284–302; and Benoît Roux, "Le pasteur Charles de Rochefort et l'*Histoire naturelle et morale des îles Antilles de l'Amérique*," *Cahiers d'Histoire de l'Amérique Coloniale* 5 (2011) = *Les Indiens des Petites Antilles. Des premiers peuplements aux débuts de la colonisation européenne*, pp. 175–216. A digital version of the 1658 edition of the book is available at https://archive.org.

20   See Theodor de Bry, *Americae nona & postrema pars* (Frankfurt: Matthaeus Becker, 1602), [part 3], plate 4, a digital version of which is available at https://archive.org. De Fer included a similar scene of alpacas in the cartouche of his map *Le Perou dans l'Amerique meridionale, dressé sur les divers relations des flibustiers et nouveaux voyageurs* (Paris: I.F. Benard, 1719), a good image of which is available at https://jcb.lunaimaging.com.

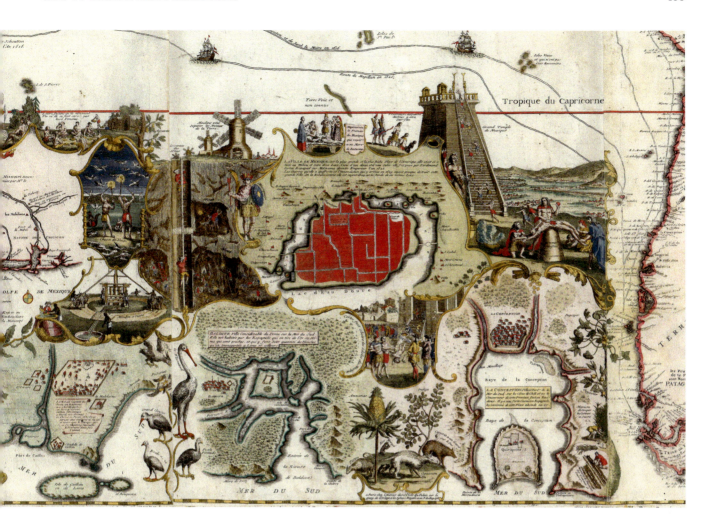

indigenous Canadians (Fig. 103) was copied from Louis Armand, Baron de Lahontan's *Nouveaux voyages* of 1703 (Fig. 104).[21]

The other scenes related to Canada seem to have been loosely inspired by Lahontan, but in some cases are intriguingly different from his illustrations, and it is not clear why this is the case. To the left of the marriage scene there are scenes of a presentation of a peace pipe (*calumet*) and the dance of the peace pipe, and below a

Canadian burial. The scene of presentation would seem to be based on Lahontan's description.[22] Lahontan illustrates the peace pipe dance as a circle of men around one man who dances while holding the pipe,[23] but the image on the map shows two men dancing around the pipe fixed to the ground. He also illustrates a Canadian burial, but shows coffins being placed on stilts,[24] rather than underground as de Fer depicts. On the other hand, the huts in

---

21   The illustration of the marriage ceremony is in Louis Armand de Lom d'Arce Lahontan, *Nouveaux voyages de mr le baron de Lahontan, dans l'Amerique septentrionale* (The Hague: Les Frères l'Honoré, 1703), vol. 2, following p. 132. On Lahontan and his work see A.H. Greenly, "Lahontan: An Essay and Bibliography," *Papers of the Bibliographical Society of America* 48.4 (1954), pp. 334–389; and David Allen Harvey, "The Noble Savage and the Savage Noble: Philosophy and Ethnography in the Voyages of the Baron de Lahontan," *French Colonial History* 11 (2010), pp. 161–191. There is an English translation of his work as Lahontan, *New Voyages to North-America*, ed. Reuben Gold Thwaites (Chicago: A.C. McClurg, 1905); in this edition the plate illustrating the marriage of indigenous Canadians is in vol. 2 following p. 492.

22   Lahontan describes the presentation of the peace pipe in ceremonies to secure peace in his *Nouveaux voyages* (see note 21), vol. 2, pp. 187–189; and his *New Voyages* (see note 21), vol. 2, pp. 508–509.

23   Lahontan illustrates the peace pipe dance in his *Nouveaux voyages* (see note 21), vol. 2, plate following p. 187, and describes the dance in vol. 2, pp. 187–189; also see vol. 1, pp. 137–144; and see and his *New Voyages* (see note 21), vol. 2, pp. 508–509, and also vol. 1, pp. 168–169.

24   For the illustration of the burial see Lahontan, *Nouveaux voyages*, vol. 2, plate following p. 148; a high-resolution image of this plate is available at https://jcb.lunaimaging.com.

FIGURE 99   Detail of the birds (an eagle attacking a parrot, a
flamingo, a brown pelican, a guineafowl, and a moorhen)
between the inset maps of Lima and Valdivia on de Fer's
Carte de la mer du Sud
COURTESY OF BARRY LAWRENCE RUDERMAN
ANTIQUE MAPS

FIGURE 101   Detail of the muskrat, a peccary, an armadillo, and an
opossum with its young between the inset maps of
Valdivia and La Concepción on de Fer's *Carte de la mer
du Sud*
COURTESY OF BARRY LAWRENCE RUDERMAN
ANTIQUE MAPS

FIGURE 100   De Fer's source for his birds: Charles de Rochefort's
Histoire naturelle et morale des iles Antilles de l'Amerique
(Rotterdam: Arnould Leers, 1658), p. 166
JOHN CARTER BROWN LIBRARY, E658 R674H (COPY 2).
COURTESY OF THE JOHN CARTER BROWN LIBRARY

FIGURE 102   De Fer's source for his animals: Charles de Rochefort's
Histoire naturelle et morale des iles Antilles de l'Amerique
(Rotterdam: Arnould Leers, 1665), p. 141
JOHN CARTER BROWN LIBRARY, E665 R674H.
COURTESY OF THE JOHN CARTER BROWN LIBRARY

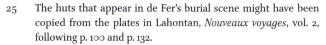

FIGURE 103   Detail of the marriage ceremony of indigenous
Canadians on de Fer's *Carte de la mer du Sud*
COURTESY OF BARRY LAWRENCE RUDERMAN
ANTIQUE MAPS

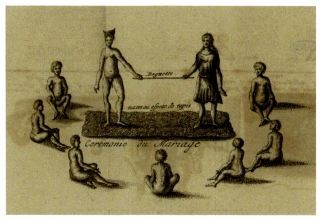

FIGURE 104   De Fer's source for his image of the marriage ceremony:
Louis Armand de Lom d'Arce Lahontan, *Nouveaux
voyages de mr le baron de Lahontan, dans l'Amerique
septentrionale* (The Hague: Les Frères l'Honoré, 1703),
vol. 2, following p. 132
JOHN CARTER BROWN LIBRARY, E703 L184N2.
COURTESY OF THE JOHN CARTER BROWN LIBRARY

the burial scene on de Fer's map are certainly copied from Lahontan.[25]

To the left of the burial there is a scene of men returning from battle with the scalps of their enemies and being welcomed back by their families.[26] Lahontan does describe warriors returning to their village with scalps, but says that the warriors carry them on their bows,[27] while de Fer depicts the men with clubs, and carrying the scalps in their hands. Below the burial there is a scene of men fishing for turtles and also catching them on the beach by turning them onto their backs. This is the artist's interpretation of Charles de Rochefort's description of the hunting of turtles.[28] To the right of the marriage there is a

scene of a feast, said to be called *vin*, in which the men are served by their wives,[29] but I find no related image or text in Lahontan, or indeed in other sources de Fer might have consulted. We see that de Fer spent considerable time reading to look for passages he wanted to illustrate in his cartouches, and was comfortable generating illustrations when the author of the book did not supply them.

To the right of the map of the Gulf of Mexico and above the map of Lima there is a striking scene of two men holding torches above their heads to hunt birds at night; this is de Fer's illustration of a passage in Nicolas Denys' *Description geographique et historique des costes de l'Amerique Septentrionale* (Paris, 1672),[30] a work that he made use of in other parts of this cartouche as well. Below this hunting scene there is an impressive, detailed image of an oxen-driven sugar mill being worked by slaves (Fig. 105); de Fer has copied this from one of the sources he used several times for this map, namely Charles de

25   The huts that appear in de Fer's burial scene might have been copied from the plates in Lahontan, *Nouveaux voyages*, vol. 2, following p. 100 and p. 132.

26   The text above the returning warriors reads *Familles restées aux habitations qui vont audevant de leurs Maris, Peres, Freres &. Vainquers de leurs Ennemis dont ils raportent les Chevelures*, that is, "Families who stayed at their dwellings who go before their husbands, fathers, brothers, etc., who defeated their enemies, whose scalps they bring back."

27   For Lahontan's description of warriors returning to their village with the scalps of their enemies see *Nouveaux voyages* (see note 21), vol. 2, p. 184; and *New Voyages* (see note 21), vol. 2, p. 505. Incidentally Guillaume Delisle includes an indigenous Canadian holding a scalp in the cartouche of his *Carte du Canada ou de la Nouvelle France et des decouvertes qui y ont été faites* (Paris: chez l'auteur, 1703). High-resolution images of later states of this map are available at https://loc.gov and https://searchworks.stanford.edu.

28   Rochefort describes the hunting of turtles in his *Histoire naturelle et morale des iles Antilles de l'Amerique* (Rotterdam: Arnould Leers, 1658), pp. 229–230. There is an earlier illustration of turning over turtles in Jean Baptiste du Tertre, *Histoire generale des Antilles habitées par les François* (Paris: T. Iolly, 1667–71), vol. 2, plate following p. 246.

29   The text accompanying the image of this feast reads *Leurs festins qu'ils nomment Vin ou ils se font servir par leurs Femmes*, that is, "Their feasts which they call 'vin,' where they are served by their wives."

30   The passage about the nocturnal hunting of birds is in Denys's *Description geographique*, vol. 2, chapter 26, pp. 442–444; and in his *The Description and Natural History of the Coasts of North America (Acadia)* (see note 6), vol. 2, chapter 26, pp. 435–436. Denys is writing about a New World tradition of hunting birds at night with lights, and incidentally there was a European tradition as well: see for example François Lacombe, *Dictionnaire du vieux langage françois* (Paris: Panckouche, 1766–67), Supplement, p. 73: "Brilleus, celui qui chasse de nuit aux oiseaux avec une lumiere."

FIGURE 105   Detail of the oxen-driven sugar mill on de Fer's *Carte de la mer du Sud*
COURTESY OF BARRY LAWRENCE RUDERMAN ANTIQUE MAPS

Rochefort's *Histoire naturelle*, specifically a plate that was not in the 1658 edition, but was added to the 1665 edition (Fig. 106).[31]

The spectacular mining scene to the right, which features men working with torches in multiple galleries, a long ladder to access the mine, and above, windmills to separate the metals from the ore, must be Potosí in what is now Bolivia, the most important silver mine in the New World, though it is not labeled, and the famous mountain is not depicted. It is not clear what source de Fer used for this image; tall ladders are prominent in many depictions of the mines of Potosí, for example the widely distributed image by Theodor de Bry,[32] and the windmills figure in an image of Potosí by Arnoldus Montanus.[33]

Further to the right, ranged around the inset map of Mexico City, are six images related to Mexico. The first depicts Magiscatzin or Maxixcatzin, Governor of the Republic of Tlaxcala, receiving baptism on his deathbed, probably based on the account in Antonio de Solís, *Histoire de la conquête du Mexique, ou de la Nouvelle Espagne* (Paris: Jeremie Bouillerot, 1691).[34] Next there is a generic scene of prisoners of war being led to sacrifice;[35] and then there is a striking image of the Templo Mayor of Mexico City (Fig. 107), adapted from that in Solís (Fig. 108).[36] The scene of human sacrifice at the bottom of the temple is also adapted from an image in Solís (Fig. 109), with the addition of a detail from Solís' text about the removal of

31   The illustration of the sugar mill is from Charles de Rochefort's *Histoire naturelle et morale des iles Antilles de l'Amerique, enrichie de plusieurs belles figures des raretez les plus considerables qui y sont d'écrites* (Rotterdam: Arnould Leers, 1658), between pages 332 and 333.

32   See Theodor de Bry, *Americae nona & postrema pars* (Frankfurt: Matthaeus Becker, 1602), [part 3], plate 3, a digital version of which is available at https://archive.org.

33   For the image of Potosí with windmills see Arnoldus Montanus, *De Nieuwe en onbekende weereld: of Beschryving van America en 't zuid-land* (Amsterdam: J. Meurs, 1671), following p. 372. A digital version of the book is available at https://loc.gov, and this image is available at https://jcb.lunaimaging.com.

34   For the account of Magiscatzin receiving baptism see Solís, *Histoire de la conquête du Mexique*, Book 5, chapter 5, p. 502; a digital version of the book is available at https://archive.org. On Solís see Frédéric Serralta, "Nueva biografía de Antonio de Solís y Rivadeneyra," *Criticón* 34 (1986), pp. 51–157; on the many editions of Solís's *Historia* see Luis A. Arocena, *Antonio de Solís, cronista indiano. Estudio sobre las formas historiográficas del barroco* (Buenos Aires: Editorial Universitaria, 1963), pp. 364–415.

35   It is probably not worth seeking a specific passage that inspired the generic scene of the prisoners of war being led to sacrifice, but one possibility would be Solís, *Histoire de la conquête du Mexique*, Book 3, chapter 12, p. 269.

36   The image of the Templo Mayor is in Solís, *Histoire de la conquête du Mexique*, Book 3, chapter 14, following p. 278.

FIGURE 106 De Fer's source for the sugar mill: the plate in Charles de Rochefort's *Histoire naturelle et morale des iles Antilles de l'Amerique* (Rotterdam: Arnould Leers, 1665), between pages 332 and 333

FIGURE 107 Detail of the Templo Mayor of Mexico City and human sacrifice on de Fer's *Carte de la mer du Sud*

FIGURE 108 De Fer's source for the image of the Templo Mayor: Antonio de Solís, *Histoire de la conquête du Mexique, ou de la Nouvelle Espagne* (Paris: Jeremie Bouillerot, 1691), following p. 278

pag. 275 L'Idole Viztzilipuztli

FIGURE 109 Image of human sacrifice in Antonio de Solís, *Histoire de la conquête du Mexique, ou de la Nouvelle Espagne* (Paris: Jeremie Bouillerot, 1691), Book 3, chapter 13, following p. 274

JOHN CARTER BROWN LIBRARY, B691 S687HP / 1-SIZE. COURTESY OF THE JOHN CARTER BROWN LIBRARY

plants and animals in the cartouche—from Rochefort's *Histoire naturelle*,[40] and scenes illustrating the planting and harvesting of sugarcane, visual renderings of a passage in Rochefort.[41]

This analysis of how de Fer composed this cartouche shows the great effort he went to both in locating illustrations he wished to copy and also in finding the textual passages he would interpret graphically. He employed a good variety of sources—De Bry, Rochefort, Denys, Solís, Le Gobien, and Lahontan, studying each work closely to determine how it could contribute to the composition. In this cartouche and the one in the South Atlantic de Fer was trying to convey to the users of his map a succinct panorama of the New World, showing its ports, its geographical features, its urban landscape, elements of its economy and culture, and its flora and fauna. Very far from being mere embellishment, the cartouche makes the map something more than a map. There is a temptation to describe maps that are rich in extra-geographical information as "encyclopedic," but as Angelo Cattaneo has noted, this would be a very loose and improper use of the word;[42] nonetheless de Fer's cartouches certainly make his map a multidisciplinary reference work.

Above the inset map of the Isthmus of Panama is the cartouche dedicating the map to Louis Alexandre de Bourbon, comte de Toulouse (1678–1737), the son of Louis XIV and his mistress Françoise-Athénaïs, the marquise de Montespan.[43] He amassed an impressive library, which was the subject of the first catalog of a private library to be issued in France in 1708.[44] Louis Alexandre owned a good selection of geographical works, atlases,

the victim's heart.[37] The view over the Valley of Mexico in the background, showing a causeway and a bridge linking the city to the mainland, is based on the right-hand part of a broader view in Solís.[38] Below the inset map of Mexico City there is a scene of Hernán Cortés having the Mexican idols destroyed, a visual representation of a passage in Solís.[39]

Finally, the right-hand border of this huge cartouche is formed by some of de Fer's rocaille embellishments above, and below, by a papaya tree copied—like the other

37 The image of human sacrifice is in Solís, *Histoire de la conquête du Mexique*, Book 3, chapter 13, following p. 274, with the detail about the removal of the victim's heart on p. 277.

38 The image of the Valley of Mexico is in Solís, *Histoire de la conquête du Mexique*, Book 3, chapter 13, following p. 272.

39 The passage about Cortés having the Mexican idols destroyed is in Solís, *Histoire de la conquête du Mexique*, Book 2, chapter 12, p. 143.

40 For the papaya tree at the right of the cartouche see Charles de Rochefort, *Histoire naturelle* (Rotterdam, 1658), p. 86.

41 The passage about sugarcane is in Rochefort's *Histoire naturelle* (Rotterdam, 1658), chapter 10, article 7, p. 106.

42 See Angelo Cattaneo, *Fra Mauro's Mappa Mundi and Fifteenth-Century Venice* (Turnhout: Brepols, 2011), pp. 244–249. For additional discussion of the status of maps as encyclopedias, see Andrea Nanetti, Angelo Cattaneo, Siew Ann Cheong, and Chin-Yew Lin, "Maps as Knowledge Aggregators: from Renaissance Italy Fra Mauro to Web Search Engines," *The Cartographic Journal* 52.2 (2015), pp. 159–167.

43 On Louis Alexandre see Jean Duma, *Les Bourbon-Penthièvre (1678–1793): une nébuleuse aristocratique au XVIIIᵉ siècle* (Paris: Publications de la Sorbonne, 1995); and Jacques Bernot, *Le Comte de Toulouse (1678–1737): Amiral de France, gouverneur de Bretagne* (Paris: F. Lanore, 2012).

44 The catalog is *Catalogue de la bibliothèque du Chateau de Rambouillet, appartenant à Son Altesse Sérénissime monseigneur le comte de Toulouse* (Paris: s.n., 1708).

and maps, and so was a sensible choice by de Fer as the dedicatee for his map.[45]

Two later adaptations of de Fer's 1713 map attest to its strong appeal. The first of these is by the Huguenot pastor Henri Abraham Chatelain (1684–1743), published in Amsterdam in 1719, and it is interesting to see how Chatelain plays up the map's features in his title, which translated into English runs "Very Curious Map of the South Sea, Containing New and Very Useful Remarks not only on the Ports and Islands of this Sea, but also on the Main Countries of Both North and South America, with the Names and Route of Travelers by Whom the Discovery was Made."[46] The second adaptation, published

in Amsterdam in about 1730, was by the engraver and publisher Andries de Leth (c.1662–1731), who reduced, reorganized, and simplified the program of cartouches. His title, translated, runs "New Map of the South Sea Drawn Up by Order of the Main Directors and Drawn from the Most Recent Accounts and the Relations of the Most Modern Navigators, both from France and from Spain, we have Attached Various Curious Remarks Regarding the Discoveries of Latitudes and Longitudes, the Manners of the Country, and Navigation."[47]

---

45   In the later edition of the catalog, *Catalogue de la bibliothèque du chasteau de Rambouillet, appartenant à son altesse serenissime Monseigneur le comte de Toulouse* (Paris: G. Martin, 1726–1734) the works on geography and that have maps are listed on pp. 277–291 and 607–611, and p. 140 in the supplement.

46   Chatelain's original title is *Carte tres curieuse de la Mer du Sud, contenant des remarques nouvelles et tres utiles non seulement sur les ports et iles de cette mer, mais aussy sur les principaux pays de l'Amerique tant Septentrionale que Meridionale, avec les noms & la route des voyageurs par qui la decouverte en a été faite*. High-resolution images of Chatelain's map are available at

https://www.digitalcommonwealth.org/search and https://catalog.princeton.edu.

47   De Leth's original title is *Carte nouvelle de la mer du Sud dressée par ordre des principaux directeurs, & tirée des memoires les plus recents et des Relations des Navigateurs les plus Modernes, tant de France, que d'Espagne, l'on ÿa joint, diverses remarques curieuses par raport aux decouvertes des Graduations des manierres du Pais que de la Navigation*. High-resolution images of two exemplars of the map are available at https://searchworks.stanford.edu. On this map see Oscar I. Norwich, Pam Kolbe, and Jeffrey C. Stone, *Norwich's Maps of Africa: An Illustrated and Annotated Carto-Bibliography*, 2nd edn., revised and edited by Jeffrey C. Stone (Norwich, VT: Terra Nova Press, 1997), pp. 366–367, no. 320.

Advertising Makes Its Entrance

George Willdey, Map of North America, *1715*

The cartouche on a map of North America by the London optical instrument maker and store-owner George Willdey (*c.*1676–1737) contains an advertisement for his shop and for the goods he had for sale, a striking entrance of commercialism into the realm of the cartouche that signals a new way that maps were sold and thought of in early eighteenth-century England. Willdey's is not the first advertisement in a cartouche: 25 years earlier, in about 1690, the prolific cartographer and able self-promoter Vincenzo Coronelli (1650–1718) made a map of the Mediterranean in which he includes a cartouche advertising his book of plans of cities and forts around the Mediterranean, which he saw as complementing the map.[1] But Coronelli's advertising cartouche is an exception: he did not make other such cartouches, and it was not a common practice among other cartographers of his epoch.[2]

Willdey was not a particularly learned man, and certainly not an expert in geography; he was a businessman dedicated to the success of a commercial enterprise. He had apprenticed as a maker of spectacles and set up his own shop in 1707 near the center of London, by St. Paul's Cathedral,[3] and in about 1709 began to sell maps and globes, initially in collaboration with the cartographers Charles Price (1679–1733) and John Senex (1678–1740), but Senex soon dropped out of the partnership. In 1710 Senex made a map of North America.[4] As we have seen before, many cartographers from the sixteenth to the eighteenth centuries placed a large cartouche in the northwestern part of the continent to conceal their ignorance of the region's geography, and Senex adhered to this same practice (Fig. 110). Senex's cartouche is unremarkable, with a feather headdress at the top, male and female native Americans (with an out-of-place parasol), and below a personification of America with a caiman and other New World animals and plants, including sugarcane and pineapples.

Willdey copied the geography of Senex's map exactly, but replaced the cartouche with a new one engraved

---

1 Coronelli's map is titled *Ristretto del Mediterraneo* (Venice, *c.*1690). A high-resolution image of the western sheet of the map, which includes the cartouche discussed here, is available at https://searchworks.stanford.edu. The text of the cartouche in the lower left-hand corner of the map, translated, reads: "Father Coronelli, maker of these two hydrographic maps, for greater elucidation of them, has published a book of more than two hundred drawings of the fortresses, cities, and other places located on the shores of the Mediterranean, which are sold both together with and separately from the other works of the same author, also in Paris, all with the privilege of publication from his Majesty. In the bookstore of I.B. Nolin in the Quay de l'Horloge du Palais, near Rue de Harlay by the sign of the Place des Victoires." The book in question is Vincenzo Coronelli, *Citta, fortezze, isole, e porti principale dell'Europa, in pianti, et in eluatione, descritte, e publicate ad uso dell'Academia cosmografica degli argonauti* (Venice: si vende da D. Padouani, 1689).

2 There is a case of a cartouche with a subtle visual advertisement for the shop of the map publisher Philip Lea (fl. 1683–1700) on his map *Spain and Portugal* of 1690: his shop was named Atlas and Hercules, and in the cartouche he depicts Atlas supporting the celestial sphere, and Hercules supporting the terrestrial sphere. See Henry G. Taliaferro, "Philip Lea and the Seventeenth-Century Map Trade," in Margaret Beck Pritchard and Henry G. Taliaferro, eds., *Degrees of Latitude: Mapping Colonial America* (Williamsburg: Colonial Williamsburg Foundation, 2002), pp. 394–412, esp. 402, 404, and 412; a high-resolution image of the map is available at https://www.digitalcommonwealth.org/search. Some other maps available at the publisher's shop are also advertised in the title cartouche of Louis Brion de la Tour's *Mappemonde ou sont marquées les nouvelles découvertes* (Paris: Esnauts & Rapilly, 1781).

3 On George Willdey see Sarah Tyacke, *London Map-Sellers, 1660–1720: A Collection of Advertisements for Maps Placed in the London Gazette, 1668–1719, with Biographical Notes on the Map-Sellers* (Tring: Map Collector Publications, 1978), pp. 146–148; Helen Clifford, "In Defence of the Toyshop: The Intriguing Case of George Willdey and the Huguenots," *Proceedings of the Huguenot Society of Great Britain and Ireland* 27.2 (1999), pp. 171–188; Laurence Worms and Ashley Baynton-Williams, *British Map Engravers: A Dictionary of Engravers, Lithographers and Their Principal Employers to 1850* (London: Rare Book Society, 2011), pp. 291–292; and David J. Bryden and Dennis L. Simms, "Trade Ephemera, Archimedes and the Opticians of London," *Atti della Fondazione Giorgio Ronchi* 62 (2007), pp. 797–838, esp. 799–800 and 807–809.

4 Senex's map is titled *North America Corrected from the Observations Communicated to the Royal Society at London, and the Royal Academy at Paris* (London, 1710); for discussion of it see Raymond Phineas Stearns, "Joseph Kellogg's Observations on Senex's Map of North America (1710)," *Mississippi Valley Historical Review* 23 (1936), pp. 345–354; for a catalog of his other maps and globes see the single sheet *A Catalogue of Globes, Maps, &c. Made by the late John Senex, F.R.S. and Continue to be Sold by his Widow Mary Senex, at the Globe, over-against St. Dunstan's Church in Fleet-Street: Where may be Had, All Maps and Globes, &c. as in Mr. Senex's Life-Time* (London: Mary Senex, 1741–1742).

© CHET VAN DUZER, 2023 | DOI:10.1163/9789004523838_024

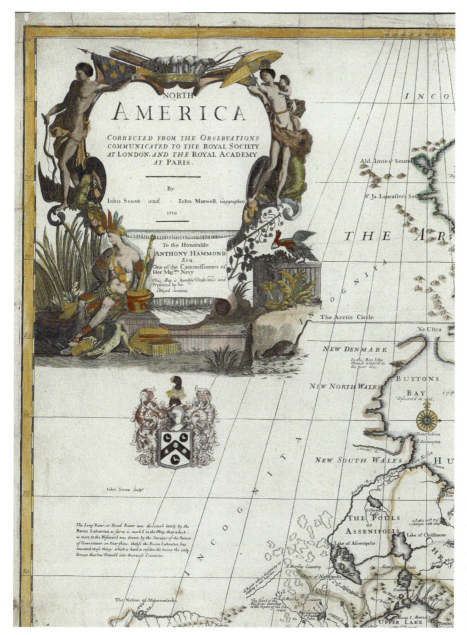

FIGURE 110
Detail of the cartouche on John Senex's
*North America Corrected from the
Observations Communicated to the Royal
Society at London, and the Royal Academy
at Paris* (London, 1710)
STANFORD UNIVERSITY, DAVID RUMSEY
MAP COLLECTION, G3301 1710 .S46.
COURTESY OF THE DAVID RUMSEY MAP
COLLECTION

by Henry Terrason (Fig. 111).[5] Above we have Fame, the god Mercury, and two *putti* holding aloft a portrait of

King George I, recently ascended to the throne, to whom Willdey dedicates the map; below there is a personification of America, with a caiman, sugarcane and pineapples as in Senex's cartouche, but Willdey adheres more closely to the personification of America in the 1603 edition of Cesare Ripa's *Iconologia* (Fig. 112). Willdey was no doubt using an intermediate source, such as a map with a personification of America that depended on Ripa, but Willdey and Ripa both have America holding an arrow pointing at herself, and both have a severed head shot through with

5   Willdey's map of North America is advertised in the *Post Man*, September 8–10, 1715, p. 2, which means that it was published that year—I thank Ashley Baynton-Williams for this reference. For discussion of the map see Margaret Beck Pritchard and Henry G. Taliaferro, *Degrees of Latitude: Mapping Colonial America* (Williamsburg, VA: Colonial Williamsburg Foundation, 2002), pp. 110–113. There are remarks on Willdey's cartouche in Gerard L. Alexander, "Willdey's Enterprising Map of North America," *Antiques* 82 (July, 1962), pp. 76–77 (he identifies many of the items advertised in the cartouche); David Bosse, "The World of Maps," *The American Magazine and Historical Chronicle* 3.2 (1987–88), pp. 60–62; Dalia Varanka, "Editorial and Design Principles in the Rise of the English World Atlases, 1606–1789," Ph.D. Dissertation, University of Wisconsin-Milwaukee, 1994, pp. 298–299; and J.B. Harley, "Power

and Legitimation in the English Geographical Atlases of the Eighteenth Century," in John A. Wolter and Ronald E. Grim, eds., *Images of the World: The Atlas Through History* (Washington, DC: Library of Congress, 1997), pp. 161–204, at 184.

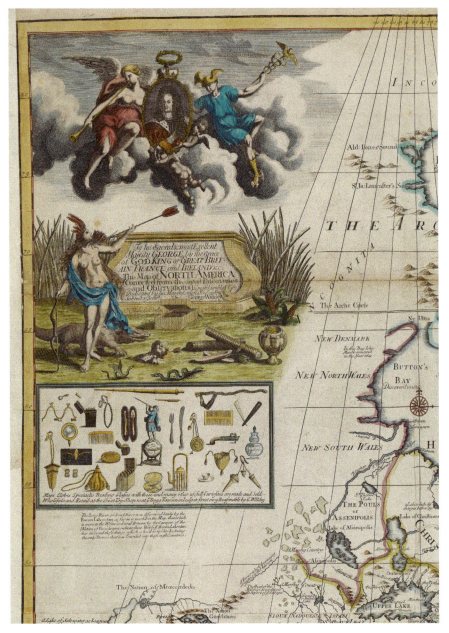

FIGURE 111
Detail of the cartouche on George Willdey's
Map of North America (*Corrected from
the latest Discoveries and Observations*)
(London, 1715)
STANFORD UNIVERSITY, DAVID RUMSEY
MAP CENTER, GLEN MCLAUGHLIN MAP
COLLECTION. COURTESY OF THE GLEN
MCLAUGHLIN MAP COLLECTION

an arrow at her feet.[6] The presence of the winged serpent is surprising, as that creature is usually associated with the Middle East or Asia, but this is another case of enthusiasm for exotica causing their appearance in geographically inappropriate contexts.[7] The personification of America gazes respectfully upward at King George, expressing the dependence of the colonies on Britain.

Further down there is a frame that displays some of the objects available for purchase in Willdey's store, including a hand mirror, spurs, buckles, a string of beads, a reticule, combs, a teapot, a pincushion, a telescope, traveling cutlery, a porcelain vase, a teacup and saucer, a razor, and so forth. The figure in the middle, of a man standing on a globe and looking through a telescope, is not an item that Willdey had for sale, but rather a representation of "Archimedes and Globe," which was one of the names of

---

6   It is worth remarking that Willdey was not using the recent English edition of Ripa, where the image of America is very different: see Cesare Ripa, *Iconologia, or, Moral Emblems*, trans. Pierce Tempest (London: Printed by Benj. Motte, 1709), between pages 53 and 54. A digital version of the book is available at https://archive.org.

7   On the transport of exotica from appropriate cartouche contexts to geographically inappropriate ones see "The Sources of Cartouches" in the Introduction above, and also Benjamin Schmidt, "Collecting Global Icons: The Case of the Exotic Parasol," in Daniela Bleichmar and Peter C. Mancall, eds., *Collecting across Cultures: Material Exchanges in the Early Modern Atlantic World* (Philadelphia:

University of Pennsylvania Press, 2011), pp. 31–57 and 292–296, esp. 292 and 296.

Willdey's shop.[8] The text below the images reads: "Maps Globes Spectacles Reading Glasses with these and many other usefull Curiosities are made and Sold—Wholesale and Retail at the Great Toy Shop next ye Dogg Tavern in Ludgate street very Reasonable by G. Willdey." I have mentioned several times that cartouches are spaces in which there can be a privileged communication between the cartographer and his audience, and here Willdey takes advantage of that special channel to make a sales pitch. While this use of the cartouche for commercial purposes may seem to sully the map, it is worth pointing out that the display of merchandise below is not so different from the display of New World commodities—sugarcane, pineapple, gold, bales of tobacco, etc.—just above, and this commodification of places in cartouches is very common.

Willdey had similar cartouches advertising his goods included on other maps he sold in his shop: on Emanuel Bowen's map of Europe of 1714,[9] on Bowen's map of Asia of 1714,[10] on Willdey's own map of Great Britain and Ireland of 1715,[11] on Bowen's map of Sweden and Norway of 1717,[12] and on Charles Price's map of Africa of 1721.[13] Willdey also

FIGURE 112   Personification of America in Cesare Ripa, *Iconologia* (Padua, 1603)
DUKE UNIVERSITY, RUBENSTEIN LIBRARY, RARE BOOKS, 8VO, N7740 .R5 1603. COURTESY OF DUKE UNIVERSITY

presents images of his goods for sale in the bottom margin of Price's world map of 1714, associated with but outside of the dedicatory cartouche at the bottom of the map.[14] But I think that the use of the cartouche to conceal geographical ignorance in his map of North America, and its juxtaposition with valuable articles from the New World, make that case particularly interesting.

Willdey was also active in advertising his shop in London newspapers. Sarah Tyacke has discussed his

8   Willdey used the name "Archimedes and Globe" in an advertisement printed in the *Daily Courant*, no. 2640, Monday, April 10, 1710, p. 4. On the name see Bryden and Simms, "Trade Ephemera" (see note 3), p. 797: "From the 1670's, a number of prominent London opticians adopted a portrait of Archimedes as their symbol, often adding instruments associated with his name. Their signs were often complemented by assorted instruments of the trade, optical goods and features drawn from the coat of arms of the Spectacle Makers' Company." Also see D.J. Bryden and D.L. Simms, "Archimedes as an Advertising Symbol," *Technology and Culture* 34 (1993), pp. 387–391.

9   Emanuel Bowen, *Europe Corrected According to ye Latest Discoveries & Observations Communicated to the Royal Society at London & ye Royal Academy at Paris* (London, 1714).

10   Emanuel Bowen, *Asia Corrected According to the Latest Discoveryes & Observations Communicated to the Royal Society at London and the Royal Academy at Paris* (London, 1714). The cartouche of goods for sale on this map is mentioned by Bryden and Simms, "Trade Ephemera" (see note 3), p. 808. An image of the map is available on the website of the Huntington Library at https://hdl.huntington.org.

11   George Willdey, *This Map of Great Britain and Ireland Corrected from the Newest & most Exact Observations* (London, 1715). The map is viewable at https://gallica.bnf.fr. The cartouche frame around the goods for sale is particularly elaborate.

12   Emanuel Bowen, *A New and Exact Map of Sweden and Norway Corrected from the Best Observations Communicated to ye Royal Society at London & the Royal Academy at Paris &c.* (London, 1717). A high-resolution image of the map is available at https://www.doria.fi.

13   Charles Price, *Africa Corrected from Observations of Mess. of ye Royal Societies at London and Paris* (London, 1721). The map is listed in Oscar Norwich, Pam Kolbe, and Jeffrey C. Stone, *Norwich's Maps of Africa: An Illustrated and Annotated Carto-Bibliography*

(Norwich, VT: Terra Nova Press, 1997), p. 92, no. 77; a high-resolution image of the map is available at https://searchworks.stanford.edu. The map is remarkable for the way Price extended the cartouche in the lower left corner of the map to the right from the image in his 1711 map, adding the man riding the crocodile and the personification of the river: this is an interesting case of cartouche revision. His earlier map is Charles Price, *Africa Corrected from Observations of Mess. of ye Royal Societies at London and Paris* (London, 1711); an image of the map is available at https://searchworks.stanford.edu.

14   Price's world map is Charles Price, *A New and Correct Map of the World Projected upon the Plane of the Horizon Laid Down from the Newest Discoveries and Most Exact Observations* (London, 1714). A high-resolution image of the map is available at https://loc.gov.

advertisements in the *London Gazette*,[15] but he also advertised in *The Post-Man and the Historical Account*, the *English Post*, the *Daily Courant*, the *Flying Post*, the *Daily Post*,[16] the *London Evening Post*, and the *Universal Spectator and Weekly Journal*. Jeffrey Wigelsworth has called Willdey "the most prolific advertiser for items of public science."[17] He ran newspaper advertisements from when he opened his shop till his death in 1737, and he no doubt did so because he found that they worked. The much higher volume of his newspaper advertisements than his advertisements on maps makes one wonder if perhaps some customers voiced objections to the latter.

Willdey's cartouche on his map of North America that advertises his wares reflects both increasing prosperity and commercialism in England after the Restoration of the monarchy in 1660 and increasing popular interest in science.[18] Given that the London cartographer and shopkeeper Philip Lea (1660–1700) had printed an advertisement for his maps and other goods on the frontispiece of his edition of *The Elements of Euclid* in 1685,[19] it was inevitable that this new commercialism would find its way onto maps. When it did in Willdey's hands, it was natural that the advertisements would end up in cartouches.[20]

---

15 On Willdey's advertising see Sarah Tyacke, *London Map-Sellers* (see note 3), pp. 146–148.

16 In one of his advertisements in the *Daily Post*, no. 3156, Friday, Oct. 31, 1729, p. 1, he lists the maps that he has available, and adds: "They are handsomely coloured, and illustrated with curious Ornaments. The Price of each Map is but 8 d. and those that buy Six shall have a Seventh gratis," an early example of a "Buy one, get one free" (now called BOGOF) type of offer. But Willdey was not the first to make this type of offer: it is used in a sale of books mentioned in the *Post Man and the Historical Account* (London) 118 (Feb. 8–11, 1696), p. 2; and the advertisement preceding the title page in the anonymous book *The Judgment of Whole Kingdoms and Nations ...* (London: T. Harrison, 1710).

17 Jeffrey R. Wigelsworth, *Selling Science in the Age of Newton: Advertising and the Commoditization of Knowledge* (Farnham, UK, and Burlington, VT: Ashgate, 2010), pp. 66–69 on Willdey, at 66. On Willdey's advertising also see D.J. Bryden, "A 1707 Advertising Skirmish between London Opticians," *Bulletin of the Scientific Instrument Society* 77 (2003), pp. 14–21.

18 Tyacke, *London Map-Sellers* (see note 3), p. xi; and Wigelsworth, *Selling Science* (see note 17).

19 On Philip Lea see Tyacke, *London Map-Sellers* (see note 3), pp. 120–122, and she reproduced the 1685 frontispiece. A good image of it is also available in the digital collections of the Wellcome Library at https://wellcomecollection.org/collections.

20 There is also an advertisement by a map publisher of goods for sale in his shop—though not in a cartouche—on William Price's *A New Plan of ye Great Town of Boston in New England in America with the Many Additionall Buildings & New Streets, to the Year, 1733* (Boston, 1733). A high-resolution image of this printing of the map is available at https://jcb.lunaimaging.com; good images of the 1769 printing are available at https://loc.gov and https://www.digitalcommonwealth.org/search/. On the advertisement see John W. Reps, "Boston by Bostonians: The Printed Plans and Views of the Colonial City by its Artists, Cartographers, Engravers, and Publishers," in *Boston Prints and Printmakers 1670–1775* (Boston: The Colonial Society of Massachusetts, 1973), pp. 3–56, at 21 and 32. Jean Baptiste de Bouge (1757–1833) on sheet 8 of his 20-sheet *Carte chorographique du Royaume des Pays-Bas* of 1823 has a cartouche with a self-portrait surrounded by the titles of maps that he has made, but this seems to be the cartographer's *cirriculum vitae*, and thus assertion of expertise, rather than an advertisement for those other maps. This cartouche is mentioned and illustrated by James A. Welu, "Cartographic Self-Portraits," in Carla Clivio Marzoli, Giacomo Corna Pellegrini, and Gaetano Ferro, eds., *Imago et mensura mundi: Atti del IX Congresso internazionale di storia della cartografia* (Rome: Istituto della Enciclopedia italiana, 1985), vol. 2, pp. 525–539; downloadable high-resolution images of the sheets of the 1828 printing of the map are available on the website of the Vilnius University Library.

CHAPTER 23

The Collapse of the Mississippi Bubble

Matthäus Seutter, Accurata delineatio Ludovicianae vel Gallice Louisiane, *c.1728*

The cartouche on Seutter's *c.*1728 map of Louisiana[1] is a particularly ambitious one, for it has as its goal to tell in one image the whole story of a dramatic and complicated economic scheme that briefly seemed capable of pulling France out of dire financial straits, but resulted instead in the ruin of many investors and decades of additional fiscal woes for the nation. This was the so-called Mississippi Bubble.

The story has its beginning in the War of the Spanish Succession (1701–14), which has figured prominently in two cartouches discussed earlier, those in Sanson's *Téatre de la Guerre en Flandre & Brabant* (1710) (Chapter 19) and in Homann's *Leopoldi Magni Filio Iosepho I* (*c.*1705–11) (Chapter 20). France succeeded in upholding Louis XIV's grandson Philip as King of Spain, but prosecution of the war required France to maintain large armies in two or three theaters on foreign soil simultaneously, with long supply chains, and the debts incurred by the French crown were enormous. By 1713, payments on these debts consumed 69% of tax revenues, a clearly unsustainable level.[2] In 1714 the war ended, and in 1715 Louis XIV died, and was succeeded by Louis XV, then just five years old, so the kingdom was ruled by Philippe II, Duke of Orléans (1674–1723), until 1723. In 1716 the government defaulted on its debts, damaging not just the nation's economic power, but also its ability to project its political power.

Dire circumstances suggest unconventional solutions, and Philippe II arranged for a foreigner, the Scotsman John Law (1671–1729), to make a presentation to the Banque Générale proposing the establishment of a private bank that could issue paper currency, then unusual, which would increase available credit, and also absorb some of the government's debt. The proposal was accepted, and Law founded the Banque Générale Privée in May of 1716. Law is an interesting man, an economist and writer who had been urging similar reforms in Scotland,[3] and whom Joseph Schumpeter, the influential political economist, has described as "in the front rank of monetary economists of all time."[4] He was tall, well-dressed, charismatic, and ambitious; he was a frequent gambler, had to flee England after killing a man in a duel in London in 1694, and could not return to England till he was pardoned in 1719.[5] After leaving England he was involved in a variety of money-making schemes on the continent, and did well for himself. The phrase that the French applied to him for decades after his economic schemes failed was *Le maudit Escossais*, "the damned Scotsman."[6]

After Law established the Banque Générale Privée in 1716 his power and responsibilities increased at a breathtaking pace. In August of 1717 Law bought the Compagnie du Mississippi, which had exclusive rights to trade in the French territories in Louisiana and the West Indies, and re-organized it as the Compagnie d'Occident ("Company

---

1 Most of Seutter's maps lack dates, and I thank Michael Ritter for supplying dates for Seutter's maps based on his examination of Seutter's manuscript stocklists of his maps, for this chapter and for my others about Seutter's maps. Ritter supplies some criteria that are useful in dating Seutter's maps in his article "Seutter, Probst and Lotter: An Eighteenth-Century Map Publishing House in Germany," *Imago Mundi* 53 (2001), pp. 130–135, at 132; also see Michael Ritter, "Hilfsmittel zu Datierung von Karten der Augsburger Verlage Seutter, Lotter und Probst," in Kurt Brunner and Thomas Horst, eds., *15. Kartographiehistorisches Colloquium, Munich 2–4 September 2010: Vorträge, Berichte, Posterbeiträge* (Bonn: Kirschbaum Verlag, 2012), pp. 247–254; and Peter H. Meurer, "Das Druckprivileg für Matthäus Seutter," *Cartographica Helvetica* 8 (1993), pp. 32–36.

2 Earl J. Hamilton, "The Political Economy of France at the Time of John Law," *History of Political Economy* 1.1 (1969), pp. 123–149, at 123; and Eugene N. White, "Long Shadow of John Law on French Public Finance: The Mississippi Bubble," in William N. Goetzmann, ed., *The Great Mirror of Folly: Finance, Culture, and the Crash of 1720* (New Haven: Yale University Press, 2013), pp. 99–105, at 99–100.

3 For Law's writings see his *Oeuvres complètes*, ed. Paul Harsin (Paris: Librairie du Recueil Sirey, 1934); Antoin E. Murphy, *John Law's 'Essay on a Land Bank'* (Donnybrook, Dublin: Aeon Pub., 1994); and Antoin E. Murphy, *John Law: Economic Theorist and Policy-Maker* (Oxford: Clarendon Press; New York: Oxford University Press, 1997), esp. pp. 111–148.

4 Joseph Schumpeter, *History of Economic Analysis* (New York: Oxford University Press. 1954), p. 295. Gavin John Adams has asserted that "John Law's *Money and Trade Considered* is the most influential but least acknowledged work in the history of economics," in *John Law: The Lauriston Lecture and Collected Writings* (Marston Gate: Newton Page, 2017), pp. 22–23.

5 The standard scholarly biography of Law is James Buchan, *John Law: A Scottish Adventurer of the Eighteenth Century* (London: MacLehose Press, 2018); Janet Gleeson's *Millionaire: The Philanderer, Gambler, and Duelist Who Invented Modern Finance* (New York: Simon & Schuster, 2000), is aimed at a broader audience and devotes more attention to Law's character.

6 See White, "Long Shadow of John Law" (see note 2), p. 103.

© CHET VAN DUZER, 2023 | DOI:10.1163/9789004523838_025

of the West"). The holders of depreciated French government bonds were permitted to exchange them for shares in the company, and the Company gave eager investors a way to share in the economic possibilities offered by the French holdings in the New World.[7] In September of 1718 the Company acquired the monopoly on French tobacco trade with Africa, and in January of 1719 Law's Banque Générale Privée was nationalized and renamed the Bank Royale—with Law as its director, giving him great control over the money supply so that he could continue his financial reforms. In May he obtained control of the French monopolies on trade with China and East Asia, and merged them with the Compagnie d'Occident to form the Compagnie des Indes, thus taking control of all trade between France and the world beyond Europe.

In August of 1719 the Compagnie des Indes arranged to take over the entirety of the national debt with a loan to the king of 1.2 billion *livres*, making it the sole creditor. It also purchased the rights to mint French coinage and collect taxes. In January of 1720 Law was appointed Contrôleur Général des Finances, and then Surintendant Général des Finances, in charge of all of the nation's financial affairs and money creation.

At this moment Law was one of the wealthiest and most powerful uncrowned people in European history,[8] and his reforms greatly increased French economic activity and trade. The financial opportunities, both real and imagined, enthralled investors, and the prices of shares in the Compagnie skyrocketed, with excited crowds often gathering on Rue Quinquempoix, the Parisian street where the Exchange was located, to hear the latest news and celebrate the rising prices of their shares. Speculation by buying shares on credit was rampant. The word "millionaire" was coined to describe the most successful investors in the Compagnie.

The collapse of Law's system, however, was as swift as its rise. Law had financed each new acquisition or enterprise by printing more bank notes and by issuing additional shares in the Compagnie, thus diluting the value of both, and inflation reached 23% per month early in 1720. Prices of the shares collapsed over the course of

the year, ruining investors and allowing control of the Compagnie to be wrested from Law. Riots broke out in the Rue Quinquempoix, and Law was forced to flee Paris by night, leaving behind for his creditors his residence on Place Vendôme and the many chateaux he had purchased. France was so traumatized by the experience that it waited some eighty years before again introducing paper currency.

The crumbling of Law's system and the grave losses suffered by investors generated an outpouring of satirical prints and literature. The speculative frenzy had reached the Netherlands, and one particularly impressive collection of satiric prints and texts was titled *Het groote tafereel der dwaasheid* ("The Great Mirror of Folly"), published in Amsterdam in 1720,[9] though the individual prints in it circulated before the date of publication. The cartouche on Seutter's map of *c*.1728 (Fig. 113),[10] which was designed by the printmaker and draftsman Gottfried Rogg,[11] is part of that same tradition.[12] Above there is a winged

7   There is a good concise account of this part of Law's career in Jon Moen, "John Law and the Mississippi Bubble: 1718–1720," *Mississippi History Now*, October 2001, available at http://www.mshistorynow .mdah.ms.gov. For an account of these years by an insider see Nicolas Dutot, *Histoire du système de John Law, 1716–1720: Publication intégrale du manuscrit inédit de Poitiers*, ed. Antoin E. Murphy (Paris: Institut national d'études démographiques, 2000).

8   Earl J. Hamilton, "John Law of Lauriston: Banker, Gamester, Merchant, Chief?" *The American Economic Review* 57.2 (1967), pp. 273–282, at 273; and Earl J. Hamilton, "Law, John," in David L. Sills, ed., *International Encyclopedia of the Social Sciences* (New York: Macmillan and The Free Press, 1968–1991), vol. 9, pp. 78–81, at 80.

9   Frans De Bruyn, "*Het groote tafereel der dwaasheid* and the Speculative Bubble of 1720: A Bibliographical Enigma and an Economic Force," *Eighteenth-Century Life* 24.1 (2000), pp. 62–87; Frans De Bruyn, "Reading *Het groote tafereel der dwaasheid*: An Emblem Book of the Folly of Speculation in the Bubble Year 1720," *Eighteenth-Century Life* 24.2 (2000), pp. 1–42; Kuniko Forrer, "*Het groote tafereel der dwaasheid*: A Bibliographical Interpretation," in William N. Goetzmann, ed., *The Great Mirror of Folly: Finance, Culture, and the Crash of 1720* (New Haven: Yale University Press, 2013), pp. 35–52; and Frans De Bruyn, "Satire in Text and Image: Bubble Publications in England and the Netherlands Compared," in William N. Goetzmann, ed., *The Great Mirror of Folly: Finance, Culture, and the Crash of 1720* (New Haven: Yale University Press, 2013), pp. 159–174.

10   On Seutter's work as a cartographer see Christian Sandler, *Matthäus Seutter (1678–1757) und seine Landkarten: ein Handbuch* (Bad Langensalza: Rockstuhl, 2001); first published in *Mitteilungen des Vereins für Erdkunde zu Leipzig* (1894), pp. 1–38; Peter H. Meurer, "Das Druckprivileg für Matthäus Seutter," *Cartographica Helvetica* 8 (1993), pp. 32–36; Michael Ritter, "Seutter, Probst and Lotter: An Eighteenth-Century Map Publishing House in Germany," *Imago Mundi* 53 (2001), pp. 130–135; and Michael Ritter, "Die Augsburger Landkartenverlage Seutter, Lotter und Probst," *Cartographica Helvetica* 25 (2002), pp. 2–10.

11   The inscription at the bottom of the cartouche indicates that Gottfried Rogg designed it, and Melchior Rein engraved it. Rogg (1669–1742) designed the cartouches on several of Seutter's maps; for a brief account of his work, see Ulrich Thieme and Felix Becker, eds., *Allgemeines Lexikon der Bildenden Künstler von der Antike bis zur Gegenwart* (Leipzig: E.A. Seemann, 1907–50), vol. 28, pp. 516–517. I thank Michael Ritter for this reference.

12   There are brief discussions of this cartouche in Donald H. Cresswell, *The American Revolution in Drawings and Prints: A Checklist of 1765–1790 Graphics in the Library of Congress* (Washington, DC: Library of Congress, 1975), pp. 302, no. 722; and Wolfgang Cillessen, "'Tot waarschouwinge voor de Nakomelinge'—Der Börsenkrach von 1720 als moralisches Lehrstück," in Philippe Kaenel and Rolf Reichardt, eds., *Interkulturelle Kommunikation in der europäischen Druckgraphik im 18. und 19. Jahrhundert = The*

FIGURE 113 Matthäus Seutter, *Accurata delineatio celeberrimae Regionis Ludovicianae vel Gallice Louisiane* (Augsburg, *c.*1728)
STANFORD UNIVERSITY, DAVID RUMSEY MAP COLLECTION, IN PROCESS (NO CALL NUMER). COURTESY
OF THE DAVID RUMSEY MAP COLLECTION

FIGURE 114   One of Seutter's likely sources, the print *Uystlag der wind negotie*, in *Het groote tafereel der dwaasheid* (Amsterdam, 1720)
JOHN CARTER BROWN LIBRARY F720 G876T2 /2-SIZE. COURTESY OF THE JOHN CARTER BROWN LIBRARY

personification of Fame blowing a trumpet to proclaim an *Aureum Seculum*, a Golden Century, as the banner indicates, but she holds a second trumpet, indicating that a second announcement of a different nature is coming. Just below, atop the pedestal containing the map's title information, is a female figure that some map dealers have identified as a personification of the Mississippi, but is actually a personification of Fortune, as her scarf and the winged ball she stands on are Fortune's typical attributes,[13] and her banner declares *Fortuna audentes juvat*, "Fortune favors the bold." Fortune holds a cornucopia from which

riches pour; the cornucopia is often one of her attributes, but in this case we are also probably to see an allusion to an early coat of arms of the Compagnie d'Occident, which involved a cornucopia from which the Mississippi River flowed.[14]

On the left, winged *putti* carry stock certificates in the Compagnie down to earth, and they are handed to happy investors by Hope personified, identifiable by her anchor, a typical attribute, and also by the banner above her, which reads *Qualis res, talis spes*, "The business justifies the hope." We should probably identify the man in the foreground as John Law: his is the only face not obscured, and it is difficult to imagine an image of the Mississippi Bubble that did not include Law. In the background there are two smiling men with a bag of gold, and

European Print and Cultural Transfer in the 18th and 19th Centuries = Gravure et communication interculturelle en Europe aux 18ᵉ et 19ᵉ siècles (Hildesheim, Zurich, and New York: Olms, 2007), pp. 295–332; for a more detailed discussion see Camille Mathieu, "An Effortless Empire: John Law and the Imagery of French Louisiana, 1683–1735," *Journal18* 10 (Fall 2020), available at https://www.journal18.org/5285. On Seutter's map see Pierluigi Portinaro and Franco Knirsch, *The Cartography of North America, 1500–1800* (New York: Facts on File, 1987), no. 117.

13   On personifications of Fortune standing on a ball see Sibylle Appuhn-Radtke, "Fortuna," in Wolfgang Augustyn, ed., *Reallexikon zur Deutschen Kunstgeschichte*, vol. 10 (Munich: In Kommission bei C.H. Beck, 2005), pp. 271–401, available in *RDK Labor* at http://www.rdklabor.de, the paragraph "Die nackte Fortuna auf der Kugel."

14   This coat of arms of the Compagnie appears on two maps: the anonymous *Louisiana by de Rivier Missisippi*, *c.*1720, which was printed in *Het groote tafereel der dwaasheid* (Amsterdam: s.n., 1720), and in *Aanmerkingen over den koophandel en het geldt, door den Hr. Law* (Amsterdam: Steenhouwer en Uytwerf, 1721); and Johann Baptist Homann's *Amplissimae regionis Mississipi seu Provinciae Ludovicianae à R.P. Ludovico Hennepin Francisc. Miss in America Septentrionali anno 1687* (Nuremberg: Homann, *c.*1720). A high-resolution image of the first map is available at https://digital.library.illinois.edu, and of the second at https://www.digitalcommonwealth.org/search.

in the distance, men are climbing a tree and falling from it, graphically illustrating the rise and fall of their hopes.[15]

To the right of the pedestal the situation is very different. A winged *putto* holds an empty bag, and the investors below are distraught: one wrings his hands, a second pulls his hair out, a third strangles himself, and the fourth prepares to fall on his sword. In the foreground in front of the pedestal two winged *putti* cut apart what seem to be freshly printed stock certificates, while a broken press for minting coins lies before them; and two unwinged *putti* blow bubbles, alluding to the Mississippi Bubble.

We cannot be sure, but it is tempting to think that Rogg drew some inspiration for his cartouche from a few of the illustrations in *Het groote tafereel der dwaasheid* ("The Great Mirror of Folly"), printed in 1720.[16] The print *Uystlag der wind negotie* ("Eruption of the Wind Trade") includes an elevated, seated man holding a cornucopia distributing stock certificates to a group of prosperous men to the right, and further to the right there is a group of men who have been ruined—the similarity to Seutter's cartouche is very striking indeed (Fig. 114).[17] The print *Vonnis van Apol*

over de bubbels ("Apollo's Verdict on the Stock-Investors") includes Hope with an anchor,[18] and the print *De inbeelding; heersseres van't rookverkopers-gild, maald Missisippi hier, 't geen Vrankryks schat verspild* ("Fancy, the Ruler of the Guild of Smoke-Sellers, Paints here Mississippi, which Wastes France's Treasures") includes a young boy blowing bubbles while two others look on.[19]

From Paris, Law had fled to Brussels at the end of 1720, and passed the next few years gambling in various cities on the continent; he returned to London in 1723, but the stay did not improve his fortunes, and he next moved to Venice, where he died a poor man in 1729, a sad end to a remarkable life. It was the economic historian Larry Neal who in 1990 began to restore Law's reputation as an economist, and this rehabilitation has been continued more recently Antoin E. Murphy.[20]

---

15   For discussion of the image of climbing the tree and falling from it in other illustrations of economic bubbles see Mathieu "An Effortless Empire" (see note 12).

16   On *Het groote tafereel* see note 9.

17   A high-resolution image of the print *Uystlag der wind negotie* is available on the website of the John Carter Brown Library, at https://jcb.lunaimaging.com; there is a detailed description of it in Frederic George Stephens, *Catalogue of Prints and Drawings in the British Museum. Division 1, Political and Personal Satires* (London: by order of the Trustees, 1870), vol. 2, pp. 444–447, no. 1627; compare his description of the English version of the print pp. 493–495, no. 1652.

18   A high-resolution image of the print *Vonnis van Apol over de bubbels* is available on the website of the John Carter Brown Library, at https://jcb.lunaimaging.com (this print is not listed in Stephens).

19   A high-resolution image of the print *De inbeelding* is available at https://jcb.lunaimaging.com; there is a detailed description of it in Stephens, *Catalogue of Prints and Drawings* (see note 17), vol. 2, pp. 502–503, no. 1657.

20   See Neal's *The Rise of Financial Capitalism: International Capital Markets in the Age of Reason* (Cambridge, England, and New York: Cambridge University Press, 1990), and the remarks by White, "Long Shadow of John Law" (see note 2), p. 102; and see Murphy's *John Law: Economic Theorist and Policymaker* (Oxford: Clarendon Press; New York: Oxford University Press, 1997) and other works.

"The Link of the Human Race for Both Utility and Pleasure"

Matthäus Seutter, Postarum seu cursorum publicorum diverticula en mansiones per Germaniam, *c.1731*

The next cartouche we will consider is also by Seutter, but concerns postal routes rather than economic systems. The production of postal route maps is limited enough that we can easily survey the cartouches on these maps that precede Seutter's to show just how extraordinary his cartouche is.[1]

The earliest European map of postal routes was created by Nicolas Sanson (1600–1667), and was the first important map he produced. He made it following the passage of a law in 1627 that insisted that French citizens pay to send their own mail using the system that had previously been restricted, at least officially, to government correspondence.[2] Sanson's map was printed in 1632,[3] its cartouche is modest and generic, and makes no allusion to the carrying of letters. About four years later Nicolas Berey published a copy of Sanson's map with depictions in the upper margin of two mail coaches, each carrying passengers, using the decoration to allude to the subject of the map.[4]

In 1689 Alexis-Hubert Jaillot, who published versions of many of Sanson's maps, printed a map of France's postal

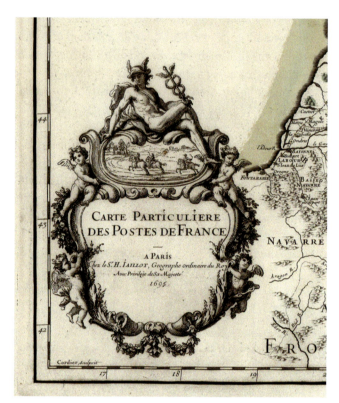

FIGURE 115   Alexis Hubert Jaillot, *Carte Particulaire de Postes de France*, in his *Atlas Francois* (Paris: Hubert Jaillot, 1695) STANFORD UNIVERSITY, DAVID RUMSEY MAP COLLECTION, G1046.F1 J3 1706 FF. COURTESY OF THE DAVID RUMSEY MAP COLLECTION

routes that showed graphically the distance between every postal station, and had a new program of decoration,[5] including a title cartouche that alludes to the map's subject matter (Fig. 115): atop the cartouche sits Mercury, the Roman god of travel, commerce, and communication, and below is an inset scene of three postal riders arriving at a station where they can change their horses. A similar but

---

1   Maps of postal routes fall into the category of thematic maps. On early maps of postal routes see Guy Arbellot, "Le réseau des routes de poste, objet des premières cartes thématiques de la France moderne," *Actes du 104e congrès des sociétés savantes, Bordeaux 1979, Histoire moderne* (Paris: Bibliothèque nationale, 1980), vol. 1, pp. 97–115; Elias Werner, "Road Maps for Europe's Early Post Routes," *The Map Collector* 16 (1981), pp. 30–34; *Landkarten und Postroutenkarten: Dokumente der Geschichte: Sonderausstellung im Bundespostmuseum 23. November 1982 bis 16. Januar 1983* (Frankfurt am Main: Bundespostmuseum, 1982); Guy Arbellot, *Autour des routes de poste: Les premières cartes routières de la France, XVIIe–XIXe siècle* (Paris: Bibliothèque Nationale de France and Musée de la Poste, 1992); and Silvia Siniscalchi, "La cartografia postale e le sue evoluzioni. Una cifra crono-spaziale dei mutamenti territoriali," *Geotema Supplemento* 2019, available at https://www.ageiweb.it /geotema/supplemento2019_siniscalchi/.

2   The law was passed October 16, 1627, but the earliest publication of the law we have is from ten years later, as *Règlement du feu sieur Alméras sur le port des lettres et pacquets* (Paris: J. Bessin, 1637).

3   Nicolas Sanson, *Carte géographicque des postes qui trauersent la France* (Paris: Melchior Tavernier, 1632). A high-resolution image of the map is available at https://catalog.princeton.edu.

4   *Carte generale de toute les poste et traverse de France* (Paris: Nicolas Berey, c.1636). This map was copied by Nicolas Langlois in about 1650, with the same title and decoration, and a zoomable image of this map may be seen at https://gallica.bnf.fr.

5   *Carte Particuliere des Postes de France* (Paris: H. Jaillot, 1689), engraved by Robert Cordier. A high-resolution image of the map is available at https://searchworks.stanford.edu. On Jaillot's career as a cartographer and map publisher see François Roland, "Alexis Hubert Jaillot, géographe du roi Louis XIV (1632–1712)," *Mémoires de l'Académie des Sciences, Belles Lettres et Arts de Besançon* (1918), pp. 45–76, also printed separately in Besançon in 1919; and see Mireille Pastoureau, "Alexis-Hubert Jaillot," in *Les atlas français: XVIe–XVIIe siècles: Répertoire bibliographique et étude* (Paris: Bibliothèque nationale de France, 1984), pp. 229–288.

FIGURE 116   Giacomo Cantelli, *L'Italia con le sue poste e strade principali* (Rome: Domenico de Rossi, 1695)
MCMASTER UNIVERSITY LIBRARY, LLOYD REEDS MAP COLLECTION, RMC 107120. COURTESY OF MCMASTER UNIVERSITY LIBRARY

FIGURE 117   Michel-Antoine Baudrand, *Carte particuliere des Postes de l'Italie* (Amsterdam: Pierre Mortier, 1695)
FROM THE AMERICAN GEOGRAPHICAL SOCIETY LIBRARY, UNIVERSITY OF WISCONSIN-MILWAUKEE LIBRARIES, 655 B-[1695?]. COURTESY OF THE AMERICAN GEOGRAPHICAL SOCIETY LIBRARY

less elaborate scene, perhaps inspired by Jaillot's, appears in the dedicatory cartouche on Giacomo Cantelli's map of the postal routes of Italy, printed in 1695 (Fig. 116),[6] and in that cartouche, the publisher remarks that the postal service has had the effect of unifying the country.[7] In 1695

Michel-Antoine Baudrand designed a map of the postal routes in Italy,[8] and his cartouche (Fig. 117) is a close copy (reversed left to right) of Jaillot's cartouche on his map of the postal routes in France, demonstrating the common practice of borrowing cartouches from other maps. Vincenzo Coronelli made a map of Italy's postal routes a few years later, about 1705,[9] and though we have seen that Coronelli was capable of wonderfully elaborate and creative cartouches, in this case he stayed with more generic iconography relevant to Italy and Rome. Even expert cartouche artists did not feel the need to give every map their best efforts.

In 1709 the famous German cartographer and map publisher Johann Baptist Homann (1663–1724) published a map of the postal routes in Germany made by Johann Peter Nell that went through multiple states,[10] and the cartouche does allude to the theme of the map

6   Giacomo Cantelli, *L'Italia con le sue poste e strade principali* (Rome: Domenico de Rossi, 1695); a high-resolution image of the map is available at https://searchworks.stanford.edu. On Cantelli's cartographic work see Laura Federzoni, "Giacomo Cantelli: la formazione e l'attività di un cartografo del XVII secolo," *Bollettino della Società Geografica Italiana* 10.4 (1993), pp. 539–554. There is an excellent bibliography of early postal cartography and geography, particularly in Italy, in Clemente Fedele, "The Postal Geography of Ottavio Codogno," in Clemente Fedele, Armando Serra, and Marco Gerosa, eds., *Europa postale: l'opera di Ottavio Codogno luogotenente dei Tasso nella Milano seicentesca* (Camerata Cornello, Bg: Museo dei Tasso e della storia postale, 2014), pp. 66–92.

7   In his dedication to Michele de Tassis, marchese di Paul and Conte di Zelo, de Rossi writes: *Se il Mare forma ancora tra le sue rupi eco di gloria al primo Inventor delle Navi, perche unì con un Legno le Provincie più divise, e diede con una Carta il Commercio à due Mondi: ben vede L.E.V. qual debito corra alla Terra di applaudire con voci di gratitudine alla sua Eccellentissma Casa, da cui coll'introduzione delle Poste, riconosce il singolarissimo beneficio di essere divenuta Patria commune,* that is, "If the sea still generates among its cliffs an echo of the glory of the first inventor of ships, because he united the most divided provinces by means of wood, and he gave trade to two worlds by means of a map, Your Excellency can see what debt the earth owes to applaud with a voice of gratitude Your excellent house, from which, through the introduction of postal service, it accrued the singular benefit of having become a common homeland."

8   Michel-Antoine Baudrand, *Carte particulière des Postes de l'Italie* (Amsterdam: Pierre Mortier, 1695); a high-resolution image of the map is available at https://uwm.edu/lib-collections/agsl-digital-map-collection/.

9   Vincenzo Coronelli, *L'Italia colle sue poste e strade viaggiate, e delineate* (Venice, *c.*1705); an image of the map is available at http://www.sardegnadigitallibrary.it.

10   Johann Peter Nell, *Postarum seu Veredariorum Stationes per Germaniam et Provincias Adiacentes = Neu-vermehrte Post-Charte durch gantz Teutschland nach Italien, Franckreich, Niederland, Preußen, Polen, und Ungarn &c.* (Nuremberg: J.B. Homann, 1709); a high-resolution image of the map is available at http://www5.kb.dk.

POSTARUM SEU VEREDARIORUM STATI

(Fig. 118).[11] The coat of arms is that of the dedicatee, Prince Karl Joseph von Paar (1654–1725), who, together with his brother Joseph Ignaz, had control of the postal system in much of the Hungarian, Austrian, and Bohemian lands at the time.[12] To the left of the coat of arms there is a *putto*—who has the winged helmet and caduceus of the god Mercury—preparing a saddle-bag full of letters, and to the right a *putto* rides a winged horse, acting as letter-carrier, and blowing his post horn to announce his arrival.

Seutter published his first map of the postal routes in Germany in about 1727 with an ambitious and spectacular cartouche, far surpassing anything that had come before (Fig. 119).[13] The cartouche was engraved by Melchior

---

11   I illustrate the revised 1714 state of Homann's map. In this state Homann adds winged *putto* in front of the winged horse who holds a banner that proclaims that the map was revised in the year that the Treaty of Rastatt was signed, i.e. 1714. Moreover, the latter part of this text is a chronogram indicating the same date. It reads *paX germanIae rastaDII paCta et sanCIta est*; choosing only the capital letters gives XMIDIICCI, and rearranging them gives MDCCXIIII, or 1714 in Roman numerals. On chronograms see James Hilton, *Chronograms, 5000 and More in Number, Excerpted out of Various Authors and Collected at Many Places* (London: E. Stock, 1882).

12   Ludwig Kalmus, *Weltgeschichte der Post* (Vienna: Göth, 1938), pp. 292–302.

13   Seutter's map of the German postal routes, first published *c.*1727, is titled *Postarum seu cursorum publicorum diverticula et mansiones per Germaniam et confin. Provincias*. I illustrate a later state printed after 1731; a high-resolution image of the map is available at https://searchworks.stanford.edu. I thank Michael

FIGURE 119 Matthäus Seutter, *Postarum seu cursorum publicorum diverticula et mansiones per Germaniam et confin. Provincias* (Augsburg, after 1731), in [Composite Seutter Atlas] (Augsburg: Matthäus Seutter, *c.*1755)
STANFORD UNIVERSITY, DAVID RUMSEY MAP COLLECTION, G1015 .S4 1755 TOM III FF. COURTESY OF THE DAVID RUMSEY MAP COLLECTION

Rein; Rein had engraved a couple of earlier cartouches for Seutter, including that on his map of Louisiana discussed just above.

Starting at the bottom of the cartouche, we have a globe representing the world, and banners with the motto *Humanae vincula gentis usui et lusui*, "The link of the human race for both utility and pleasure," and Seutter takes this phrase about the postal service as the theme of the cartouche. Two ribbons attach the globe to two letter-writers at their desks just above, a human one on the left, and the god Mercury on the right. Additional ribbons link the globe to letter-carriers further above, three mortals on their horses, each blowing his post horn as he gallops across the countryside, with a small settlement visible in the distance on either side. Another ribbon links the globe to a personification of Fame, blowing her trumpet as she carries letters—the trumpet seems to have a function

similar to that of the post horns, announcing the arrival of important communications.

The presence of the globe and the ribbons joining the actors make the cartouche a dramatic illustration of the global reach and the power and of the postal network to unify us all. The image is not without its mysteries: whom does Mercury represent exactly? And how does Fame deliver letters? Or are we to understand that letters bring Fame with them? The larger meaning seems to be that the postal service is greater in its effects than a purely human enterprise should be. The cartouche is all about the power of the network, a very modern message.

Sometime before 1741 Seutter developed a new cartouche for his map of German postal routes, one much less elaborate and philosophical than his earlier one, designed to fit a smaller map in an atlas (Fig. 120).[14] At

---

Ritter for valuable information about the different states of this map and their dates, and also the dates of other maps by Seutter.

14   Matthäus Seutter, *Postarum seu cursorum publicorum diverticula et mansiones per Germaniam et confin. Provincias* (Augsburg, before 1741). A high-resolution image of the map is available at https://searchworks.stanford.edu.

FIGURE 120

Seutter's new cartouche on his *Postarum seu cursorum publicorum diverticula et mansiones per Germaniam et confin. Provincias* (Augsburg, before 1741) in his *Atlas Novus* (Augsburg: Matthäus Seutter, *c.*1735)

the top of the design, above the double-headed eagle symbolizing the Holy Roman Empire, particularly the Habsburg Monarchy, is the motto *Provido auspicio*, "With a forward-looking beginning," a phrase I have not found used elsewhere. On the left is a personification of Fame blowing on a trumpet, and below, a king at his desk who has just written a letter, and below him, a well-to-do man at his desk hands to a servant a letter to be posted. On two banners we again read the phrase *Humanae vincula gentis usui et lusui*, "The link of the human race for both utility and pleasure." On the right, Mercury, the god of communication and travel, holds out letters for delivery, and in the landscape we see several horsemen, some blowing their post horns, some pulling carts, out carrying the mail. So the scene is divided between the composition of letters on the left, and their delivery on the right.

Seutter's new cartouche shares many elements with its predecessor: the frame around the title has a similar shape and position, and the double-headed eagle and the mottos are the same; in both cases we have two letter-writers, multiple letter-carriers, and Fame and Mercury. At the same time, the new, smaller cartouche is very different indeed, and is a much less clear visualization of the motto it shares with the earlier cartouche.

One wonders whether Seutter decided that the noble image of the postal service conveyed by these two cartouches did not agree with practical experiences with the service, for in 1740 he made a new map of Germany's postal routes with a cartouche that makes no lofty claim that the postal service unites humanity. The map was engraved by his son-in-law Tobias Conrad Lotter (1717–1777), who worked with Seutter,[15] and the cartouche on this

map[16] is completely different from the earlier ones, and remarkably banal: it merely shows mounted letter-carriers and a coach setting out from a walled city, with the frame around the title details tilted over at an inelegant angle to fit between the cartouche decoration and the coastline (Fig. 121). Lotter produced his own map of Germany's postal routes in 1769, whose cartouches also lack the inspiration of Seutter's earlier efforts: the title cartouche shows Mercury on the left holding a letter, the imperial coat of arms above, and letter-carriers and a coach bearing mail across the countryside, and a cartouche in the map's lower corner shows a *putto* blowing a postal horn while he rides a winged horse to deliver mail, and letters, a saddle, and postal horns below.[17]

The dazzling cartouche that first appeared on Seutter's map of *c*.1727 is of a whole different level of imaginative sophistication from the cartouches on postal route maps that preceded it, and also from those that followed it.[18]

---

15 Michael Ritter, "Seutter, Probst and Lotter: An Eighteenth-Century Map Publishing House in Germany," *Imago Mundi* 53

(2001), pp. 130–135; and Michael Ritter, *Die Welt aus Augsburg: Landkarten von Tobias Conrad Lotter (1717–1777) und seinen Nachfolgern* (Berlin: Deutscher Kunstverlag, 2014), esp. "Tobias Conrad Lotter als Mitarbeiter von Matthäus Seutter," pp. 36–40.

16 The map with the new cartouche is Matthäus Seutter, *Postarum seu Cursorum Publicorum diverticula et mansiones per Germaniam et Confin. Prov.* (Augsburg: Matthäus Seutter, 1744).

17 Tobias Conrad Lotter, *Mappa Geographica exhibens Postas omnes tam vehiculares quam veredarias Totius Germaniae cum earum accurata distantia* (Augsburg: Lotter, 1769). Ritter discusses and illustrates the cartouche on this map in his "Seutter, Probst and Lotter" (see note 15) at 133; and *Die Welt aus Augsburg* (see note 15), at 214–215.

18 Incidentally Mary Sponberg Pedley, *Bel et utile: The Work of the Robert de Vaugondy Family of Mapmakers* (Tring, England: Map Collector Publications, 1992), p. 66, shows the cartouches illustrating the carrying of letters in the road maps in Robert de Vaugondy's *Atlas Universel* of 1757.

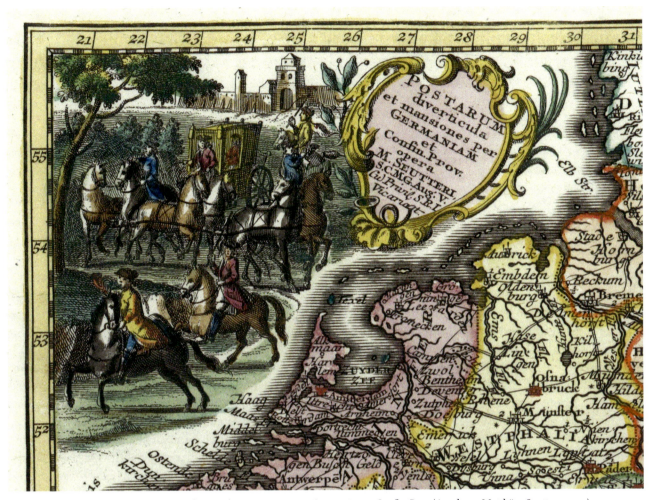

FIGURE 121 Matthäus Seutter, *Postarum diverticula et mansiones per Germaniam et Confin. Prov.* (Augsburg: Matthäus Seutter, c.1740)
COURTESY OF ANTIQUARIAT NORBERT HAAS

CHAPTER 25

Kill the Cannibals and Convert the Rest

Jean-Baptiste Nolin, II, L'Amerique dressée sur les relations les plus recentes, *1740*

Earlier we examined the large and elaborate cartouche on Jean-Baptiste Nolin's map of the Canal du Midi, titled *Le canal royal de Languedoc* (1697); Nolin died in 1708 and passed his map publishing firm on to his son, Jean-Baptiste Nolin, II (1686–1762). Most of the son's cartouches are unexceptional: he certainly saw the value of having decoration on his maps, but generally he did not devote much thought to his cartouches. One exception is the cartouche on his *Carte des cinq provinces de l'Assistance de France, des RR. PP. de la Compagnie de Jésus* (Paris, 1705), where the cartouche texts are on the topsail and mainsail of a beautifully rendered small carrack off the Atlantic coast of France. The title information is on the topsail, while on the mainsail there is a long paragraph about the organization of the Jesuit order both in France and abroad, the number of people working in the different regions, and a list of the Frenchmen who have led the Jesuit order in various regions. The use of a ship's sails as the frames of the cartouche texts of course suggests oceanic travel and thus alludes to the global reach of the Jesuit mission. Remarkably, more than a century later the German historian Friedrich Schöll cites the text of this cartouche as evidence for the way the Jesuit order was organized in the seventeenth century—a rare use of cartouche text as historical documentation.[1]

Nolin also deployed particularly rich cartouches on his wall map of the Americas, which he first published in 1740. This was part of a set of wall maps Nolin made of each of the continents then recognized, Europe,[2] Asia,[3]

Africa,[4] in addition to the Americas, and for these wall maps Nolin created more elaborate cartouches than usual.

One of the cartouches on Nolin's wall map of the Americas involves cannibals, and in order to fully appreciate that cartouche, we will look briefly at two earlier cartouches that involve cannibals on maps made by Nolin the father. The first of these was on a map of South America made by the elder Nolin in collaboration with Vincenzo Coronelli in 1689.[5] The cartouche (Fig. 122) shows a woman and man roasting and eating a human head and arm on the left, and a man cutting wood on the right. The wood can only be brasil wood, which was one of the most valuable commodities that Europeans took from South America,[6] though the colorist of this map failed to paint it red. Reports of cannibals in the Caribbean islands and particularly in Brazil go back to the accounts of Columbus and Amerigo Vespucci,[7] and they had long been portrayed on maps as typical inhabitants of South America. Often they were represented within South America, cooking parts of human bodies over fires, hanging those parts on

---

1 A zoomable image of Nolin's *Carte des cinq provinces de l'Assistance de France* is available at https://gallica.bnf.fr. For Schöll's citation of the text from the title cartouche of this map see Maximilian Samson Friedrich Schöll, *Cours d'histoire des états européens, depuis le bouleversement de l'Empire romain d'Occident jusqu'en 1789* (Paris: A. Pihan-Delaforest, Gide fils; and Berlin: Duncker et Humblot, 1830–1834), vol. 23, pp. 308–309.

2 Nolin's wall map of Europe is titled *L'Europe dressée sur les nouvelles observations faites en toutes les parties de la terre rectifiée par M.rs de l'Academie Royale des Sciences* (Paris: J.B. Nolin, 1740). No images of this map are available online; there are exemplars at the Library of Congress, the Bibliothèque nationale de France, the Bayerische Staatsbibliothek, and the Staatliche Bibliothek Regensburg.

3 I do not find an exemplar of Nolin's wall map of Asia that he printed, but there is a later state published by Jean-Baptiste Crépy, titled *L'Asie dressée sur les nouvelles observations faites en toutes*

les parties de la terre et rectifiées par M.rs de l'Académie Royle des Sciences (Paris: Crépy, 1767).

4 Nolin's wall map of Africa is titled *L'Afrique dressée sur les relations les plus récentes et rectifiées sur les dernières observations dédiée et présenté à sa majesté très chrestienne, Louis XV* (Paris: J.B. Nolin, 1740). There is an exemplar of this, the first state of the map, at the Library of Congress.

5 Vincenzo Coronelli and Jean-Baptiste Nolin, *L'Amerique meridionale ou la partie meridionale de indes occidentales dressée sur les memoires les plus nouvelles et dediée a monsieur Jacques Colombo Secretaire de la Serenissime Republique de Venise* (Paris: J.B. Nolin, 1689).

6 On depictions of the harvesting of brasil wood on maps see Yuri T. Rocha, Andrea Presotto and Felisberto Cavalheiro, "The Representation of *Caesalpinia echinata* (Brazilwood) in Sixteen-and Seventeenth-Century Maps," *Anais da Academia Brasileira de Ciências* 79.4 (2007), pp. 751–765.

7 See for example Peter Hulme, "Columbus and the Cannibals: A Study of the Reports of Anthropophagy in the Journal of Christopher Columbus," *Ibero-Amerikanisches Archiv* 4 (1978), pp. 115–139, reprinted in his *Colonial Encounters: Europe and the Native Caribbean, 1492–1797* (London: Methuen, 1986), pp. 1–43; and Michael Palencia Roth, "Cannibalism and the New Man of Latin America in the 15th and 16th Century European Imagination," *Comparative Civilizations Review* 12 (1985), pp. 1–27.

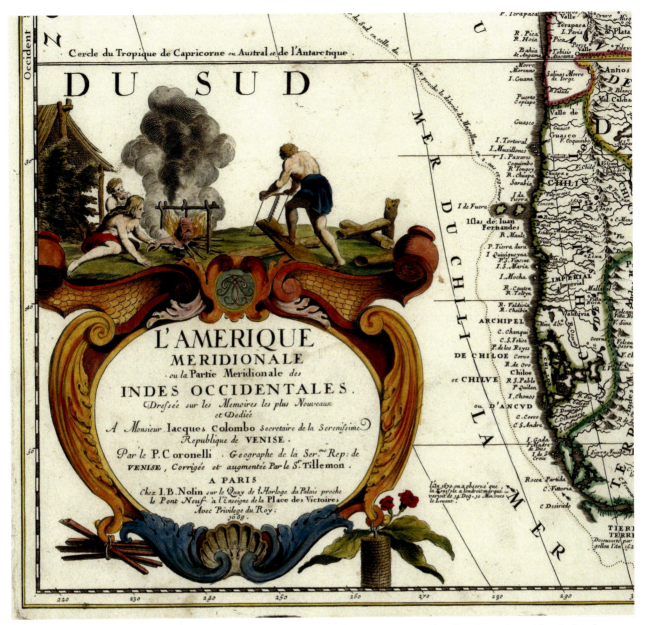

FIGURE 122   The cartouche from Vincenzo Coronelli and Jean-Baptiste Nolin, *L'Amerique meridionale ou la partie meridionale de indes occidentales dressée sur les memoires les plus nouvelles et dediée a monsieur Jacques Colombo Secretaire de la Serenissime Republique de Venise* (Paris: J.B. Nolin, 1689)
COURTESY OF BARRY LAWRENCE RUDERMAN ANTIQUE MAPS

trees, and eating them.[8] It seems that on this map Coronelli and Nolin moved this typical scene from the body of the map into the cartouche as a way to save space within South America.

Nolin's other earlier map that has an image related to cannibalism in its cartouche was also a collaboration with Coronelli, namely their map of western Canada first

8   For general accounts of images of cannibals on maps see Cynthia A. Chambers, "Cannibalism in a Cultural Context: Cartographic Imagery and Iconography of the New World Indigenous Peoples During the Age of Discovery," Ph.D. Dissertation, The University of Texas at Arlington, 2006; Cynthia A. Chambers, "The Geography of Cannibalism: Specificity in Sixteenth-Century New World Cartography and Literature," *Terrae Incognitae* 39.1 (2007), pp. 52–67; and James Walker, *From Alterity to Allegory: Depictions of Cannibalism on Early European Maps of the New World* (Washington, DC: Philip Lee Phillips Map Society Publication, 2015). Also see Carlos A. Jáuregui, *Canibalia: Canibalismo, calibanismo, antropofagia cultural y consumo en América Latina* (Madrid: Iberoamericana and Vervuert, 2008), pp. 102–108; and for images of Latin American cannibals in other media, see Nasheli Jiménez del Val, "Seeing Cannibals: European Colonial Discourses on the Latin American Other," Ph.D. Dissertation, Cardiff University, 2009.

FIGURE 123   Cartouche in the upper right corner of Vincenzo Coronelli and Jean-Baptiste Nolin, *Partie occidentale du Canada ou de la Nouvelle France ou sont les Nations des Ilinois, de Tracy, les Iroquois, et plusieurs autres peuples; avec la Louisiane nouvellement decouverte etc.* (Paris: J.B. Nolin, 1688)

printed in 1688.[9] In the upper right corner there is a cartouche containing the multiple different scales of miles. Some of the cartouche's strapwork supports a pot over an open fire, and in front of the fire, more of the strapwork supports a spit on which a man whose arms have been chopped off is roasting (Fig. 123). Roasting a man on a spit had been part of the iconography of cannibalism, cartographic and otherwise, from the beginning.[10]

On the younger Nolin's map of the Americas from 1740 the two cartouches are thematically related to each other in an interesting way. The cartouche in the upper left corner (Fig. 124) is a fairly standard cartouche about New World evangelization.[11] In the upper left, Faith personified reads from the Bible to bare-chested inhabitants of the New World, who receive her words enthusiastically. In the upper right, two more inhabitants of the New World

---

9   Vincenzo Coronelli and Jean-Baptiste Nolin, *Partie occidentale du Canada ou de la Nouvelle France ou sont les Nations des Ilinois, de Tracy, les Iroquois, et plusieurs autres peuples; avec la Louisiane nouvellement decouverte etc.* (Paris: J.B. Nolin, 1688). A high-resolution image of the map is available at https://jcb .lunaimaging.com.

10   In addition to the reference about cartographic images of cannibals just cited see Surekha Davies, "Spit-Roasts, Barbecues

and the Invention of the Brazilian Cannibal," in her *Renaissance Ethnography and the Invention of the Human: New Worlds, Maps and Monsters* (Cambridge and New York: Cambridge University Press, 2016), pp. 65–108.

11   I have studied some other colonialist cartouches in my article "Colonialism in the Cartouche: Imagery and Power in Early Modern Maps," *Figura: Studies on the Classical Tradition* 9.2 (2021), pp. 90–130.

FIGURE 124
The title cartouche on Jean-Baptiste Nolin,
II, *L'Amerique dressée sur les relations les
plus recentes, rectifiées sur les dernieres
observations, dediée et presentée a sa Majesté
tres chrestienne Louis XV* (Paris, *c*.1740)
YALE UNIVERSITY, BEINECKE LIBRARY 70
1740A. COURTESY OF THE BEINECKE RARE
BOOK AND MANUSCRIPT LIBRARY

burn an offering, smoke a peace pipe, and look reverently at the sun—this representing the highest form of worship thought possible in what was called natural theology, meaning religion unenlightened by Christianity. In the middle register a Dominican and a Franciscan friar preach to more New World natives, two of whom wear the feathered headdresses of chiefs. Below there are scenes illustrating the natural bounty of the Americas: two native men bring up what seems to be gold ore from a mine,[12] a pineapple appears on the left, and to the right, beavers,

valuable for their fur, are at work, a theme common in cartouches on maps of the New World.[13]

The scene in the cartouche around the scales of miles in the lower left corner (Fig. 125) is startling. In a New World landscape with a palm tree, a banana tree, a pineapple, a cactus, and a cotton plant, native people hold a cannibal feast, their poses and gestures based on European models, as was often the case in European images of Native Americans at this time.[14] A woman places more human

---

12   These same two miners appeared in a cartouche on an earlier map made by Vincenzo Coronelli and Jean-Baptiste Nolin, *Le Nouveau Mexique appelé aussi nouvelle Grenade et Marata. Avec Partie de Californie* (Paris, *c*.1688). A high-resolution image of the map is available at https://jcb.lunaimaging.com.

13   See Edward H. Dahl, "The Original Beaver Map: De Fer's 1698 Wall Map of America," *The Map Collector* 29 (1984), pp. 22–26; and François-Marc Gagnon, "La première iconographie du castor," *Scientia Canadensis* 31.1–2 (2008), pp. 12–26.

14   On European artists using traditional poses and gestures from European art in depicting Native Americans see William C. Sturtevant, "First Visual Images of Native America," in Fredi Chiappelli, Michael J.B. Allen, and Robert Louis Benson, eds., *First Images of America: The Impact of the New World on the Old*

FIGURE 125   The cartouche containing the scale of miles on Jean-Baptiste Nolin, II, *L'Amerique dressée sur les relations les plus recentes, rectifiées sur les dernieres observations, dediée et presentée a sa Majesté tres chrestienne Louis XV* (Paris, c.1740)
YALE UNIVERSITY, BEINECKE LIBRARY 70 1740A. COURTESY OF THE BEINECKE RARE BOOK AND MANUSCRIPT LIBRARY

body parts on the fire (which is similar to that in the 1689 map illustrated just above), a man eats some of the cooked flesh, another man dismembers a body tied to a post, and one more man runs away to the right. He runs away because two French soldiers fire a musket and pistol at the feasters from behind the plinth that displays the scales of miles. In between them stands Mars, the god of war, holding a shield bearing the fleurs-de-lis of France, looking on and supporting their aggression. The French soldiers are not only positioned higher than the cannibals, but they both lean on and are protected by a European structure

marked with measurements of the European cartographic enterprise—a tool of colonial control.[15]

While the cartouche in the upper left corner of the map shows the process of evangelization in the New World, this cartouche shows what happens when evangelization does not succeed. Specifically it alludes to a doctrine according to which Europeans were justified in making war against New World cannibals. Previously slavery had been illegal in the Americas, but in 1503 Queen Isabella of Castile passed a law that made it legal for Spaniards in the newly discovered lands to enslave cannibals.[16] What had been permission to enslave was interpreted as

———————

(Berkeley, CA and London: University of California Press, 1976), vol. 1, pp. 417–454, esp. 418 and 420; Paul H. Hulton, "Realism and Tradition in Ethnological and Natural History Imagery of the 16th Century," in Allan Ellenius, ed., *The Natural Sciences and the Arts: Aspects of Interaction from the Renaissance to the 20th Century* (Uppsala: Imqvist & Wicksell International, 1985), pp. 18–31; Jean Michel Massing, "Early European Images of America: The Ethnographic Approach," in Jay A. Levenson, ed., *Circa 1492: Art in the Age of Exploration* (Washington, DC: National Gallery of Art; New Haven: Yale University Press, 1991), pp. 515–520, and particularly Henry Keazor, "Theodore De Bry's Images for *America*," *Print Quarterly* 15.2 (1998), pp. 131–149.

15   See for example Raymond B. Craib, "Cartography and Power in the Conquest and Creation of New Spain," *Latin American Research Review* 35.1 (2000), pp. 7–36; Matthew Edney, "The Irony of Imperial Mapping," in James R. Akerman, ed., *The Imperial Map: Cartography and the Mastery of Empire* (Chicago: University of Chicago Press, 2009), pp. 11–45, with very good bibliography; and Nate Probasco, "Cartography as a Tool of Colonization: Sir Humphrey Gilbert's 1583 Voyage to North America," *Renaissance Quarterly* 67.2 (2014), pp. 425–472.

16   Michael Palencia-Roth, "The Cannibal Law of 1503," in Jerry M. Williams and Robert E. Lewis, eds., *Early Images of the Americas: Transfer and Invention* (Tucson: University of Arizona Press, 1993), pp. 21–63, esp. 22–27.

permission to make war against the cannibals, and in fact the word "cannibal" came to be applied to any peoples in the New World who resisted the Spanish, as a way of justifying violence against them.[17]

In the years that followed, as the Spanish encroachments and colonization in the New World encountered more and more violent resistance, the rhetoric turned to that of a "just war" against the cannibals, invoking a medieval legal doctrine that a war against "enemies of Christ" was justified. In particular the Spanish humanist Juan Ginés de Sepúlveda (1494–1573) wrote a dialogue in 1547 titled *Democrates secundus, de iustis belli causis* ("The Second Democrates, or, On the Just Causes of War") in which he argued that war against the native peoples of the New World was justified specifically in order to stop them from practicing cannibalism.[18] In Valladolid in 1550–1551 Sepúlveda had a public debate on his doctrines with Bartolomé de las Casas (1484–1566), the great advocate of the rights of the peoples of the Americas, which is to say, a debate on the justice of the methods by which Spain expanded its empire in the New World.[19]

Sepúlveda did not win the debate, but the idea that the sins committed by inhabitants of the Americas justified European violence against them continued to be a subtext of colonial activities for many years, and not just in the Iberian Peninsula. The lower cartouche alludes to French thoughts about invading Brazil, which was believed to be densely populated with cannibals: the French had invaded Rio de Janeiro in 1711 and the island of Fernando de Noronha in 1736, and had planned other invasions.[20]

So the two cartouches on Nolin's map have an important political dimension that is not obvious at first glance. A small inscription in the cartouche in the lower left corner of the map indicates that Nolin had hired F. Dubercelle to design and engrave it, an artist about whom we have no biographical information, and not even his first name. He was active from about 1716 to 1743, and does not seem to have worked with Nolin again—not even to make the cartouches on Nolin's other three wall maps of the continents—but he did make two other maps and also a view of Besançon.[21]

The National Library of France has a proof-state of Nolin's map that was printed with the text for the cartouche in the upper left corner, but without the elaborately decorated frame.[22] This version of the cartouche text lists Nolin's address as on the Quay de l'Horloge du Palais, where several mapmakers had their shops, while

17   Palencia-Roth, "The Cannibal Law" (see note 16), pp. 42–44; on the wider application of the word "cannibal" see Neil L. Whitehead, "Carib Cannibalism: The Historical Evidence," *Journal de la Société des Américanistes* 70 (1984), pp. 68–87, at 76; and Jáuregui, *Canibalia* (see note 8), esp. pp. 84, 87, 102, and 106.

18   Sepúlveda's dialogue *Democrates secundus* was not printed during his lifetime, but circulated widely in manuscript. For an edition of the work see Juán Ginés de Sepúlveda, *Demócrates segundo, o, De las justas causas de la guerra contra los indios*, ed. Ángel Losada (Madrid: Consejo Superior de Investigaciones Científicas, 1984), with a discussion of manuscripts and attempts to publish the work on pp. xii–xxvi.

19   Ángel Losada, "The Controversy between Sepúlveda and Las Casas in the Junta of Valladolid," in Juan Friede and Benjamin Keen, eds., *Bartolomé de Las Casas in History. Toward an Understanding of the Man and His Work* (DeKalb: Northern Illinois University Press, 1971), pp. 279–307; Anthony Pagden, *The Fall of Natural Man: The American Indian and the Origins of Comparative Ethnology* (New York: Cambridge University Press, 1982), pp. 27–56 ("The Theory of Natural Slavery") and 110–118; Alfonso Maestre Sánchez, "'Todas las gentes del mundo son hombres': El gran debate entre Fray Bartolomé de las Casas (1474–1566) y Juan Ginés de Sepúlveda (1490–1573)," *Anales del seminario de historia de la filosofía* 21 (2004), pp. 91–134; Carla Forti, "La disputa sulla 'guerra giusta' nella conquista spagnola dell'America," *Critica storica* 28.2 (1991), pp. 251–296; and David M. Lantigua, "The Politics of Natural Law at Valladolid, 1550–1551," in his *Infidels and Empires in a New World Order: Early Modern Spanish Contributions to International Legal Thought* (Cambridge and New York: Cambridge University Press, 2020), pp. 141–186. Also see Giuseppe Tosi, "La teoria della schiavitù naturale nel dibattito sul Nuovo Mondo (1510–1573). 'Veri domini' o 'servi a natura'?" *Divus Thomas* 105.3 (2002), pp. 9–258, who has a useful chronology of the wider debate pp. 237–258.

20   On French invasions of Brazil, and plans to invade it, in the early eighteenth century see Louis de Chancel de Lagrange, *A tomada do Rio de Janeiro em 1711 por Duguay-Trouin*, ed. Mário Ferreira França (Rio de Janeiro: Departamento de Imprensa Nacional, 1967); Ricardo Vieira Martins and Carlos Alberto Lombardi Filgueiras, "A Invasão Francesa ao Rio de Janeiro em 1711 sob a análise da Cartografia Histórica," in *Anais do 1° Simpósio Brasileiro de Cartografia Histórica* (Paraty, 2011), pp. 1–16 (online resource); Aníbal Barreto, *Fortificações no Brasil (Resumo Histórico)* (Rio de Janeiro: Biblioteca do Exército Editora, 1958), pp. 124–125; and Júnia Ferreira Furtado, *Oráculos da geografia iluminista: Dom Luís da Cunha e Jean-Baptiste Bourguignon d'Anville na construção da cartografia do Brasil* (Belo Horizonte: Editora UFMG, 2012), chapter 6.

21   Dubercelle's maps are in François Ignace Dunod de Charnage, *Histoire des sequanois et de la province sequanoise des bourguignons et du premier royaume de Bourgogne de l'Eglise de Besançon* (Besançon: Charmet, 1735); and Gillet de Moyvre, *La Vie et les amours de Tibulle, chevalier romain, et de Sulpicie, dame romaine: leurs poésies et quelques autres traduites en vers François* (Paris: S. Jorry, 1743); his view of Besançon, titled *Veue de Besançon dessinée de la Croix d'Arênes*, is in the second book.

22   The proof-state of Nolin's wall map of the Americas, *L'Amérique dressée sur les relations …*, is in Paris, Bibliothèque nationale de France, Cartes et plans, GE C-2404; an image of the map is available at https://gallica.bnf.fr. On the page describing the map it is incorrectly dated to 1720.

the other printings of the map indicate Rue St. Jacques, the center of printing and printmaking in Paris.[23] It seems that in 1740 Nolin had shops on both streets, and decided while he was working on his wall map of the Americas that he would sell it from his shop on the more prestigious Rue St. Jacques. So he had the engraver change his address and add both the elaborate decoration to the cartouche that shows the evangelization of the New World, and the indication of his legal privilege to print the map. Thus the cartouches give us some insights into the cartographer's creative process, decisions, and life.

23   On Nolin's two different establishments see Mary Sponberg Pedley, *The Commerce of Cartography: Making and Marketing Maps in Eighteenth-Century France and England* (Chicago: University of Chicago Press, 2004), p. 107.

CHAPTER 26

The Cartographer and the Shogun

Matthäus Seutter, Regni Japoniae nova mappa geographica, *c.1745*

In presenting a third cartouche by Seutter, this one embellishing one of his maps of Japan, I reveal my strong admiration for his work in this arena: for me at least, he and Coronelli—or the artists whose work they contracted and supervised—are among the top designers of cartouches.

In order to give context to the cartouche on Seutter's map of Japan of *c.*1745, I begin with an earlier map he made of those islands. The Dutch scholar and cartographer Adriaan Reland (1676–1718) is best known for his books and maps relating to the Middle East, but he was also interested in Asia: he had written about the languages of Asia, including Japan,[1] and in 1715 made a map of Japan based on Japanese maps, particularly a map by Ishikawa Ryūsen in the library of Benjamin Dutry, a former director of the Dutch East India Company.[2] Reland

used Sino-Japanese characters to indicate the names of each of the 66 provinces of Japan, the first time this had been done on a European map, and his map was widely copied, including by Seutter.

In his version of the map, first printed *c.*1738 (Fig. 126),[3] Seutter generally followed Reland very closely, but he did make some changes. He removed the dedication Reland had placed in the central cartouche, filling it instead with Reland's description of his sources (which the earlier cartographer had squeezed into the lower margin), and replaced the dedicatee's coat of arms above Reland's cartouche with personifications of Fame and Asia and the god Mercury—rather generic decoration.[4] Seutter copied Reland's other decorations, including the scenes of daily life in Japan and the numerous pieces of Japanese porcelain. The presence of the porcelain is easy to explain: it was one of the main reasons Europeans were interested in trading with Japan.[5]

Some years later Seutter produced a new map of Japan, copying from a different source, and in this case adding a remarkable cartouche. The new map he copied from was produced as a result of the visit to Japan by the German naturalist, traveler, and physician Engelbert Kaempfer

---

1   Adriaan Reland, *Dissertationum miscellanearum pars tertia et ultima* (Utrecht: G. Broedelet, 1708), pp. 103–119 on the Japanese language, in the section "De linguis insularum quarumdam orientalium." On Reland see Alastair Hamilton, "Adrianus Reland (1676–1718), Outstanding Orientalist," in Hervé Jamin, ed., *Zes keer zestig: 360 jaar universitaire geschiedenis in zes biografieën* (Utrecht: Universiteit Utrecht, 1996), pp. 22–31; and Bart Jaski, Christian Lange, Anna Pytlowany, and Henk J. van Rinsum, eds., *The Orient in Utrecht: Adriaan Reland (1676–1718), Arabist, Cartographer, Antiquarian and Scholar of Comparative Religion* (Leiden and Boston: Brill, 2021), particularly Bart Jaski, Christian Lange, Anna Pytlowany, and Henk J. van Rinsum, "Adriaan Reland (1676–1718): Early Modern Humanist, Philologist and Scholar of Comparative Religion," pp. 1–13; and Toon van Hal, "Adriaan Reland's Fascination with the Languages of the World," pp. 146–172.

2   Reland's map of Japan is titled *Imperium Japonicum per regiones digestum sex et sexaginta atque ex ipsorum Japonesium mappis descriptum* (Amsterdam: I. Ottens, 1715). The map is discussed by Jason C. Hubbard, *Japoniae insulae: The Mapping of Japan: Historical Introduction and Cartobibliography of European Printed Maps of Japan to 1800* (Houten: HES & De Graaf Publishers, 2012), pp. 282–286, no. 68; Marcia Yonemoto, "Envisioning Japan in Eighteenth-Century Europe: The International Career of a Cartographic Image," *Intellectual History Newsletter* 22 (2000), pp. 17–35; Marcia Yonemoto, "The European Career of Ishikawa Ryūsen's Map of Japan," in Kären Wigen, Sugimoto Fumiko, and Cary Karacas, eds., *Cartographic Japan: A History in Maps* (Chicago and London: University of Chicago Press, 2016), pp. 37–40; and Tobias Winnerling, 'Geleerdster der Landbeschryveren'? Adriaan Reland Mapping Persia and Japan, 1705–1715," in Jaski et al., eds., *The Orient in Utrecht* (see note 1), pp. 219–242. A high-resolution image of the map is available at http://www5.kb.dk. Reland borrowed the images of everyday Japanese life in the lower part of his map, and of the emperor to the right, from Arnoldus Montanus, *Gedenkwaerdige gesantschappen*

der Oost-Indische maatschappy (Amsterdam: J. Meurs, 1669), pp. 54, 57, 83, 184, and 194. This book is available in digital format at https://archive.org.

3   Seutter's map that he based on Reland's is Matthäus Seutter, *Imperium Japonicum per sexaginta et sex regiones digestum atque ex ipsorum Japonesium mappis descriptum* (Augsburg, c.1730). A high-resolution of the map is available at https://www.digitale-sammlungen.de.

4   The text in the left-hand cartouche on Seutter's (and Reland's) map is translated into English by Yonemoto, "Envisioning Japan" (see note 2), p. 24; and Yonemoto, "The European Career" (see note 2), p. 38; the longer text about Reland's sources is transcribed and summarized by George Kiss, "The Cartography of Japan during the Middle Tokugawa Era: A Study in Cross-Cultural Influences," *Annals of the Association of American Geographers* 37.2 (1947), pp. 101–119, at 103.

5   On Europe's trade in Japanese porcelain see T. Volker, *The Japanese Porcelain Trade of the Dutch East India Company after 1683* (Leiden: E.J. Brill, 1959); and Oliver Impey, "The Trade in Japanese Porcelain" and "Japanese Export Porcelain," in John Ayers, Oliver Impey, and J.V.G. Mallet, eds., *Porcelain for Palaces: The Fashion for Japan in Europe, 1650–1750* (London: Oriental Ceramic Society, 1990), pp. 18–21 and 25–36, respectively.

© CHET VAN DUZER, 2023 | DOI:10.1163/9789004523838_028

FIGURE 126   Matthäus Seutter, *Imperium Japonicum per sexaginta et sex regiones digestum atque ex ipsorum Japonesium mappis descriptum*
(Augsburg, *c.*1730–60)
MUNICH, BAYERISCHE STAATSBIBLIOTHEK, 2 MAPP. 168–2#99. COURTESY OF THE BAYERISCHE STAATSBIBLIOTHEK

(1651–1716), who stayed in Nagasaki from 1690 to 1692.[6] Europeans were generally confined to the small island of Deshima in Nagasaki harbor, but Kaempfer visited Edo (later Tokyo) twice and met the shogun Tokugawa Tsunayoshi (1646–1709), taking every opportunity to learn about the country. In addition to a study of the plants of Japan[7] he wrote a history of the country that addresses politics and religion in detail, gives a careful account of Nagasaki, and also describes the country's minerals, plants, animals, insects, and fish. He died before the work could be published, and the manuscript made its way to

England and was first printed in an English translation in 1727,[8] and then in French and Dutch in 1729.[9]

6   Detlef Haberland, *Engelbert Kaempfer, 1651–1716: A Biography*, trans. Peter Hogg (London: British Library, 1996).

7   Kaempfer's *Flora Japonica* is part 5 of his *Amoenitatum exoticarum politico-physico-medicarum* (Lemgo: Heinrich Wilhelm Meyer, 1712).

8   The title of the English translation of Kaempfer's work is *The History of Japan, giving an Account of the Ancient and Present State and Government of that Empire; of its Temples, Palaces, Castles and other Buildings; of its Metals, Minerals, Trees, Plants, Animals, Birds and Fishes; of the Chronology and Succession of the Emperors, Ecclesiastical and Secular; of the Original Descent, Religions, Customs, and Manufactures of the Natives, and of their Trade and Commerce with the Dutch and Chinese* (London: Printed for the Translator, 1727). It is available in electronic format at https://archive.org. There is a more recent and much superior English translation of Kaempfer's book in Beatrice M. Bodart-Bailey, *Kaempfer's Japan: Tokugawa Culture Observed* (Honolulu: University of Hawaii Press, 1999).

9   On the history of Kaempfer's manuscript, its movements, and its translations see Derek Massarella, "The History of *The History*: The Purchase and Publication of Kaempfer's *History of Japan*,"

FIGURE 127 Engelbert Kaempfer, *Imperium Japonicum in sexaginta et octo provincias divisum: Ex ipsorum Japonensium mappis & observationibus Kaempferianis* (London, 1727)
COURTESY OF BARRY LAWRENCE RUDERMAN ANTIQUE MAPS

Kaempfer's book includes a map of Japan titled *Imperium Japonicum in sexaginta et octo provincias divisum: Ex ipsorum Japonensium mappis & observationibus Kaempferianis* ("The Japanese Empire Divided in Sixty-Eight Provinces, Made from the Maps of the Japanese Themselves and Kaempfer's Observations") (Fig. 127).[10] The map, which

was actually made from Japanese maps by Johann Caspar Scheuchzer, who translated Kaempfer's book into English, is decorated with inset maps of the Kamchatka Peninsula and Hokkaido and an image of a Japanese compass with a table of distances to various places, mostly in Asia, from Japan. At the left there is an illustration of Japanese "rosaries," actually Buddhist prayer beads, and below there is a cartouche dedicating the map to Sir Hans Sloane (1660–1753), who had purchased Kaempfer's manuscripts and had them brought to England and arranged for

Transactions of the Asiatic Society of Japan 8 (1993), pp. 9–43; reprinted in Beatrice M. Bodart-Bailey and Derek Massarella, eds., *The Furthest Goal: Engelbert Kaempfer's Encounter with Tokugawa Japan* (Sandgate: Japan Library, 1995), pp. 96–131; and also Beatrice M. Bodart Bailey, "Kaempfer Restor'd," *Monumenta Nipponica* 43.1 (1988), pp. 1–33.

10 Kaempfer's map of Japan is Plate 8 in his book; for discussion of it see Lutz Walter, "Engelbert Kaempfer and the European Cartography of Japan," in Lutz Walter, ed., *Japan: A Cartographic Vision: European Printed Maps from the Early 16th to the 19th Century* (Munich and New York: Prestel-Verlag, 1994), pp. 61–68; and

Jason C. Hubbard, *Japoniae insulae: The Mapping of Japan: Historical Introduction and Cartobibliography of European Printed Maps of Japan to 1800* (Houten: HES & De Graaf Publishers, 2012), nos. 77 and 79. Kaempfer's map of Nagasaki is Plate 19 in his book.

their translation—the text in the cartouche was written by Scheuchzer. The cartouche is flanked by "Tossitoku" (Toshitoku), the Japanese god of good fortune, and on the right, "Jebis" (Ebisu), the Japanese god of the sea. In the lower right corner of the map is an image of Daikoku, the Japanese god of wealth.[11]

In making his new map in about 1745 Seutter copied Kaempfer's cartography very closely, and he indicates his debt in his title: *Regni Japoniae nova mappa geographica, ex indigenarum observationibus delineata ab Engelberto Kaempfero recusa et emendata a Matth. Seuttero* ("New Geographical Map of the Kingdom of Japan, Drawn by Engelbert Kaempfer from the Observations of Local Peoples, and Revised by Matthäus Seutter").[12] But Seutter changed the decorative program entirely. At the bottom of the map he replaced Kaempfer's cartouche and Japanese deities with images of Japanese family crests borrowed from the frontispiece of the English translation of Kaempfer's book, and borrowed images of Japanese coins from Kaempfer's map of Nagasaki.[13] At the top he removes Kaempfer's inset maps and the image of the compass and adds part of the Kamchatka Peninsula (which should have appeared on Kaempfer's map) and an elaborate cartouche in the upper left corner (Fig. 128).

This cartouche takes some time to interpret. At the top, seated on a throne, we have the shogun, specifically Tokugawa Tsunayoshi (1646–1709), for the triple holly-hock emblem above is that of the Tokugawa clan,[14] and Kaempfer had met Tokugawa. The shogun's vest represents Japanese armor. His throne—intriguingly—looks more like a cartouche frame than anything Japanese, but then Seutter was no expert on Japan. The man to the right of the shogun takes from him a stylus, and the fact that the shogun had been holding a stylus indicates that the map of

Japan that he holds forth in his other hand was made under his authority.[15] The man on the left in European clothes to whom the shogun shows the map of Japan is Kaempfer, and Kaempfer copies information from the shogun's map onto his own map. In this remarkable image we see the cartographer in action, his map coming to life, something rarely depicted even in an idealized way like this,[16] and the cartouche emphasizes the reliability of Kaempfer's work by his use of Japanese maps—specifically, Japanese maps that had been created under the shogun's authority.[17] The accuracy of Kaempfer's map is thus unimpeachable, and of course Seutter's map, which he based on Kaempfer's, shares that same accuracy. The cartouche tells the story of the map's genesis.

On his earlier map that he had copied from Reland, Seutter did not even mention Reland, giving him no credit at all, but here he not only includes Kaempfer's name in the title, but also depicts him, a remarkable change. Seutter had perhaps realized that the minor decorative changes he had made to Reland's map, specifically the addition of the generic figures of Mercury and personifications of Fame and Asia, were a lost opportunity—that he could have created a cartouche that conveyed much more about the map. The tradition of visually citing sources on maps goes back to the Hereford *mappamundi* of *c*.1300, which has a scene of the Roman Emperor Augustus ordering the world to be mapped, with the implication that the Hereford map derives from that cartographic heritage.[18] Another famous example is Martin Waldseemüller's world map of 1507, where he includes in the upper margin portraits of two of his most important sources and maps of the areas they had knowledge of: Claudius Ptolemy with a Ptolemaic world map, and Amerigo Vespucci with a map

---

11   These Japanese gods are described in Kaempfer's *The History of Japan* (1727), Book 3, chapter 3, p. 224. The decoration of Kaempfer's map is discussed by Marcia Yonemoto, "Envisioning Japan in Eighteenth-Century Europe: The International Career of a Cartographic Image," *Intellectual History Newsletter* 22 (2000), pp. 17–35, esp. 28.

12   On Seutter's map of *c*.1745 see Jason C. Hubbard, *Japoniae insulae: The Mapping of Japan: Historical Introduction and Cartobibliography of European Printed Maps of Japan to 1800* (Houten: HES & De Graaf Publishers, 2012), no. 81.

13   Again, Kaempfer's *History of Japan* (1727) is available at https://archive.org, and both the frontispiece and the map of Nagasaki (Plate 19) are viewable there.

14   The hollyhock emblem is identified as the *Insignia imperatoris japonici*, the insignia of the Emperor of Japan (rather than that of the Shogun), on the frontispiece of the 1727 English translation of Kaempfer's work, and this identification is confirmed on pp. 392 and 119—but Kaempfer often uses the word emperor for the shogun.

15   I thank Michael Ritter for the interpretation of the stylus.

16   Some other examples of depictions of cartographers in action are supplied by Rodney Shirley, "The Face of the Maker: Portraits of Cartographers Concealed in Maps and Title Pages," *Mercator's World* 1.4 (1996), pp. 14–19; and on representations of cartographers at work see Michael Bischoff, "Geographia: Representations of Mapmaking in the Early Modern Period," *IMCoS Journal* 152 (2018), pp. 14–23.

17   Kaempfer mentions his use of Japanese maps in his *History of Japan* (1727), on Plates 8 and 19 following p. 392, in addition to the reference in the title of his map of Japan. Incidentally there is mention of gifts of European maps to the shogun in Kees Zandvliet, *Mapping for Money: Maps, Plans, and Topographic Paintings and their Role in Dutch Overseas Expansion during the 16th and 17th Centuries* (Amsterdam: Batavian Lion International, 1998), pp. 122 and 124.

18   Diarmuid Scully, "Augustus, Rome, Britain and Ireland on the Hereford *mappa mundi*: Imperium and Salvation," *Peregrinations: Journal of Medieval Art and Architecture* 4.1 (2013), pp. 107–133, esp. 115–118.

FIGURE 128   Matthäus Seutter, *Regni Japoniae nova mappa geographica, ex indigenarum observationibus delineata ab Engelberto Kaempfero recusa et emendata a Matth. Seuttero* (Ausgburg, c.1740)
COURTESY OF BARRY LAWRENCE RUDERMAN ANTIQUE MAPS

of the more recently discovered parts of the world, eastern Asia, Japan, and the New World.[19] Also see the discussion of Pieter van den Keere's portraits of some of authorities he had consulted in his *Nova totius orbis mappa, c.*1611 in Chapter 5 above.

The scene of the boat on the left in Seutter's cartouche he borrows from his earlier map of Japan, where it appears to the right of the principle cartouche at the bottom;[20] the man sitting below holding a tablet with Japanese characters he borrowed from the frontispiece of the French or Dutch edition of Kaempfer's *History of Japan*, where the characters are better formed and much easier to read

(Fig. 129).[21] The characters were copied from Plate 15 of Kaempfer's book, where they are identified as the "twelve celestial signs," but they are actually the twelve celestial branches of the sexagenary cycle.[22] It also seems possible that this frontispiece provided some general inspiration to Seutter in designing his cartouche: the central figure, History personified, is writing while she receives

19   On these portraits on Waldseemüller's 1507 map see my *Martin Waldseemüller's Carta marina of 1516: Study and Transcription of the Long Legends* (New York: Springer, 2019), pp. 5 and 15.

20   Seutter had borrowed the scene of the boat on his *Imperium Japonicum* from Reland's map, and Reland borrowed it from Arnoldus Montanus, *Gedenkwaerdige gesantschappen der Oost-Indische maatschappy* (Amsterdam: J. Meurs, 1669), p. 54.

21   The French translation is Engelbert Kaempfer, *Histoire naturelle, civile, et ecclésiastique de l'empire du Japon* (The Hague: P. Gosse and J. Neaulme, 1729), and the Dutch is Engelbert Kaempfer, *De Beschryving van Japan* (Amsterdam: Balthasar Lakemann, 1729). The Dutch edition, but not the French, has a poem by Claas Bruin (1671–1731) explaining the frontispiece. Both editions are available in electronic format at https://archive.org. On the frontispieces in these editions see Marion Kintzinger, *Chronos und Historia: Studien zur Titelblattikonographie historiographischer Werke vom 16. bis zum 18. Jahrhundert* (Wiesbaden: Harrassowitz, 1995), pp. 193–194 and fig. 172.

22   The Japanese characters for the twelve celestial signs in the frontispiece are copied from Kaempfer's Plate 15.

information from Truth personified, who pulls back the cover from a globe with Japan prominently displayed, with the triple hollyhock emblem of the Tokugawa clan above. In both images we have a transfer of information and the recording of that information (History writing, Kaempfer making his map), cartography (the globe, the maps of Japan), the Tokugawa emblem above—and the man with the tablet in the lower left. And Seutter's new cartouche, like both his earlier map and the frontispiece in Kaempfer's book, has several pieces of Japanese porcelain depicted in it, which was the Japanese product of the greatest interest to Europeans.

Studying Seutter's new cartouche allows us to see how he brought together elements from multiple sources to create it, and demonstrates, incidentally, that he had at least two different editions of Kaempfer's book in his workshop, both the English translation, whose frontispiece is the source of the Japanese coats of arms on his map, and either the French or the Dutch translation, whose frontispiece he also used as a source. Moreover, he makes a bold graphic claim for the authority of Kaempfer's map, suggesting that it derived from Japanese maps made under the shogun's authority, and thus gives full credit to his predecessor and source.[23]

Seutter's cartouche should be seen in the context of *chinoiserie*, a strong interest by European artists in East Asian subjects and fanciful imaginings of East Asian decoration.[24] This style resulted in the production of model books of *chinoiserie* cartouches around the middle of the eighteenth century, for example, Alexis Peyrotte's *Nouveaux cartouches chinois* ("New Chinese Cartouches") and *Second livre de cartouches chinois* ("Second Book of Chinese Cartouches") (Paris: Huquier, *c.*1742),[25] and Jean Pillement, *Oeuvres de fleurs, ornements, cartouches, figures et sujets chinois, très utiles pour les manufactures d'étoffes de soyes, d'indiennes, de perses, de péquins et de papiers de tantures, les peintres* [*sic*, for *peintures*] *les ameublements et belvederes dans le goût chinois* (Paris: chez Le Père et Avaulez, s.d.).[26] There was also an eighteenth-century model book titled *A Book of Compartments in the Chinese Taste, Useful for all Artificers* that does not survive.[27]

But none of these model book cartouches has the iconographic and historic richness of Seutter's.

23   It had been very common for cartographers to copy maps by other cartographers, usually with no indication of credit, but it is worth mentioning that there had recently been a legal case in France involving cartographic plagiarism: see Numa Broc, "Une affaire de plagiat cartographique sous Louis XIV: le procès Delisle-Nolin," *Revue d'histoire des sciences et de leurs applications* 23 (1970), pp. 141–153, and the discussion in Mary Sponberg Pedley, *The Commerce of Cartography: Making and Marketing Maps in Eighteenth-Century France and England* (Chicago: University of Chicago Press, 2005), pp. 107–110.

24   Anita Brookner, "Chinoiserie in French Painting," *Apollo: The International Magazine for Collectors* 65 (1957), pp. 253–257; Hugh Honour, *Chinoiserie, The Vision of Cathay* (New York: E.P. Dutton & Co., Inc., 1961); Dawn Jacobson, *Chinoiserie* (London: Phaidon Press Ltd., 1993).

25   On Peyrotte's model books—not all of whose cartouches involve *chinoiserie*, despite the title—see Désiré Guilmard, *Les maîtres ornemanistes* (Paris: E. Plon, 1880–81), p. 192; and Gauvin Alexander Bailey, *The Spiritual Rococo: Decor and Divinity from the Salons of Paris to the Missions of Patagonia* (Burlington: Ashgate, 2014), p. 196. The model books are available in electronic format at https://bibliotheque-numerique.inha.fr/idurl /1/22128.

26   The title of Pillement's model book translates as "Works of Flowers, Ornaments, Cartouches, Figures and Chinese Subjects, Very Useful for the Manufacture of Silk, Indian, Persian, and Pekin Fabrics, and Dyed Papers, Paintings, Furnishings, and Belvederes in the Chinese Taste." For discussion of the model book see Désiré Guilmard, *Les maîtres ornemanistes* (Paris: E. Plon, 1880–81), p. 188; Álvaro Samuel Guimarães da Mota, "Gravuras de chinoiserie de Jean-Baptiste Pillement," M.A. Thesis, Faculdade de Letras da Universidade do Porto, 1997, vol. 1, p. 71, and vol. 2, p. 130. Pillement also made *A New Book of Chinese Ornaments* (London, 1755): see *Sayer & Bennett's Enlarged Catalogue of New and Valuable Prints, in Sets, or Single, Also Useful and Correct Maps and Charts, Likewise Books of Architecture, Views of Antiquity, Drawing and Copy Books* (London: Sayer & Bennett, 1775), p. 112, no. 14; and Maria Gordon-Smith, "The Influence of Jean Pillement on French and English Decorative Arts Part One," *Artibus et Historiae* 21.41 (2000), pp. 171–196, at 174, 175, and 177.

27   On the lost model book of Chinese cartouches see *Sayer & Bennett's Enlarged Catalogue of New and Valuable Prints* (see note 26), p. 113, no. 18; and Terry F. Friedman, "Two Eighteenth-Century Catalogues of Ornamental Pattern Books," *Furniture History* 11 (1975), pp. 66–75, at 70, no. 178.

FIGURE 129 The frontispiece in Engelbert Kaempfer, *De beschryving van Japan* (The Hague: P. Gosse en J. Neaulme; Amsterdam: Balthasar Lakeman, 1729)
UNIVERSITY OF CALIFORNIA AT BERKELEY, EAST ASIAN RARE, 3409.9.2048. COURTESY OF THE UNIVERSITY OF CALIFORNIA

The Illusionistic Roll of the Cartouche

Gilles and Didier Robert de Vaugondy, Carte de la terre des Hebreux ou Israelites, *1745*

Two important French cartographers of the eighteenth century were a father and son team, Gilles Robert de Vaugondy (1688–1766) and Didier Robert de Vaugondy (c.1723–1786), and they had a strong appreciation of the importance of cartouches. They inherited and acquired the printing plates for many of the maps of Nicolas Sanson (1600–67), a few of whose works were mentioned above, which they both reprinted and used as the foundations of their own revised maps.[1] Among their better-known works is their *Atlas Universel* of 1757,[2] and they made it clear in their advertisements for the atlas that the cartouches were a priority. Theirs was the first atlas published in France by subscription,[3] which entailed the need for advertising to attract subscribers, and an advertisement published five years before the publication specifies that the cartouches will be designed and engraved by a well-known artist:[4] *La Gravure est du sieur de la Haye & de ses deux fils. Les Cartouches sont dessinés & gravés par le sieur Babel* ("The engraving is by the Sieur de la Haye and his two sons. The cartouches are drawn and engraved by Mr. Babel.")

This is Pierre-Edmé Babel (1720–1775),[5] who a later, similar advertisement for the atlas said was *célèbre par ses Ouvrages d'Ornemens*, "famous for his ornamental works,"[6] and who had made two model books of cartouches (though curiously he did not sign any of the cartouches in the *Atlas Universel*).[7] The continuing interest in cartouches by the Robert de Vaugondys and their publisher Antoine Boudet[8] is also demonstrated by two notices for the 1779 edition of their atlas, in which they write: *La derniere livraison de l'Atlas Universel de Messieurs Robert de Vaugondy, retouché quant à la gravure des Cartouches, & contenant 108 Cartes de grandeur uniforme,* "The latest edition of the *Atlas Universel* of Messrs Robert de Vaugondy, touched up as to the engraving of the

---

1   On the son see Frank Arthur Kafker, "Robert de Vaugondy, Didier," in *The Encyclopedists as Individuals: A Biographical Dictionary of the Authors of the Encyclopédie* (Oxford: Voltaire Foundation at the Taylor Institution, 1988), pp. 330–333; the essential work on father and son is Mary Sponberg Pedley, *Bel et utile: The Work of the Robert de Vaugondy Family of Mapmakers* (Tring, England: Map Collector Publications, 1992), who addresses the Robert de Vaugondys' acquisition of the plates for Sanson's maps on p. 21.

2   On the *Atlas Universel* see George Fordham, *Studies in Carto-Bibliography, British and French, and in the Bibliography of Itineraries and Road-Books* (Oxford: Clarendon Press, 1914; London: Dawsons, 1969), pp. 165–168; Pedley, *Bel et utile* (see note 1), pp. 51–68; and Mary Sponberg Pedley, "'Commode, complet, uniforme, et suivi': Problems in Atlas Editing in Enlightenment France," in Joan Winearls, ed., *Editing Early and Historical Atlases: Papers Given at the Twenty-Ninth Annual Conference on Editorial Problems, University of Toronto, 5–6 November 1993* (Toronto and Buffalo: University of Toronto Press, 1995), pp. 83–108, esp. 95–99.

3   Mary Sponberg Pedley, "The Subscription List of the 1757 *Atlas Universel*: A Study in Cartographic Dissemination," *Imago Mundi* 31 (1979), pp. 66–77.

4   The advertisement for the *Atlas Universel* is in the *Journal des Sçavans* for April 1752, pp. 254–255. The journal is available in digital format at https://gallica.bnf.fr.

5   On Babel see Désiré Guilmard, *Les maîtres ornemanistes. Dessinateurs, peintres, architectes, sculpteurs et graveurs. Écoles française, italienne, allemande et des Pays-Bas* (Paris: E. Plon, 1880–81), vol. 1, pp. 173–175; Julius Meyer, ed., *Allgemeines Künstler-Lexikon* (Leipzig: Verlag von Wilhelm Engelmann, 1872–1885), vol. 2, pp. 500–502; Marcel Roux, *Inventaire du fonds français: graveurs du dix-huitième siècle* (Paris: Bibliothèque nationale de France, 1930), vol. 1, pp. 368–382; and Peter Fuhring, "Some Newly Identified Drawings of Ornament From the Seventeenth and Eighteenth Centuries in the Nationalmuseum, Stockholm: Lucas Kilian, Nicolas II Loir, Alexis Loir, Jacques de Lajoüe and Pierre-Edme Babel," *Nationalmuseum Bulletin* (Stockholm) 17.3 (1993), pp. 11–25, esp. 21–23.

6   This other advertisement for the *Atlas Universel* is in the *Affiches, annonces, et avis divers*, January 16, 1754, pp. 9–10; Didier Robert de Vaugondy uses the same phrase in the prospectus for the *Atlas*: Gilles Robert de Vaugondy, *Atlas universel ... proposé par souscription* (Paris: chez les auteurs, quai de l'Horloge du Palais, 1757), p. 3. The prospectus is available on https://archive.org.

7   Pierre-Edmé Babel, [Collection of cartouches] (Paris: Jacques Chereau, 1740); and Pierre-Edmé Babel, *Cartouches pour estre acompagnés de suports et trophées* (Paris: chez Huquier fils, 1750). On the latter model book see Guilmard, *Les maîtres ornemanistes* (see note 5), p. 173.

8   On Antoine Boudet see Jacques Guinard, "Le livre dans la Péninsule Ibérique au XVIIIᵉ siècle: témoinage d'un libraire français," *Bulletin hispanique* 49 (1957), pp. 176–198, esp. 176–179; Robert Favre, "Boudet, Antoine," in Jean Sgard, ed., *Dictionnaire des journalists (1600–1789)* (Oxford: Voltaire Foundation, 1999), vol. 1, no. 95; Frédéric Barbier, Sabine Juratic, and Annick Mellerio, "Boudet, Antoine Chrétien," in *Dictionnaire des imprimeurs, libraires et gens du livre à Paris (1701–1789)* (Geneva: Droz, 2007–), vol. 1, pp. 274–280; and Gabriel Sánchez Espinosa, "Los libreros Ángel Corradi y Antoine Boudet, y la importación de libros franceses para la Academia de San Fernando," *Bulletin hispanique* 114.1 (2012), pp. 195–216, esp. 205 and 211–212.

© CHET VAN DUZER, 2023 | DOI:10.1163/9789004523838_029

cartouches, and containing 108 maps of uniform size."[9] The cartouches are the first thing mentioned, even before the number of the maps.

We have no records of discussions between the cartographers, their publisher, and the cartouche designers that indicate who was making decisions regarding the maps' cartouches. But it is certainly worth examining some cartouches by this team who had a full appreciation of the value and importance of cartouches in selling maps. We will examine their maps of the Holy Land because the father, Gilles, had a particular interest in that region: he revised a book about the geography of the Holy Land,[10] and produced eleven maps of the Holy Land for a Bible in 1748–49.[11] One of the advantages of maps of the Holy Land from the decorative point of view is that the coastline leaves ample open space in the Mediterranean for a cartouche.

It turns out that most of the cartouches on the maps of the Robert de Vaugondys, despite their appreciation of the genre, are not of any particular symbolic or allegorical richness. They exemplify the florid ornateness, writhing structure, and asymmetrical design typical of the rococo or rocaille,[12] and are very finely engraved, but allegory was not an aspect of cartouche design that appealed to these cartographers. They had a different conception of the functions of cartouches than the other cartographers whose works we have been examining.

Gilles published a map of the Holy Land in 1743 titled *Terre de Chanaan ou terre promise à Abraham et à sa postérité*, that is, "The Land of Canaan or Land Promised to Abraham and his Posterity."[13] In addition to the main map with its title cartouche, we have an inset map (cartouche) with its title cartouche,[14] and an inset plan (cartouche) of the camp of the Israelites around the Ark of the Covenant (Numbers 1:3–4). The title cartouche of the main map (Fig. 130) is signed at the top by "Gobin," that is, Jean-Baptiste Gobin, an artist whose only signed works are the cartouches on maps by the Vaugondys. In the long text following the map's title Gilles explains that he has placed the lands of the sons of Canaan as well as he can; says that the map shows the 42 places the Israelites stopped on the Exodus; notes that the map is intended to help with the reading of the first five books of the Bible; and says that he made it based on manuscript maps by Guillaume Sanson.[15]

At the bottom of the title cartouche Gobin depicts the drunkenness of Noah, and helpfully supplies the biblical reference (Genesis 9:22–23) below. Noah's son Ham points to his father, while his other two sons prepare to cover him, though strangely, he is already covered, probably out of Gobin's desire for decorousness. A large grapevine grows up the right-hand side of the frame: in this case the vegetal decoration is part of the theme of the cartouche. The drunkenness of Noah is an appropriate theme for the cartouche because Ham was the father of Canaan, and when Noah awoke he cursed Canaan and his descendants—and the map is of the Land of Canaan.[16] So the cartouche depicts a decisive moment in the history of the peoples of the Holy Land.

The decoration of the cartouche is appropriate to the map's subject, and the fact that the map was specifically designed for teaching is interesting, but there is no rich

9   For the advertisement for the 1779 edition of the *Atlas Universel* see *Affiches, annonces, et avis divers* for August 4, 1779, p. 123. Similar text about the 1779 edition appears in *L'on distribue chez Boudet, libraire-imprimeur du Roi, rue S. Jacques* (Paris: Boudet, 1779), but there it is added that the cartouches had to be touched up because the atlas has sold so well that the printing plates become worn.

10   Gilles Robert de Vaugondy, *Géographie sacrée, et historique de l'Ancien et du Nouveau Testament* (Paris: Durand, 1747). The three volumes are available on https://archive.org.

11   Augustin Calmet, *La Sainte Bible en latin et en françois avec des notes litterales, critiques et historiques* (Paris: chez Gabriel Martin, J.B. Coignard & Ant. Boudet, Pierre-Jean Mariette, Hippolyte-Louis Guerin, 1748–1750); some volumes of the Bible are available on https://archive.org. The son Didier mentions his father's making the maps for the bible in the *Atlas Universel*, p. 20, col. 2. The maps in this Bible were reprinted in the *Atlas biblique ou cartes et figures de la bible* (Avignon: François-Barthelemi Merande, 1784). It is worth mentioning that none of these maps has a cartouche: perhaps that embellishment was thought unnecessary in a didactic context.

12   See the discussion of rocaille or rococo cartouches in the Introduction.

13   On Gilles' 1743 map, which was engraved by Jean Lattré, see Pedley, *Bel et utile* (see note 1), p. 198, no. 391. A high-resolution image of Gilles' 1743 map is available at https://loc.gov.

14   The inset map's title is *Carte des voiages d'Abraham faits par l'ordre de Dieu, en Asie et en Egypte où sont les pays dont il lui promit la possession et à sa postérité en récompence de son obeisance*, "Map of the Journeys of Abraham Made by the Order of God, in Asia and in Egypt, where are the Countries of which God Promised Possession and to him and his Posterity as a Reward for his Obedience."

15   The title cartouche in Gilles' 1743 map reads: *Terre de Chanaan ou terre promise a Abraham et a sa postérité. On a chiffré les noms des onze fils de Chanaan selon leur ordre, quelques uns d'entr'eux ont plusieurs fois changé de demeure. On a aussi marqué la sortie du Peuple d'Israel hors de l'Egypte et ses 42 demeures dans le desert pendant 40 ans. Cette Carte sert pour la lecture du Pentateuque. Elle est dressée sur les manuscrits de G. Sanson Géog. du Roi par le Sr. Robert Géog ord. du Roi.*

16   For discussion of early modern interpretations of the Curse of Ham see David M. Whitford, *The Curse of Ham in the Early Modern Era: The Bible and the Justifications for Slavery* (Farnham, England, and Burlington, VT: Ashgate, 2009).

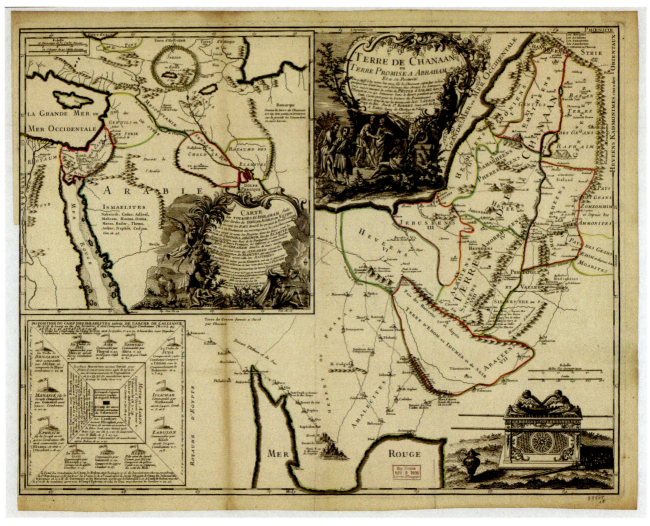

FIGURE 130   Gilles Robert de Vaugondy, *Terre de Chanaan ou Terre Promise a Abraham, et a sa Posterite de G. Sanson Geographe du Roy*, first published in 1743, and this is the 1797 printing

LIBRARY OF CONGRESS, GEOGRAPHY AND MAP DIVISION, G7500 1743 .R6. COURTESY OF THE LIBRARY OF CONGRESS

symbolism here. Most of the cartouches on the maps by the Robert de Vaugondys are similar in this regard.

Two years later, in 1745, Gilles published another map of the Holy Land titled *Carte de la terre des Hebreux ou Israelites partagée selon l'ordre de Dieu aux douze tribus descendantes des douze fils de Jacob*, "Map of the Land of the Hebrews or Israelites Shared According to the Order of God to the Twelve Tribes Descended from the Twelve Sons of Jacob."[17] It has a large inset map occupying the eastern Mediterranean, that is, the upper left corner of the main map. The map appeared in two different states: in the first state printed in 1745 the inset map is presented with the *trompe-l'oeil* illusion that it is on a separate piece of paper, with its edge curling up, and its title cartouche is elaborately decorated (Fig. 131), while in a later state printed around 1773 (though it still bears the 1745 date) the inset map has a plain linear border, and its title cartouche

has a plain border.[18] It seems that some additional decoration was contemplated for the less elaborate state, since the engraver left space free of the meridians and parallels along the diagonal part of the cartouche's frame, but such decoration was never added, and the less elaborate version was reprinted years later.[19]

Both the main map and the inset map have title cartouches, but again, neither has decoration of any profundity. In the title cartouche of the main map (Fig. 132), at the top we have the Hebrew name of God written in a triangle

---

17   On Gilles' 1745 map Pedley, *Bel et utile* (see note 1), p. 198, no. 392.

18   A note on the less elaborate state of the map says that it would serve to accompany reading of Jean-Baptiste-Sébastien Colomme, *Notice de l'Écriture Sainte, ou Description topographique, chronologique, historique et critique des royaumes, provinces … dont il est fait mention dans la Vulgate* (Paris: L. Prault, 1773). A zoomable image of this map is available at https://gallica.bnf.fr.

19   A high-resolution image of a 1797 printing of the map is available at https://ufdc.ufl.edu.

FIGURE 131 Gilles Robert de Vaugondy, *Carte de la Terre des Hebreux ou Israelites partagée selon l'ordre de Dieu aux douze tribus descendantes des Douze Fils de Jacob* (Paris: chez l'auteur, 1745)

COURTESY OF OLD WORLD AUCTIONS, GLEN ALLEN, VIRGINIA

that symbolizes the Trinity that shines with light; on the left sits Moses holding the Tablets of the Law, with the "horns of light" on his head deriving from Exodus 34:29–35, and on the right the high priest Aaron, his brother.[20]

The title of the inset map (Fig. 133) is *La monarchie des Hebreux sous Salomon, ou, Le royaume d'Israel distingué en douze gouvernemens*, "The Monarchy of the Hebrews under Solomon, or, The Kingdom of Israel Distinguished in Twelve Governments," which is to say that it shows the Holy Land at a very different period in history than the main map, about 1000 years later.[21] At the right-hand side of the title cartouche Fame, blowing her trumpet, brings an olive branch to the land, indicating the peace that prevailed during the monarchy (1 Kings 4:20 and 24–25). The small scene at the bottom of the cartouche, which is

20   The text in the main title cartouche on Gilles' 1745 map reads: *Carte de la terre des Hebreux ou Israelites partagée selon l'ordre de Dieu aux douze tribus descendantes des douze fils de Jacob, savoir au delà du Jourdain, deux portions qui furent accordées aux tribus de Ruben, et de Gad, et une demie aux fils de Manasse (Deut. ch. 3 v. 12 ecc, Josué ch. 12. v. 62), au deçà du Jourdain, une portion à la tribu de Juda, une à celle d'Ephraim, et une demie aux fils et aux filles de Manassé, (Josué ch. 15.16.et 17) sept portions qui échurent au sort aux tribus de Benjamin, Simeon, Zabulon, Issachar, Aser, Nephtali, et Dan, (Jos. ch. 18 et 19) les villes que l'on désigna dans chaque tribu pour la demeure de ceux de la tribu de Levi, et les six villes de refuge (Jos. ch. 20) Dressée pour la lécture de l'Ecriture Sainte sur les cartes, et manuscrits des Srs. Sanson, par le Sr. Robert, Geographe ordinaire du roy*. The design of the cartouche seems to have drawn inspiration from that on Alexis Hubert Jalliot, *Iudaea seu Terra Sancta, quae Hebraeorum sive Israelitarum in suas duodecim tribus divisa* (Paris: Jalliot, 1691); a high-resolution image of the map is available at https://uwm.edu/lib-collections/.

21   The text in the inset map's title cartouche on Gilles' 1745 map reads: *La monarchie des Hebreux sous Salomon, ou, Le royaume d'Israel distingué en douze gouvernemens d'après les manuscrits de Nicolas et Guillaume Sanson, par le sr. Robert, geog. ord. du roy. Ce Royaume a duré depuis l'an du monde 2909 jusquen 3029, ce qui fait 120 ans, savoir 40 ans sous Saul, 40 ans sous David, et 40 ans sous Salomon, après lequel il fut divisé en Rme. de Juda, et Rme. D'Israel. Le Roy Salomon possedoit tous les pais qui est au deçà du Fleuve [d'Euphrate] depuis Thapsa jusquà la ville de Gaza, et aux frontieres d'Egypte. Tous les rois de ces regions lui obeissoient, il étoit en paix avec tous ses voisins. du 3e Livre des Roys ch. 4.*

FIGURE 132 Detail of the title cartouche from Gilles Robert de Vaugondy, *Carte de la Terre des Hebreux ou Israelites partagée selon l'ordre de Dieu aux douze tribus descendantes des Douze Fils de Jacob* (Paris: chez l'auteur, 1745)
COURTESY OF OLD WORLD AUCTIONS, GLEN ALLEN, VIRGINIA

very finely rendered, depicts the judgement of Solomon, in which he adjudicated between two women who both claimed to be the mother of a child (1 Kings 3:16–26).

But Gilles' 1745 map of the Holy Land is nonetheless interesting in terms of its cartouches. The map's composition gives it a striking *mise en abyme* or nested character: we have the main map of the Holy Land, and off its coast a cartouche with an inset map of the Holy Land, and off

its coast the title cartouche of the inset map. The nestedness, emphasized by the placement of the phrase GRANDE MER OCCIDENTALE in the same position and orientation on both "outer" and "inner" map, is very striking, so much so that it is difficult to think that Gilles was not conscious of it. We saw this same consciousness of the recursive possibilities offered by cartouches, of their potential for *mise en abyme* composition, in Willem Hondius's *Nova*

FIGURE 133   Detail of the inset map from Gilles Robert de Vaugondy, *Carte de la Terre des Hebreux ou Israelites partagée selon l'ordre de Dieu aux douze tribus descendantes des Douze Fils de Jacob* (Paris: chez l'auteur, 1745)

COURTESY OF OLD WORLD AUCTIONS, GLEN ALLEN, VIRGINIA

totius Brasiliae … descriptio of 1635, discussed in Chapter 8 above.

The production of the map in two different versions, one with the *trompe-l'oeil* illusion that the inset map is on a separate piece of paper, the other where the cartouche border is a simple line, raises interesting questions about the ontology of cartouches. At the same time that the *trompe-l'oeil* suggests that the cartouche of the inset map is an object separate from the main map, the pyramid and its rays at the top of the main title cartouche just below extend upward onto the inset map, breaking the illusion created by the curling edge of paper, and affixing the inset map to the main map. While one cartouche—the inset map—asserts its independence and declares its separate existence, another—the title cartouche below—denies this claim, identifies the illusion as illusion, and binds the maps together. More precisely, it is the Tetragrammaton, the name of God in the shining pyramid, that accomplishes this, and this name was thought to be of magical

power for centuries.[22] The location of the Tetragrammaton precisely on the border between what might otherwise be two separate maps, holding them together, is certainly no accident. It is God who binds together the two maps of the Holy Land that depict it at times more than 1000 years apart, just as it was God who supported the Israelites during those centuries.[23]

---

22   See Robert J. Wilkinson, "The Tetragrammaton in Renaissance Magic and among the Later Christian Kabbalists," in his *Tetragrammaton: Western Christians and the Hebrew Name of God: From the Beginnings to the Seventeenth Century* (Leiden and Boston: Brill, 2015), pp. 416–460; also see his pp. 365–381 on the Tetragrammaton in illustrations.

23   Remarkably, Robert de Vaugondy published another version of this map very similar to the one discussed here, but without the pyramid and Tetragrammaton within the image of the sun. The map is Gilles Robert de Vaugondy, *Carte de la Terre des Hebreux ou Israelites partagée selon l'ordre de Dieu* (Paris: chez l'auteur, 1745). A zoomable image of the map is available at https://gallica .bnf.fr.

The *trompe-l'oeil* is unlike anything else on the Robert de Vaugondys' maps, as is the use of the Tetragrammaton.[24] Thus, the cartographers most likely commissioned a special artist to plan the map's cartouches. In the lower left corner of the map there is an inscription indicating that Guillaume Delahaye (1725–1802) engraved the map,[25] but unfortunately there is no mark indicating who designed the map's extraordinary program of cartouches.

---

24   The Robert de Vaugondys published a new map of the Holy Land in 1750, *La Judée ou Terre Sainte divisée en ses douze tribus*, and its two cartouches have no remarkable symbolism or philosophical profundity. High-resolution images of the map may be found at https://searchworks.stanford.edu.

25   The Robert de Vaugondys would later have a dispute with the Delahayes about the quality of some of their lettering on maps in their *Atlas Universel*: see Pedley, *Bel et utile* (see note 1), pp. 49–51.

A Cartographic Balancing Act

Matthäus Seutter, Partie orientale de la Nouvelle France ou du Canada, *c.1756*

In Seutter's map of Japan discussed above he indicated his reliance on Engelbert Kaempfer's map in his title, and used the cartouche to emphasize the authority of Kaempfer's map, and thus of his own. That is to say, the cartouche gives more detail about something that he had stated in the title. In Seutter's later map of Canada, on the other hand, the title gives no hint as to what the cartographer regarded as one of its main selling points: this information is only conveyed in the striking cartouche. The map thus demonstrates that in the eighteenth century, study of the cartouche was an expected part of considering the purchase of a map: the cartographer could rely on customers to understand the map's advantages by interpreting the cartouche, and as a result, those advantages did not always need to be spelled out in the title.

The full title of Seutter's map of Canada is *Partie orientale de la Nouvelle France ou du Canada avec l'Isle de Terre-Neuve et de Nouvelle Escosse, Acadie et Nouv. Angleterre avec fleuve de St. Laurence*, that is, "The Eastern Part of New France or Canada, with the Islands of Newfoundland and Nova Scotia, Acadia, and New England, with the St. Lawrence River." It makes no explicit reference to the competing claims of France and Britain in the region, and yet, as we shall see, the cartouche makes it clear that those competing claims are in fact the focus of the map.[1] The map was drawn by Seutter's son Albrecht Carl, and it is difficult to know how the work of making the map was divided between son and elderly father.

France and Britain had long had clashing territorial ambitions in North America, and those ambitions were frequently expressed cartographically.[2] To mention just one specific earlier example, Nicolas de Fer (1646–1720) on his 1698 wall map of America titled *L'Amerique, divisee selon l'etendue de ses principales parties* places great

emphasis on the accomplishments of French explorers and takes every opportunity to expand French claims, even marking part of the Carolinas as French territory.[3] The competition between French and British interests in North America found physical expression in King George's War (1744–48), which was the New World part of the War of the Austrian Succession (1740–48). This war generated numerous skirmishes between French and British colonists mainly in New York, New Hampshire, Massachusetts Bay, and Nova Scotia, as well as the privateering of French ships by New Yorkers.[4] The most momentous event of the war was the taking of the French fortress of Louisbourg on Cape Breton Island by irregular soldiers following a 47-day siege in 1745.[5] The conflict ended with the Treaty of Aix-la-Chapelle (1748), which returned Louisbourg to France and restored all colonial borders to their locations before the fighting began, that is, to the locations specified in the Treaty of Utrecht of 1713.

Unfortunately the locations of the borders had never been clear, and in 1749 the two countries established a boundary commission to examine all of the relevant documents, such as land grants and treaties, to determine where the borders should be. The commission also consulted maps, though both sides expressed serious reservations both about the legal value of the information in maps, and about their impartiality.[6] A few years later, while the dispute between France and Britain continued, the author of a letter to the editor of a London newspaper wrote as follows:[7]

1 I thank Michael Ritter for supplying the date for Seutter's map (*c.*1756) based on his examination of Seutter's manuscript stocklists of his maps.

2 W.F. Reddaway, "Rivalry for Colonial Power, 1714–1748," in J. Holland Rose, A.P. Newton, and E.A. Benians, eds., *The Cambridge History of the British Empire* (New York: The Macmillan Company; Cambridge, UK: The University Press, 1929–1959), vol. 1, pp. 346–376; Seymour I. Schwartz, "European Claims in America: 1700–1750," in Seymour I. Schwartz and Ralph E. Ehrenberg, *Mapping of America* (New York: H.N. Abrams, 1980), pp. 132–155.

3 On de Fer's 1698 map of the Americas see Edward H. Dahl, "The Original Beaver Map: De Fer's 1698 Wall Map of America," *The Map Collector* 29 (1984), pp. 22–26.

4 On King George's War see Robert Leckie, *A Few Acres of Snow: The Saga of the French and Indian Wars* (New York: J. Wiley & Sons, 1999), pp. 243–261; on the privateering of French ships by New Yorkers see James G. Lydon, "The Great Capture of 1744," *New-York Historical Society Quarterly* 52.3 (1968), pp. 255–269.

5 Robert Emmet Wall, Jr., "Louisbourg, 1745," *New England Quarterly* 37.1 (1964), pp. 64–83; Raymond R. Baker, "A Campaign of Amateurs: The Siege of Louisbourg, 1745," *Canadian Historic Sites* 18 (1978), pp. 5–58.

6 Mary Pedley, "Map Wars: The Role of Maps in the Nova Scotia/Acadia Boundary Disputes of 1750," *Imago Mundi* 50.1 (1998), pp. 96–104.

7 Cited by Pedley, "Map Wars" (see note 6), p. 99; I quote from *Read's Weekly Journal* (London), no. 1066, November 9, 1754, p. 1; reprinted

© CHET VAN DUZER, 2023 | DOI:10.1163/9789004523838_030

PARTIE
ORIENTALE
de la
NOUVELLE FRANCE
ou du
CANADA
avec
l'Isle de TERRE-NEUVE
et de
NOUVELLE ESCOSSE
ACADIE
et
NOUV. ANGLETERRE
avec
FLEUVE de St. LAURENCE
representé
par M. ATH. SEUTTER.
Geogr. de S.M. Imper.
d'Augsbourg.

FIGURE 134

The title cartouche on Matthäus Seutter, *Partie orientale de la Nouvelle France ou du Canada* (Augsburg, *c*.1750)

UNIVERSITY OF SOUTHERN MAINE, OSHER MAP LIBRARY AND SMITH CENTER FOR CARTOGRAPHIC EDUCATION, SMITH COLLECTION, NO. 1905. COURTESY OF THE OSHER MAP LIBRARY

"The King of France has always ten or a dozen geographers, devoted to his ministers, who are continually contriving how to corrupt and cook up their maps most to the advantage of their own nation, and prejudice of the English. This all the maps can testify which have appeared at Paris since the peace of Utrecht, when Mr. De L'Isle, the King's premier geographer, began to curtail the British dominions in that continent more than ever, and reduced Nova Scotia to less than the Peninsula, which is hardly a third part of the whole."

Tensions between the English and French in North America remained high, and on July 3, 1754, French and Indian forces attacked a young George Washington and Virginian and British troops at Fort Necessity, southeast of the future site of Pittsburgh, and forced their surrender. This action sparked the French and Indian War (1754–63) between the colonies of New France and British America, and it was in this geopolitical context that Seutter made his map of the eastern part of North America.[8] Again, though the title of the map contains no reference to the war, the cartouche makes very clear the cartographer's goal of impartially depicting the French and English claims.

At the top of the cartouche (Fig. 134) there is a Native American chief holding a bow in one hand, while there is a leash around his other hand, which very disturbingly is held by the European man to his right, probably an attempt to indicate the alliances between European and Indian forces on both sides of the war. To the left the chief's foot touches the arm of Diana, the goddess of the hunt, who also holds a bow and has a quiver of arrows, and to her left there is a landscape in which men on horseback and dogs hunt a deer, and we see other deer and two beavers nearby. So the chief, together with Diana, represent the gathering of the terrestrial natural resources, particularly meat and fur, available in Canada. Meanwhile on the other side of the cartouche just below the European man is Neptune, the god of the sea, who rides a sea monster while holding his trident and an anchor, and he also has a fishing pole and a seine net. To the right there are several European ships at sea, as well as a scene of fishing using a seine net, so the European man, together with Neptune,

represents trade with the New World and the bounty of the sea. That is, the upper part of the cartouche represents the resources at stake in the contest between France and Britain and their colonies in North America.

Below there is a woman wearing a diadem, an elaborate brooch, and a wide metal belt. She holds a map in her lap, and with her right hand she is measuring a distance on it with a divider. The map is of eastern Canada, and is very similar indeed to Seutter's. With her other hand she holds the scales of justice, and below her feet we see the coat of arms of England with its three lions, and the coat of arms of France with its three fleurs-de-lis, so it is the interests of England and France that are being balanced. It seems that Seutter is representing himself as a personification of Justice while making his map of eastern Canada, in which he carefully balances the interests of England and France. This is a very interesting case of a cartographer depicting himself on a map:[9] here we see the cartographer at work creating his map, so that the map contains an image of its own production. It is also an unusual case of a map-within-a-map where the "inner" and "outer" maps are the same.

Looking over the cartographer's shoulders we see Mercury the god of travel and communication on the left, and a general in armor on the right. Mercury seems quite benign, with a merely intellectual interest in the proceedings, but the general sits closer and has his sword out in one hand, and his spear in his other—and his spear sticks menacingly up into the title of the map above, splitting apart Seutter's first name and also his title. The image alludes of course to the military and commercial interests who have stakes in the production of an equitable map.

But the threat posed to the cartographer by the general's weapons is some invented drama, just as the cartographer's claims to impartiality are probably exaggerated. Seutter's interest was in selling maps. The cartouche is attractive and intriguing, but Seutter gives no indication of how he arrived at the boundaries he indicates, and the map would never have any evidentiary value in the dispute between France and England. His thought was

---

in *The Pennsylvania Gazette* (Philadelphia), no, 1364, Feb. 11, 1755, and in the *New-York Mercury*, Feb. 24, 1755, pp. 1–2.

8 Matthäus Seutter, *Partie orientale de la Nouvelle France ou du Canada* (Augsburg, c.1756). High-resolution images of the map, but without the cartouche hand-colored, are available at https://loc.gov, https://jcb.lunaimaging.com, and https://www.davidrumsey.com. For discussion of the map see Kenneth A. Kershaw, *Early Printed Maps of Canada* (Ancaster, Ontario: Kershaw Pub., 1993–1998), vol. 2, pp. 18–19, no. 343.

9 We saw a cartographer's self-portrait earlier in Georg Vischer's *Archiducatus Austriae inferioris* of 1670; for discussion of other maps that include self-portraits by cartographers see James A. Welu, "Cartographic Self-Portraits," in Carla Clivio Marzoli, Giacomo Corna Pellegrini, and Gaetano Ferro, eds., *Imago et mensura mundi: Atti del IX Congresso internazionale di storia della cartografia* (Rome: Istituto della Enciclopedia italiana, 1985), vol. 2, pp. 525–539; and Rodney Shirley, "The Face of the Maker: Portraits of Cartographers Concealed in Maps and Title Pages," *Mercator's World* 1.4 (1996), pp. 14–19. On representations of cartographers at work see Michael Bischoff, "Geographia: Representations of Mapmaking in the Early Modern Period," *IMCoS Journal* 152 (2018), pp. 14–23.

probably that sophisticated customers knew that English maps of Canada favored English claims, and French maps favored French claims, and they would appreciate a map that lacked those nationalistic distortions. This map was probably one of the last maps Seutter made before his death in 1757.

The challenge of balancing France's and Britain's competing claims in maps was a current topic when Seutter made his map. The boundary commission that had been established to weigh their claims had been unable to reach an agreement, and published their findings in 1755 with two separate maps, one representing the French claims, and the other the English.[10] Seutter's map continued

to have life: in 1762 his son-in-law Tobias Conrad Lotter obtained the plates of many of Seutter's maps, including this one, and reprinted the map, modifying the plate to substitute his name for Seutter's as the map's creator.[11]

10   The two maps produced by the boundary commission that show the French and English claims in North America are *Mémoires des commissaires du Roi et de ceux de Sa Majesté britannique, sur les possessions & les droits respectifs des deux couronnes en Amérique* (Paris: L'imprimerie Royale, 1755–1757); and *The Memorials of the English and French Commissaries Concerning the Limits of Nova Scotia or Acadia* (London: s.n., 1755). On the different maps see Pedley, "Map Wars" (see note 6). The

Paris publishing firm Lopez and Cruz also adopted this strategy of publishing two separate maps to represent the French and English claims, both with the title *Mapa de la America Septentrional dividido en dos partes delineado por Lopez y Cruz* (Paris: Lopez y Cruz, 1755). High-resolution images of both maps are available at https://jcb.lunaimaging.com.

11   On Lotter's acquisition of Seutter's plates in 1762 see Michael Ritter, "Seutter, Probst and Lotter: An Eighteenth-Century Map Publishing House in Germany," *Imago Mundi* 53 (2001), pp. 130–135, at 133; and Michael Ritter, "Die Augsburger Landkartenverlage Seutter, Lotter und Probst," *Cartographica Helvetica* 25 (2002), pp. 2–10, at 7–8. Lotter's reprint of Seutter's map is Tobias Conrad Lotter, *Partie orientale de la Nouvelle France ou du Canada avec l'isle de Terre-Neuve et de Nouvelle Escosse, Acadie et Nouv. Angleterre avec fleuve de St. Laurence represénté par T. Conr. Lotter, graveur et géogr. d'Augsbourg* (Augsburg, c.1762). A high-resolution image of Lotter's map is available at https://www.digitalcommonwealth.org/search.

Impartial Border, Partisan Cartouche

Juan de la Cruz Cano y Olmedilla, Mapa geográfico de America Meridional, *1775*

In 1764 Jerónimo Grimaldi (1710–1789), the Spanish Minister of State, ordered the cartographers Tomás López (1730–1802) and Juan de la Cruz Cano y Olmedilla (1734–1790) to make a large new map of South America, one important goal of which was to indicate the border between the Spanish and Portuguese colonies in the continent.[1] López soon found that his and his colleague's ideas about the project differed, and he gave him all of his notes and allowed him to take full responsibility for the project.[2] Cruz Cano spent ten years making the map, consulting the accounts of explorers, missionaries, and colonists, as well the cartographic resources of the Secretaria del Estado de América Meridional (Secretary of State for South America) and the Archivo de Indias, the Spanish governmental department that administered their empire in the Americas and the Philippines.[3] The resulting map (Fig. 135), printed on eight sheets in 1775, measures more than seven by five feet (220 × 162 cm),[4] was the most important and authoritative map of the continent made in the eighteenth century, and continued to be consulted with regard to border disputes well into the twentieth century.[5]

The title cartouche is remarkable for its size, stretching the height of the map from neat line to neat line, more than six feet high, and thus much larger than the cartouche on Nolin's map *Le canal royal de Languedoc* of 1697, discussed in Chapter 15. Also, the map is one of the few cases in which we have remarks from the cartographer himself about the interpretation of the cartouche.

Cruz Cano's map of South America stands apart from the other maps he made not only in terms of its size and the amount of time he devoted to it, but also in terms of the elaborateness of its cartouche. Indeed, looking at his other maps, whose cartouches are all plain and unimaginative,[6] we might be forgiven for thinking that he had hired a specialized artist to design the cartouche on his monumental map, but he did engrave scenes similar to the contents of the cartouche on his map of South America in other contexts, such as elaborate allegorical title pages for books and coats of arms.[7] The large cartouche is indeed his own creation: at the bottom of sheet 1 of the map he says that he designed, engraved and illustrated the map,[8] and he was paid for the map's decoration,

---

1   For an account of the long-continued problems regarding the border between Spanish and Portuguese possessions in South America see Ángel Antonio Pozuelo Reina, *Las fronteras en América del Sur, 1750–1900: Herencia de un conflicto de la época señorial* (Saarbrücken: Editorial Académica Española, 2011).

2   On López's work as a cartographer see Gabriel Marcel, "Le géographe Thomas Lopez et son oeuvre: Essai de biographie et de cartographie," *Revue Hispanique* 16 (1907), pp. 137–243; on the early arrangements regarding the making of the map, see Cesáreo Fernández Duro, *Armada española desde la unión de los reinos de Castilla y de León* (Madrid: Est. tipográfico 'Sucesores de Rivadeneyra,' 1895–1903), vol. 7, pp. 399–415, an account which is summarized in Marcel's article, pp. 179–180. Grimaldi's continuing interest in the question of the boundary between Spanish and Portuguese colonies in South America is reflected in his authorship of the *Respuesta a la memoria que presentó en 16 de enero de 1776 el Exmo Señor Don Francisco Inocencio de Souza Coutiño, embaxador de S.M.F. cerca del Rei N.S. relativa a la negociacion entablada para tratar del arreglo y señalamiento de límites de las posesiones españolas y portuguesas en América Meridional* (Madrid, 1776).

3   For discussion of Cruz Cano's sources see Fernández Duro, *Armada española* (see note 2), vol. 7, p. 401; Thomas Smith, "Cruz Cano's Map of South America, Madrid, 1775: Its Creation, Adversities and Rehabilitation," *Imago Mundi* 20 (1966), pp. 49–78, at 56–57; and José Andrés Jiménez Garcés, "La obra del cartógrafo Cano y Olmedilla y su mapa de la América Meridional de 1775," Tesis doctoral, Universidad Complutense, 2016, pp. 453–465, available at https://eprints.ucm.es/37926/.

4   The map is Juan de la Cruz Cano y Olmedilla, *Mapa geográfico de America Meridional, dispuesto y gravado por D. Juan de la Cruz Cano*

y Olmedilla (Madrid: s.n., 1775). A good high-resolution image of Cruz Cano's map is available at https://searchworks.stanford.edu.

5   On the use of the map in border disputes see Smith, "Cruz Cano's Map" (see note 3), pp. 72–73; Mariano Cuesta Domingo, "Cartografía de América del Sur. Juan de la Cruz," in *Milicia y sociedad ilustrada en España y América (1750–1800): actas XI Jornadas Nacionales de Historia Militar, Sevilla, 11–15 de noviembre de 2002* (Madrid: Deimos, 2003), vol. 2, pp. 209–238, at 235; and in more detail, Jiménez Garcés, "La obra del cartógrafo Cano y Olmedilla" (see note 3), pp. 549–555.

6   On Juan de la Cruz's other maps see Jiménez Garcés, "La obra del cartógrafo Cano y Olmedilla" (see note 3), pp. 71–145, with illustrations.

7   Jiménez Garcés, "La obra del cartógrafo Cano y Olmedilla" (see note 3), illustrates some such title pages and coats of arms in his illustrations 13, 21, 77, and 93; also see for example the title page of Diego Velasco, *Curso theorico-practico de operaciones de cirugia* (Madrid: Joachin Ibarra, 1763); and the frontispiece in each volume of Francisco de Alesón, *Annales del Reyno de Navarra* (Pamplona: Pascual Ibañez, 1766).

8   The text at the bottom of sheet 1 of the map reads *Hoja 1a de la America Meridional, construida gravada, è illustrada por Dnr. Juan de la Cruz Geografo Pensionado por S.M. y Academico de Merito en*

© CHET VAN DUZER, 2023 | DOI:10.1163/9789004523838_031

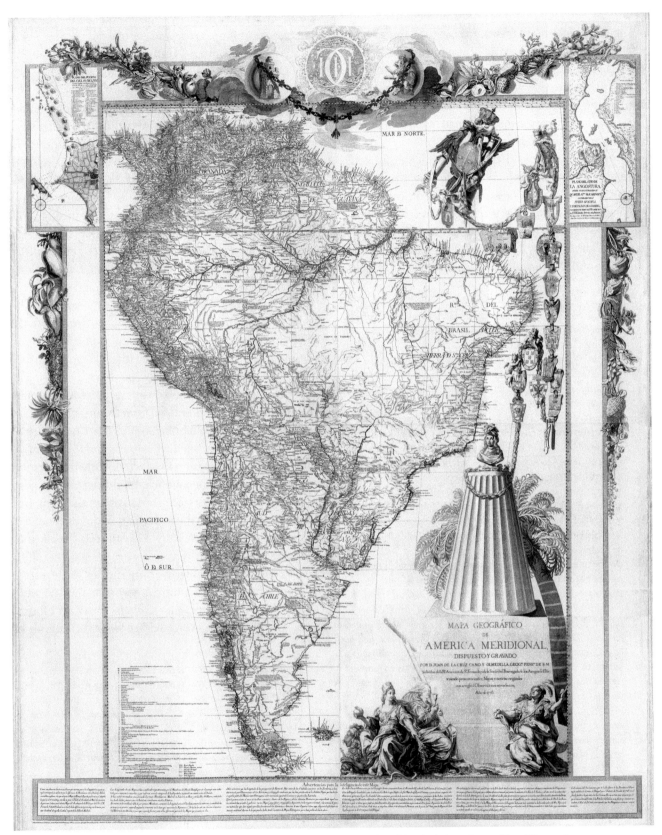

FIGURE 135 Juan de la Cruz Cano y Olmedilla, *Mapa geográfico de America Meridional* (Madrid: Cruz Cano y Olmedilla, 1775)
STANFORD UNIVERSITY, DAVID RUMSEY MAP COLLECTION, G1700 .C7 1775 FF. COURTESY OF THE DAVID RUMSEY MAP COLLECTION

specifically 3000 *reales* "for the illustration of natural history and coats of arms of the country, with a large allegorical title cartouche."[9] In terms of appreciating the value of 3000 *reales*, the intended sale price of the map was 64 *reales*,[10] so the payment for designing the vegetation in the map's margins (the "natural history"), the coats of arms, and the title cartouche was equal to the sale price of about 47 exemplars of the map.

In order to understand the title cartouche we must begin in the map's upper margin.[11] The map symbolically proclaims Spanish political control of South America: at the head of the map there is a detailed scientific image of the sun, complete with sunspots, containing the monogram of Charles III of Spain (1716–1788). So the Spanish king is the sun shining above South America.[12] On either side are orbs with symbols of Castile and León—the kingdoms whose union was the nucleus of what became Spain and the Spanish Empire—united by the collar of the chivalric Order of the Golden Fleece, which was part of the coat of arms of the king of Spain.

I mentioned that Juan de la Cruz left some notes on the map's decoration, and with regard to this part of the decoration, he writes, "The exterior decoration shows the sun with the figure of our lord the King who illuminates the two worlds, producing the wealth of the Golden Fleece."[13] The interpretation that the two orbs represent the two hemispheres is not one that would have occurred to me, but spheres representing the two hemispheres do appear in some versions of the royal achievement of the Indies.[14] The presence of the collar of the Order of the Golden Fleece seems well explained by the fact that it was part of the coat of arms of Spain; the idea that it represents the wealth that the king would generate is abstruse at best. On either side of the orbs grows a garland of plants native to the New World that extends down either side of the map.[15]

The title cartouche has three main parts. First, a garland with the coats of arms of various cities and regions of South America extends down from the upper margin of the map to a bust of Columbus; second, there is the bust of Columbus atop a large tapering column; and third, there is a stone base for the column in which the title information is chiseled, and three personifications at the bottom edge of the map with a palm tree growing up on the right. Just as the garland connects the upper part of the cartouche to the bust of Columbus, the palm tree connects the allegorical figures to the bust as well.

The coats of arms (Fig. 136) are mostly those of cities founded in Spanish South America in the sixteenth century. Juan de la Cruz Cano explains the coats of arms thus: "The interior [decoration] shows the triumph of

la Rl. de Sn. Fernando; impresa y gravada la letra por Hipolito Ricarte año 1771. A separate scan of sheet 1 is available at https://searchworks.stanford.edu.

9 Ricardo Donoso, "El mapa de América Meridional de don Juan de la Cruz Cano y Olmedilla," *Revista Chilena de Historia y Geografía* 131 (1963), pp. 121–175, at 138: "Por la ilustración de Historia natural y Blasones del País, con un tarjetón alegórico, tres mil [*reales*]." The word *tarjeta*, normally meaning "card," is used in the sense of *membrete de los mapas y cartas*, literally "the letterhead of maps or letters." The augmentative "-ón" adds the sense of "large," so *tarjetón* is here "a large title cartouche." This information about the cost of the decoration is also cited by Smith, "Cruz Cano's Map" (see note 3), p. 75; and Isidoro Vázquez de Acuña, *Don Juan de la Cruz, su mapa de América Meridional (1775) y las fronteras del reino de Chile* (Santiago: Instituto de Investigaciones del Patrimonio Territorial de Chile, Universidad de Santiago, 1984), p. 83.

10 On the intended sale price of the map see Donoso, "El mapa de América Meridional" (see note 9), p. 139.

11 The map's decoration has been described several times, for example by Vázquez de Acuña, *Don Juan de la Cruz* (see note 9), pp. 22–23; Maria Ignez Mantovani Franco, *A arte nos mapas na Casa Fiat de Cultura: uma viagem pelos quatro cantos do mundo: exposição de 12 de agosto a 05 de outubro de 2008* (Nova Lima: MG Casa Fiat de Cultura, 2008), pp. 22–23; and Jiménez Garcés, "La obra del cartógrafo Cano y Olmedilla" (see note 3), pp. 344–348—but it has never been interpreted.

12 Louis XIV of France had associated himself with the sun at every opportunity, but there was also a rich tradition of association between Spanish kings and solar imagery: see Víctor Manuel Mínguez Cornelles, *Los reyes solares: iconografía astral de la monarquía hispánica* (Castelló de la Plana: Universitat Jaume I, 2001). The image of the sun on Cruz Cano's map seems to have been inspired by that in Athanasius Kircher's *Mundus Subterraneus* (Amsterdam, 1665), vol. 1, following p. 64. On cartography under Charles III see Horacio Capel, "Los programas científicos: Geografía y cartografía," in Manuel Sellés, José Luis Peset, and Antonio Lafuente, eds., *Carlos III y la ciencia de la Ilustración* (Madrid: Alianza Editorial, 1988), pp. 99–126. Ludovico Ariosto described the empire of Charles V as one on which the sun never set in his *Orlando furioso*, Canto 15, stanzas 25–26, first published in 1516, and this flattering description was widely disseminated.

13 Donoso, "El mapa de América Meridional" (see note 9), p. 155: "La ilustración del ornato exterior demuestra el sol con la cifra del Rey nuestro señor que alumbra los dos mundos produciendo la riqueza del Toison de oro." This passage is also supplied by Isidoro Vázquez de Acuña, *Don Juan de la Cruz* (see note 9), p. 77. The letter containing this passage is in Madrid, Archivo Histórico Nacional, Consejos, Leg. 11284, carpeta no. 1, expediente no. 1, doc. no. 46.

14 For an example of the royal achievement of the Indies in which the spheres represent the two hemispheres see the title page of Juan de Larrinaga Salazar, *Memorial discursivo sobre el oficio de protector general de los Indios del Piru* (Madrid: Imprenta Real, 1626); and the frontispiece of the *Real ordenanza para el establecimiento é instruccion de intendentes de exército y provincia en el reino de la Nueva-España* (Madrid, 1786). A good image of the former is available in https://jcb.lunaimaging.com.

15 Many of the plants in these garlands are identified by Jiménez Garcés, "La obra del cartógrafo Cano y Olmedilla" (see note 3), pp. 345–346.

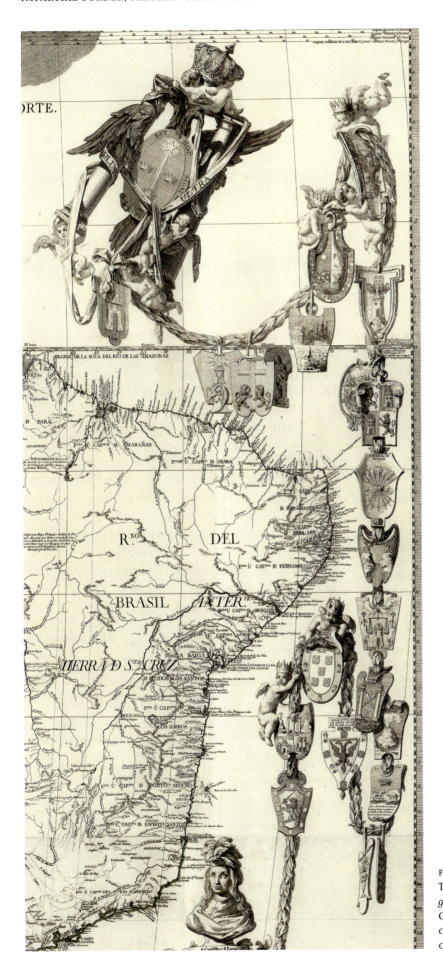

FIGURE 136
The coats of arms from Cruz Cano's *Mapa geográfico de America Meridional* (Madrid: Cruz Cano y Olmedilla, 1775)
COURTESY OF THE DAVID RUMSEY MAP COLLECTION

Columbus as the first discoverer of that continent, linked with the coats of arms granted to the cities founded by other heroes who succeeded him."[16] His emphasis on the founders of the cities and their role as followers of Columbus is not something that would occur just from studying the map, but perhaps it reflects the source Cruz Cano was using. He had a deep knowledge of South America, and certainly could have assembled a list of such cities from other sources, but it seems likely that he took most of them (the names of the cities and founders, not the coats of arms) from the catalog of the founders of the principal cities of South America in Giovanni Domenico Coleti's *Dizionario storico-geografico dell'America meridionale* ("Historical-Geographical Encyclopedia of South America") (Venice: Stamperia Coleti, 1771).[17]

The first coat of arms, that of Lima, the capital of Spanish South America, is presented in its full heraldic achievement, flanked by the Pillars of Hercules with the motto *Plus ultra*, "Still further," the Habsburg two-headed eagle, and the king's crown above,[18] while for the others Cruz Cano just shows the coats of arms proper. Beginning from the top, those are (with the modern country in which they are located and the founder and year of foundation from Coleti):

1. Lima, Peru, Francisco Pizarro, 1535.
2. Cusco, Peru, Francisco Pizarro, 1534.[19]
3. Santa María de la Antigua del Darién, Colombia, Martín Fernández de Enciso, 1509.[20]
4. Cartagena, Colombia, Pedro de Heredia, 1533.
5. Venezuela is not a city but a region, and the image is not a coat of arms, but rather a dark image of the Virgin, so this is an outlier on the list. The region was explored by Alonso de Ojeda.[21]
6. Santa Marta, Colombia, Rodrigo de Bastidas, 1525. In this case, curiously, the coat of arms does not bear the name of the city.[22]
7. Panama City, Panama, Pedro Arias Dávila, 1518. The coat of arms should have two ships rather than one, and a yoke in place of the anchor.
8. Bogotá, Colombia, Gonzalo Jiménez de Quesada y Rivera, 1538.
9. Quito, Ecuador, Sebastián de Benalcázar, 1534.
10. Popayán, Colombia, Sebastián de Belalcázar, 1537.
11. Tunja, Colombia, Gonzalo Suárez Rendón, 1539.[23]
12. San Sebastián de Mariquita, Colombia, Francisco Núñez Pedroso, 1551.
13. Villa de San Cristóbal de los Llanos, Mexico. The city is in North America, so it is not on the map, and its presence among the coats of arms is difficult to explain. The town was founded as Villa Real de Chiapa in 1528 by Diego de Mazariegos and Andrés de la Tovilla.[24]
14. San Miguel de Piura, Peru, Francisco Pizarro, 1531.
15. Trujillo, Peru, Francisco Pizarro, 1535.[25]
16. Arequipa, Peru, Francisco Pizarro, 1534.[26]
17. La Paz, Bolivia, Alonso de Mendoza, 1548.

16   Donoso, "El mapa de América Meridional" (see note 9), p. 155: "la del interior un triunfo a Colón como primer descubridor de aquella tierra firme, enlazado con los blasones concedidos a las ciudades que fundaron otros héroes que le sucedieron." This passage is also transcribed by Vázquez de Acuña, *Don Juan de la Cruz* (see note 9), p. 77.

17   The catalog of founders of cities is in Coleti's vol. 1, pp. 13–15. On Coleti's encyclopedia see Gabriel Giraldo Jaramillo, "El Padre Juan Domingo Colety y su *Diccionario Histórico-Geográfico de la América Meridional*," *Boletín de la Sociedad Geográfica de Colombia* 10.1 (1952), pp. 1–22; and Donatella Ferro, "Giandomenico Coleti e le 'Nazioni barbare'," in her *Studi di letteratura ibero-americana offerti a Giuseppe Bellini* (Rome: Bulzoni, 1984), pp. 169–179.

18   This form of Lima's coat of arms may be seen in Gil González Dávila, *Teatro eclesiastico de la primitiva iglesia de las Indias occidentales* (Madrid: Diego de la Carrera, 1649), vol. 2; the arms appear in a similar style on a map by Joseph Mulder, *Lima, Ciudad de los Reyes, Corte y Emporio del Imperio Peruano* (s.l., c.1688). Images of both are available on https://jcb.lunaimaging.com. The initials "I" and "K" at the top of the Pillars of Hercules might seem like the initials of an engraver or artist, but they are part of Lima's coat of arms, representing the first letters of the names of Queen Joanna and King Charles V, who had granted the arms to the city. The documents granting some of the coats of arms on Cruz Cano's maps are transcribed in Santiago Montoto, *Nobiliario de reinos, ciudades y villas de América española* (Madrid: Compañía Ibero-Americana de Publicaciones, 1928).

19   Cusco is not in Coleti's list on vol. 1, pp. 13–15, but he describes it in his vol. 1, p. 123.

20   Coleti writes Baldazzar Enciso in place of Martín Fernández de Enciso. On the coat of arms of Santa María de la Antigua del Darién see Enrique Ortega Ricaurte, *Heráldica colombiana* (Bogotá: Editorial Minerva, 1952), p. 7.

21   Coleti discusses Venezuela in his vol. 2, pp. 177–178.

22   On the coat of arms of Santa Marta see Enrique Ortega Ricaurte, *Heráldica colombiana* (Bogotá: Editorial Minerva, 1952), p. 11; and Arturo Bermúdez, *Materiales para la historia de Santa Marta* (Bogotá: Fondo Mixto de Promoción de la Cultura y las Artes del Magdalena, 1997), p. 256.

23   Tunja is not in Coleti's list on vol. 1, pp. 13–15, but he describes it in vol. 2, pp. 169–170.

24   The coat of arms here is indeed that of San Cristóbal de los Llanos, Mexico: see Teodoro Amerlinck y Zirion, "Heráldica municipal en la Nueva España durante el siglo XVI," *Revista hidalguía* 232–233 (1992), pp. 499–511, at 503–504.

25   Trujillo was actually founded by Diego de Almagro.

26   Arequipa was actually founded by Garcí Manuel de Carbajal in 1540.

18.   The panel is turned away from the viewer, so no coat of arms is visible.

19.   Consulado de Lima, the merchants' guild, founded in 1613; it is not a city or region, so it is an outlier on this list.[27]

20.   Concepción, Chile, Pedro Gutiérrez de Valdivia, 1551.

21.   Brazil is a region rather than a city, and a colony of Portugal rather than a kingdom of Spain, so it is definitely an outlier on this list. Moreover, the arms are those of Portugal rather than those of colonial Brazil.

22.   Charcas, Bolivia, Sebastián de Benalcázar, 1538, listed by Coleti as La Plata, its original name.[28]

23.   Santiago, Chile, Pedro de Valdivia, 1541.

There is no geographical or chronological order to the list. The presence of the arms of Portugal / Brazil (no. 21) at least acknowledges the Portuguese presence in the continent in a cartouche that is otherwise all about Spanish colonial activities, but its presence in this list of Spanish foundations is nonetheless puzzling. The presence of the arms of the Consulado de Lima (no. 19) gives Lima additional presence in the cartouche, but it is not easy to imagine why Cruz Cano included them. Nor is it easy to explain the strange darkened image for Venezuela (no. 5), or the arms of a city that does not appear on the map, Villa de San Cristóbal de los Llanos, in what is now Mexico (no. 13). The cartographer must have had a connection with or particular interest in the city, but we have no evidence of that connection. One also wonders why Cruz Cano omitted some cities from the list, such as Buenos Aires, which was founded in 1536 by Pedro de Mendoza.[29]

The garland of coats of arms of Spanish foundations in the New World ends with a flower by the bust of Columbus atop a tall tapering column (Fig. 137). Just below the bust are the lines *A Castilla, y a Leon / Nuevo mundo dió Colon*, "To Castile and to León Columbus gave a New World." These lines, first mentioned in a slightly different form by Gonzalo Fernández de Oviedo in 1535 in his *Historia*

General de las Indias,[30] were thought—incorrectly—to be part of Columbus's coat of arms,[31] but their importance here is that they emphasize in the strongest possible terms that Columbus gave the New World to Spain, with no mention of Portugal.

The structure supporting the bust of Columbus is very large, suggesting that it has some special significance, and it does: it is in the shape of a border marker (in Spanish, a *mojón* or *marco*), alluding to the principal goal of the map, which is to delineate the border between Spanish and Portuguese possessions in South America (though it should be said that the border is difficult to follow on the map). This structure has not been identified as a border marker in previous literature. This general design of a square base and a tapering upper structure had been used for elaborate border markers in the Luso-Hispanic world for at least a century, and a similar design was prepared for the implementation of the 1750 Treaty of Madrid that attempted to settle the border between Spanish and Portuguese possessions in South America (Fig. 138).[32] In imagining a border marker between Spanish and Portuguese lands in South America that proclaims that Columbus had given the New World to Spain, and that is connected with memorials of the many Spanish conquests and foundations in the

27   On the Consulado de Lima see José Antonio Pejovés Macedo, *El Tribunal del Consulado de Lima: antecedentes del arbitraje comercial y marítimo en el Perú* (Lima: Universidad de Lima, Fondo Editorial, 2018).

28   Felipe Guaman Poma de Ayala in his *Nueva corónica y buen gobierno*, written in 1615, has an image of the coat of arms of La Plata (now Charcas), in Copenhagen, Det Kongelige Bibliotek, GKS 2232 4°, f. 1066r. See http://www5.kb.dk/permalink/2006/poma/1066/es/text/, where however the arms are incorrectly identified as those of Potosí in the online commentary.

29   On the historical populations of cities in Latin America see Woodrow Borah, "Latin American Cities in the Eighteenth Century: A Sketch," *Urban History Review—Revue d'histoire urbaine*, special volume (1980), pp. 7–14.

30   Gonzalo Fernández de Oviedo y Valdés, *Historia General de las Indias* (Seville: Juan Cromberger, 1535), book 1, chapter 7, f. 10v.

31   For discussion of this phrase about Columbus see Henry Harrisse, *Christophe Colomb devant l'histoire* (Paris: H. Welter, 1892), vol. 2, pp. 177–179; and Henry Vignaud, *Études critiques sur la vie de Colomb avant ses découvertes* (Paris: H. Welter, 1905), pp. 83–93. For a more recent discussion of Columbus's coat of arms see Félix Martínez Llorente, "El escudo de armas de Cristóbal Colón: Estudio de un acrecentamiento heráldico," in Jesús Varela Marcos and María Montserrat León Guerrero, eds., *Actas del Congreso Internacional 'v Centenario del muerte del Almirante,' Valladolid, 15 a 19 de mayo de 2006* (Valladolid: Instituto Interuniversitario de Iberoamérica, Universidad de Valladolid and Ayuntamiento de Valladolid, 2006), vol. 1, *Cristóbal Colón y el Descubrimiento del Nuevo Mundo*, pp. 233–268.

32   The post-1750 design for the border marker is in Simancas, Archivo General de Simancas, Estado, Legajos, 07374, 19, and has the assigned title *Modelo de los marcos ....* For discussion of the design see Concepción Alvarez Terán, *Mapas, planos y dibujos* (Valladolid: Archivo de Simancas, 1980–1990), vol. 1, p. 676; and Juan Vicente Bachiller Cabria, *Cartografía manuscrita de Brasil en las colecciones españolas (1500–1822) = Cartografia manuscrita do Brasil nas coleçoes espanholas (1500–1822)* (Salamanca: Universidad de Salamanca, Centro de Estudios Brasileños, 2008), pp. 102–103, no. 92, and fig. 92. Another map that shows a border marker is *Mapa Geografico da 3a partida de divizoes que comprehende do Salto grande do Parana the aboca de Rio Jaurú*, 1754, Penalva do Castelo, Casa da Ínsua (CI-CG62), illustrated in Inácio Guerreiro, "Fronteiras do Brasil colonial: a cartografia dos limites na segunda metade do século XVIII," *Océanos* (Lisbon) 40 (1999), pp. 24–44, at 28.

FIGURE 137 The border marker with the bust of Columbus from Cruz Cano's *Mapa geográfico de America Meridional* (Madrid: Cruz Cano y Olmedilla, 1775)
COURTESY OF THE DAVID RUMSEY MAP COLLECTION

continent, the cartographer makes it all too clear where his sympathies lie, or at least for which government he was working.

At the base of the border marker, and at the lower edge of the map, we have a lion, three personifications, and a crocodile (Fig. 139). Cruz Cano says that these are

"Religion placed between Spain and America represented by an Inca."[33] To supply a bit more detail and precision: on the left we have a personification of Spain, with the

---

33 Donoso, "El mapa de América Meridional" (see note 9), p. 155: "Religión colocada entre España y América representada por un

FIGURE 138 The post-1750 design for the border marker between
Portuguese and Spanish possessions in South America
is in the possession of the Spanish Ministerio de
Educación, Cultura y Deporte, in Simancas, Archivo
General de Simancas, Estado, Legajos, 07374, 19
COURTESY OF THE MINISTERIO DE EDUCACIÓN,
CULTURA Y DEPORTE

pomegranate—*granada* in Spanish—representing the
Nasrid Kingdom of Granada that Spain had conquered
in 1492.[34] She is seated on the back of a sceptered lion
that represents Spanish royal power;[35] the lion faces away
from the other figures, perhaps to indicate a lack of hostility toward them. Beside Spain sits a personification of

Religion, veiled and holding a tall cross and a chalice,[36]
representing Spain's goal of spreading Christianity in the
New World. Across from Spain and Religion sits a personification of America, riding a crocodile (as she often does)
in a spirited pose, holding a hatchet with its head downward, indicating a peaceful attitude. It is noteworthy that
America is not naked, as personifications of the continent
often were, and her solar brooch is probably intended to
give her the Inca identity Cruz Cano ascribes to her.

European artists usually depict personifications of
America as subservient to personifications of Europe, but
here while Spain and Religion look tranquilly across at
America, she does not return their gaze, instead looking
and pointing upward at the border marker and the bust
of Columbus—and the palm tree beside her emphasizes
this upward orientation. The border marker and bust of
Columbus are of course signs of Spanish control and possession of the New World, but it is interesting that Cruz
Cano shows at least a hint of—dare we say independence?—in the personification of America, particularly
on a map where the imagery of Spanish power and control
is otherwise so pronounced.[37]

Despite the cartographer's emphasis on the imagery of
Spanish authority and control in South America, and his
minimizing of Portugal, he depicted the border between
the Spanish and Portuguese claims objectively. In 1775
Cruz Cano started printing the map and had copies sent
to the king and select ministers and ambassadors. The
cartographer's colleague Tomás López reported that the
Spanish government, which was beginning new nego-
tiations with Portugal about their possessions in South
America, decided that Cruz Cano's map did not favor the
Spanish position adequately, and ordered its printing sus-
pended and the copies that had been distributed to be
recalled.[38] In fact Cruz Cano's delineation of the border

Inca." This passage is also transcribed by Vázquez de Acuña, *Don
Juan de la Cruz* (see note 9), p. 77.

34 The pomegranate was added to the bottom of the coat of arms
of the Catholic Monarchs in 1492 following their reconquest of
Granada and has appeared on the arms of every Spanish mon-
arch since.

35 Víctor Mínguez Cornelles, "'Leo fortis, rex fortis': el león y la
monarquía hispánica," in Manuel Chust Calero and Víctor
Mínguez Cornelles, eds., *El imperio sublevado: monarquía y
naciones en España e Hispanoamérica* (Madrid: CSIC, 2004),
pp. 57–94.

36 The veil and the cross are both found in the personification of
Religion by Cesare Ripa in his *Iconologia*, for example in the
Rome edition of 1603, p. 430. In including a personification of
Religion the cartographer may have drawn inspiration from his
teacher Jean-Baptiste d'Anville, who includes a similar figure
on his map of *Amérique méridionale publiée sous les auspices de
Monseigneur le Duc d'Orleans* of 1748; a high-resolution image of
this map is available at https://jcb.lunaimaging.com.

37 On cartouches used to symbolize political control of a region see
for example G.N.C. Clarke, "Taking Possession: The Cartouche
as Cultural Text in Eighteenth-Century American Maps,"
Word & Image 4.2 (1988), pp. 455–474; and Christine M. Petto,
"Semblance of Sovereignty: Cartographic Possession in Map
Cartouches and Atlas Frontispieces of Early Modern Europe,"
in Gary Backhaus and John Murungi, eds., *Symbolic Landscapes*
(Dordrecht: Springer, 2009), pp. 227–250.

38 On the government's dissatisfaction with Cruz Cano's map
see Fernández Duro, *Armada Española* (see note 2), vol. 7,

was quickly revised in multiple early printings of the map.[39] The facts that his map, the fruit of ten years' work for which he was very poorly paid, saw so little circulation, and that its most important feature was immediately deemed unsatisfactory, must have been enormously frustrating for the cartographer.

Cruz Cano's map saw new life and wider diffusion in a version printed in London in 1799—though in this version it was stripped of its cartouche and other decoration. The US statesman and future president Thomas Jefferson (1743–1826) had a strong interest in maps and entertained vague hopes that the revolutionary ideas he helped develop in North America might also take hold in South America.[40] Through the assistance of William Carmichael, a US diplomat in Spain, Jefferson acquired an exemplar of Cruz Cano's map in 1786 and thought it should be printed in a new version.[41] Jefferson arranged

to have the new version of the map published by William Faden in London, and sent him his exemplar of the map, together with his "Observations for the Republication of the Map of South America by Don Juan de la Cruz Cano," in which he suggested that it be printed on fewer sheets, including diagrams for how this might be accomplished, and advises "getting rid of the margin," by which he meant all of the decoration.[42]

In another letter he sent with the map in December of 1786 Jefferson writes, "I send the map of S. America for which I will pray you to take arrangements with Faden or any other. He is the best. For his gain he will wish to make the map large. For that of the public and for their convenience I wish to debarrass it of all useless margins."[43] To debarrass means to remove something that causes shame or embarrassment, so Jefferson comes out very strongly against Cruz Cano's more than six-foot-long cartouche proclaiming the primacy of Spain in South America—a desire that reflects his wish for a detailed image of South America that showed the possibility of freedom from European control. So cartouches can support one political program, yet fall victim to another. The new, reduced size, and cartouche-less version of Cruz Cano's map was finally published in 1799.[44]

---

pp. 402–404. Smith, "Cruz Cano's Map" (see note 3), pp. 67–69, casts doubt on López's account, but without sufficient reason, it seems to me. Jiménez Garcés, "La obra del cartógrafo Cano y Olmedilla" (see note 3), p. 202, suggests that the government realized that the map's great accuracy would make it valuable to Spain's enemies, and for that reason publicly questioned the map's quality and had it recalled.

39   The revisions to Cruz Cano's map with regard to the border between Spanish and Portuguese claims are detailed by Smith, "Cruz Cano's Map" (see note 3), pp. 64–67 and 75–77.

40   On Jefferson's interest in maps see Joel Kovarsky, *The True Geography of Our Country: Jefferson's Cartographic Vision* (Charlottesville: University of Virginia Press, 2014); on his interest in South America see Claude Gernade Bowers, "Thomas Jefferson and South America," *Bulletin of the Pan American Union* 77 (1943), pp. 183–191; Esteban Ponce, "Fragmentos de un discurso no amoroso: Thomas Jefferson y la América Hispana. Una aproximación a las relaciones sur-norte," *Procesos: Revista Ecuatoriana de Historia* 30.2 (2009), pp. 5–24; and Jiménez Garcés, "La obra del cartógrafo Cano y Olmedilla" (see note 3), pp. 541–550. More generally see Piero Glijeses, "The Limits of Sympathy: The United States and the Independence of Spanish America," *Journal of Latin American Studies* 24.3 (1992), pp. 481–505.

41   On Jefferson's acquisition of Cruz Cano's map and efforts to have it published anew see Walter Ristow, "The Juan de la

Cruz map of South America, 1775," in Merle C. Prunty, Jr., ed., *Festschrift: Clarence F. Jones* (Evanston, IL: Dept. of Geography, Northwestern University, 1962), pp. 1–12, esp. 4–10.

42   Julian P. Boyd, ed., *The Papers of Thomas Jefferson* (Princeton: Princeton University Press, 1950–), vol. 10, pp. 216–217; see https://founders.archives.gov/documents/Jefferson/01-10-02-0143.

43   Julian P. Boyd, ed., *The Papers of Thomas Jefferson* (Princeton: Princeton University Press, 1950–), vol. 10, p. 640; see https://founders.archives.gov/documents/Jefferson/01-10-02-0471.

44   Faden retained the title of Cruz Cano's map, and it was published as *Mapa geográfico de America Meridional, dispuesto y gravado por D. Juan de la Cruz Cano y Olmedilla* (London: William Faden, 1799). A high-resolution image of the map is available at https://searchworks.stanford.edu. It not only lacks Cruz Cano's elaborate cartouche, but in addition, the title information in the lower right-hand corner is unframed.

FIGURE 139 The personifications of Spain, Religion, and America from Cruz Cano's *Mapa geográfico de America Meridional* (Madrid: Cruz Cano y Olmedilla, 1775)

CHAPTER 30

A Tactile Illusion That Legitimates the Map

Henry Pelham, A Plan of Boston in New England with its Environs, *1777*

The American painter, engraver, and cartographer Henry Pelham (1749–1806)[1] had advantages when he began his work as an artist: he was the son of Peter Pelham (*c.*1697–1751), a painter and engraver, and though his father died when he was just two years old, his elder half-brother was the accomplished painter John Singleton Copley (1738–1815). Henry's production as a cartographer was small, but his 1777 map of his native Boston is regarded as the finest printed map of the city to date.

Pelham did his surveying for the map in 1775 and 1776 while Boston was occupied by the British and besieged by the Continental Army during the Revolutionary War. The cartographer was loyal to the British, and made the map for them;[2] the British were naturally interested in the American fortifications and positions, and General James Urquhart, the Town-Major (the officer charged with keeping order in an occupied city) gave him a permit that allowed him to cross the lines so as to include in his map the "rebel" positions. In a letter to his half-brother dated January 27, 1776, Pelham describes havoc he encountered during his surveying excursions:[3]

"Not a hillock 6 feet high but what is entrench'd, not a pass where a man could go but what is defended by cannon; fences pulled down, houses removed, woods grubed up, fields cut into trenches and molded into ramparts, are but a part of the changes the country has gone thro. Nor has Boston been free from the effects of war. An hundred places you might be brought to and you not know where you were. I doubt if you would know the town at all. Charlestown I am sure you would not. there not a tree, not an house, not even so much as a stick of wood as large as your hand remains."

In March of 1776 the Continental Army under George Washington fortified Dorchester Heights, a commanding position over the city, and in the face of this potent threat the British evacuated. Pelham left the city in August and traveled to London, where the printing plates for the map were prepared by Francis Jukes using a combination of line engraving and aquatint, the latter process allowing a great range of tones in the shading,[4] and the map was printed in June of 1777.[5] It was dedicated to Lord George Germain (1716–1785), the British Secretary of State for America during the Revolutionary War, perhaps in the hope of additional cartographic commissions. Unfortunately Germain was not a map enthusiast.[6]

---

1 The standard biography is Peter Harbison, "Henry Pelham (1749–1806): Painter, Engraver, Engineer, Map-Maker and Illustrator of Clare's Antiquities," in Ciarán Ó Muchadha, ed., *County Clare Studies: Essays in Memory of Gerald O'Connell, Seán Ó Murchadha, Thomas Coffey and Pat Flynn* (Ennis: Clare Archaeological Society, 2000), pp. 72–100; also see Denison R. Slade, "Henry Pelham, the Half-Brother of John Singleton Copley," *Publications of the Colonial Society of Massachusetts* 5 (1902), pp. 193–211.

2 The British actually assisted Pelham in the early stages of his survey: see Pelham's letter to Susanna Copley of July 23, 1775, in John Singleton Copley, *Letters & Papers of John Singleton Copley and Henry Pelham, 1739–1776* (Boston: Massachusetts Historical Society, 1914), pp. 344–347, at 346.

3 Copley, *Letters & Papers of John Singleton Copley* (see note 2), pp. 364–369, at 368.

4 Henry's father Peter Pelham had been the first to introduce the competing process of mezzotint to America: see David McNeely Stauffer, *American Engravers upon Copper and Steel* (New York: Grolier Club, 1907), vol. 1, pp. 206–208.

5 The full details of the map are Henry Pelham, *A Plan of Boston in New England with its Environs, Including Milton, Dorchester, Roxbury, Brooklin, Cambridge, Medford, Charlestown, Parts of Malden and Chelsea with the Military Works Constructed in Those Places in the Years 1775 and 1776* (London: Publish'd according to Act of Parliament June 2d 1777, by Henry Pelham). A high-resolution image of the map is available at https://loc.gov. For discussion of the map see John W. Reps, "Boston by Bostonians: The Printed Plans and Views of the Colonial City by its Artists, Cartographers, Engravers, and Publishers," in *Boston Prints and Printmakers, 1670–1775: A Conference held by the Colonial Society of Massachusetts, 1 and 2 April 1971* (Boston: Colonial Society of Massachusetts, 1973), pp. 3–56, at 52–56; also see William Archer Butterfield, *A Key to Pelham's Plan of Boston in New England and its Environs during 1775–1776, with Notes of Historic Personages, their Residences, in Colonial Times, Men who Fell during the Revolution and the Entrenchment of Both Armies during the Siege of Boston, Showing their Relative Positions Today* (Boston: W.A. Butterfield, 1930).

6 A phrase Germain wrote in 1770 seems to reflect an appreciation of maps, but in fact reveals his naive lack of appreciation of the importance of geography: "a man may be well acquainted with the face of a country, and its divisions, as laid down in a map, without knowing a step of the road to a single market town," from "Debates in a New-Established Society," *The Gentleman's and London Magazine* (Sept., 1770), pp. 534–537, at 536. Germain's collection of maps, preserved at the Clements Library at the University of Michigan, is much smaller than (for example) that of Jean-Baptiste-Donatien

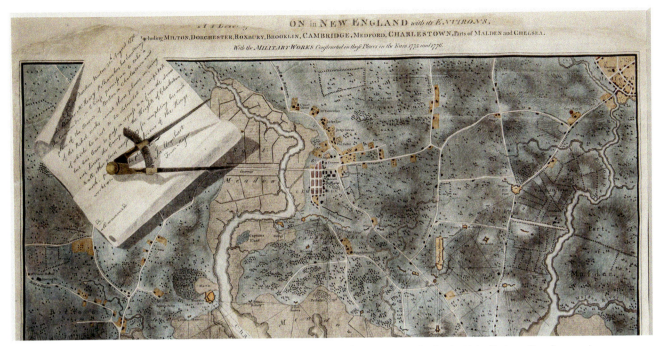

FIGURE 140 Detail of the *trompe-l'oeil* cartouche in Henry Pelham, *A Plan of Boston in New England with its Environs* (London, 1777)
GEORGE WASHINGTON'S MOUNT VERNON, MAP-4835. COURTESY OF THE MOUNT VERNON LADIES' ASSOCIATION

Pelham's brilliant cartouche (Fig. 140), in which he brings his considerable artistic skills to bear, shows the pass that allowed him to traverse the British lines to make his survey for the map, and also his dividers, used for measuring distances on a map. They are presented in *trompe-l'oeil*, creating the illusion that they are separate objects resting on top of the map, with the edges of the permit curling up, and with wonderfully realistic shadows made possible by the aquatint engraving process. The pass not only sits astride the map's border, but also encroaches on the map's title, which adds to the illusion that it is a separate piece of paper. The text of the pass reads as follows (parts of the text near the end are covered by the dividers):[7]

"Head Quarters Boston 28th August 1775.
The Bearer Mr. Henry Pelham has his Excellency the Commander in Chief's permission to take a plan of the Towns of Boston & Charlestown and of the Rebel works round those places in doing of which he is not to be obstructed or impeded but has leave to pass & repass to

& from the advanced lines, the Camps [o]n the Heights of Charlestown & all the other places neces[sa]ry for completing his said work p[...] views of the Kings Works &c he pl[...] to.

Ja: Urquhart, Town Major
To all concerned"

The pass is a wonderful example of a cartographer using a cartouche to speak directly to the viewer: here Pelham demonstrates his map's authority, showing that his project had the support of the British government and that he had special access in order to make it, supplying information about how he made it, and exhibiting one of the tools he used to make it. The cartouche gives the viewer insight into the cartographer's methods in creating the map, and the history of its production. Also, the pass is the only place on the map where Pelham's name is printed. It does not form part of the printed dedication at the bottom of the map,[8] where the cartographer intended to sign his name by hand, which he did on about half of the map's surviving copies.

de Vimeur, comte de Rochambeau (1725–1807), commander of the French expeditionary army (1780–82) that participated in the Revolutionary War, which is now divided between the Library of Congress and the Beinecke Library.

7 The text of Pelham's pass is transcribed in "Appendix J: A Supplementary List of Maps Relating to Boston, Subsequent to 1600, Copies of which are in Possession of Collectors of the Same," in *Thirty-Seventh Annual Report of the City Engineer Boston for the Year 1903* (Boston: Municipal Printing Office, 1904), pp. 112–206, at 132.

8 The dedication of Pelham's map reads "To the Right Honourable Lord George Germain, One of his Majesty's Principal Secretaries of State &c. &. &c. this Plan is dedicated with the greatest respect, by his Lordship's most obedient and much obliged humble servant."

Pelham's only other surviving maps, of County Clare, Ireland, printed in 1787,[9] and of Bere Island and Bere Haven in southwest Ireland,[10] have no imaginative cartouches—indeed the title and dedication on both are cartoucheless—and the question arises as to the source of Pelham's inspiration. As it happens, a plausible source of inspiration is not far to seek, and the comparison between this source and what Pelham produced is instructive.

Henry's father Peter Pelham had engraved just one map, more than thirty years earlier, in 1745.[11] It was also related to a war in the American colonies, namely King George's War, waged between the forces of the French and British colonies in North America from 1744 to 1748. The most important event of the war was the siege and capture of the French fortress of Louisbourg on Cape Breton Island in Nova Scotia;[12] the attack had been urged by William Shirley (1694–1771), governor of the Province of Massachusetts Bay, and was commanded by Sir William Pepperrell (1696–1759). Following the capture of the fortress in June of 1745 both were heroes; Peter Pelham painted their portraits, and he made a mezzotint of a map of the fortress and town of Louisbourg that had been drawn by the engineer Richard Gridley (1710–1796) from his own observations of the site (Fig. 141).[13]

The senior Pelham presents the inset map of the harbor with some *trompe-l'oeil* effects, as if it is a separate piece of paper: in the upper corners, tacks seem to hold the inset in place, the edge of the inset is slightly uneven all the way around, there is shading along the left and lower edges, and the lower right corner is turned up. Moreover, he includes in a cartouche in the upper right a letter written by Richard Gridley, the map's creator, dedicating the work to Governor Shirley, who, as Gridley emphasizes, was one of the prime movers of the siege.[14]

There are other earlier maps with *trompe-l'oeil* cartouches[15]—including Gilles and Didier Robert de Vaugondy's *Carte de la terre des Hebreux ou Israelites* discussed earlier—but it is tempting to think that Henry Pelham drew inspiration for his cartouche from those on his father's map, combining the ideas of the *tromp-l'oeil* inset map and the letter into one, and adding the dividers on top of the pass. Henry's use of *trompe-l'oeil* is much bolder, from the oblique angle of the permit with respect to the main map and the fact that it crosses the map's neatline and encroaches on the map's title to its more curled edges, and he makes much better use of the opportunity offered by cartouches to communicate with the viewer about his map. Gridley was present at and involved in the siege at Louisbourg, but he does not say this in his letter, nor does he quite say that he made the map, or give any hint as to how he made it. Henry displays his pass which both shows the support that his project had from the British government and gives details about the type of surveying he did, and his dividers clearly allude to the process of making the map.

Gridley's letter makes public his respect to the governor for organizing the siege, and the subtle *trompe-l'oeil* effects

9   Pelham's other surviving map is Henry Pelham, *The County of Clare in the Province of Munster and Kingdom of Ireland* (London: W. Faden, 1787); a good resolution image of the map is available via the online catalog of the Harvard University Library. We also have a partial copy of Pelham's map of Kerry, but it does not show any cartouches: see Jean B. Archer, "Henry Pelham's Lost Grand Jury Map of Kerry (c.1800): A Newly Found Derivative," *Imago Mundi* 58.2 (2006), pp. 183–197.

10   Pelham's map of Bere Island and Bere Haven, dated 1804 and titled *Map of Bear Haven and the Great Bear Island*, survives in a manuscript copy in the Scottish Records Office, RHP 3194. See Archer, "Henry Pelham's Lost Grand Jury Map of Kerry" (see note 9), pp. 188 and 194.

11   On Peter Pelham see William Henry Whitmore, *Notes Concerning Peter Pelham, the Earliest Artist Resident in New England, and his Successors Prior to the Revolution* (Cambridge, MA: J. Wilson, 1867); Frederick W. Coburn, "More Notes on Peter Pelham," *Art in America* 20 (1932), pp. 143–154; and Andrew Oliver, "Peter Pelham (c. 1697–1751): Sometime Printmaker of Boston," *Boston Prints and Printmakers, 1670–1775: A Conference Held by the Colonial Society of Massachusetts, 1 and 2 April 1971* (Boston: Colonial Society of Massachusetts, 1973), pp. 132–173.

12   For discussion of the siege see Robert Emmet Wall, Jr., "Louisbourg, 1745," *New England Quarterly* 37.1 (1964), pp. 64–83; and Raymond R. Baker, "A Campaign of Amateurs: The Siege of Louisbourg, 1745," *Canadian Historic Sites* 18 (1978), pp. 5–58.

13   The full details of the map are Richard Gridley, *A Plan of the City and Fortress of Louisbourg with a Small Plan of the Harbour* (Boston: Sold by J. Smibert in Queen Street, 1746); for discussion

of it see Oliver, "Peter Pelham" (see note 11), pp. 154–155 and 171; and James C. Wheat and Christian F. Brun, *Maps and Charts Published in America before 1800: A Bibliography* (New Haven: Yale University Press, 1969), no. 75. A high-resolution image of the map is available at https://www.digitalcommonwealth.org /search.

14   Gridley writes "To his Excellency William Shirley ... by whom the late expedition against that place was projected and undertaken[,] and under whose commission, orders, & directions the land & sea forces employ'd therein by this province were rais'd and euqipp'd in fifty days[,] the siege of this fortress was form'd & supported, & the reduction of it to the obedience of his Britannic Majesty, after a siege of forty nine days most happily effected on the seventeenth day of June 1745."

15   In 2017–18 David Weimer curated an exhibition at the Harvard Map Collection held titled "Look But Don't Touch: Tactile Illusions on Maps" that featured several maps with *trompe-l'oeil* cartouches. There is an excellent website devoted to the exhibition.

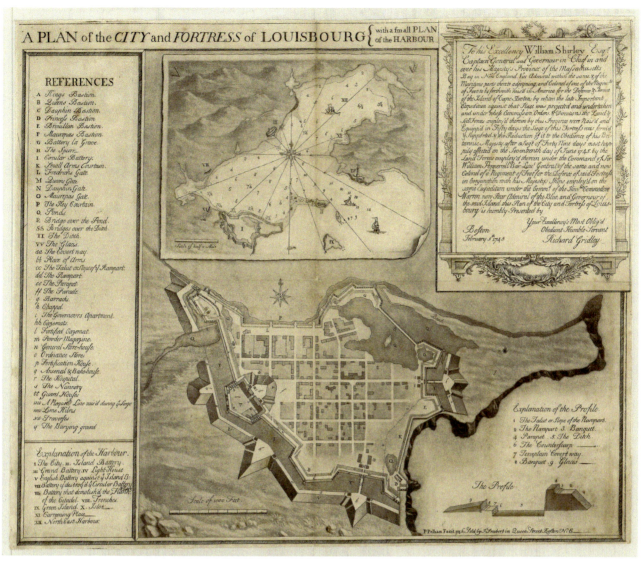

FIGURE 141   Richard Gridley, *A Plan of the City and Fortress of Louisbourg with a Small Plan of the Harbour* (Boston: Sold by J. Smibert in Queen Street, 1746)

BOSTON, MASSACHUSETTS HISTORICAL SOCIETY, SPECIAL COLLS. MAPS 1746. COURTESY OF THE MASSACHUSETTS HISTORICAL SOCIETY

on the inset map merely demonstrate Peter Pelham's artistic skills as an engraver. The bold illusionistic effects in the engraving of Henry Pelham's pass attract and beguile the viewer's eye, and then the contents of the pass, together with his dividers, bring the viewer into the world of his map. Paradoxically it is the fact that the cartouche seems physically separate from the map that draws the viewer into it.

CHAPTER 31

Fighting Back against Colonial Cartography

José Joaquim da Rocha, Mappa da Comarca do Sabará pertencente a Capitania de Minas Gerais, c.*1778*

We have examined several cartouches that express Europe's superiority to its trading partners or control over its colonies;[1] we will now consider a cartouche that portrays resistance to colonial aggression, specifically resistance to mapping by colonial powers, for cartography has long been one of the prime tools for consolidating power over a territory.

Gold was discovered in the mountains of southeastern Brazil in 1693, producing the longest-continuing gold rush in history, which resulted in a huge influx of both Portuguese settlers and African slaves to dig for gold, in a region that came to be called Minas Gerais, which means "General Mines."[2] In the eighteenth century Portugal established a large bureaucracy to try to control the production of gold and also to extend its political control of the land.[3] José Joaquim da Rocha (c.1740–1807),[4] a military engineer and cartographer, had been born in the village of São Miguel da Vila de Souza, south of the coastal city of Aveiro, in northern Portugal, and arrived in Brazil in the 1760s.[5] He wrote three geographical-historical reports about Minas Gerais for the governors of the Captaincy in 1780, 1783, and 1788, designed to help them in administering the region—and also in the interest of securing a job for himself.[6] He also made manuscript maps for the Portuguese administrators, both of the whole of Minas Gerais and more detailed maps of its divisions.[7]

Some of Rocha's maps have the plainest of cartouches, with unadorned rectangles around the title and dedication; in others this information is framed by carefully painted trees accompanied by additional native plants and animals,[8] while still others have the trees and also images of indigenous people with placid expressions, even if they are holding spears or bows and arrows.[9]

1　I have studied some other colonialist cartouches in my article "Colonialism in the Cartouche: Imagery and Power in Early Modern Maps," *Figura: Studies on the Classical Tradition* 9.2 (2021), pp. 90–130.

2　Regarding the source of the name Minas Gerais, the cartographer we will be considering here, José Joaquim da Rocha, wrote that *as Minas Gerais tomaram este nome por serem suas faisqueiras continuadas, em as quais se acha ouro com mais ou menos conta,* that is, "Minas Gerais took its name from its continuous veins of gold, in which gold is found of greater or lesser quantity." See José Joaquim da Rocha, *Geografia histórica da capitania de Minas Gerais,* ed. Maria Efigênia Lage de Resende (Belo Horizonte: Fundação João Pinheiro, 1995), p. 78. A digital version of this book is available at http://www.bibliotecadigital.mg.gov.br.

3　For discussion of a plan for the reconquest of part of Minas Gerais by Antonio de Noronha, the Captain General of the Captaincy of Minas Gerais, see Laura de Mello e Souza, "Dom Antonio de Noronha and the Secret Plan for the Cuieté," *Tempo* 20 (2014), pp. 1–15.

4　The cartographer is not to be confused with José Joaquim da Rocha (c.1737–1807), a Brazilian painter and restorer who worked on religious art; or José Joaquim da Rocha (1777–1848), a Brazilian lawyer and politician.

5　For biographical information on Rocha see Rocha, *Geografia Histórica* (see note 2), pp. 200–207.

6　On Rocha's geographical-historical reports on Minas Gerais, which were not published during his lifetime, see Júnia Ferreira Furtado, "Iluminuras da Sedição: a cartografia de José Joaquim da Rocha e a Inconfidência Mineira," in Fernando Pedro da Silva, ed., *Atas do IV Congresso Internacional do Barroco Íbero-Americano, Ouro Preto, 2006* (Belo Horizonte: C/Arte, 2008) pp. 981–1003, at 984–991; and Júnia Ferreira Furtado, "Rebellious Maps: José Joaquim da Rocha and the Proto-Independence Movement in Colonial Brazil," in Martin Brückner, ed., *Early American Cartographies* (Chapel Hill, NC: University of North Carolina Press for the Omohundro Institute of Early American History and Culture, 2011), pp. 116–142, at 126–127. The first report was published in 1995, with notes about the differences between it and Rocha's two subsequent reports: see note 2.

7　On Rocha's maps see Cristina Ávila, Juliana Souza Duarte, Maria do Carmo Andrade Gomes, Maria Luísa Thomasi, and Renata Hanriot, "Cartografia e inconfidência: Considerações sobre a obra de José Joaquim da Rocha," *Análise & Conjuntura* (Belo Horizonte) 4.2–3 (1989), pp. 373–392; and Antônio Gilberto Costa et al., "Os mapas de José Joaquim da Rocha," in Antônio Gilberto Costa, ed., *Cartografia da conquista do território das Minas* (Belo Horizonte: Editora da UFMG; Lisbon: Editorial Kapa, 2004), pp. 145–151. Some of his maps are well reproduced as flyleaf inserts in Rocha, *Geografia Histórica* (see note 2); in the digital edition of the book these images follow p. 144. Also see José Flávio Morais Castro, "Georreferenciamento e Cartometria dos mapas da Capitania de Minas Gerais elaborados por José Joaquim da Rocha em 1778 e 1793," *Sociedade & Natureza* 25.3 (2013), pp. 581–593.

8　For examples of Rocha's cartouches framed by trees with native produce and animals see for example José Joaquim da Rocha, *Mappa da Comarca do Rio das Mortes, pertencente a Capitania das Minas Gerais que mandou descrever o Ilustrissimo e Excelentissimo Senhor D. Antonio de Noronha Governador e Cap. am General da mesma Capitania segundo as mais exactas informaçõens,* 1777, in the Biblioteca Nacional in Rio de Janeiro, with a digital image available at http://bndigital.bn.gov.br/acervodigital.

9　For an example of one of Rocha's maps with placid native people see his *Mappa da Capitania de Minas Geraes: que mandou fazer o Illmo. e Exmo. senhor D. Anto. de Noronha, governador e capitão genal. da mesma capitania,* 1777, in the Biblioteca Nacional in

FIGURE 142 The title cartouche on José Joaquim da Rocha, *Mappa da Comarca do Sabará pertencente a Capitania de Minas Gerais, c.1777–78*
RIO DE JANEIRO, BIBLIOTECA NACIONAL, ARC.030,01,033—CARTOGRAFÍA. COURTESY OF THE BIBLIOTECA NACIONAL

Two of his cartouches are very different from those just mentioned; both of them are on maps of the District of Sabará, more commonly called Rio das Velhas county (*comarca*), in the western part of Minas Gerais. He made one of the maps in 1778, and it is titled *Mappa da Comarca do Sabara* ("Map of the District of Sabará").[10] The other map bears no date, but since it shows an entirely different geography of the District, and Rocha says that he made the map based on new information from his own survey, it must be somewhat later. Its title adds that Sabará is part of the Captaincy of Minas Gerais, and it is dedicated to its governor, Antonio de Noronha.[11]

These cartouches (Fig. 142 and 143) are more famous than most, as they have been often reproduced, including on the covers of two books,[12] and they have also been dis-

_____

Rio de Janeiro, with a digital image available at http://bndigital.bn.gov.br/acervodigital.

10 Rocha's 1778 map of Sabará is in Belo Horizonte, Arquivo Público Mineiro, Seção Colonial (Secretaria de Governo—Colônia), SC-005. A high-resolution image of the map is available at http://www.siaapm.cultura.mg.gov.br.

11 Rocha's later map of Sabará is titled *Mappa da Comarca do Sabará pertencente a Capitania de Minas Gerais*, that is, "Map

of the District of Sabará which Pertains to the Captaincy of Minas Gerais." A cartouche at the bottom of the map adds *Esta descripsão a mandou fazer o Ill.mo e ex.mo Senhor D. Antonio de Noronha Governador, e Capitão General da mesma Capitania conforme as mais certas de novas observacoens feitas com grande trabalho do seu autor*, that is, "This map was commissioned by the most illustrious and excellent Sir D. Antonio de Noronha, Governor and Captain General of the same Captaincy, in accordance with the most certain of the new observations made with much work by the author." The map is in the Biblioteca Nacional in Rio de Janeiro, with a digital image available at http://bndigital.bn.gov.br/acervodigital. The map is discussed by Ávila et al., "Cartografia e inconfidência" (see note 7), pp. 389–392.

12 See the covers of Martin Brückner, ed., *Early American Cartographies* (Chapel Hill, NC: University of North Carolina Press, 2011); and Beatriz Piccolotto Siqueira Bueno, *Desenho e desígnio, o Brasil dos engenheiros militares (1500–1882)* (São Paulo: Editora da Universidade de São Paulo, 2011).

FIGURE 143   The title cartouche on José Joaquim da Rocha, *Mappa da Comarca do Sabará*, 1778
BELO HORIZONTE, ARQUIVO PÚBLICO MINEIRO SC-005. COURTESY OF THE ARQUIVO PÚBLICO MINEIRO

cussed before,[13] but more remains to be said about them. In both cartouches the title is framed by two trees and the ground.[14] On the left a naked Indian man holding a

bow kneels beside a tree and aims an arrow across the cartouche at a seated man who wears a Portuguese uniform. The man is measuring a distance on the map with dividers, probably to be understood as a representation of making a map, and is unaware of the danger he is in. The Portuguese soldier making the map no doubt represents the Rocha himself, so we have here another example of a

13   Hal Langfur, "Uncertain Refuge: Frontier Formation and the Origins of the Botocudo War in Late Colonial Brazil," *Hispanic American Historical Review* 82.2 (2002), pp. 215–256, at 235–236; Bueno, *Desenho e desígnio* (see note 12), p. 26; Furtado, "Iluminuras da Sedição" (see note 6), p. 998; Júnia Furtado, "Um cartógrafo rebelde? José Joaquim da Rocha e a cartografia de Minas Gerais," *Anais do Museu Paulista* 17.2 (2009), pp. 155–187, at 178; and Furtado, "Rebellious Maps" (see note 6), pp. 138–139.

14   In Rocha's *Mappa da Comarca do Sabará pertencente a Capitania de Minas Gerais* both trees are probably *pau-jacaré* (*Piptadenia gonoacantha*)—which is called *monjolo* in Minas Gerais—while

on his *Mappa da Comarca do Sabara* the palm on the left is *macaúba* (*Acrocomia aculeata*), and the tree on the right again *pau-jacaré*. I thank Dr. Pedro Lage Viana, Curador do Herbário do Museu Paraense Emílio Goeldi, Belém, Brazil, for these identifications.

cartographer's self-portrait in a cartouche.[15] Rocha makes no reference to such an episode in his account of Sabará,[16] but if the image does represent something the cartographer experienced, there would not necessarily be any reason to relate the episode in a historical-geographical account of the district.

There are interesting differences between the two cartouches: in the earlier cartouche the Indian is larger and more muscular, the tree beside him is a palm, the ground is depicted in more detail, and the cartographer is shown in profile; while in the later image the Indian is smaller, which shifts emphasis from his physicality to the arrow, the two trees are the same, and we see the cartographer's whole face, making him more sympathetic. It is possible that an Indian attacked a Portuguese soldier who happened to be a cartographer,[17] but it is tempting and reasonable to read the image as representing indigenous resistance to European mapping projects—that is, to read the image as a representation of indigenous awareness that when Europeans come making maps, the local peoples are certain to suffer, that cartographic knowledge of a region entails political power over it, and a determination to halt the Portuguese mapping of Minas Gerais. Here the cartographic self-consciousness we have seen in other cartouches is deployed with a very different purpose, to expose a conflict inescapable in any colonial mapping program.[18]

For we have other records of violence against surveyors and cartographers working on colonial mapping projects.[19] Between 1536 and 1691 England conquered Ireland and settled it with Protestant colonists in an attempt to change the religion of the island. On August 28, 1609, Sir John Davies, the Attorney-General of the colonial administration, wrote to Robert Cecil, Earl of Salisbury, the Secretary of State of England, recalling an episode that happened in 1603:[20]

"though the country be now quiet and the heads of greatness gone, yet [our] geographers do not forget what entertainment the Irish of Tyrconnell gave to a map-maker about the end of the late great rebellion; for one Barkeley being appointed by the late Earl of Devonshire to draw a true and perfect map of the north parts of Ulster (the old maps being false and defective), when he came into Tyrconnell, the inhabitants took off his head, because they would not have their country discovered."

An anonymous nineteenth-century writer, introducing this episode, writes:[21]

"At that time it was, indeed, as will be seen, as dangerous for an Englishman to attempt a general survey in the country as to take arms in a general conquest, the Gaelic people having been as hostile to a map maker as a soldier; for, to their minds, the appearance of either surely portended confiscation."

In his letter Sir John Davies got the name of the cartographer wrong, it was not Barkeley but rather Richard Bartlett (d. 1603), a cartographer working for the English general Charles Blount, Baron Mountjoy, who had been tasked with subduing Ulster—and his maps emphasize defensive structures such as castles and forts.[22]

15   Langfur, "Uncertain Refuge" (see note 13), p. 235; and Furtado, "Iluminuras da Sedição" (see note 6), p. 998, both identify the cartographer as Rocha. On self-portraits by cartographers see James A. Welu, "Cartographic Self-Portraits," in Carla Clivio Marzoli, Giacomo Corna Pellegrini, and Gaetano Ferro, eds., *Imago et mensura mundi: Atti del IX Congresso internazionale di storia della cartografia* (Rome: Istituto della Enciclopedia italiana, 1985), vol. 2, pp. 525–539; and Rodney Shirley, "The Face of the Maker: Portraits of Cartographers Concealed in Maps and Title Pages," *Mercator's World* 1.4 (1996), pp. 14–19.

16   For Rocha's account of Sabará see Rocha, *Geografia Histórica* (see note 2), pp. 106–114.

17   For a good account of conflicts between Indians and settlers in Minas Gerais see Maria Leônia Chaves de Resende, "Gentios brasílicos: Índios coloniais em Minas Gerais setecentista," Ph.D. Dissertation, Universidade de Campinas, 2003, particularly pp. 302 and 361–362.

18   Compare the self-portrait by Georg Vischer in his map *Archiducatus Austriae inferioris*, 1670 / 1697, discussed in Chapter 9 above: there the cartographer went armed with pistols to defend himself against landowners who thought that his maps would entail tax increases; the anti-cartographic hostility in Rocha's map is related, but explicit and both political and economic, rather than purely economic.

19   In addition to the examples of violence against surveyors described here, see those cited at the end of Chapter 9 above.

20   C.W. Russell and John P. Pendergrast, eds., *Calendar of the State Papers, Relating to Ireland, of the Reign of James I, 1608–1610, Preserved in Her Majesty's Public Record Office, and Elsewhere* (London: Longman et al., 1874), p. 280; also see George Hill, *An Historical Account of the Plantation in Ulster at the Commencement of the Seventeenth Century, 1608–1620* (Belfast: M'Caw, Stevenson & Orr, 1877), p. 169.

21   See "Notes on Old Irish Maps," *Ulster Journal of Archeology* 4 (1856), pp. 118–127, at 118.

22   On Bartlett and his cartographic work see Gerard Anthony Hayes-McCoy, *Ulster and Other Irish Maps, c. 1600* (Dublin: Stationery Office for the Irish Manuscripts Commission, 1964) (reproductions of 12 of Bartlett's maps); John H. Andrews, *The Queen's Last Map-Maker: Richard Bartlett in Ireland, 1600–3* (Dublin: Geography Publications, 2008); and Gearóid Ó Tuathail, "Introduction: Geo-Power," in his *Critical Geopolitics: The Politics*

There was also substantial, if less violent, resistance to British colonial mapping in India in the nineteenth century, particularly during the Great Trigonometrical Survey begun in 1802. Lancelot Wilkinson (1805–1841), a British civil servant and scholar in the service of the East India Company in India, wrote:[23]

"The officers employed on the grand trigonometrical and other surveys, have always experienced, in almost every part of India, the greatest obstructions in the discharge of their duties, from the prejudices and ignorance of the people and their native princes. At Kotah, no less ignorance and prejudice had been displayed than elsewhere: so strong were the suspicions entertained by the late Ráj Ráná Madhu Singh, of the designs of the British Government, when Captain Paton, the Deputy Quarter-Master General at Nímach, entered his territories to survey certain roads, &c. and so reiterated his objections in reply to the Agent, Captain Ross's assurances, that the last-mentioned officer was at length obliged to request Captain Paton to withdraw."

It is only to be expected that Wilkinson, an officer of the colonial enterprise, would attribute the Indians' resistance to the survey to their "prejudices and ignorance."

What is so remarkable about Rocha's cartouche is that it supplies a graphic representation of indigenous resistance to colonial mapping, that that representation appears on a map, that it is on a map made by a colonial cartographer, and that it shows the violence being threatened against that very cartographer. It is possible that resistance to colonial authority was not so very far from Rocha's thoughts, for several years after he made the maps of Sabará he was accused of having made maps in support of a movement called the Inconfidência Mineira ("Minas Gerais Conspiracy") that sought independence from Portugal and the creation of a Brazilian republic.[24] The authorities were satisfied with hanging the leader of the movement, and Rocha, together with most of the other accused conspirators, was acquitted, and it seems that we will never know whether he was actually involved in the plot.

A more recent technique that indigenous groups have employed to resist colonial mapping programs is "counter-mapping," a term coined by Edward Said in 1993 which refers to maps made by those indigenous groups that reflect their own interests, claims, and power structures, rather than those of the colonizing or oppressing state.[25]

---

of Writing Global Space (Minneapolis: University of Minnesota Press, 1996), pp. 1–20.

23 Lancelot Wilkinson, "On the Use of the Siddhantas in the Work of Native Education," *Journal of the Asiatic Society of Bengal* 3 (1834), pp. 504–519, at 511–512, quoted in part in Matthew Edney's good discussion of Indian resistance to British mapping in his *Mapping an Empire: The Geographical Construction of British India, 1765–1843* (Chicago: University of Chicago Press, 1997), pp. 325–332.

24 See Furtado, "Um cartógrafo rebelde" (see note 13), Furtado, "Iluminuras da Sedição" (see note 6), and Furtado, "Rebellious Maps" (see note 6).

25 On counter-mapping see Edward Said, *Culture and Imperialism* (New York: Alfred A. Knopf, 1993), p. 77; Edward Said, "Facts, Facts, and More Facts," in his *Peace and Its Discontents: Essays on Palestine in the Middle East Peace Process* (New York: Vintage, 1996), pp. 26–31 (the essay was written in 1993); Nancy Lee Peluso, "Whose Woods are These? Counter-Mapping Forest Territories in Kalimantan, Indonesia," *Antipode* 27.4 (1995), pp. 383–406; Dorothy L. Hodgson and Richard A. Schroeder, "Dilemmas of Counter-Mapping Community Resources in Tanzania," *Development and Change* 33.1 (2002), pp. 79–100; Joel Wainwright and Joe Bryan, "Cartography, Territory, Property: Postcolonial Reflections on Indigenous Counter-Mapping in Nicaragua and Belize," *Cultural Geographies* 16.2 (2009), pp. 153–178; and Tony Syme, "Localizing Landscapes: A Call for Respectful Design in Indigenous Counter Mapping," *Information, Communication & Society* 23:8 (2020), pp. 1106–1122. On efforts to decolonize maps more generally see Raymond B. Craib, "Cartography and Decolonization," in James R. Akerman, ed., *Decolonizing the Map: Cartography from Colony to Nation* (Chicago: University of Chicago Press, 2017), pp. 11–71, as well as the other essays in the book.

CHAPTER 32

The Actors Begin to Leave the Stage

Jean Janvier, Maps of 1761, 1769, and 1774; Robert de Vaugondy, Map of 1778; John Purdy, Map of 1809

Just as with maps, so often with cartouches: what is not present can be very revealing. In this chapter we will examine some cartouches that reveal an important trend in the second half of the eighteenth century and the early part of the nineteenth, namely the removal of personifications from cartouche decoration, as part of a movement towards plainer, less elaborate cartouches. First it is necessary to distinguish a type of cartouche that is visually similar to, and yet very different from those we will focus on.

Some eighteenth-century cartouches depict several weapons and pieces of armor in the foreground or above the frame; these are often intended to represent trophies of war, that is, captured enemy arms and armor, and the presence of these pieces of equipment turn the cartouche itself into a war trophy, or a monument or memorial on the battlefield composed of or decorated with these items. By good fortune there is a cartouche in a model book by Pierre-Edmé Babel (1720–1775), a cartouche artist mentioned a couple of times above,[1] that exemplifies this type and explicitly identifies the arms and armor as trophies. The cartouche was printed in about 1738, is titled *Cartouche avec des trophées et piramide* ("Cartouche with trophies and a pyramid") and is signed *Babel delineavit et Sculp.* ("Babel designed and engraved it") (Fig. 144).[2]

FIGURE 144 Pierre-Edmé Babel, *Cartouche avec des trophées et piramide*, c.1738
COOPER HEWITT COOPER HEWITT SMITHSONIAN DESIGN MUSEUM 1921-6-231-10. COURTESY OF THE SMITHSONIAN INSTITUTION

The cartouches we will be examining in this chapter also present collections of weapons and clothing, and thus are superficially similar to these displays of war trophies, but in fact have an entirely different derivation and meaning.

We have seen cartouches that contain personifications of the continents, for example Jodocus Hondius's 1608 world map (see Chapter 4), and these representations continued in the seventeenth and eighteenth centuries. For instance, in 1696 Pierre Mortier in Amsterdam published a double-hemisphere world map that he attributed to the

---

1   On the cartouche artist and engraver Pierre-Edmé Babel see Désiré Guilmard, *Les maîtres ornemanistes. Dessinateurs, peintres, architectes, sculpteurs et graveurs. Écoles française, italienne, allemande et des Pays-Bas* (Paris: E. Plon, 1880–81), vol. 1, pp. 173–175; Julius Meyer, ed., *Allgemeines Künstler-Lexikon* (Leipzig: Verlag von Wilhelm Engelmann, 1872–1885), vol. 2, pp. 500–502; Marcel Roux, *Inventaire du fonds français: graveurs du dix-huitième siècle* (Paris: Bibliothèque nationale de France, 1930), vol. 1, pp. 368–382; and Peter Fuhring, "Some Newly Identified Drawings of Ornament From the Seventeenth and Eighteenth Centuries in the Nationalmuseum, Stockholm: Lucas Kilian, Nicolas II Loir, Alexis Loir, Jacques de Lajoüe and Pierre-Edme Babel," *Nationalmuseum Bulletin* (Stockholm) 17.3 (1993), pp. 11–25, esp. 21–23.

2   Babel's cartouche with trophies appears separately in some collections, such as the Metropolitan Museum and the Cooper Hewitt Smithsonian Design Museum, and in an assembled collection of cartouches by Babel in Paris at the Bibliothèque de l'Institut National d'Histoire de l'Art, Collections Jacques Doucet, which has been assigned the title [*Ornements, cartouches, fontaines*] (Paris: Jacques Chéreau, c.1720–1769), which has the shelfmark NUM FOL EST 486, and is available in digital format. On this cartouche see Désiré Guilmard, *Les maîtres ornemanistes, dessinateurs, peintres, architectes, sculpteurs et graveurs* (Paris: E. Plon, 1880–1881), vol. 1,

p. 173; and *Catalogue des ouvrages d'ornementation et d'architecture des XVIᵉ, XVIIᵉ et XVIIIᵉ siècles* (Paris: Georges Rapilly, 1908), p. 23, no. 138.

FIGURE 145 Title cartouche from Gilles Robert de Vaugondy, *Mappemonde ou description du globe terrestre ou l'on trouve en général la rapport que toutes les parties ont avec les cieux et entr' elles par les Srs. Sanson, géog: ord. du roi* (Paris: Ches le Sr. Robert, Quai de l'Horloge du Palais, 1743)
COURTESY OF THE BARTELE GALLERY, MANDARIN ORIENTAL HOTEL, JAKARTA

famous cartographer Nicolas Sanson, who had passed away in 1667. Mortier probably commissioned the title cartouche from a specialized artist; nestled between the two circular hemispheres, the cartouche is adorned with personifications of Europe, Asia, Africa, and America.[3] The design proved popular, and in 1700 Guillaume Delisle (1675–1726) published a double-hemisphere world map whose title cartouche has a similar layout and similar personifications.[4] Delisle used this same cartouche design on several of his later double-hemisphere world maps, and it was also used by other cartographers, for example Charles Price (fl. 1680–1720).[5]

Pierre Mortier's cartouche also inspired the title cartouche on a double-hemisphere world map made in 1743 by Gilles Robert de Vaugondy (1688–1766), the father in the father-and-son team we met earlier (Fig. 145).[6] Africa, almost naked, is in the upper left with her lion, Asia is in the upper right, wearing a turban, America is in the lower left with a feather headdress and parasol, and Europe is in the lower right wearing a crown and holding a bouquet of flowers. Traditional iconography ascribes several attributes to each personification that we do not see here, but nonetheless each is easily recognizable, and they help emphasize the map's global scope.[7]

3   The details regarding Mortier's double-hemisphere world map are Nicolas Sanson, *Mappe-monde, dressé sur les observations de mrs. de l'Academie royale des sciences et quelques autres et sur les memoires les plus recens* (Amsterdam: Pierre Mortier, 1696); a high-resolution image of the map is available at https://loc.gov.

4   Guillaume Delisle, *Mappe-monde, dressé sur les observations de mrs. de l'Academie royale des sciences et quelques autres et sur les memoires les plus recens* (Paris: chez l'auteur, rue des Canettes, pres de St. Sulpice, 1700); a high-resolution image of the map is available at https://loc.gov.

5   Charles Price, *A New and Correct Map of the World Projected upon the Plane of the Horizon Laid Down from the Newest Discoveries and*

Most Exact Observations (London: Sold by G. Willdey, 1714); a high-resolution image of the map is available at https://loc.gov.

6   Gilles Robert de Vaugondy, *Mappemonde ou description du globe terrestre ou l'on trouve en général la rapport que toutes les parties ont avec les cieux et entr' elles par les Srs. Sanson, géog: ord. du roi: Revue augmentée et assujeties aux observations astronomiques* (Paris: ches le Sr. Robert, Quai de l'Horloge du Palais, 1743). There is an exemplar of this rare map at the Clements Library at the University of Michigan. On this map see Mary Sponberg Pedley, *Bel et utile: The Work of the Robert de Vaugondy Family of Mapmakers* (Tring, England: Map Collector Publications, 1992), pp. 133–134, no. 4.

7   Incidentally on Robert de Vaugondys' 1743 map, in addition to the female personifications of the continents, the ribbon that runs

FIGURE 146 Title cartouche from Gilles and Didier Robert de Vaugondy, *Mappe monde, ou carte générale du globe terrestre dessinée suivant les regles de la projection des cartes réduites* (Paris: Fortin, 1812)
MAP FIRST PUBLISHED IN 1778. COURTESY OF ARADER GALLERIES

Some years later the Robert de Vaugondys made another world map, this one on the Mercator projection, titled *Mappe monde, ou carte générale du globe terrestre dessinée suivant les regles de la projection des cartes réduites* ("World Map, or General Map of the Terrestrial Globe Drawn According to the Rules of the Projection for Reduced Maps") (Paris: chez l'auteur, 1760).[8] It has a large cartouche in the Southern Ocean, designed by Arrivet, an engraver about whom we know very little,[9] and it too represents the four continents, but in a very different way (Fig. 146). Europe is represented at the top of the cartouche, the position of superiority. The shield with the cow's head alludes to the myth of Zeus, in the form of a bull, carrying away

___

across the top of the map alludes to a survey of the earth. It reads: *Josué ordonna qu'on choisisse trois hommes de chaque Tribu pour faire le tour et la Description de la Terre. Ils partirent & reconnurent avec soin & la Diviserent en sept parts qu'ils ecrivirent dans un Livre. Josue ch. 18 v. 4, 8, 9,* that is, "Joshua ordered that three men from each tribe be chosen to go make a tour and description of the earth. They set out and carefully surveyed it and divided it into seven parts, which they wrote in a book. Joshua 18:4 and 8–9."

8 On the Robert de Vaugondys' 1760 *Mappe monde* see Pedley, *Bel et utile* (see note 6), p. 135, no. 10. A high-resolution image of the 1778 state of the map is available at https://loc.gov.

9 The 1778 map was engraved by E. Dussy, a frequent collaborator with the Robert de Vaugondys, who signed it in the lower left corner, while beneath the cartouche, Arrivet wrote *Arrivet inv. & sulp.,* indicating that he both designed and engraved it. Arrivet designed and signed almost all the cartouches in Gilles Robert de Vaugondy, *Nouvel atlas portatif* (Paris: Chés le S. Robert, 1762).

Europa. The caduceus and winged helmet of Mercury, god of travelers and merchants, and a globe, a map, books, and tools for surveying, indicate Europe's mastery of learning and of the tools of colonial power. The bird at the right is intended to represent an eagle as a symbol of both the Roman Empire and the Holy Roman Empire.

At the lower left we have Chinese porcelain, a camel and a parasol representing Asia; in the register in the center below there are African animals (an elephant, a lion, and a rhinoceros attacking an elephant) and coral, though the connection between coral and Africa is tenuous.[10] Finally on the right there is a Native American feather headdress, a feathered neckband, a bow and arrow, and a small shield, representing America.[11] The crocodile below is conveniently between the African animals and the American artifacts, for the animal was associated with both continents. So the cartographer and cartouche artist manage to represent the four continents through products and animals from those regions and equipment and attributes of their inhabitants, without using personifications. In particular, America is represented chiefly by the clothing and weapons that either a personification of America, or an American Indian, might have worn in a cartouche, and these items are not trophies here.[12]

Other cartouche artists in the second half of the eighteenth century use this same method of representing a continent or region by means of the attributes of a personification or of a "typical" resident, without the personification. For example, Jean Janvier (fl. 1746–1776) made a map

titled *L'Amerique, divisee en ses principaux etats* ("America Divided into its Main States") (Paris: Jean Lattré, 1760) that has a cartouche of exactly this type that was designed by Pierre-Philippe Choffard (1730–1809)—an artist we encountered in the Introduction above (Fig. 147).[13] We have a bow, a quiver of arrows, a feather headdress, and a small shield, exactly the things we might expect to see an American Indian holding and wearing in a cartouche, piled on the ground, very much as in the Robert de Vaugondys' map of the same year.

Janvier and Choffard also use this method on Janvier's map of the German Empire titled *L'Empire d'Allemagne divise par cercles subdivises en leurs etats et souverainetes* ("The German Empire Divided into Districts which are Subdivided into their States and Sovereignties") (Paris: Jean Lattré, 1761) (Fig. 148).[14] Here, beneath the imperial eagle above, we see lying on the ground the crown, orb, scepter, and sword of the Holy Roman Emperor, instead of a depiction of him wearing and holding these items.[15] This cartouche is not signed by Choffard, but it was copied from a cartouche in one of his model books.[16]

The same cartographer and artist created a double-hemisphere world map whose cartouche probably inspired that designed by Robert de Vaugondy and Arrivet a few years later. Janvier's map is titled *Mappe monde, ou description du globe terrestre assujettie aux observations astronomiques* ("World map, or Description of the Terrestrial Globe in Accordance with Astronomical Observations") (Paris: Jean Lattré, 1774);[17] an inscription at the base of the left-hand hemisphere reads *PP Choffard fecit ornamenta 1760*, "P.P. Choffard made the ornaments in 1760." It is surprising that Janvier would wait fourteen years, from 1760

---

10   Coral was fished along the North African coast, but the most important centers of coral fishing were in European waters, particularly near Livorno, Naples, Genoa, and Marseilles. See Marlise Rijks, "'Unusual Excrescences of Nature': Collected Coral and the Study of Petrified Luxury in Early Modern Antwerp," *Dutch Crossing: Journal of Low Countries Studies* 43.2 (2019), pp. 127–156, esp. 130; and Francesca Trivellato, "The Exchange of Mediterranean Coral and Indian Diamonds," in *The Familiarity of Strangers: The Sephardic Diaspora, Livorno, and Cross-Cultural Trade in the Early Modern Period* (New Haven: Yale University Press, 2009), pp. 224–250 and 362–374.

11   On Native American feathered neckbands see Elizabeth Hill Boone, "Seeking Indianness: Christoph Weiditz, the Aztecs, and Feathered Amerindians," *Colonial Latin American Review* 26.1 (2017), pp. 39–61, esp. 46, 51, and 55.

12   The son Didier Robert de Vaugondy and his cartouche engraver Arrivet used similar but much more concise iconography to represent the continents in another world map, *Mappemonde suivant la projection des cartes reduites* (Paris: s.n., 1761)—so concise, in fact, as to be almost incomprehensible without comparison with the 1760 map discussed here. On this map see Pedley, *Bel et utile* (see note 6), p. 136, no. 15. An image of the 1761 map is available at https://gallica.bnf.fr; a high-resolution image of the 1778 state, on which the cartouche was re-engraved by Charles Jacques Groux, is available in the Clements Library Image Bank at https://quod.lib.umich.edu/w/wclic.

13   A high-resolution image of Janvier's 1760 map *L'Amerique, divisee en ses principaux etats* is available at https://digitalcollec tions.nypl.org, and has the signature "P.P. Choffard fecit, 1760" below the cartouche. This signature is included on the 1769 state of the map, but not on the 1774 state.

14   A high-resolution image of Janvier's 1761 map *L'Empire d'Allemagne* is available at https://searchworks.stanford.edu.

15   Jean Janvier, or his unnamed cartouche artist, uses a similar strategy in his *L'Italie, divisee en ses differents etats, royaumes et republiques* (Paris: Jean Lattre, 1763): at the bottom of the cartouche we see the papal tiara and the keys of St. Peter on the right, and a cardinal's hat and staff on the left—but the dignitaries themselves are not depicted. A high-resolution image of the map is available at https://searchworks.stanford.edu.

16   See the volume with the assigned title [Cartouches] that includes Choffard's works from all six of his *cahiers* of cartouches in Paris at the Bibliothèque de l'Institut National d'Histoire de l'Art, Collections Jacques Doucet, NUM FOL RES 103, which is available in digital format, p. 13.

17   A high-resolution image of Janvier's 1774 *Mappe monde* available at https://loc.gov.

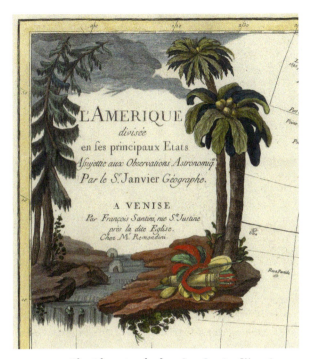

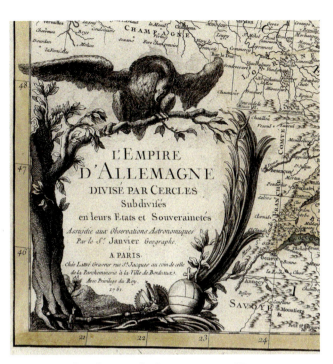

FIGURE 147 The title cartouche from Jean Janvier, *L'Amerique, divisee en ses principaux etats*, first published in Paris in 1769, the copy illustrated here is of a later state (Venice: François Santini, 1784) with recent hand-coloring
COURTESY OF OLD WORLD AUCTIONS, GLEN ALLEN, VIRGINIA

FIGURE 148 The title cartouche from Jean Janvier, *L'Empire d'Allemagne divise par cercles subdivises en leurs etats et souverainetes* (Paris: Jean Lattré, 1761)
STANFORD UNIVERSITY, DAVID RUMSEY MAP COLLECTION, G1015 .L3 1763 F. COURTESY OF THE DAVID RUMSEY MAP COLLECTION

to 1774, to use Choffard's cartouche, but there is no sign of an earlier printing of this map.[18]

The decoration symbolizing the four continents sits atop the superstructure with the labels *Hémisphere Occidental* (Fig. 149) and *Hémisphere Oriental* (Fig. 150). Choffard makes the interesting compositional choice of placing the items representing Asia and Europe, which he saw as having richer material cultures—and thus more items to display—closer to the center of the map, on either side of the title, and the items representing America and Africa at the left and right edges, respectively. Beginning at the left, with the items representing America, we see a palm tree, a bow, a club, a feather headdress and loincloth, and a chest-covering of metal disks—all but the palm tree, of course, things we would expect to see a "typical" Native American carrying or wearing. Asia is represented by a carpet, a hatchet, a dragon banner, a feather headdress, a book with an Islamic crescent, pearls, a scepter with an Islamic crescent, and two censers. Again, we can easily imagine an image of an Asian potentate wearing the

headdress and holding the scepter, and standing beside the book and the censers.

In the section representing Europe we have a rifle, a cannon, a plumed helmet, flags, a ship's sail and rigging, an armillary sphere, a painter's palette, and a sculpted bust, indicating the continent's military, navigational, and artistic accomplishments. Here there is less emphasis on clothing and personal arms. Finally, in the section representing Africa we see a palm tree, an ivory tusk,[19] a lion's pelt, and a large spear. It is easy to imagine a version of this scene that involved an African native holding the spear and standing beside the tree.[20]

18 Janvier printed a double-hemisphere world map in 1762 with a different cartouche program, namely his *Mappe-monde, ou description du globe terrestre assujettie aux observations astronomiques* (Paris: Jean Lattré, 1762). The similarity of the titles of several of these eighteenth-century world maps makes it challenging to distinguish them.

19 There is, of course, a close association between elephants and Africa that goes back centuries, and personifications of Africa often wore a sort of hat with the trunk of an elephant on the front: see Joaneath Spicer, "The Personification of Africa with an Elephant-Head Crest in Cesare Ripa's *Iconologia* (1603)," in Walter S. Melion and B.A.M. Ramakers, eds., *Personification: Embodying Meaning and Emotion* (Leiden and Boston: Brill, 2016), pp. 675–715.

20 Representations of the continents very similar to those in Janvier's *Mappe monde* of 1774 are deployed in Rigobert Bonne's *Mappe monde, ou description du globe terrestre drojettée e assujettie au ciel* (Paris: Jean Lattré, 1778)—also printed by Lattré. Interestingly, whoever was responsible for the map's decoration seems not to have understood the continental significance of the decoration above the two hemispheres, for the map also has personifications of the continents—as four male children—in

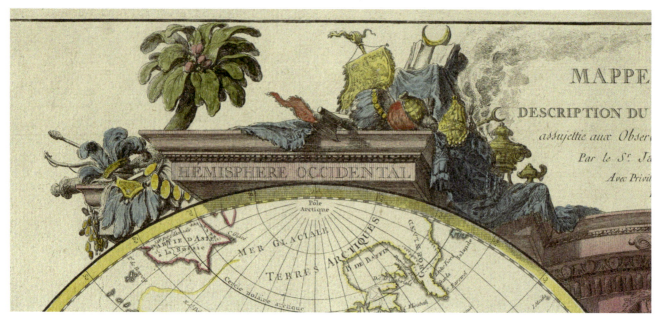

FIGURE 149 Detail of the title cartouche in the western hemisphere in Jean Janvier, *Mappe monde, ou description du globe terrestre assujettie aux observations astronomiques* (Paris: Jean Lattré, 1774)
YALE UNIVERSITY, BEINECKE LIBRARY, 11 1774. COURTESY OF THE BEINECKE RARE BOOK AND MANUSCRIPT LIBRARY

FIGURE 150 Detail of the title cartouche in the eastern hemisphere in Jean Janvier, *Mappe monde, ou description du globe terrestre assujettie aux observations astronomiques* (Paris: Jean Lattré, 1774)
YALE UNIVERSITY, BEINECKE LIBRARY, 11 1774. COURTESY OF THE BEINECKE RARE BOOK AND MANUSCRIPT LIBRARY

This same system of representing places with the attributes of personifications, but without the personifications themselves, was adopted by other cartographers.[21] For

example, the English cartographer John Purdy (1773–1843) in his 1809 map *The Continent and Islands of Africa, with all*

the four corners of the map. A high-resolution image of the map is available at https://loc.gov.

21   A spectacularly clear example of this use of the attributes of personifications of the continents, but not the personifications themselves, appears on the title page of the *Atlas moderne ou collection de cartes sur toutes les parties du globe terrestre*

par plusieurs auteurs (Paris: Lattre et Jean Thomas Herissant, 1762). The title page was designed by "Mounet," i.e. Charles Monnet (1732–after 1808), and engraved by Benoît-Louis Prévost (c.1733–1816); an image of the title page is available at https://searchworks.stanford.edu. The atlas was printed again in 1791 with the same title page, but with the artist's name corrected to "Monnet."

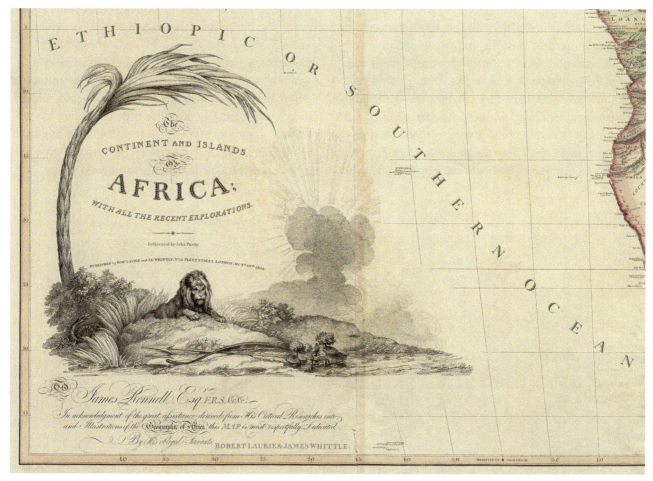

FIGURE 151   John Purdy, *The Continent and Islands of Africa, with all the Recent Explorations* (London: Laurie & Whittle, 1809)
YALE UNIVERSITY, BEINECKE LIBRARY, 60 1809. COURTESY OF THE BEINECKE RARE BOOK AND MANUSCRIPT LIBRARY

the Recent Explorations (London: Laurie & Whittle, 1809) has a title cartouche framed by the land below, a palm tree, clouds, and sunbeams (Fig. 151).[22] A serpent lurks in the bushes and a lion sits atop a low eminence looking ahead to where a bow and two arrows lie on the ground, and near them is a marsh where some lotus grows. The lion's gaze is intent, and I think both he and the map's viewer know that something we might have expected to

see, namely an African man holding the bow and arrow, a typical inhabitant of the region, is missing.

There was always diversity in the styles of cartouches in favor in different countries and with different cartographers; nevertheless, the cartouches we have considered in this section speak volumes about the direction cartouches were headed in the late eighteenth and early nineteenth centuries. The personifications and typical inhabitants that had been staples of cartouche decoration have vanished, leaving their clothes and weapons and attributes behind—and these items were evidently felt to be adequate representations of their regions, by both the makers and the consumers of maps. The person wearing the clothes and holding the weapons, who gave them life, was no longer thought necessary or desirable, and indeed an interest in ethnographic illustrations on maps, facile and racist as they may have been, was falling by the wayside. As discussed in the Introduction, in some circles at least, a new Neoclassical aesthetic was taking

22   A high-resolution image of Purdy's map of Africa is available in the Digital Collections of the Beinecke Library. On Purdy see Albert Frederick Pollard, "Purdy, John," in Leslie Stephen and Sidney Lee, eds., *Dictionary of National Biography* (London: Smith, Elder, & Co., 1885–1901), vol. 47, p. 46; Hugh Robert Mill, *Catalogue of the Library of the Royal Geographical Society, Containing the Titles of All Works up to December 1893* (London: J. Murray, 1895), pp. 385–386; and Susanna Fisher, *The Makers of the Blueback Charts: A History of Imray, Laurie, Norie & Wilson Ltd* (St. Ives, Cambridgeshire: Imray, Laurie, Norie & Wilson Ltd., 2001), pp. 65–67.

over, favoring smaller, less elaborate, less complex, less populated cartouches. When the accurate determination of longitude became possible and triangulation surveys were completed in some European countries, ideas about what maps should be were changing.

In the Introduction I suggested that the deployment of cartouches populated with people marked an important moment in cartographic history, namely when maps began to achieve the theatrical character that Abraham Ortelius had implied they should have by the title of his 1570 atlas, *Theatrum orbis terrarum*, "The Theater of the World." We have seen soldiers and sovereigns, gods and personifications, native peoples and cartographers, sailors, skeletons, *putti*, and letter-carriers enliven many a cartographic stage with their deeds and silent gestures, but now, in these late eighteenth-century cartouches, they are taking their exits. The fact that they leave their clothes, weapons, and other possessions in heaps in the middle of the stage makes their departure seem hasty and even precipitous, and it is now far too late to applaud them.

A Map on a Map on a Map

John Randel, Jr., The City of New York as Laid Out by the Commissioners, *1821*

I end the body of the book with a map from the early nineteenth century that makes striking use of cartouches even while showing that this artistic genre was in steep decline. The map was made by John Randel, Jr. (1787–1865), an energetic surveyor, cartographer, and inventor who had been hired by the Commissioners of the city of New York to survey northward from the settlement at the southern tip of Manhattan and lay out a grid of streets that would give order to and facilitate the development of the island.[1] The idea of organizing cities on a grid was an old one,[2] but the Commissioners' project was very much of the Enlightenment, a plan to force the irregular hills, valleys, swamps, streams, forests, farmsteads, and roads into a leveled Cartesian coordinate system.[3] Randel's map was thus designed to further a project that had sprung from the same intellectual movement that tended to reduce elaborate cartouche decoration on maps, and Randel himself was a man of the Enlightenment, with an intense dedication to the accuracy of his work.

Despite his years of painstaking effort on the project, going so far as to invent his own new surveying instruments to improve the quality of his work, it took quite some time for Randel's map to be published. The Commissioners hired Randel in 1807, and in March of 1811 he delivered to the city three copies of his hand-drawn

map of Manhattan, measuring 2.4 × 8.9 feet (73 × 272 cm).[4] I.N. Phelps Stokes, referring to this map, wrote that "The year 1811 marks the end of the little old city and the beginning of the great modern metropolis,"[5] and Edward Spann calls it "the masterplan of the first great American metropolis."[6] Randel anticipated printing a version of his map, but the unscrupulous surveyor William Bridges took much of Randel's data, hired the skilled engraver Peter Maverick (1780–1831) to engrave six printing plates, and published a detailed map of the island in 1811, without giving Randel any credit.[7] Randel complained bitterly in the press, but the damage was done.[8] The map, like many others of its time, presents its title without a cartouche.

4   Randel's 1811 manuscript map is titled *A Map of the City of New York by the Commissioners Appointed by an Act of the Legislature passed April 3rd 1807*, and high-resolution digital images of the exemplar in the New York Public Library are available at https://digitalcollec tions.nypl.org. The other two exemplars are in the New York City Municipal Archives and the Bureau of Land Management in Albany. For discussion of the map see I.N. Phelps Stokes, *The Iconography of Manhattan Island, 1498–1909* (New York: Robert H. Dodd, 1915–1928), vol. 1, pp. 470–473 and plate 79, which precedes p. 413; Edward Spann, "The Greatest Grid: The New York Plan of 1811," in Daniel Schaffer, ed., *Two Centuries of American Planning* (Baltimore: Johns Hopkins University Press. 1988), pp. 11–39; and Holloway, *The Measure of Manhattan* (see note 1), pp. 54–66.

5   Stokes, *The Iconography of Manhattan Island* (see note 4), vol. 1, pp. 407–408.

6   Spann, "The Greatest Grid" (see note 4), p. 14.

7   Bridges' 1811 map, which measures about 2 × 7.5 feet (58 × 228 cm), is titled *This Map of the City of New York and Island of Manhattan, as Laid Out by the Commissioners Appointed by the Legislature, April 3d, 1807 is Respectfully Dedicated to the Mayor, Aldermen and Commonalty Thereof*; a high-resolution image of a hand-colored exemplar of the map is available at https://loc.gov. Bridges accompanied the map with a pamphlet titled *Map of the City of New York and Island of Manhattan with Explanatory Remarks and References* (New York: printed for the author by T. & J. Swords, 1811). For discussion of the map see Stokes, *The Iconography of Manhattan Island* (see note 4), vol. 3, pp. 543–549.

8   Randel's and Bridges' letters in the press about credit for the information in Bridge's 1811 map are transcribed by Stokes (see the previous note); for discussion see Holloway, *The Measure of Manhattan* (see note 1), pp. 102–110. Incidentally Bridges had engaged in cartographic piracy before: in making his *Plan of the City of New-York with the Recent and Intended Improvements* (New York: Isaac Riley, 1807) he had borrowed from an 1801 map by Casimir Goerck and Joseph François Mangin titled *Plan of the City of New-York, Drawn from Actual Survey*. Both of these maps were engraved by Peter Maverick.

1   The standard biography of Randel is Marguerite Holloway, *The Measure of Manhattan: The Tumultuous Career and Surprising Legacy of John Randel Jr., Cartographer, Surveyor, Inventor* (New York: W.W. Norton & Company, 2013). Also see Hilary Ballon, *The Greatest Grid: The Master Plan of Manhattan, 1811–2011* (New York: Columbia University Press, 2012), particularly the chapters "The Commissioners' Plan of 1811" and "Surveying the City." Ballon's book is the catalog of a 2011–2012 exhibition of the same name at the Museum of the City of New York, the online version of which can be seen at http:// thegreatestgrid.mcny.org. And see Peter Marcuse, "The Grid as City Plan: New York City and Laissez-Faire Planning in the Nineteenth Century," *Planning Perspectives* 2.3 (1987), pp. 287–310.

2   See Dan Stanislawski, "The Origin and Spread of the Grid-Pattern Town," *Geographical Review* 36.1 (1946), pp. 105–120; and Reuben S. Rose-Redwood, "Genealogies of the Grid: Revisiting Stanislawski's Search for the Origin of the Grid-Pattern Town," *Geographical Review* 98.1 (2008), pp. 42–58.

3   Gerard Koeppel, *City on a Grid: How New York became New York* (Boston: Da Capo Press, 2015), p. xvi.

Randel continued to make surveys for the commissioners, refining and adding to his data, and in 1814 prepared a new map of New York. This manuscript map survives;[9] instead of being oriented along the north-south axis of the island as his 1811 map was, it is oriented to north, meaning that Manhattan is at an angle, and he takes advantage of this to show more detail of the Hudson and East Rivers and the lands beyond them, and also of the harbor and Bay of New York. He includes as a decoration accompanying the title the 1784 seal of the City of New York,[10] evidently to indicate the official nature of the map. In March of 1814 Randel placed advertisements in the *Evening Post* declaring that his map would soon be published:[11]

"In the hands of the engraver, and shortly will be published, Randel's Map of Manhattan Island, with the opposite shores, the harbor, bay and narrows. Containing the plan of the city of New York, as laid out by the commissioners: also the villages of Brooklyn, Jersey and Hoboken .... The size of the map is 22 by 34 inches, and will be delivered to subscribers at the moderate price of $2.50 coloured, non subscribers will pay $4."

He goes on to cite a letter from Gouverneur Morris, one of the commissioners, praising the map, and notes that Bridges' map was much more expensive, at $8 uncolored. But the map was never printed: the War of 1812 was underway, and it was thought that the map would give valuable intelligence to the British.[12] So once again Randel's plans to publish a map of the city came to naught.

In the following years he continued surveying for the commissioners, and from 1818 to 1820 he produced a huge manuscript map of the island on 92 sheets at a scale of 100 feet to the inch (1:12,000); when the sheets are assembled the map is almost 50 feet long.[13] And in 1821 he finally published a map of Manhattan. He realized that this map would be "the enduring, widely disseminated record" of his work on the island,[14] and he took pains to make sure that it would be an impressive monument worthy of his years of effort.[15] He had the plate engraved by Peter Maverick, the same engraver who had made the plates for Bridges' 1811 map; he secured special paper from Morris & Kingsland; he ran different advertisements for the map multiple times each, and offered versions of the maps at multiple price points.[16] His design for the map was a striking departure from his earlier work, for he presented three maps in one, depicted in *trompe-l'oeil* as if each were lying on top of the other. That is to say, he presents the map with two nested inset maps, or two nested cartouches (Fig. 152).

The "base" map is titled *A Map of the States of Connecticut and Rho[de Island] with part[s of] New York, Mas[sachusettes, and New Jersey]*—parts of the title are covered by the map that lies on top of it. This map shows the geographical and political context of Manhattan. One might ask why the island is at the left-hand edge of the map rather than at its center, but this is because Randel emphasizes his use of the Prime Meridian of New York City by making that meridian the left-hand edge of the map,[17] and in fact he leaves a gap in the scale of latitude so that that scale will not cover up part of Manhattan

9   Randel's 1814 manuscript map is titled *The City of New York as Laid Out by the Commissioners with the Surrounding Country*, measures 81 × 52 cm, and is held by the New-York Historical Society. For discussion and illustration of the map see Stokes, *The Iconography of Manhattan Island* (see note 4), vol. 3, pp. 874 and 543–544 and A. Plate 15, following p. 855.

10   On the 1784 seal of the City of New York see John B. Pine, *Seal and Flag of the City of New York* (New York: G.P. Putnam's Sons, 1915), pp. 55–63.

11   From the *Evening Post* (New York), March 21, 1814, p. 3; the ad ran again in the *Evening Post* on March 30, 1814, p. 1.

12   Holloway, *The Measure of Manhattan* (see note 1), p. 109.

13   These are Randel's so-called Farm Maps, which are fascinating as they show simultaneously the topographical details of the island (including many farms) and also the planned grid of streets and avenues, that is, the island both as it is and as it would be. These maps are held in the Manhattan Borough President's Office and were digitized and are viewable online as part of the exhibition

"The Greatest Grid": see again https://thegreatestgrid.mcny.org. Also see Holloway, *The Measure of Manhattan* (see note 1), p. 120.

14   I borrow the phrase from Holloway, *The Measure of Manhattan* (see note 1), p. 132.

15   On Randel's 1521 map see Stokes, *The Iconography of Manhattan Island* (see note 4), vol. 1, p. 473; Paul E. Cohen and Robert T. Augustyn, *Manhattan in Maps, 1527–1995* (New York: Rizzoli International Publications, 1997), pp. 108–109; and Holloway, *The Measure of Manhattan* (see note 1), pp. 125–133. A high-resolution image of the Library of Congress's hand-colored copy of the map is available at https://loc.gov.

16   The announcement of Randel's map was first published in the *Evening Post* (New York) March 3, 1821, p. 3, and a more detailed description of the map followed in the *Evening Post*, April 23, 1821, p. 3, where the prices for the different versions of the map are listed as follows: the map in sheets, uncolored, $3.62; in sheets, colored, $4.00; colored and mounted on muslin rollers, $5.00; colored, on rollers, and varnished, $5.50; with extra molding and gilt twist and knobs, $6.00; and with gilt molding and knobs, $6.75. Randel revised these prices upwards in the advertisement in the *Evening Post*, May 1, 1821, p. 1. The only two surviving copies of Randel's map that are hand-colored are those in the Library of Congress and in Trinity College Library in Hartford, CT.

17   On the New York meridian, which usually went through City Hall, see Joseph Hyde Pratt, "American Prime Meridians," *Geographical Review* 32.2 (1942), pp. 233–244, at 240–243; the first map to use it is Claude Joseph Sauthier, *A Map of the Province of New-York Reduc'd from the Large Drawing of that Province ....* (London: William Faden, 1776), a high-resolution image of which

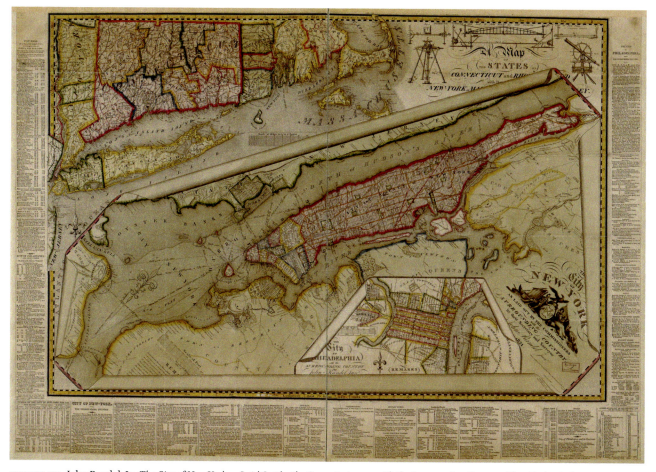

FIGURE 152 John Randel, Jr., *The City of New York as Laid Out by the Commissioners with the Surrounding Country* (New York, 1821)
LIBRARY OF CONGRESS, GEOGRAPHY AND MAP DIVISION, G3804.N4G45 1821 .R3. COURTESY OF THE LIBRARY OF CONGRESS

and the Hudson River. The base map thus places a strong emphasis on the grid and the centrality of Manhattan in that grid.

In the upper right-hand corner of the map around the map's title there are detailed drawings of the instruments Randel invented to make his survey as accurate as possible (Fig. 153), his various measuring rods, his theodolite, and his water level,[18] and we read "Instruments invented and used by John Randel Jun[r]. while Surveying the City of New

York: see accompanying description." Randel intended to publish a pamphlet to accompany his map—as Bridges had with his 1811 map—but this never came to pass.[19] The images of Randel's instruments proclaim his dedication to the accuracy of his surveying, and thus to the accuracy of his map, and speak directly to the viewer in a way we have seen other cartographers do in their cartouches, but while the instruments are ranged around the map's title, they are not part of a title cartouche: there is no frame around the title, no title cartouche at all.

A map that is really three nested maps presents an interesting problem for catalogers: under which of the three titles should the map be listed? Logic would suggest using

is available at https://loc.gov. Randel also indicated the New York City Hall Prime Meridian on his 1814 map.

18 For discussion of these depictions of Randel's instruments see Holloway, *The Measure of Manhattan* (see note 1), pp. 75–88. For other maps with illustrations of surveying instruments see David Smith, "The Cartographic Illustration of Land Surveying Instruments and Methods," *Bulletin of the Society of Cartographers* 26.1 (1992), pp. 11–20. One such map is Vincenzo Coronelli, *Parte Occidentale della China* (Venice, 1696), a hand-colored copy of which is available at https://searchworks.stanford.edu; also see a map mentioned above, Georg Matthäus Vischer's *Archiducatus Austriae Superioris geographica descriptio* (Augsburg: Melchior Küsell, 1669). A good zoomable image of the map is available at https://gallica.bnf.fr.

19 Part of the text at the bottom of Randel's map reads: "Note.—The Pamphlet accompanying this Map, contains—1. A description of the Instruments used in surveying the streets and avenues, with the method of using them; their particular adaptation to the measure of a degree of latitude, and the facilities which the ice on Hudson's River presents for such an operation, will be illustrated. It is known, from experience, that a line measured twice with these instruments on such a field, will not in any case differ more than one inch in five miles."

FIGURE 153 Detail of Randel's custom surveying instruments on his *The City of New York*
COURTESY OF THE LIBRARY OF CONGRESS

the title of the outer or base map, and indeed Randel himself lists the title of the outer map first,[20] but most modern catalogers have cited the map under the title of the first inset map, that of Manhattan, perhaps influenced by the fact that the title is unobscured and includes the map's date (Fig. 154). This title runs: *The City of New York as Laid Out by the Commissioners with the Surrounding Country by their Secretary and Surveyor, John Randel Junr. 1821.*[21] This map is similar to Randel's 1814 map of the island: it is oriented to the north, the cartographer refers to the meridian of New York in the upper and lower margins of the map, he shows both current topographical features of the island and the proposed grid, and he includes the seal of the City of New York with the title.[22] We might say that the coat of arms in the center of the seal of the City of New York qualifies the title of the map as a cartouche, but the

title is certainly unframed, again indicating the decline in elaborate cartouche decoration in the late eighteenth and early nineteenth centuries.

The frame of the inset map of New York, on the other hand, is very clear: all four corners of the map are rolled inward, in two cases so that the edges of the rolls are coincident with the neatlines of the outer map; and these four edges, together with the four small parts of the map's neatlines, form an octagonal cartouche. At the right end of the lower roll, in a part purporting to show the back of the first inset map, Randel has written "This Paper made by Morris & Kingsland, New York," assuring the viewer of the quality materials of the inset map, but leaving us to wonder about the paper upon which the outer and innermost maps were printed.

The second inset map (Fig. 155) is titled *The City of Philadelphia, with the Surrounding Country, by John Randel, Junr*. The question naturally arises as to why a cartographer who had spent so many years and so much effort mapping New York would place a map of Philadelphia as the central, most nested item on his map. The answer is that Philadelphia was also designed on a grid, but earlier: the original plan for Philadelphia's grid was prepared by Thomas Holme in 1683, and approved by William Penn, the founder of the Province of Pennsylvania.[23] In

---

20   See again Randel's advertisement for his 1821 map in the *Evening Post*, March 3, 1821, p. 3.

21   At the time of writing the only library to catalog Randel's 1821 map under the title of its outer map is the Smithsonian's Dibner Library.

22   On the seal of New York see Pine, *Seal and Flag of the City of New York* (see note 10), pp. 55–63. The earliest map I know that shows the seal of the City of New York is Bernard Ratzer, *Plan of the City of New York, in North America, Surveyed in the Years 1766 and 1767* (London: Jefferys & Faden, 1776); a high-resolution image of this map is available at https://digitalcollections.nypl.org. The map publisher Matthew Dripps continued to display the city's seal beside the titles of his maps of New York into the middle of the nineteenth century.

23   Thomas Holme's 1683 map of Philadelphia's planned grid is titled *A Portraiture of the City of Philadelphia in the Province of Pennsylvania in America* (London: Sold by Andrew Sowle in

his advertisement for his 1821 map Randel notes that he depicts New York and Philadelphia on the same scale,[24] an interesting and otherwise totally unsuspected detail which means that he intended the viewer to compare the two grids, and see that the one that he had established in New York was much larger. Indeed, the fact that the lower parts of the two inset maps are depicted as rolled up together helps suggest connection and comparison between them.

Again, there is no frame around the title of the map of Philadelphia, reflecting the disappearance of such decoration in the late eighteenth and early nineteenth century; at the same time, the frame of the inset map of Philadelphia is well defined by the rolls and sections of neatlines around it. So while eschewing traditional cartouche decoration—not incorporating the images of his surveying instruments into a title cartouche, for example—Randel deploys nested cartouches of inset maps to show the geographical context of Manhattan and to offer a comparison of the grids of New York and Philadelphia to demonstrate the superior scale of his own accomplishments. In this sense, Randel does use these

cartouches to communicate directly with the viewer of the map.

Unfortunately Randel's map did not sell well. There was too much of the cartographer in it: potential buyers of the map would no doubt want to focus on the details of Manhattan, but instead of providing a large-scale map of the island, Randel chose a smaller format on expensive paper, and indulged in an egocentric comparison with Philadelphia, which viewers no doubt found to be a confusing distraction. The Finance Committee of the city's Common Council, in their report of September 4, 1820, said that they had seen Randel's map, but found "that the scale on which it is drawn is too small for the ordinary purposes of reference."[25] As an encouragement to Randel they agreed to buy 24 copies of the map for their members, but crucially, for the map traditionally given to new members of the Council to aid them in the discharge of their public duties, they chose not Randel's map, but rather one by John Longworth, probably his map of 1817, which shows only the southern part of Manhattan, that is, the part already densely settled.[26]

The financial failure of his map was hard on Randel—and this disappointment came on top of the difficulties he had in his two earlier unsuccessful attempts to publish maps of Manhattan. The great surveyor never made another important map.[27]

Shoreditch, 1683); a high-resolution image of the map is available at https://digitalcollections.nypl.org. For discussion of the Philadelphia grid see John W. Reps, *The Making of Urban America* (Princeton: Princeton University Press, 1965), pp. 157–174; and Perry L. Norton, "William Penn Plans his City," *Pennsylvania Heritage* 11.2 (1985), pp. 26–31.

24   For Randel's statement that the map of Philadelphia is on the same scale as that of New York see again the *Evening Post*, April 23, 1821, p. 3: "To this is added, on a separate scroll, a representation of the city of Philadelphia, with its surrounding villages, on the same scale with the city of New York." Both inset maps have scales of feet, but it would not occur to most viewers to compare the scales and realize that they are the same.

25   From the *Minutes of the Common Council of the City of New York, 1784–1831* (New York: City of New York, 1917), vol. 11, p. 299, quoted by Holloway, *The Measure of Manhattan* (see note 1), p. 132.

26   David Longworth, *This Actual Map and Comparative Plans Showing 88 Years Growth of the City of New York* (New York: David Longworth, 1817); a high-resolution image of the map is available at https://digitalcollections.nypl.org.

27   Holloway, *The Measure of Manhattan* (see note 1), p. 132.

FIGURE 154 Detail of Randel's inset map of New York on his *The City of New York*
COURTESY OF THE LIBRARY OF CONGRESS

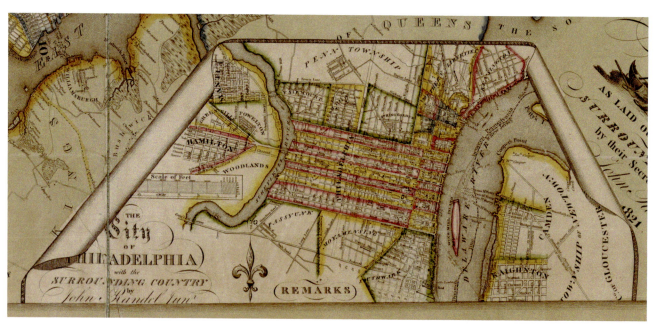

FIGURE 155 Detail of Randel's inset map of Philadelphia on his *The City of New York*
COURTESY OF THE LIBRARY OF CONGRESS

Conclusions

In the body of the book we have seen cases in which cartographers decorated cartouches with the tools of surveying,[1] and even depicted themselves or another cartographer working on maps:[2] these cartouches allude visually to the process of creating maps. One cartouche goes further and illustrates the process of drawing a cartouche on a map: the cartouche shows its own creation. This is a manuscript map made in 1789 by the Spanish military engineer and cartographer Francisco Requena (1743–1824)[3] which shows part of what is now southern Colombia where multiple rivers meet before flowing into the Japurá River.[4]

The title cartouche (Fig. 156) shows a cliff on which the map's title and the cartographer's name seem to be carved; the writing is a bit muddled as Requena wrote most of the words twice, first in pencil and then in ink, and he also made some corrections to the inked text. At the top (Fig. 157) a surveyor, no doubt Requena himself, takes a sighting with help from an assistant. In the lower left corner of the cartouche an Indigenous man holding a spear and shield looks placidly across the cartouche at a European man in the lower right-hand corner.

That European man, who is seated on a rock (Fig. 158), looks upward at the cliff and draws the scene before him. In particular, at the top of his sketch we can see the top of

the cliff, the surveyor, and his assistant. That is, the man in the lower right-hand corner of the cartouche is drawing the cartouche. Both the surveyor and the artist represent the cartographer, and so in this remarkable cartouche, the cartographer gives equal weight to the gathering of geographical data and to cartouche design in the creation of a map: he places the cartouche on a par with the map itself. Moreover, the fact that within his cartouche the cartographer depicts himself drawing the cartouche creates a wonderful *mise en abyme*, with the theoretical possibility of an infinite sequence of nested images of the cartographer drawing the cartouche, in which the cartographer draws the cartouche, and so on.

• • •

In this book I have tried to illustrate some of the richness, variety, and importance of cartouches. They are often the most engaging parts of maps; the symbolism of the more complex examples is stimulating and satisfying to interpret; cartouches illustrate all aspects of the human condition and all parts of the natural world; and they are essential to interpreting maps—to understanding the cartographer's outlook and intentions, and how the cartographer's outlook influenced his or her depiction of part of the earth's surface. Cartouches are supplements (*parerga*) to maps, and frames demarcate them as separate from the cartographic space, and yet these supplements' richness transforms the maps on which they appear and reveal their true natures. Cartouches function as a sort of legend to the map[5] that guides the viewer not in interpreting the symbols representing lighthouses, railways, and tidal flats, but rather in understanding the cartographer's influences, politics, and hopes.

In the Introduction I outlined the development of cartouches over time, from the almost unadorned examples of the fourteenth and fifteenth centuries, to the advent of cartouches with strapwork, knotwork, and vegetal motifs in the early sixteenth century, to the rise of cartouches that display local peoples, animals, and goods, and that

---

1   For maps whose cartouches are decorated with surveying tools see Chapter 9 on Vischer's *Archiducatus Austriae inferioris* of 1670 / 1697, and also Chapter 33 on Randel's *The City of New York* of 1821.

2   For cartouches that include a portrait of a cartographer working with a map see Chapter 26 on Seutter's *Regni Japoniae nova mappa geographica* of 1740, Chapter 28 on Seutter's *Partie orientale de la Nouvelle France ou du Canada* of 1750, and Chapter 31 on Rocha's two maps titled *Mappa da Comarca do Sabará* made around 1778.

3   On the donation of Requena's maps to the Library of Congress see Lawrence Martin, "South American Cartographic Treasures," *The Library of Congress Quarterly Journal of Current Acquisitions* 1.3 (1944), pp. 30–39; and Lawrence Martin and Walter W. Ristow, "South American Historical Maps," in Walter W. Ristow, ed., *A la Carte: Selected Papers on Maps and Atlases* (Washington, DC: Library of Congress, 1972), pp. 189–203, esp. 198–200. On Requena himself see Eric Beerman, "Bosquejo biográfico de Don Francisco Requena y su Descripción de la Provincia de Guayaquil en 1774," *Revista del Archivo Histórico de Guayas* 14 (1978), pp. 3–22; and Eric Beerman, "Pintor y cartógrafo en las amazonas, Francisco Requena," *Anales, Museo de América* 2 (1994), pp. 83–97. The map under discussion here is mentioned by Robert C. Smith, "Requena and the Japurá: Some Eighteen Century Watercolors of the Amazon and Other Rivers," *The Americas* 3.1 (1945), pp. 31–65, at 33–34.

4   Francisco Requena's map is titled *Mapa de una parte de los Rios de los Engaños o Commiari, Mesay, Cuñaré, Jauiyá y Rufari: los quales, unidos todos, entran por una sola boca en el Rio Yapurá* (1789). A high-resolution image of the map is available at https://loc.gov.

5   For discussion of the history of legends on maps see Günter Schilder, "Historische ontwikkeling van legenda's: een verkenning" [Historical Development of Legends: An Exploration], *Kartografisch Tijdschrift* 9.1 (1983), pp. 19–28. Also see the interesting article by Peter van der Krogt and Ferjan Ormeling, "Een handleiding voor kaartgebruik met een legenda landje uit 1554" [A Manual for the Use of Maps with a 'Legend-Map' from 1554], *Caert-Thresoor* 21 (2002), pp. 41–46.

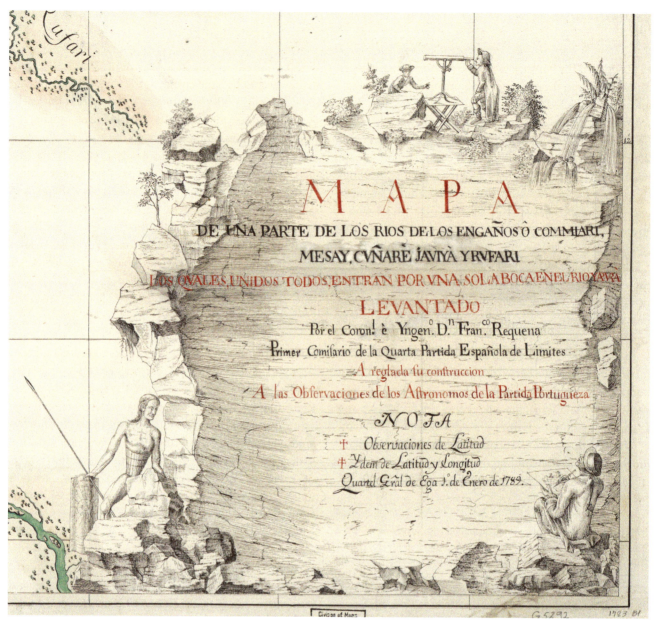

FIGURE 156 The title cartouche on Francisco Requena's *Mapa de una parte de los Rios de los Engaños o Commiari, Mesay, Cuñaré, Jauiyá y Rufari:*
los quales, unidos todos, entran por una sola boca en el Rio Yapurá, 1789
LIBRARY OF CONGRESS, GEOGRAPHY AND MAP DIVISION, G5292.Y2 1789 .R4. COURTESY OF THE LIBRARY OF CONGRESS

include personifications and elaborate symbolism, in the latter part of the sixteenth century. As early as the sixteenth century some cartographers favored simpler and less elaborate cartouches, but this preference became widespread in the late eighteenth century with the rise of Neoclassicism. We witnessed an important stage in the reduction of cartouche imagery in Chapter 32, where we saw some cartographers of the late eighteenth and early nineteenth centuries omit the personifications of regions that we would have been present in earlier cartouches, but still representing those regions through the attributes of those personifications, such as their typical clothes and weapons.

It is worth highlighting here two cartographers whose maps contain some of the finest and richest cartouches, namely Vincenzo Coronelli (1650–1718) and Matthäus Seutter (1678–1757). The huge terrestrial globe that Coronelli made for Louis XIV in 1681–83 is one of his earliest surviving cartographic works,[6] and it evinces a strong

---

6 On Coronelli's huge terrestrial globe, which is in Paris, BnF, GE A-500 (RES), see Monique Pelletier, "Les globes de Louis XIV: les sources françaises de l'oeuvre de Coronelli," *Imago Mundi* 34 (1982), pp. 72–89; Catherine Hoffmann and Hélène Richard, eds., *Les globes de Louis XIV: étude artistique, historique et matérielle* (Paris: Bibliothèque nationale de France, 2012); and Marica Milanesi,

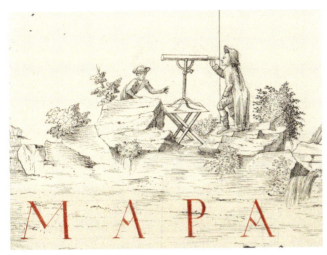

FIGURE 157 Detail of the surveyor (representing Requena) on Requena's *Mapa de una parte de los Rios de los Engaños o Commiari ...*
COURTESY OF THE LIBRARY OF CONGRESS

FIGURE 158 Detail of the artist (representing Requena) drawing the cartouche on Requena's *Mapa de una parte de los Rios de los Engaños o Commiari ...*
COURTESY OF THE LIBRARY OF CONGRESS

interest in cartouches, but at the same time the cartouches lack the symbolic richness of his later work in this genre.

The cartouche describing "La Florida," which means "abounding in flowers," is framed by flowers, and the cartouche about fishing for pearls in the Arabian Sea is in the shape of a seashell, and is surrounded by pearls (compare Fig. 30 above). The decoration fits the texts' subjects well, and is beautifully executed, but is not particularly imaginative. Coronelli does have cartouches with allegorical figures elsewhere on the globe, particularly in the hypothetical southern continent—as mentioned earlier, in the dedicatory cartouche to Louis XIV, the monument with a bust of Louis XIV is surrounded by women who personify the arts and sciences, and Louis XIV is being crowned by Victory while Fame blows a trumpet.[7] But again, this is pretty standard cartouche decoration.

Coronelli's huge terrestrial globe also has a cartouche at the source of the Nile. On the left is an image of the nilometer, a post with marks to measure the height of the river's water during flood season, and on the right an obelisk engraved with hieroglyphics. The upper part of the frame consists of two cornucopias representing the agricultural abundance generated by the Nile when it floods; the left and right parts of the frame are formed by sphinxes with serpentine tails that end in lotus flowers. Below is the bust of a personification of the Nile as an old man. The text in the cartouche is a long discourse about the history of the search for the sources of the Nile, some remarks on the representation of the river on maps, and a description of the nilometer on the island of Roda.[8] The decoration of the cartouche is beautifully painted, but it lacks the symbolic complexity and richness of storytelling in his cartouche about the Nile on his printed globe of 1688, and the very similar cartouche on his map *L'Africa divisa nelle sue parti* of 1689, examined above in Chapter 12.[9]

Vincenzo Coronelli Cosmographer (1650–1718) (Turnhout: Brepols, 2016), pp. 47–132.

7 For discussion of the allegorical figures by the dedication on Coronelli's huge terrestrial globe see Marica Milanesi, "The Dedication and Allegorical Figures," in her *Vincenzo Coronelli Cosmographer (1650–1718)* (Turnhout: Brepols, 2016), pp. 114–116.

8 The long text in the cartouche about the Nile on Coronelli's globe made for Louis XIV is transcribed by [François Le Large], *Recueil des inscriptions des remarques historiques et géographiques qui sont sur le globe terrestre de Marly*, Paris, Bibliothèque nationale de France, MS fr. 13365, pp. 112–120; a digital version of the manuscript is available at https://gallica.bnf.fr. On this manuscript see Gabrielle Duprat, "Deux manuscrits inédits, décrivant le globe terrestre de Marly, construit et dessiné par Coronelli (1681 à 1683)," *Der Globusfreund* 25–27 (1977–79), pp. 203–208.

9 High-resolution scans of the gores of Coronelli's terrestrial globe of 1688 are viewable at https://www.davidrumsey.com and https://searchworks.stanford.edu. The text about the Nile on Coronelli's 1688 terrestrial globe and his 1689 map *L'Africa divisa nelle sue parti* is a much abbreviated version, with some changes of emphasis, of the text on his 1681–83 globe made for Louis XIV.

Many of the cartouches on Coronelli's printed terrestrial globe of 1688 are in the same locations and their texts address the same subjects as those on his manuscript terrestrial globe of 1681–83.[10] A detailed comparison of the decoration of the corresponding cartouches on these globes would be very revealing of Coronelli's development from a cartographer who was interested in cartouches and well versed in current principles of cartouche design to one of the foremost practitioners of the art.

Matthäus Seutter is the other cartographer who, together with his occasional collaborator as cartouche designer, Gottfried Rogg,[11] was a particularly gifted designer of visually engaging and symbolically rich cartouches. Seutter began his cartographic career as an apprentice of the cartographer and publisher Johann Baptist Homann (1663–1724) in Nuremberg sometime after 1697,[12] then worked for the print and map publisher Jeremias Wolff (1663–1724),[13] and established his own map publishing

company in 1707.[14] Homann created some extraordinary cartouches—see Chapter 20 above, for example—but in general his cartouches are less elaborate and symbolically rich than Seutter's. A comparison of the cartouches on Homann's and Seutter's maps of the same regions could be very illuminating in terms of Seutter's place among his contemporaries in cartouche design, and how he built on or deviated from Homann's cartouches.[15]

There is a whole additional dimension of Seutter's engagement with cartouches that requires mention. Like other cartographers, he sold his maps both in atlases and individually, and maps sold individually were often protected by slipcases. Map slipcases do not survive well, but throughout the history of cartography, most of the slipcases that have survived are quite plain. But Seutter decorated his slipcases with title cartouches—cartouches that are different from the title cartouches on the maps inside the slipcases (Fig. 159).[16] The fact that Seutter chose to decorate his slipcases with cartouches at all is a remarkable testament to his interest in the genre. The fact that he was willing to design (or pay to have designed) a second title cartouche for each map he sold individually declares very clearly his belief in the attractiveness of cartouches to customers, and raises very interesting questions about the relationship between the two title cartouches (i.e. that on the map and that on the slipcase). Are both to be seen as equally valid in revealing the cartographer's interests?[17] Can we say that we have fully interpreted the

---

10   It is worth remarking that the cartouches on Coronelli's terrestrial globe of 1681–83 are much more elaborate than those in two of his important sources, the maps of Nicolas Sanson (1600–1667), who famously preferred that his maps have minimal decoration, and Joan Blaeu's *Atlas Maior* (Amsterdam, 1662–1672). On Coronelli's use of Blaeu and Sanson in making his globes for Louis XIV see Marica Milanesi, "A 'Special Geography' for the King: Animals and Human Beings on the Terrestrial Globe Made by Vincenzo Coronelli for Louis XIV (1681–1683)," *Globe Studies: The Journal of the International Coronelli Society* 53–54 (2005–06) (2007), pp. 11–23, at 11. For more on Coronelli's sources in making the globes, see Monique Pelletier, "Les globes de Louis XIV: les sources françaises de l'oeuvre de Coronelli," *Imago Mundi* 34 (1982), pp. 72–89, esp. 80–82.

11   On Gottfried Rogg (1669–1742) see Ulrich Thieme and Felix Becker, eds., *Allgemeines Lexikon der Bildenden Künstler von der Antike bis zur Gegenwart* (Leipzig: E.A. Seemann, 1907–50), vol. 28, pp. 516–517.

12   On Homann see Christian Sandler, *Johann Baptista Homann, Matthäus Seutter und ihre Landkarten: ein Beitrag zur Geschichte der Kartographie* (Amsterdam: Meridian Publishing, 1964); Markus Heinz, "A Programme for Map Publishing: The Homann Firm in the Eighteenth Century," *Imago Mundi* 49 (1997), pp. 104–115; Michael Hochedlinger, "Die Ernennung von Johann Baptist Homann zum kaiserlichen Geographen im Jahre 1715," *Cartographica Helvetica* 24 (2001), pp. 37–40; and Steven M. Zahlaus, "Vom rechten Glauben und von guten Geschäften: der Kupferstecher, Kartograf und Verleger Johann Baptist Homann," in Michael Diefenbacher, Brigitte Korn, and Steven M. Zahlaus, eds., *Von nah und fern: Zuwanderer in die Reichsstadt Nürnberg; Begleitband zur gleichnamigen Ausstellung im Stadtmuseum Fembohaus vom 29. März bis 10. August 2014* (Petersberg: Michael Imhof Verlag, 2014), pp. 205–212.

13   On Wolff's printing company and map production see Werner Schwarz, "Vom 'simplen' Uhrmacher zum Kunstverleger. Jeremias Wolff und seine Nachfolger," in Helmut Gier, ed., *Augsburger Buchdruck und Verlagswesen. Von den Anfängen bis zur Gegenwart* (Wiesbaden: Harrassowitz, 1997), pp. 587–618; and

Michael Ritter, "Die Landkarten von Jeremias Wolff und Johann Friedrich Probst," *Cartographica Helvetica* 35 (2007), pp. 21–30.

14   On Seutter's firm see Peter H. Meurer, "Das Druckprivileg für Matthäus Seutter," *Cartographica Helvetica* 8 (1993), pp. 32–36; Michael Ritter, "Seutter, Probst and Lotter: An Eighteenth-Century Map Publishing House in Germany," *Imago Mundi* 53 (2001), pp. 130–135; and Michael Ritter, "Die Augsburger Landkartenverlage Seutter, Lotter und Probst," *Cartographica Helvetica* 25 (2002), pp. 2–10.

15   For example, one might compare the title cartouche on Homann's map of Italy, *Statuum totius Italiae novissima repraesentatio geographica, simul exhibens Insulas Siciliae, Sardiniae, Corsicae et Maltae* (Nuremberg, c.1715), with that on Seutter's map of Italy, *Nova totius Italiae cum adiacentibus maioribus et minoribus insulis, accuratissima delineatio* (Augsburg, c.1740). Both cartographers made other maps of Italy as well, but these two have the same dimensions, making it reasonable to compare their degrees of decoration.

16   Several of Seutter's maps are viewable with their slipcases in the digital repository of the Biblioteca Nacional do Brasil, at http://acervo.bn.br/sophia_web/. Also the Osher Map Library has Seutter's *Atlas historique* of 1730, a boxed collection of twelve maps by Seutter, each with its slipcase. The slipcases and the maps are viewable on https://oshermaps.org.

17   Other maps with two title cartouches may be found among the production of Frederik de Wit (1629–1706), who included in

FIGURE 159 Slipcase with title cartouche for Matthäus Seutter, *Nova totius Italiae cum adiacentibus maioribus et minorib.*
Insulis accuratiss. delineatio (Augsburg, *c.*1730)

UNIVERSITY OF SOUTHERN MAINE, OSHER MAP LIBRARY AND SMITH CENTER FOR CARTOGRAPHIC
EDUCATION, SMITH COLLECTION, G1015.S475 1730. COURTESY OF THE OSHER MAP LIBRARY

title cartouche on one of Seutter's maps if we have not seen the cartouche on the slipcase? How do we interpret the cartouches if there are significant differences between their messages?[18]

While writing this book I was constantly impressed by the number of opportunities for further work on cartouches. The subject often seems endless. There are myriad

---

some maps one title cartouche in Latin, and the other in Dutch, with different decoration. To cite just one example, see his map *Occidentalior tractus Maris Mediterranei / Wester gedeelte van de Middelandse Zee* (Amsterdam, c.1680). On this map see George Carhart, *Frederick de Wit and the First Concise Reference Atlas* (Leiden and Boston: Brill and Hes & De Graaf, 2016), pp. 460–461.

18 Tobias Conrad Lotter (1717–1777), Seutter's son-in-law, continued this tradition of slipcases illustrated with cartouches: see Michael Ritter, *Die Welt aus Augsburg: Landkarten von Tobias Conrad Lotter (1717–1777) und seinen Nachfolgern* (Munich: Deutscher Kunstverlag, 2014), pp. 180–181 who discusses and illustrates a couple of slipcases for maps from Lotter's *Atlas minor*.

individual cartouches that cry out for interpretation, and cases in which a cartographer changed the cartouche on a new version of a map, or in which another cartographer copied a map but changed the cartouche, that offer very promising avenues for research. Further study of the use of cartouche model books in the production of maps would certainly be rewarding. Considering together all of the works of specific cartouche artists would be very fruitful, and—cutting in a different direction—investigating changes in the perception of a region through changes in the cartouches on maps of that area over time offers the prospect of insights into cartouche development and chains of influence, in addition to shedding light on attitudes to the region, its geography, its culture, and its inhabitants.

I bring this book to a close with the hope that it will inspire and facilitate multitudinous new explorations of cartouches.

Index

Page numbers in *italics* refer to illustrations.